Universal Human Rights
in Theory and Practice

Universal Human Rights

in Theory and Practice

Jack Donnelly

Second Edition

(Published in collaboration with Cornell University Press)

Manas Publications

New Delhi - 110 002 (India)

MANAS PUBLICATIONS
(We Convert Fighters into Writers)
(Publishers, Library Suppliers, Importers & Exporters)

4402/5-A, Ansari Road (Opp HDFC Bank)
Darya Ganj, New Delhi-110 002 (India)
Off.: 23260783, 23265523, Fax: 011-23272766
E-mail: manaspublications@gmail.com
manaspublications@yahoo.com

2nd Impression 2013 (FP-2005)

ISBN: 81-7049-258-0

Rs. 595/-

Designed at
Manas Publications

Printed in India at
Rajdhani Printers, Delhi.
and published by Mrs Suman Lata for
Manas Publications, 4402/5-A,
Ansari Road (Opp HDFC Bank),
Darya Ganj, New Delhi-110 002 (INDIA)

Contents

PREFACE TO THE SECOND EDITION ix

INTRODUCTION 1

Part I. Toward a Theory of Universal Human Rights

1. THE CONCEPT OF HUMAN RIGHTS 7

1. How Rights "Work" 7
2. Special Features of Human Rights 10
3. Human Rights and Human Nature 13
4. The Question of Foundations 18

2. THE UNIVERSAL DECLARATION MODEL 22

1. The Universal Declaration Model 23
2. Individual Rights 23
3. Interdependence and Indivisibility 27
4. The State and International Human Rights 33

3. EQUAL CONCERN AND RESPECT 38

1. Hegemony and Settled Norms 38
2. An Overlapping Consensus on International Human Rights 40
3. Moral Theory, Political Theory, and Human Rights 41
4. Equal Concern and Respect 43
5. Toward a Liberal Theory of Human Rights 46
6. Consensus: Overlapping but Bounded 51

Part II. Cultural Relativism and International Human Rights

4. MARKETS, STATES, AND "THE WEST" 57

1. The Evolution of Lists of Human Rights 57
2. Markets, States, and Political Equality 58

3. Expanding the Subjects and Substance of Human Rights 60
4. Linking "The West" and Human Rights 61
5. States, Citizens, and the Legal Order 64
6. Economic and Social Rights and the Welfare State 64
7. Inside, Outside, and the Society of States 65
8. Global Markets 67
9. Historical Analysis and the Genetic Fallacy 69

5. NON-WESTERN CONCEPTIONS OF HUMAN RIGHTS 71

1. Islam and Human Rights 72
2. The Premodern West 76
3. Traditional Africa 78
4. Traditional Confucian China 79
5. Caste and Human Rights 81
6. The Relevance of Human Rights 84
7. Culture and Human Rights 86

6. CULTURAL RELATIVISM AND UNIVERSAL HUMAN RIGHTS 89

1. Defining Cultural Relativism 89
2. Relativity and Universalism: A Necessary Tension 90
3. Internal Versus External Judgments 92
4. Concepts, Interpretations, Implementations 93
5. Explaining the Persistence of Culturalist Arguments 99
6. Culture and Politics 100
7. Dialogue over Real Differences 103

7. HUMAN RIGHTS AND "ASIAN VALUES" 107

1. Sovereignty and International Human Rights 108
2. The Demands of Development 109
3. Economic and Social Rights 110
4. Individuals and Society 112
5. Rights and Duties 114
6. Traditional Order and Human Rights 115
7. Human Rights and "Asian Values" 119

Part III. Human Rights and International Action

8. INTERNATIONAL HUMAN RIGHTS REGIMES 127

1. International Regimes 127
2. The Global Human Rights Regime 129

3. Political Foundations of the Global Regime 135
4. Regional Human Rights Regimes 138
5. Single-Issue Human Rights Regimes 145
6. The Evolution of Human Rights Regimes 151

9. HUMAN RIGHTS AND FOREIGN POLICY 155

1. Human Rights: A Legitimate Concern of Foreign Policy? 155
2. International Human Rights and National Identity 159
3. Trade-offs 162
4. Choice of Means 164
5. The Purposes of International Human Rights Policies 166
6. Selectivity and Consistency 168
7. Toward More Effective International Human Rights Policies 171

10. THE PRIORITY OF NATIONAL ACTION 173

1. The Limits of Multilateral Action 173
2. The Limits of Bilateral Action 177
3. The Limits of International Action 179

Part IV. Essays on Contemporary Theory and Practice

11. DEMOCRACY, DEVELOPMENT, AND HUMAN RIGHTS 185

1. The Contemporary Language of Legitimacy 186
2. Defining Democracy 188
3. Democracy and Human Rights 191
4. Defining Development 194
5. Development-Rights Trade-offs 196
6. Development and Civil and Political Rights 199
7. Markets and Economic and Social Rights 200
8. The Liberal Democratic Welfare State 202

12. GROUP RIGHTS AND HUMAN RIGHTS 204

1. Individual and Community 204
2. Liberal Approaches to Group Difference 205
3. Group Human Rights: A Skeptical View 208
4. Women 211
5. Minorities 212
6. Protecting Group Identity 214
7. Indigenous Peoples 215
8. Group Rights in a Human Rights Framework 217

9. Cultural Rights 218
10. A Right to Cultural Identity 220
11. Appendix: The Right of Peoples to Self-Determination 221

13. NONDISCRIMINATION FOR ALL: THE CASE OF SEXUAL MINORITIES 225

1. The Right to Nondiscrimination 225
2. Nondiscrimination and Political Struggle 227
3. Discrimination against Sexual Minorities 229
4. Nature, (Im)Morality, and Public Morals 233
5. Strategies for Inclusion 237

14. GENOCIDE AND HUMANITARIAN INTERVENTION 242

1. Intervention and International Law 242
2. Humanitarian Intervention and International Law 243
3. The Moral Standing of the State 244
4. Politics, Partisanship, and International Order 247
5. Changing Conceptions of Security and Sovereignty 249
6. Justifying the Antigenocide Norm 251
7. Changing Legal Practices 252
8. "Justifying" Humanitarian Intervention 254
9. Mixed Motives and the Problem of Consistency 255
10. Politics and the Authority to Intervene 257
11. Judging the Kosovo Intervention 258

REFERENCES 261

INDEX 287

Preface to the Second Edition

Pierre Vidal-Naquet, one of the great classicists of our time (although perhaps better known for his human rights work as a historian of French crimes during the Algerian war), observed that "for reasons that are my own and are probably not too 'rational,' in Greek studies the article is much easier for me than the book" (1986: xv). Much the same is true of my writings on human rights: the "natural" unit seems to be more or less self-contained segments of about 8000 words. The first edition of *Universal Human Rights in Theory and Practice* represented the coalescence of several essays written in the early and mid-1980s that were linked by their defense of a conception of "universal" human rights that acknowledges and incorporates the obvious historical contingency of both the idea of human rights and its dominant international expressions. This second edition both continues that accumulation of essays and responds to the aging of the first edition.

When I delivered the final manuscript of the first edition in the fall of 1988 I had not the slightest idea of what would occur in Central and Eastern Europe the following fall. Not surprisingly, that book bore the stamp of the Cold War. For that I offer no apologies. One of the book's attractive features, I believe, is that although primarily theoretical it directly engaged issues of immediate political significance. Because the political context has now changed, however, the continued engagement of theory with international political practice requires major changes. By the spring of 2001, it seemed to me that I had the material to make such changes effectively. Thus this new edition was written.

I have deleted half a dozen chapters, added eight that are entirely or primarily new, and substantially revised much of the remaining material. The result is a second edition that is about two thirds new. It is, however, a genuine second edition (rather than a fundamentally new book), with the same substantive focus, the same basic arguments, a similar structure, and much the same feel. Those who liked the first edition will, I think, find this a rejuvenated version of the book they have known. Those who did not like it will, I am sure, find fresh provocations. I hope this edition will attract some readers not familiar with the first and have a useful life of another dozen years.

Like most authors, I have accumulated numerous debts in writing. The community of scholars working in and around the field of human rights is particularly congenial and supportive, and I have taken advantage of the goodwill of many friends, colleagues, and acquaintances. In the first edition, my list included Philip Alston, Paul Brietzke, Charlie Brockett, Herman Burgers, Shelly Feldman, Dave Forsythe, Gary Gereffi, Ernie Haas, Glenn Hayslett, Rhoda Howard, Ed Kent, Steve Leonard, Ted Lewellen, Alan McChesney, Craig Murphy, Hanna Pitkin, Addie Pollis, Cran Pratt, Jane Sweeney, John Vincent, and Claude Welch. For this second edition I want to acknowledge, again, Dave Forsythe and Rhoda Howard-Hassmann and add Peter Baehr, Will Bain, Joanne Bauer, Daniel Bell, Joseph Chan, Tim Dunne, Hurst Hannum, Laura Hebert, Jennifer Jackson Preece, Ed Kolodziej, Gene Lyons, James Mayall, Chandra Muzaffar, Neil Stammers, Peter Van Ness, Kees Waaldijk, Alex Wendt, Dan Wessner, Nick Wheeler, Daniel Whelan, and Richard Wilson. This book is much better for their comments, criticisms, and advice—and would have been better still if I had listened more attentively. I also thank my research assistants over the last several years, especially Bassem Hassan, Laura Hebert, Jacek Lubecki, Matt Weinert, Dan Wessner, and Daniel Whelan. Roger Haydon, my editor at Cornell for both editions, has been, as always, helpful and supportive. Peg Markow did a wonderful job of copy editing under difficult circumstances. Each I think can see his or her own mark on the manuscript.

Permission to reprint material that appeared previously, usually in somewhat different form, has been granted by: the American Political Science Association, which gave permission to reprint here as Chapter 5 a revised version of "Human Rights and Human Dignity: An Analytic Critique of Non-Western Human Rights Conceptions," *American Political Science Review* 76 (June 1982); The Johns Hopkins University Press, which gave permission to reprint here (a) as Chapter 6 a revised version of "Cultural Relativism and Universal Human Rights," *Human Rights Quarterly* 6 (November 1984), and (b) as Chapter 11 a revised version of "Human Rights, Democracy, and Development," *Human Rights Quarterly*, 21 (August 1999); and MIT Press, which gave permission to reprint as Chapter 9 a much shortened version of "International Human Rights: A Regime Analysis," *International Organization* 40 (Summer 1986).

I dedicate this book, which roughly spans the time of our marriage, to Cathy. With no regrets. Considerable gratitude. And, still, much love.

JACK DONNELLY

Denver, Colorado

Universal Human Rights in Theory and Practice

Introduction

The universality of human rights is the central theme of this volume. My principal aim is to explicate and defend an account of human rights as universal rights. I do not, however, argue that human rights are timeless, unchanging, or absolute; any list or conception of human rights—and the idea of human rights itself—is historically specific and contingent. Organized around the competing claims of the universality, particularity, and relativity of human rights, this book demonstrates that the historical contingency and particularity of human rights is compatible with a conception of human rights as universal rights.

If human rights are the rights one has simply because one is a human being, as they usually are thought to be, then they are held "universally," by all human beings. They also hold "universally" against all other persons and institutions. As the highest moral rights, they regulate the fundamental structures and practices of political life, and in ordinary circumstances they take priority over other moral, legal, and political claims. These dimensions encompass what I call the *moral universality* of human rights.

Human rights in the contemporary world are universal in another sense: they are almost universally accepted, at least in word, or as ideal standards. All states regularly proclaim their acceptance of and adherence to international human rights norms,[1] and charges of human rights violations are among the strongest complaints that can be made in international relations. Three quarters of the world's states have undertaken international legal obligations to implement these rights by becoming parties to the International Human Rights Covenants, and almost all other nations have otherwise expressed approval of and commitment to their content. I call this the *international normative universality of* human rights.

Part I of this book tries to outline a theory of human rights that captures this universality without denying historical particularity. Part II turns to the

1. The most widely known international document, cited with almost universal approval by both states and human rights activists, is the Universal Declaration of Human Rights (1948).

historical particularity of human rights. I begin by emphasizing the special connection between human rights and the rise and consolidation of "liberalism" in the modern West, but proceed to argue that this does not preclude their near-universal applicability in contemporary international society.

Part III turns from the "moral universality" of human rights, the fact that human rights are held by all human beings with respect to all persons and institutions, to one aspect of the "international normative universality" of human rights, namely, the multilateral institutions and bilateral foreign policy practices that seek to realize internationally recognized human rights. Part IV concludes the volume by examining four areas of contemporary international controversy: the relationship between human rights, development, and democracy; group rights; discrimination against homosexuals; and humanitarian intervention.

There are two general themes to which I want to draw attention. The first is methodological: the necessarily multidisciplinary character of the study of human rights. The second is more substantive: the interaction of theory and practice.

Consider the range of issues covered by the Universal Declaration of Human Rights, which recognizes personal rights to life, nationality, recognition before the law, protection against torture, and protection against discrimination on such bases as race and sex; legal rights to a fair trial, the presumption of innocence, and protections against ex post facto laws, arbitrary arrest, detention or exile, and arbitrary interference with one's family, home, or reputation; a comparable variety of civil liberties and political rights; subsistence rights to food and health care; economic rights to work, rest and leisure, and social security; social rights to education and protection of the family; and the right to participate in the cultural life of the community. A comprehensive account of these rights would require that we combine, at minimum, the perspectives of law, political science, economics, and sociology, plus philosophy, if we want to understand the conceptual foundations of human rights and the justifications for this particular list.

The study of human rights is an inherently multidisciplinary enterprise.[2] One of my principal aims is to take seriously this often-stated but rarely heeded methodological dictum. To do justice to the scope and complexities of human rights, and to increase understanding of human rights, material and perspectives from various disciplines and subfields are offered. Within my own discipline of political science, I draw principally from the subfields of political theory and international relations. I also draw heavily from work in philosophy

2. The leading scholarly journal in the field, *Human Rights Quarterly* (which began its life as *Universal Human Rights*), bills itself as "A Comparative and International Journal of the Social Sciences, Humanities, and Law."

and international law. The result, I hope, concretely illustrates the fruitfulness, even necessity, of approaching human rights issues without regard to conventional disciplinary boundaries.

The importance of the interaction of theory and practice is especially striking when we consider the practical implications of the theoretical arguments of relativism considered in Part II. The way in which we think about a problem does not determine the way we act, but it may influence our behavior. The way problems are conceptualized may also be important for justifying actions and policies. For example, if it can be established that the sacrifice of human rights is not an imperative of development, but merely a convenience for those who control development policy (or even simply a cover for their self-enrichment), then repressive regimes are deprived of one important defense of their human rights violations.

Clear thinking about human rights is not the key to the struggle to implement them. It may not even be essential to successful political action on their behalf. In fact, such a utopian belief in the power of ideas is itself a dangerous impediment to effective political action. Nonetheless, conceptual clarity, the fruit of sound theory, can facilitate action. At the very least it can help to unmask the arguments of dictators and their allies.

This book thus aspires not merely to analyze the interaction of theory and practice but also to contribute in some small way to improving practice. This hope underlies, and perhaps even justifies, not only this book but much of the scholarly literature on human rights.

PART I

Toward a Theory of Universal Human Rights

1/ The Concept of Human Rights

Human rights—*droits de l'homme, derechos humanos, Menschenrechte,* "the rights of man"—are, literally, the rights that one has because one is human. What does it mean to have a right? How are being human and having rights related? The first three sections of this chapter consider these questions, examining how human rights "work" and how they both rest on and help to shape our moral nature as human beings. The final section considers the problem of philosophical foundations of substantive theories of human rights, to which we will turn in Chapters 2 and 3.

1. How Rights "Work"

What is involved in having a right to something? How do rights, of whatever type, "work"?

A. BEING RIGHT AND HAVING A RIGHT

"Right" in English, like equivalent words in several other languages, has two central moral and political senses: rectitude and entitlement (compare Dworkin 1977: 188–190). In the sense of rectitude, we speak of "the right thing to do," of some*thing being* right (or wrong). In the narrower sense of entitlement, we typically speak of some*one having* a right.

Rectitude and entitlement both link "right" and obligation, but in systematically different ways. Claims of rectitude (righteousness)—"That's wrong," "That's not right," "You really ought to do that"—focus on a standard of conduct and draw attention to the duty-bearer's obligation under that standard. Rights claims, by contrast, focus on the right-holder and draw the duty-bearer's attention to the right-holder's special title to enjoy her right.[1]

1. Rights in this sense thus are sometimes called "subjective rights"; they have as their focus a particular subject (who holds them) more than an "objective" standard to be followed or state of affairs to be realized.

To have a right to *x* is to be *entitled* to *x*. It is owed to you, belongs to you in particular. And if *x* is threatened or denied, right-holders are authorized to make special claims that ordinarily "trump" utility, social policy, and other moral or political grounds for action (Dworkin 1977: xi, 90).

Rights create—in an important sense "are"—a field of rule-governed interactions centered on, and under the control of, the right-holder. "A has a right to *x* (with respect to B)" specifies a right-holder (A), an object of the right (*x*), and a duty-bearer (B). It also outlines the relationships in which they stand. A is entitled to *x* (with respect to B). B stands under correlative obligations to A (with respect to *x*). And, should it be necessary, A may make special claims upon B to discharge those obligations.

Rights are not reducible to the correlative duties of those against whom they are held. If Anne has a right to *x* with respect to Bob, it is more than simply desirable, good, or even right that Anne enjoy *x*. She is entitled to it. Should Bob fail to discharge his obligations, besides acting improperly (i.e., violating standards of rectitude) and harming Anne, he violates her rights, making him subject to special remedial claims and sanctions.

Neither is having a right reducible to enjoying a benefit. Rather than a passive beneficiary of Bob's obligation, Anne is actively in charge of the relationship, as suggested by the language of "exercising" rights. She may assert her right to *x*. If he fails to discharge his obligation, she may press further claims against Bob, choose not to pursue the matter, or even excuse him, largely at her own discretion. Rights empower, not just benefit, those who hold them.

B. EXERCISING, RESPECTING, ENJOYING, AND ENFORCING RIGHTS

Claiming a right can "make things happen" (Feinberg 1980: 150). When Anne exercises her right, she activates Bob's obligations, with the aim of enjoying the object of her right (which in some cases may require coercive enforcement). Exercise, respect, enjoyment, and enforcement are four principal dimensions of the practice of rights.

When we consider how rights "work," though, one of the more striking facts is that we typically talk about rights only when they are at issue. If I walk into the supermarket and buy a loaf of bread, it would be odd to say that I had a right to my money, which I exchanged for a right to the bread. Only in unusual circumstances would we say that those who refrained from stealing my money or bread were respecting my rights. Rights are actually put to use, and thus important enough to talk about, only when they are at issue, when their enjoyment is questioned, threatened, or denied.

Three major forms of social interaction involving rights can be usefully distinguished:

1. "*Assertive exercise*": the right is exercised (asserted, claimed, pressed), activating the obligations of the duty-bearer, who either respects the right or violates it (in which case he is liable to enforcement action).
2. "*Active respect*"[2]: the duty-bearer takes the right into account in determining how to behave, without it ever being claimed. We can still talk of the right being respected and enjoyed, even though it has not been exercised. Enforcement procedures are never activated, although they may have been considered by the duty-bearer.
3. "*Objective enjoyment*": rights apparently never enter the transaction, as in the example of buying a loaf of bread; neither right-holder nor duty-bearer gives them any thought. We perhaps can talk here about the right—or at least the object of the right—being enjoyed. Ordinarily, though, we would not say that the right has been respected. Neither exercise nor enforcement is in any way involved.

From the point of view of society, objective enjoyment must be the norm. The costs, inconveniences, discontent, or tension associated with even active respect of a right must be the exception rather than the rule. Right-holders too would prefer not to have to exercise their rights. In an ideal world, rights would remain not only out of sight but out of mind as well.

Nonetheless, the ability to claim rights, if necessary, distinguishes having a right from simply being the (rights-less) beneficiary of someone else's obligation. Paradoxically, then, "having" a right is of most value precisely when one does not "have" (the object of) the right—that is, when active respect or objective enjoyment is not forthcoming. I call this the "possession paradox": "having" (possessing) and "not having" (not enjoying) a right at the same time, with the "having" being particularly important precisely when one does not "have" it.

We thus should be careful not to confuse possessing a right with the respect it receives or the ease or frequency with which it is enforced. In a world of saints, rights would be widely respected, rarely asserted, and almost never enforced. In a Hobbesian state of nature, rights would never be respected; at best disinterest or self-interest would lead duty-bearers not to deny the right-holder the object of her right.[3] Only an accidental coincidence of interests (or self-help enforcement) would allow a right-holder to enjoy her right.

Such differing circumstances of respect and enforcement, however, tell us

2. In the first edition, I used the label "direct enjoyment," which now seems to me not only less informative but also actually misleading in drawing attention to the right-holder's enjoyment rather than the duty-bearer's respect for the right.

3. If rights are social relations, one might think that there would be no rights in the state of nature. His state of nature, however, is a world without government, not a world without ordered social interaction (however rudimentary and anarchical that society may be).

nothing about who *has* what rights. To have a right to *x* is to be specially entitled to *x*, whether the law that gave you a legal right is violated or not; whether the promise that gave rise to the contractual right is kept or not; whether others comply with the principles of righteousness that establish your moral right or not.

I have a right to my car whether it sits in my driveway; is borrowed without my permission, for good reason or bad; is stolen but later recovered; or is stolen, never to be seen again by me (whether or not the thief is ever sought, apprehended, charged, tried, or convicted). Even if the violation ultimately goes unremedied and unpunished, the nature of the offense has been changed by my right. Violations of rights are a particular kind of injustice with a distinctive force and remedial logic.

2. Special Features of Human Rights

Human rights are, literally, the rights that one has simply because one is a human being.[4] In the third section in this chapter, Human Rights and Human Nature, we will consider the relationship between being human and having (human) rights. In this section we will focus on the special characteristics of human rights.

Human rights are *equal* rights: one either is or is not a human being, and therefore has the same human rights as everyone else (or none at all). They are also *inalienable* rights: one cannot stop being human, no matter how badly one behaves nor how barbarously one is treated. And they are *universal* rights, in the sense that today we consider all members of the species *Homo sapiens* "human beings," and thus holders of human rights.

Much of the remainder of this book explores the political implications of rights that are equal, inalienable, and universal. Here I will stress the implications of human rights being rights (in the sense discussed above) and their function as standards of political legitimacy.

A. HUMAN RIGHTS AS RIGHTS

The thorny problem of the things to which we have human rights will be addressed in Chapter 2. Here I simply note that we do not have human rights to all things that are good, or even all *important* good things. For example, we are not entitled—do not have (human) rights—to love, charity, or compassion. Parents who abuse the trust of children wreak havoc with millions of lives every

4. I emphasize the differences between (human) rights and other social practices and grounds for action. The similarities are perceptively emphasized in Nickel (1987), which is available on line at *http://spot.colorado.edu/~nickelj/msohr-welcome.htm*. Chapters 2 and 3 in particular make a good complement to the argument I develop here.

day. We do not, however, have a human right to loving, supportive parents. In fact, to recognize such a right would transform family relations in ways that many people would find unappealing or even destructive.

Most good things are not the objects of human rights. The emphasis on human rights in contemporary international society thus implies selecting certain values for special emphasis. But it also involves selecting a particular mechanism—rights—to advance those values.

Human rights are not just abstract values such as liberty, equality, and security. They are rights, particular social practices to realize those values. A human right thus should not be confused with the values or aspirations underlying it or with enjoyment of the object of the right.

For example, protection against arbitrary execution is an internationally recognized human right. The fact that people are not executed arbitrarily, however, may reflect nothing more than a government's lack of desire. Even active protection may have nothing to do with a right (title) not to be executed. For example, rulers may act out of their sense of justice or follow a divine injunction that does not endow subjects with any rights. And even a right not to be arbitrarily executed may rest on custom or statute.

Such distinctions are more than scholastic niceties. Whether citizens have a right (title) shapes the nature of the injury they suffer and the forms of protection and remedy available to them. Denying someone something that it would *be* right for her to enjoy in a just world is very different from denying her something (even the same thing) that she is entitled (*has* a right) to enjoy. Furthermore, whether she has a human right or a legal right contingently granted by the state dramatically alters her relationship to the state and the character of her injury.

B. HUMAN RIGHTS, LEGAL CHANGE, AND POLITICAL LEGITIMACY

Human rights traditionally have been thought of as moral rights of the highest order. They have also become, as we will see in more detail later, international (and in some cases national and regional) legal rights. Many states and local jurisdictions have human rights statutes. And the object of many human rights can be claimed as "ordinary" legal rights in most national legal systems.

Armed with multiple claims, right-holders typically use the "lowest" right available. For example, in the United States, as in most countries, protection against racial discrimination on the job is available on several grounds. Depending on one's employment agreement, a grievance may be all that is required, or a legal action based on the contract. If that fails (or is unavailable), one may be able to bring suit under a local ordinance or a state nondiscrimination statute. Federal statutes and the Constitution may offer remedies at still higher levels. In unusual cases, one may (be forced to) resort to international human rights claims. In addition, a victim of discrimination may appeal to considerations of justice or righteousness and claim moral (rather than legal) rights.

One can—and usually does—go very far before human rights arguments become necessary. An appeal to human rights usually testifies to the absence of enforceable positive (legal) rights and suggests that everything else has been tried and failed, leaving one with nothing else (except perhaps violence).[5] For example, homosexuals in the United States often claim their human right against discrimination because U.S. courts have held that constitutional prohibitions of discrimination do not apply to sexual preference.

Rights are a sort of "last resort"; they usually are claimed only when things are not going well. Claims of human rights are the final resort in the realm of rights; no higher rights appeal is available.

Claims of human rights thus ultimately aim to be self-liquidating, giving the possession paradox a distinctive twist. Human rights claims characteristically seek to challenge or change existing institutions, practices, or norms, especially legal practices. Most often they seek to establish (or bring about more effective enforcement of) a parallel "lower" right. For example, claims of a human right to health care in the United States typically aim to create a legal right to health care. To the extent that such claims are politically effective, the need to make them in the future will be reduced or eliminated.

A set of human rights can be seen as a standard of political legitimacy. The Universal Declaration of Human Rights, for example, presents itself as a "standard of achievement for all peoples and all nations." To the extent that governments protect human rights, they are legitimate.

No less important, though, human rights authorize and empower citizens to act to vindicate their rights; to insist that these standards be realized; to struggle to create a world in which they enjoy (the objects of) their rights. Human rights claims express not merely aspirations, suggestions, requests, or laudable ideas, but rights-based demands for change.

We must therefore not fall into the trap of speaking of human rights simply as demands for rights, what Joel Feinberg calls rights in a "manifesto sense" (1980: 153). Human rights do imply a manifesto for political change. That does not, however, make them any less truly rights. Claiming a human right, in addition to suggesting that one ought to have or enjoy a parallel legal right, involves exercising a (human) right that one already has. And in contrast to other grounds on which legal rights might be demanded—for example, justice, utility, self-interest, or beneficence—human rights claims rest on a prior moral (and international legal) entitlement.

Legal rights ground legal claims to protect already established legal entitle-

5. The "higher" claims are always available, but in practice rarely are appealed to until lower-level remedies have been tried (if not exhausted).

ments. Human rights ground moral claims to strengthen or add to existing legal entitlements.[6] That does not make human rights stronger or weaker, just different. They are human (rather than legal) rights. If they did not function differently, there would be no need for them.[7]

3. Human Rights and Human Nature

We can now turn from the "rights" to the "human" side of "human rights." This involves charting the complex relationship between human rights and "human nature."

A. THE SOURCE OF HUMAN RIGHTS

From where do we get human rights? Legal rights have the law as their source. Contracts create contractual rights. Human rights would appear to have humanity or human nature as their source. With legal rights, however, we can point to statute or custom as the mechanism by which the right is created. With contractual rights we have the act of contracting. How does "being human" give one rights?

Human needs are a common candidate: "needs establish human rights" (Bay 1982: 67); "a basic human need logically gives rise to a right" (Green 1981: 55); "it is legitimate and fruitful to regard instinctoid basic needs . . . as *rights*" (Maslow 1970: xiii).[8] Unfortunately, "human needs" is almost as obscure and controversial a notion as "human nature."

Science reveals a list of empirically validated needs that will not generate anything even approaching an adequate list of human rights. Even Christian Bay, probably the best-known advocate of a needs theory of human rights, admits that "it is premature to speak of any empirically established needs beyond sustenance and safety" (1977: 17). And Abraham Maslow, whose expansive conception of needs comes closest to being an adequate basis for a plausible set of human rights, admits that "man's instinctoid tendencies, such as they are, are far weaker than cultural forces" (1970: 129; compare 1971: 382–388).

Without a grounding in hard empirical science, though, "needs" takes on a

6. Viewing human rights as international legal (rather than moral) rights requires adding "municipal" or "national" before "legal" in this and the preceding sentence.

7. This discussion, along with the earlier discussion of the possession paradox, implicitly criticizes the "legal positivist" claim that there are no rights without remedies and no remedies except those provided by law or the sovereign. (The classic locus of this argument is Austin 1954 [1832]). Whatever the grounds for stipulating such a definition, it is inconsistent with ordinary usage and understandings, which readily comprehend moral and unenforced (even unenforceable) rights. (It also has highly controversial moral implications, ruling out certain kinds of claims by definitional fiat.) That a right is not legally enforceable often is an important fact about that right, but it is a fact about a right, not about some other kind of claim.

8. Compare Benn (1967), Pogge (2001 [1995]: 193) Gordon (1988: 728).

metaphorical or moral sense that quickly brings us back to philosophical wrangles over human nature.[9] There is nothing wrong with philosophical theory—as long as it does not masquerade as science. In fact, to understand the source of human rights we must turn to philosophy. The pseudoscientific dodge of needs will not do.[10]

The source of human rights is man's moral nature, which is only loosely linked to the "human nature" defined by scientifically ascertainable needs. The "human nature" that grounds human rights is a *prescriptive* moral account of human possibility. The scientist's human nature says that beyond this we cannot go. The moral nature that grounds human rights says that beneath this we must not permit ourselves to fall.

Human rights are "needed" not for life but for a life of dignity. "There is a human right to *x*" implies that people who enjoy a right to *x* will live richer and more fully human lives. Conversely, those unable to enjoy (the objects of) their human rights will to that extent be estranged from their moral nature.

We have human rights not to the requisites for health but to those things "needed" for a life of worthy of a human being. What these things are—what is on a defensible list of human rights—is addressed in Chapter 2. Here I focus on exploring how "human nature" (whatever its substance) gives rise to, and is in turn acted upon by, human rights.

B. HUMAN RIGHTS AND THE SOCIAL CONSTRUCTION OF HUMAN NATURE

The scientist's human nature sets the "natural" outer limits of human possibility. Human potential, however, is widely variable: the world seems to be populated by at least as many potential rapists and murderers as potential saints. Society plays a central role in selecting which potentials will be realized. Today this selection is significantly shaped by the practice of human rights, which is rooted in a substantive vision of man's moral nature.

Based on a moral vision of human nature, human rights set the limits and requirements of social (especially state) action. But the state and society, guided by human rights, play a major role in realizing that "nature." When human rights claims bring legal and political practice into line with their demands, they create the type of person posited in that moral vision.

9. Needs have even been defined in terms of rights! "We can initially define human needs, in a *minimal* sense, as that amount of food, clean water, adequate shelter, access to health services, and educational opportunities to which every person is entitled by virtue of being born" (McHale and McHale 1979: 16).

10. One might even suggest that it is positively dangerous to insist that rights are rooted in needs but then be unable to come up with a list of needs adequate to produce an attractive set of human rights.

"Human nature" is a social project more than a presocial given.[11] Just as an individual's "nature" or "character" arises from the interaction of natural endowment, social and environmental influences, and individual action, human beings create their "essential" nature through social action on themselves. Human rights provide both a substantive model for and a set of practices to realize this work of self-creation.

Human rights theories and documents point beyond actual conditions of existence—beyond the "real" in the sense of what has already been realized—to the possible, which is viewed as a deeper human moral reality. Human rights are less about the way people "are" than about what they might become. They are about *moral* rather than natural or juridical persons.

The Universal Declaration of Human Rights, for example, tells us little about life in many countries. And where it does, that is in large measure because those rights have shaped society in their image. Where theory and practice converge, it is largely because the posited rights have shaped society, and human beings, in their image. And where they diverge, claims of human rights point to the need to bring (legal and political) practice into line with (moral) theory.

The Universal Declaration, like any list of human rights, specifies minimum conditions for a dignified life, a life worthy of a human being. Even wealthy and powerful countries regularly fall far short of these requirements. As we have seen, however, this is precisely when, and perhaps even why, having human rights is so important: they demand, as rights, the social changes required to realize the underlying moral vision of human nature.

Human rights are at once a utopian ideal and a realistic practice for implementing that ideal. They say, in effect, "Treat a person like a human being and you'll get a human being." But they also say "Here's how you treat someone as a human being," and proceed to enumerate a list of human rights.

Human rights thus can be seen as a self-fulfilling moral prophecy: "Treat people like human beings—see attached list—and you will get truly human beings." The forward-looking moral vision of human nature provides the basis for the social changes implicit in claims of human rights. If the underlying vision of human nature is within the limits of "natural" possibility, and if the derivation of a list of rights is sound, then implementing those rights will make "real" that previously "ideal" nature.

Human rights seek to fuse moral vision and political practice. The relationship between human nature, human rights, and political society is "dialectical." Human rights shape political society, so as to shape human beings, so as

11. In Donnelly (1985a: 37–44), I argue that within the Western tradition of political theory, Marx and Burke provide important examples of such a theory of human nature. As these exemplars suggest, such a conception is not tied to any particular political perspective.

to realize the possibilities of human nature, which provided the basis for these rights in the first place.

In an earlier work (1985a: 31–43), I described this as a "constructivist" theory of human rights.[12] One might also use the language of reflexivity. The essential point is that "human nature" is seen as a moral posit, rather than a fact of "nature," and a social project rooted in the implementation of human rights. It is a combination of "natural," social, historical, and moral elements, conditioned, but not simply determined, by objective historical processes that it simultaneously helps to shape.

Human rights thus are constitutive no less than regulative rules.[13] We are most immediately familiar with their regulative aspects: "No one shall be subjected to torture or to cruel, inhuman or degrading treatment or punishment"; "Everyone has the right to work, to free choice of employment, to just and favorable conditions of work and to protection against unemployment." No less important, however, human rights *constitute* individuals as a particular kind of political subject: free and equal rights-bearing citizens. And by establishing the requirements and limits of legitimate government, human rights seek to constitute states of a particular kind.

C. ANALYTIC AND SUBSTANTIVE THEORIES

The theory I have sketched so far is substantively empty (compare Morsink 1987: 131–133)—or, as I would prefer to say, conceptual, analytic, or formal. I have tried to describe the character of any human right, whatever its substance, and some of the basic features of the practice as a whole, but I have yet to argue for the existence of even a single particular human right.

The obvious "solution" of presenting and defending a theory of human nature linked to a particular set of human rights, however, forces us to confront that fact that few issues in moral or political philosophy are more contentious or intractable than theories of human nature. There are many well-developed and widely accepted philosophical anthropologies: for example, Aristotle's

12. Had I been more prescient about the rise of "social constructivism" in international relations (and the social sciences more broadly), I would have done much more with the label. My route to that characterization, however, arose not out of an engagement with postmodern or post-structural social theory, or even constructivist sociology of knowledge (à la Berger and Luckmann 1967) but rather from my own work within the tradition of Wittgenstein and Anglo-American ordinary language philosophy, with the support and guidance of my dissertation supervisor Hanna Pitkin. Holt (1997: chap. 1) provides a recent argument that gets at much of what I find attractive about Wittgenstein for thinking about human rights—although I find her ultimate appeal to Oakeshott (1997: 128–141) unattractive and unpersuasive. On Wittgenstein and political theory more broadly, see Pitkin (1972). The immediate impetus was John Rawls's Howison Lecture, delivered at Berkeley in 1979 when I was working on my dissertation. It was first published as Rawls (1980) and appeared in a refined version as Lecture III of *Political Liberalism* (1996).

13. The classic formulation of this distinction is Rawls (1955), reprinted in Rawls (1999a).

zoon politikon; Marx's human natural being who distinguishes himself by producing his own material life; Mill's pleasure-seeking, progressive being; Kant's rational being governed by an objective moral law; and feminist theories that begin by questioning the gendered conceptions of "man" in these and most other accounts. Each of us probably has a favorite that, up to a certain point, we would defend. But there are few moral issues where discussion typically proves less conclusive. I doubt that there is much really new that can be said in defense of any particular theory of human nature. I am certain that I have nothing significant to add.

Philosophical anthropologies are much more like axioms than theorems. They are more assumed (or at best indirectly defended) starting points than the results of philosophical argument. This does not make substantive theories of human rights pointless or uninteresting. They simply are contentious in ways, or at least to a degree, that a good analytic theory is not.

If we were faced with an array of competing and contradictory lists of human rights clamoring for either philosophical or political attention, this inability to defend a particular theory of human nature might be a serious shortcoming. Fortunately, there is a remarkable international normative consensus on the list of rights contained in the Universal Declaration and the International Human Rights Covenants (see Chapters 2 and 3). Furthermore, in the philosophical literature on lists of human rights there are really only two major issues of controversy (other than whether there are such things as human rights): the status of economic and social rights and the issue of group human rights (which are addressed in §2.3 and Chapter 12, respectively).

Finally, although it may sound perverse, let me suggest that the "emptiness" of a conceptual theory is one of its great attractions. Given that philosophical anthropologies are so controversial, there are great dangers in tying one's analysis of human rights to any particular theory of human nature. The account of human rights I have sketched is compatible with many (but not all) theories of human nature. It is thus available to provide (relatively) "neutral" theoretical insight and guidance across (or within) a considerable range of positions.

A conceptual theory delimits a field of inquiry and provides a *relatively* uncontroversial (because substantively thin[14]) starting point for analysis. It also helps to clarify what is (and is not) at stake between competing substantive theories. But ultimately—in fact, rather quickly—we must move on to a substantive theory, and as soon as we do we must confront the notorious problem of philosophical "foundations."

14. A conceptual theory cannot be *entirely* empty. For example, "human" and "rights" are substantive moral concepts. But they can be effectively neutral notions in discussions across a considerable range of substantive theories.

4. The Question of Foundations

If the preceding account is even close to correct, "human nature" cannot be the foundation, in any strong sense of that term, for human rights. I want to conclude this chapter by suggesting that there is no other foundation either.

A. THE FAILURE OF FOUNDATIONAL APPEALS

In a weak, largely methodological, sense of the term every theory or social practice has a "foundation," a point beyond which there can be no answer to questions of "Why?" ("Because I'm the mom!") Usually, though, we talk about foundations in a strong, substantive sense as something "beyond" or "beneath" social convention or reasoned choice. A (strong) foundation can compel assent, not just ask for or induce agreement. In this sense, human rights have no foundation.

Historically, though, most human rights advocates and declarations have made foundational appeals. For example, both Locke and the American Declaration of Independence appealed to divine donation: to paraphrase Jefferson, we have all been endowed by our Creator with certain inalienable rights. The Universal Declaration of Human Rights makes an apparently foundational appeal to "the inherent dignity . . . of all members of the human family." Needs, as we saw earlier, are often advanced as an "objective" foundation.

Such grounds have often been accepted as persuasive. None, however, can through logic alone force the agreement of a skeptic. Beyond the inevitable internal or "epistemological" challenges, foundational arguments are vulnerable to external or "ontological" critique. Consider the claim that God gives us human rights. Questions such as "Are you sure?" or "How do you know that?" ask for evidence or logical argument. They pose (more or less difficult) challenges from within an accepted theoretical or ontological framework. The external question "What God?" raises a skeptical ontological challenge from outside that framework. To such questions there can be no decisive response.

"Foundational" arguments operate within (social, political, moral, religious) communities that are defined in part by their acceptance of, or at least openness to, particular foundational arguments.[15] For example, all the major parties in the English Civil War took for granted that God was a central source of rights and that the Bible provided authoritative evidence for resolving political disputes. Their disagreements, violent as they ultimately became, were "internal" disputes over who spoke for Him, when, and how, and what He desired. To English and Scottish Christians in the 1640s, asking whether God had granted political rights to kings, to men (and if so, which men), or both—and

15. The examples in this section are Western, in part to emphasize that the issue has nothing to do with difference between cultures or civilizations (which are the subject of Part II).

if both, how He wanted their competing claims to be resolved—was "natural," "obvious," even "unavoidable." But through argument alone they would have been unable to compel the assent of a skeptical atheist (had he dared raise his head) who rejected appeals to the Bible or divine donation.

Natural law theories today face much the same problem. John Finnis's *Natural Law and Natural Rights* (1980) is a brilliant account of the implications of neo-Thomist natural law for questions of natural (human) rights. To those of us outside of that tradition, the "foundational" appeals to nature and reason are more or less attractive, interesting, or persuasive. For Finnis, though, operating within that tradition, they are definitively compelling. Having accepted Finnis's starting point we may be rationally compelled to accept his conclusions about natural rights.[16] But a skeptic cannot be compelled by reason alone to start there.

Or consider Arthur Dyck's appeal to "the natural human relationships and responsibilities on which human rights are based" (1994: 13). His effort to ground human rights on "what is logically and functionally necessary, and universally so, for the existence and sustenance of communities" (1994: 123) fails because there is very little that is empirically universal about, and almost nothing that is truly logically necessary for the existence of, human communities.

Hadley Arkes, another contemporary natural law theorist, correctly identifies the situation when he writes of "The Axioms of Public Policy" (1998). Without accepting certain axiomatic propositions *that we are rationally free to reject*, no moral or political argument can go very far. Unfortunately, Arkes goes on to treat his axioms as though they were indisputable facts about the world.

Consider a very different contemporary example. The International Human Rights Covenants make a vague but clearly foundational appeal to "the inherent dignity of the human person." The very category "human being" or "human person," however, is contentious. Those who do not draw a sharp categorical distinction between *Homo sapiens* and other creatures are not irrational, however substantively misguided we may take them to be. Neither are those who draw categorical moral distinctions between groups of human beings—as in fact most societies throughout most of history have done. Many societies have denied the moral centrality, even the existence, of our common humanity on thoughtful and carefully justified grounds.

Moral and political arguments require a firm place to stand. But that place appears firm largely because we have agreed to treat it as such. "Foundations"

16. More precisely, the debate shifts to internal ("epistemological") questions. For example, Maritain (1943) provides a somewhat different neo-Thomist derivation of human rights. And Fortin (1982) offers a critique from within the Thomist camp that stresses the difference between natural rights and natural law. See also Fortin (1996).

"ground" a theory only through an inescapably contentious decision to *define* such foundations as firm ground.[17]

"Foundational" arguments reflect contingent and contentious agreements to cut off certain kinds of questions. What counts as a "legitimate" question is itself unavoidably subject to legitimate (external) questioning. There is no strong foundation for human rights—or, what amounts to the same thing, there are multiple, often inconsistent, "foundations."

In the following chapters I will argue that this is less of a practical problem than one might imagine. Nonetheless, it does counsel a certain degree of caution about the claims we make for human rights. Even if we consider ourselves morally compelled to recognize and respect human rights, we must remember that the simple fact that someone else (or another society) rejects human rights is not necessarily evidence of moral defect or even error. Part II of this book is devoted to problems of arguing and acting across such moral divides.

B. COPING WITH CONTENTIOUS "FOUNDATIONS"

The common complaint that nonfoundational theories leave human rights "vulnerable"[18] is probably true but certainly irrelevant. The "invulnerability" of a strong foundation is, if not entirely illusory, then conventional, a matter of agreement rather than proof. Foundations do provide reasoned assurance for moral beliefs and practices by allowing us to root particular arguments, rules, or practices in deeper principles. But this is the reassurance of internal consistency, not of objective external validation.[19]

Chris Brown correctly notes that

> virtually everything encompassed by the notion of "human rights" is the subject of controversy. . . . the idea that individuals have, or should have, "rights" is itself contentious, and the idea that rights could be attached to individuals by virtue solely of their common humanity is particularly subject to penetrating criticism. (1999: 103)

We can say precisely the same thing, though, about all other moral and political ideas and practices. While recognizing that human rights are at their root con-

17. A useful analogy might be drawn with the "hard core" of a Lakatosian research program (Lakatos 1970; 1978).

18. See, for example, Freeman (1994), which gives considerable critical attention to my "relativist" position. I should perhaps note, though, that in conversation Freeman has indicated that he no longer holds these views in the strong form in which he presents them in this essay.

19. Even Alasdair MacIntyre, who remains committed to the idea of the rational superiority of particular systems of thought (1988: chaps. 17–19), in his Gifford Lectures (1990) speaks of Thomism as a tradition, and even titles one chapter "Aquinas and the Rationality of Tradition." I take this to be very close to an admission that "foundations" operate only within discursive communities.

ventional and controversial, we should not place more weight on this fact than it deserves.

Human rights ultimately rest on a social decision to act as though such "things" existed—and then, through social action directed by these rights to make real the world that they envision. This does not make human rights "arbitrary," in the sense that they rest on choices that might just as well have been random. Nor are they "*merely* conventional," in roughly the way that driving on the left is required in Britain. Like all social practices, human rights come with, and in an important sense require, justifications. But those justifications appeal to "foundations" that are ultimately a matter of agreement or assumption rather than proof. Problems of "circularity" or "vulnerability" are common to all moral concepts and practices, not specific to human rights.

Moral arguments can be both uncertain in their foundations and powerful in their conclusions and implications. We can reasonably ask for good grounds for accepting, for example, the rights in the Universal Declaration of Human Rights. But such grounds—for example, their desirable consequences, their coherence with other moral ideas or practices, or the supporting authority of a revealed religious text—are not unassailable. They operate within rather than across communities or traditions.[20] And we must recognize that there are other good grounds not only for these principles and practices but also for different, even "competing," practices.

Faced with inescapably contending and contentious first principles, we not only can but should interrogate, evaluate, and judge our own. Working both "up" from "foundational" premises to particular conclusions, and back "down" from particular practices, we can both explore the implications of foundational assumptions that have previously remained obscure and attempt to ascertain whether particular judgments and practices are "reasonable" or "well justified."[21] Through such work, moral progress, in a very real sense of that term, may be possible—even if it is progress only within an ultimately conventional set of foundational assumptions.

Whatever their limits, substantive theories of human rights are both necessary and possible. The next two chapters offer my efforts to provide substantive content to the analytic theory offered earlier by arguing that we have a variety of good (although not unassailable) moral and political reasons for accepting the system of human rights outlined in the Universal Declaration of Human Rights.

20. This does not mean that there are no points of agreement across traditions. (On overlapping consensus, see §3.2.) But any such overlaps are not evidence for a higher metatheory that is "natural" rather than conventional.

21. Compare Rawls's notion of reflective equilibrium (1971: 20–21, 48–51).

2/ The Universal Declaration Model

This chapter begins to sketch a particular substantive theory of human rights that I call the "Universal Declaration model," in recognition of the central role of the Universal Declaration of Human Rights[1] in establishing the contours of the contemporary consensus on internationally recognized human rights. Adopted by the United Nations General Assembly on December 10, 1948, by a vote of 48–0 (with eight abstentions), the Universal Declaration has been endorsed, regularly and repeatedly, by virtually all states. For the purposes of international action, "human rights" means roughly "what is in the Universal Declaration of Human Rights."[2] This chapter outlines its main features. Chapter 3 begins to offer a substantive defense.

1. The best study of the development and substance of the Universal Declaration is Morsink (1999). See also Samnoy (1990) and Eide and Swinehart (1992).

2. It is often argued that the Universal Declaration is distinctively Western and thus not really universal. On the dangers of confusing origins with substance, see §4.10. But even the claim that the West played a dominant role is problematic.

The principal drafters were Canadian (John Humphrey) and French (Rene Cassin), and the American representative on the Commission on Human Rights, Eleanor Roosevelt, played a leading role in ushering the Declaration through the UN machinery. But important contributions in the drafting were also made by Charles Malik (Lebanon), P. C. Chang (China), Hernan Santa Cruz (Chile) and Alexi Pavlov (USSR). See Morsink (1999: 28–34)and Samnoy (1990: chap. 7). On the important role of small states, see Waltz (2001).

In addition to twenty Latin American states, thirteen "non-Western" countries voted for the Universal Declaration: Afghanistan, Burma, China, Egypt, Ethiopia, India, Iran, Iraq, Lebanon, Pakistan, Philippines, Syria, and Turkey. In other words, "Western" states, understood as the states of Europe plus the United States, Canada, Australia, and New Zealand, made up only about a third of the votes for the Universal Declaration. Muslim states provided half as many votes to the final total as Western states.

There simply was no North-South split in 1948. Quite the contrary, countries from what would later be called the Third World were at least as enthusiastic about the Universal Declaration as Western countries. The only serious disagreement was *within* the West, as the Soviet bloc countries abstained because they wanted greater emphasis on economic and social rights. (Saudi Arabia's abstention rested primarily with disagreements with parts of Articles 16 and 18.) Just one country, South Africa, could be seen as fundamentally opposed to the Declaration (Morsink [1999: 21–28]).

1. The Universal Declaration Model

The Universal Declaration of Human Rights includes a short but substantial list of rights that has been further elaborated, with modest additions, in a variety of later treaties, most notably the 1966 International Human Rights Covenants. Table 2.1 provides a list of the rights recognized in these documents.

In addition to the substance of these internationally recognized human rights, to which we will return in Chapter 3, four structural features of the Universal Declaration model merit emphasis.

First, (universal) rights—entitlements—are the mechanism for implementing such values as nondiscrimination and an adequate standard of living. The implications of this choice were discussed in Chapter 1.

Second, all the rights in the Universal Declaration and the Covenants, with the exception of self-determination of peoples, are rights of individuals, not corporate entities. §2 examines the logic behind this restriction and addresses some common misconceptions about individual human rights. We will return to the issue of group rights in Chapter 12.

Third, internationally recognized human rights are treated as an interdependent and indivisible whole, rather than as a menu from which one may freely select (or choose not to select). §3 explores this dimension of the Universal Declaration model, with special attention to the relation of civil and political rights to economic, social, and cultural rights.

Fourth, although these are universal rights, held equally by all human beings everywhere, states have near exclusive responsibility to implement them for their own nationals. §4 explores the special place of the state in the contemporary practice of human rights.

2. Individual Rights

With the exception of the right to self-determination,[3] all the rights in the Universal Declaration and the Covenants are the rights of individuals. Enumerations of rights thus typically begin "Every human being . . . ," "Everyone has the right . . . ," "No one shall be . . . ," "Everyone is entitled. . . ." Even where one might expect groups to appear as right-holders, they do not. For example, Article 27 of the International Covenant on Civil and Political

---

Ashlid Samnoy correctly notes that the debate in the United Nations in 1948 "gives an impression of a massive appreciation of the Declaration. The events were characterised as 'the most important document of the century' (Ecuador), 'a world milestone in the long struggle for human rights' (France), 'a decisive stage in the process of uniting a divided world' (Haiti), 'an epoch-making event' (Pakistan) and 'a justification of the very existence of the United Nations' (the Philippines)" (1990: 210).

3. For the remainder of this chapter, I omit further reference to this exception, to which we will return in §12.11.

TABLE 2.1 The Substance of the Universal Declaration Model*

Nondiscrimination (U2, E2, C2)
Life (U3, C6)
Liberty and security of person (U3, C9)
Protection against slavery (U4, C8)
Protection against torture (U5, C7)
Legal personality (U6, C16)
Equal protection of the law (U7, C14, C26)
Legal remedy (U8, C2)
Protection against arbitrary arrest, detention, or exile (U9, C9)
Access to independent and impartial tribunal (U10, C14)
Presumption of innocence (U11, C14)
Protection against ex post facto laws (U11, C15)
Privacy (U12, C17)
Freedom of movement (U13, C12)
Nationality (U15, C24)
Marry and found a family (U16, C23)
Protection and assistance of families (U16, E10, C23)
Marriage only with free consent of spouses (U16, E10, C23)
Equal rights of men and women in marriage (U16, C23)
Freedom of thought, conscience, and religion (U18, C18)
Freedom of opinion and expression (U19, C19)
Freedom of assembly (U20, C21)
Freedom of association (U20, C22)
Participation in government (U21, C25)
Social security (U22, E9)
Work (U23, E6)
Just and favorable conditions of work (U23, E7)
Trade unions (U23, E8, C22)
Rest and leisure (U24, E7)
Adequate standard of living (U25, E11)
Education (U26, E13)
Participation in cultural life (U27, E15)
Self-determination (E1, C1)
Protection of and assistance to children (E10, C24)
Freedom from hunger (E11)
Health (E12, U25)
Asylum (U14)
Property (U17)
Compulsory primary education (E14)
Humane treatment when deprived of liberty (C10)
Protection against imprisonment for a debt (C11)
Expulsion of aliens only by law (C13)
Prohibition of war propaganda and incitement to discrimination (C20)
Minority culture (C27)

* This list includes all rights that receive explicit mention in both the Universal Declaration and one of the Covenants or receives a full article in one of these three instruments.

References are to the article, by number is the Universal Declaration (U), International Covenant on Civil and Political Rights (C) or International Covenant on Economic Social and Cultural Rights (E).

Rights reads, "In those States in which ethnic, religious or linguistic minorities exist, persons belonging to such minorities shall not be denied the right, in community with the other members of their group, to enjoy their own culture, to profess and practise their own religion, or to use their own language." Individuals belonging to minorities, not minorities (collective entities), have these rights.

If human rights are the rights that one has simply as a human being, then only human beings have human rights; if one is not a human being, by definition one cannot have human rights. Because only individual persons are human beings, it would seem that only individuals can have human rights.

Collectivities of all sorts have many and varied rights. But these are not—cannot be—human rights, unless we substantially recast the concept. Although it is worth taking seriously claims for radical revisions of the Universal Declaration model, this chapter is explicitly restricted to explicating that model and beginning to lay out some of its attractions. In Chapter 12 I argue against the idea of group human rights and defend the general adequacy of an individual human rights approach.

Society does have legitimate claims against individuals. Individuals do have important duties to society,[4] many of which correspond to rights of society. But from none of this does it logically follow that society, or any other social group, has *human* rights.

Human rights, however, are not held by atomistic individuals, nor are they necessarily corrosive to community.[5] In addition to being separate persons, individuals are participants in many associations and members of a variety of communities. And individual rights are a *social* practice.

As we saw in Chapter 1, all (human) rights are embedded in a social context and have important social dimensions. A's right to *x* with respect to B establishes and operates through social relationships. Individual and group rights differ in who holds the right—individuals or corporate actors—not in their sociality.

In fact, many individual human rights are characteristically exercised, and can only be enjoyed, through collective action. Political participation, social insurance, and free and compulsory primary education, for example, are rights that would be of little significance, or even be incomprehensible, in the absence of community. Freedom of association, obviously, is a right of collective action.

4. These duties, however, are not a condition for the possession or enjoyment of human rights (except in some very limited instances, such as restrictions on the enjoyment of personal liberty of those convicted of serious crimes). One has the same human rights whether or not one discharges one's duties to society. One is a human being, and thus has the same human rights as any other human being, whether or not one is a good citizen or even a contributing member of society.

5. See Howard (1995) for an account of human rights that emphasizes their compatibility with strong communities.

Workers' rights, family rights, and minority rights are enjoyed by individuals as members of social groups or occupants of social roles.[6]

Even where group membership is essential to the definition of a human right, however, the rights are held by individual members of protected groups and not by the group as a collective entity. Families, for example, are protected by a number of internationally recognized human rights. From a human rights perspective, however, the family is a social group that is valued only because its intermediation typically protects, helps to develop, or enriches the life of individual family members.[7] Furthermore, the human rights of families, understood as associations of rights-holding individuals, apply only against the broader society. Families may not exercise their rights in ways that infringe on the human rights of their members (or on any other persons). Families may not, for example, deny their adult members freedom of religion or the right to participate in politics.

The Universal Declaration envisions individuals deeply enmeshed in "natural" and voluntary groups, ranging from families through the state. Due process and equal protection, for example, make no sense except in the context of a political community; speech, work, and politics take place only in communities; torture and education alike occur only in a social context.[8]

The very ideas of respecting and violating human rights rest on the idea of the individual as part of a larger social enterprise. Rights-bearing individuals alone cannot effectively implement their rights. Alone, individuals cannot make for themselves a life worthy of human beings. Any plausible account of human dignity must include membership in society. To paraphrase Aristotle, outside of society, one would be either a god or a beast. Or, as Hobbes put it, life would be solitary, poor, nasty, brutish, and short.

6. These rights, however, are universal in the sense that they refer to anyone who should happen to be in that class, the membership of which is in principle open to all (in the sense that it is not defined by achievement or ascription).

7. Families, of course, have other (perhaps even more important) dimensions. The love between spouses or the often heroic sacrifices parents make for their children lie outside the realm of human rights. In much the same vein, freedom of religion and the associational rights of churches and religious communities fail to exhaust—even fail to scratch the surface of—the meaning and significance of religion. We must not confuse human rights with all good things.

8. At the risk of belaboring the point, consider a few more examples from the Universal Declaration. Human beings "should act towards one another in a spirit of brotherhood" (Art. 1). "Everyone has the right to own property alone as well as in association with others" (Art. 17). "Everyone has the right . . . to seek, receive and impart information and ideas through any media and regardless of frontiers" (Art. 19). "Everyone has the right to take part in the government of his country" (Art. 21). "Everyone, as a member of society, has the right to social security" (Art. 22). "Everyone who works has the right to just and favourable remuneration ensuring for himself and his family an existence worthy of human dignity, and supplemented, if necessary, by other means of social protection" (Art. 23). "Everyone has the right to a standard of living adequate for the health and wellbeing of himself and of his family" (Art. 25). "Everyone has the right freely to participate in the cultural life of the community" (Art. 27).

Nonetheless, a human rights conception of human dignity and political legitimacy rests on the fact that human beings have an essential, irreducible moral worth and dignity independent of the social groups to which they belong and the social roles that they occupy. We will return to this point in Chapter 3.

3. Interdependence and Indivisibility

The Universal Declaration model treats internationally recognized human rights holistically, as an indivisible structure in which the value of each right is significantly augmented by the presence of many others. As Article 5 of the 1993 Vienna Declaration puts it, "All human rights are universal, indivisible and interdependent and interrelated."

During the Cold War, this doctrine was regularly challenged. In particular, the relationship between civil and political rights and economic, social, and cultural rights was a matter of intense and lively, although not particularly productive or illuminating, controversy. Commentators and leaders in all Soviet bloc and most Third World countries regularly disparaged most civil and political rights. Conversely, many Western (especially Anglo-American) conservatives and philosophers—but, significantly, only the government of the United States—disparaged most economic and social rights.

Such debates have largely receded from international discussions,[9] but their legacy remains in the persistence of the categories of civil and political and economic, social, and cultural rights. We should also note that in some Western circles a lingering suspicion of economic and social rights persists.[10] This is particularly true in the United States, where skepticism persists across much of the mainstream political spectrum.

A. THE STATUS OF ECONOMIC AND SOCIAL RIGHTS

In international discussions it has become almost a reflex to talk of "civil and political rights" and "economic, social, and cultural rights." Although I too occasionally use these categories, they are seriously misleading. A dichotomous

9. For example, as of October 22, 2001, only ten states were party to just one of the Covenants (and five of those had signed but not yet ratified the other). One hundred forty states were parties to both (and an additional four had signed but not yet ratified both). http://www.unhchr.ch/pdf/report.pdf.

10. The continuing policy relevance of the debate is suggested by a recent issue of *The Economist* (August 18–24, 2001), which devotes its cover, the principal leader, and a three-page Special Report to the status of economic and social rights. Given that newspaper's position on the right of the European political spectrum, it is of some significance that the leader accepts (with only moderate reluctance) the reality of economic and social human rights—although it does question the practicality of implementing many and claims that "the moral imperative to stop poverty or disease is . . . not as convincing as the moral imperative to stop torture" (2001: 19).

division of any complex reality is likely to be crude and easily (mis)read to suggest that the two categories are antithetical. This is especially true because the dichotomy between civil and political rights and economic, social, and cultural rights was born of political controversy, first in working-class political struggles in the nineteenth and early twentieth centuries and then in Cold War ideological rivalry. But the argument against economic and social rights has also been philosophical, not merely political or polemical.

Maurice Cranston offers the most widely cited argument that whereas traditional civil and political rights to life, liberty, and property are "universal, paramount, categorical moral rights" (1964: 40), economic and social rights "belong to a different logical category" (1964: 54)—that is, they are not truly human rights.[11] As Chapter 1 suggests, I accept universality and paramountcy as central indicators of rights that might appropriately be considered human rights. But Cranston is simply wrong that internationally recognized economic, social, and cultural rights fail to meet these tests.

Cranston notes that the right to work, like many other economic and social rights, refers directly to a particular class of people rather than all human beings (1973: 67). Many civil and political rights, though, also fail such a test of universality. For example, only citizens who have attained a certain age and completed any necessary formalities of registration have the right to vote.

As for (lack of) paramountcy, Cranston singles out the right to periodic holidays with pay (1973: 66–67). But is such a right any less important than, say, the right of juveniles to separate prison facilities, a right recognized in the International Covenant on Civil and Political Rights? Questions concerning paramountcy arise in both cases because the right in question has been specified in rather detailed terms (compare §6.4). In the case of paid holidays, the full right recognized is a right to "rest, leisure, and reasonable limitation of working hours and periodic holidays with pay." Denial of this right would indeed be a serious affront to human dignity; it was, for example, one of the most oppressive features of unregulated nineteenth century capitalism.

In any case, the right to periodic holidays with pay is hardly the typical economic and social right. For example, the right to work is arguably as important as most basic civil and political rights; the psychological, physical, and moral effects of prolonged enforced unemployment may be as severe as those associated with denial of, say, freedom of speech. A right to education may be as essential to a life of dignity as freedom of speech or religion. (Economic and social) rights to food and health care may be as essential for protecting life as the (civil or political) right to life.

Cranston's appeal to (im)practicality is more complex. "'Political rights'

11. Cranston goes so far as to claim that such rights "[do] not make sense," and he suggests that claims of such rights probably are not even "intelligible" (1973: 65, 69).

can be readily secured by legislation.[12] The economic and social rights can rarely, if ever, be secured by legislation alone" (1964: 37). In fact, however, no right can be reliably realized through legislation alone. Unless legislation is backed by enforcement, the right is likely to be legally and politically insecure.

"There is nothing essentially difficult about transforming political and civil rights into positive rights," whereas realizing economic and social rights is "utterly impossible" in most countries (Cranston 1973: 66). "To guarantee civil and political rights is relatively cheap, whereas to guarantee economic and social rights is potentially enormously costly" (Economist 2001: 20). Both sides of such claims are problematic.

There are in fact severe impediments to establishing an effective positive right to, say, freedom of speech, press, or assembly in North Korea, Liberia, Cuba, China, or Burma. Only in particular kinds of political circumstances—for example, where there has already been considerable progress in implementing many internationally recognized human rights—are civil and political rights likely to be systematically easier to implement. Even then, the differences are more matters of degree than kind. And they vary considerably from right to right and with time and place.

If we insist on the standards of, say, Sweden, it may not be false to say that realizing most economic and social rights is "impossible" in most countries. But Northern European standards for civil and political rights would be nearly as "impossible." Resource shortages, as even the most conservative international financial institutions have come to understand, usually are largely attributable to poor governance. The problems to which Cranston points are matters of *political* economy, not natural scarcity.

Because rights impose correlative duties and, as the old moral maxim puts it, "ought implies can"—no one has an obligation to attempt what is truly impossible—Cranston argues that it is logically incoherent to hold that economic and social "rights" are anything more than utopian aspirations (1973: 68). The "can" in "ought implies can," however, refers to physical impossibility; unless it is physically impossible, one may still be obliged to try to do something that proves to be "impossible." The impediments to implementing most economic and social rights, however, are political. For example, there is more than enough food in the world to feed everyone; widespread hunger and malnutrition exist not because of a physical shortage of food but because of political decisions about its distribution.[13]

This leaves Cranston with little more than an argument that civil and polit-

12. He even claims that civil and political rights "generally . . . can be secured by fairly simple legislation" (1973: 66).

13. In fact, over the past half century famines have occurred only in places where there was enough food for everyone within the borders of the famine-stricken country (Sen 1981; Dreze and Sen 1990).

ical rights are relatively easy to implement. Hugo Adam Bedau advances a similar "argument from indifference to economic contingencies" (1979: 36–37). Even granting such empirically dubious claims, I cannot see why ease or expense of implementation should have any conceptual or moral significance. It seems odd to me to suggest that something is a real human right only if it is relatively easy to implement. Ease of implementation is certainly irrelevant to determining moral paramountcy.

B. "POSITIVE" AND "NEGATIVE" RIGHTS

Underlying many criticisms of economic and social rights is the distinction between "negative" rights, which require only forbearance on the part of others, and "positive" rights, which require others to provide goods, services, or opportunities. Henry Shue (1979; 1980), however, has shown that this distinction is of little moral significance and in any case fails to correspond to the distinction between civil and political rights and economic and social rights.

The right to protection against torture is usually advanced as the archetypal negative right: it requires "nothing more" than that the state refrain from incursions on personal liberty and bodily integrity. But protecting people against torture always requires positive endeavors by the state. Guaranteeing this "negative" right as a practical political matter requires major "positive" programs to train, supervise, and control the police and security forces. In many countries this would be not only extremely expensive but also politically "impossible" (without changing the regime).

Conversely, in some circumstances government restraint may be the key to realizing the positive-sounding right to food. Consider government development programs that in numerous Third World countries have encouraged producing cash crops for export rather than traditional food crops for local consumption. In such cases, the right to food would have been better realized if the government had done "nothing more" than refrain from interfering with agricultural incentives (compare Shue 1980: 41–45).

All human rights require both positive action and restraint on the part of the state.[14] Furthermore, whether a right is relatively positive or negative usually depends on historically contingent circumstances. For example, the right to food is more of a negative right in the wheat fields of Kansas than in Watts or East Los Angeles. Equal protection of the law is somewhat more positive in the South Bronx than in Stockholm. In Argentina, protection against torture was a very positive right indeed in the late 1970s. Today it is a much more negative right.

14. Shue (1980: 52–60) usefully distinguishes duties to avoid depriving, duties to protect from deprivation, and duties to aid the deprived. Most rights demand all three kinds of duties in at least some circumstances.

Even if all civil and political rights were entirely negative, though, they would not therefore deserve priority. Cranston (1964: 38) and Bedau (1979: 38) suggest that "negative" civil and political rights deserve priority because their violation involves the direct infliction of injury (an act of commission), whereas violating "positive" economic and social rights usually involves only the failure to confer a benefit (an act of omission). Even accepting this (false) description of the rights, Shue shows that often there is little moral difference.

Imagine a man stranded on an out-of-the-way desert island with neither food nor water. A sailor from a passing ship comes ashore but leaves the man to die. This act of omission is as serious a violation of human rights as strangling him, an act of commission. It is killing him, plain and simple—indirectly through "inaction" but just as surely, and perhaps even more cruelly (Shue 1979: 72–75). The moral difference lies not in the essential character of the acts per se but in contingent, empirical circumstances. In each case, culpable killing occurs.

C. THE RIGHT TO PROPERTY

Finally, we can note that most critics of economic and social rights do not in fact reject all such rights. Quite the contrary, almost all accept a right to private property.

For example, Cranston, like Locke, offers a list of exactly three basic human rights, to life, liberty, and property ("estates" in Locke's older terminology).[15] But Cranston never thinks to challenge the status of the (economic) human right to private property.[16] Quite the contrary, he concludes his property chapter by insisting that property "is inseparable from liberty" (1973: 50).[17]

Advocates of such a view face the insurmountable task of providing a plausible theoretical ground that yields precisely this one economic right. For example, property is often defended because it provides needed resources and space for the effective exercise of liberty. A right to work, however, seems at least as plausible a way to ensure resources for every person, given what we know about the tendency of private property to be very unevenly distributed and readily alienated in most legal systems.

This is not to criticize a limited right to property. Such a right can make an

15. From a more explicitly libertarian perspective, Tibor Machan devotes considerable effort to arguing for "the nonexistence of basic welfare rights" (Machan [1989: 100–123, 193–205]) while giving centrality of place in his scheme to the right to property. Compare Boaz (1997: 60–68).

16. This suggests that he, quite bizarrely, considers it a civil or political right. Compare Machan (1999: 4, 86). This is occasionally even argued explicitly (e.g., Yates [1995: 123]; Hernandez-Truyol [1996–1997: 224]). But if private property is not an economic right—and an often extravagant one at that—it is hard to imagine what is.

17. Even if true, this is largely irrelevant. Enough food to remain alive and guaranteed rest and leisure are also inseparable from liberty, but Cranston denies human rights to these things. That *a* is essential to the enjoyment of *x*, to which we have a human right, does not make *a* a human right.

important contribution to a life of dignity. But this single economic right alone simply cannot provide economic security and autonomy for all. In fact, for many people—in the Western world, most people, whose principal "property" is their labor power or skills—other economic and social rights would seem to be a better mechanism to realize economic security and autonomy.

D. TRANSCENDING THE DICHOTOMY

The conventional dichotomy also obscures the immense diversity within each of its two classes. Consider the great variety of rights in the category of civil and political rights. Rights to life, protection against discrimination, prohibition of slavery, recognition before the law, protection against torture, and nationality provide bodily, legal, and moral integrity to individuals. Rights to habeas corpus, protection against arbitrary arrest and detention, the presumption of innocence, and protection against ex post facto laws provide procedural guarantees for individuals in their dealings with the legal and political system, and especially the criminal law. The rights to freedom of thought, conscience, speech, press, association, and assembly define both a private sphere of conscience and belief and a public space in which these "private" issues, as well as public concerns, can be freely discussed, criticized, and advocated. The right to popular participation in government, and many public aspects of civil liberties such as the freedoms of speech, press, and assembly, empower citizens to participate in politics and exercise some control over the state.

Economic, social, and cultural rights are no less varied. The rights to food and access to health care provide survival and minimal physical security against disease or injury. Rights to social security, work, rest and leisure, and trade unions reflect not only the material necessity of labor but also the fact that meaningful work is in itself highly satisfying and can be central to personal dignity and development. The rights to education, to found and maintain a family, and to participate in the cultural life of the community provide social and cultural membership and participation.

In fact, affinities are often as striking across as within the conventional categories. The right to work, for example, is a right to economic participation that is instrumentally and intrinsically valuable in ways very much like the right to political participation. Cultural rights are perhaps most closely related to individual civil liberties, given the integral place of religion, public speech, and the mass media in the cultural life of most communities. The social or cultural right to education is intimately connected with the civil or political rights to freedom of speech, belief, and opinion, and so forth.

Abandoning the conventional dichotomy can give us a clearer picture of the nature and range of human rights and allow us to see much more clearly their manifold interrelationships.[18] Our lives—and the rights we need to live them

18. For one alternative typology, see Donnelly and Howard (1988).

with dignity—do not fall into largely separate political and socioeconomic spheres. Economic and social rights usually are violated by or with the collusion of elite-controlled political mechanisms of exclusion and domination. Poverty in the midst of plenty is a political phenomenon. Civil and political rights are often violated to protect economic privilege. We must think about, and categorize, human rights in ways that highlight rather than obscure such social realities.

In particular, we must overcome the dangerous illusion—shared by conservative critics of economic and social rights, radical critics of civil and political rights, and authoritarian regimes of various types—that the state can be a neutral instrument of technocratic management and an impartial arbiter of politically neutral rules of social order. Those who wield political power often do not rise above their personal, group, party, or class interests. Rarely do they exercise their power completely uninfluenced by such affiliations.

How one thinks about human rights does not and cannot determine political practice. Nonetheless, certain ways of thinking, such as about the traditional dichotomy, can help to support widely prevalent patterns of human rights violations. In every country where ruling elites have been able to enforce such a dichotomization of human rights, the consequence has been the systematic violation of a wide range of internationally recognized human rights.[19] Conversely, well-conceived theory, even at the very basic level of classificatory schemes, can aid in the struggle for greater respect for human rights.

The careful reader will note that this section has not directly defended the interdependence and indivisibility of the rights recognized in the Universal Declaration. (Section 3.4 begins to make such an argument, which is pursued further in the discussions of cultural relativism in Part II.) By undermining the conventional dichotomy between civil and political rights and economic, social, and cultural rights, however, it has addressed one of the principal philosophical and political challenges posed to this central element of the Universal Declaration model.

4. The State and International Human Rights

If human rights are held universally—that is, equally and by all—one might imagine that they hold (universally) against all other individuals and groups. Such a conception is inherently plausible and in many ways morally attractive. It is not, however, the dominant contemporary international understanding (compare §4.10).

19. As an American, I want to note explicitly that this includes the United States, where economic and social rights are systematically violated in significant measure because they still are seen as not really matters of rights (entitlement) but as considerations of justice, charity, or utility.

A. NATIONAL IMPLEMENTATION OF INTERNATIONAL HUMAN RIGHTS

Internationally recognized human rights impose obligations on and are exercised against sovereign territorial states. "Everyone has a right to *x*" in contemporary international practice means "Each state has the authority and responsibility to implement and protect the right to *x* within its territory." The Universal Declaration presents itself as "a common standard of achievement for all peoples and nations"—and the states that represent them. The Covenants create obligations only for states, and states have international human rights obligations only to *their own* nationals (and foreign nationals in their territory or otherwise subject to their jurisdiction or control).

Human rights norms have been largely internationalized. Their implementation, however, remains almost exclusively national. As we will see in Chapter 8, contemporary international (and regional) human rights regimes are supervisory mechanisms that monitor relations between states and citizens. They are not alternatives to a fundamentally statist conception of human rights. Even in the strong European regional human rights regime, the supervisory organs of the European Court of Human Rights regulate relations between states and their nationals or residents.

The centrality of states in the contemporary construction of international human rights is also clear in the substance of recognized rights. Some, most notably rights of political participation, are typically (although not universally) restricted to citizens. Many obligations—for example, to provide education and social insurance—apply only to residents. Virtually all apply to foreign nationals only while they are subject to the jurisdiction of that state.

Foreign states have no internationally recognized human rights obligation to protect foreign nationals abroad from, for example, torture. They are not even at liberty to use more than persuasive means on behalf of, for example, foreign victims of torture. Current norms of state sovereignty still prohibit states from acting coercively abroad against torture and virtually all other violations of human rights.[20]

This focus on state-citizen relations is also embedded in our ordinary language. The human rights of a person who is beaten by the police have been violated, but it is an ordinary crime, not a human rights violation, to receive an otherwise identical beating at the hands of a thief or an irascible neighbor. Internationally, we distinguish human rights violations from war crimes. Even when comparable suffering is inflicted on innocent civilians, we draw a sharp categorical distinction based on whether the perpetrator is (an agent of) one's own government or a foreign state.

Although neither necessary nor inevitable, this state-centric conception of

20. Genocide seems to be emerging as an exception. See Chapter 14.

human rights has deep historical roots. The idea of human rights received its first mature expression in, and remains deeply enmeshed with, liberal social contract theory, the only major tradition of political theory that assumes that individuals are endowed with equal and inalienable rights. And the contractarian notion of the state as an instrument for the protection, implementation, and effective realization of natural rights is strikingly similar to the conception of the state in international human rights instruments. Both measure the legitimacy of the state largely by its performance in implementing human rights.

The restriction of international human rights obligations to nationals, residents, and visitors also reflects the central role of the sovereign state in modern politics. Since at least the sixteenth century, states have struggled, with considerable success, to consolidate their internal authority over competing local powers. Simultaneously, early modern states struggled, with even greater success, to free themselves from imperial and papal authority. Their late modern successors have jealously, zealously, and (for all the talk of globalization) largely successfully fought attempts to reinstitute supranational authority.

With power and authority thus doubly concentrated, the modern state has emerged as both the principal threat to the enjoyment of human rights and the essential institution for their effective implementation and enforcement. Although human rights advocates have generally had an adversarial relationship with states, both sides of this relationship between the state and human rights require emphasis.

B. PRINCIPAL VIOLATOR AND ESSENTIAL PROTECTOR

Early advocates of natural (human) rights emphasized keeping the state out of the private lives and property of its citizens. In later eras, working men, racial and religious minorities, women, and the colonized, among other dispossessed groups, asserted their human rights against states that appeared to them principally as instruments of repression and domination. In recent decades, most human rights advocates, as symbolized by the work of groups such as Amnesty International, have focused on preventing state abuses of individual rights. Given the immense power and reach of the modern state, this emphasis on controlling state power has been, and remains, both prudent and productive.

The human rights strategy of control over the state has had two principal dimensions. Negatively, it prohibits a wide range of state interferences in the personal, social, and political lives of citizens, acting both individually and collectively. But beyond carving out zones of state exclusion, human rights place the people above and in positive control of their government. Political authority is vested in a free citizenry endowed with extensive rights of political participation (rights to vote, freedom of association, free speech, etc.).

Precisely because of its political dominance in the contemporary world, however, the state is the central institution available for effectively implementing internationally recognized human rights. "Failed states" such as Somalia suggest that one of the few things as frightening in the contemporary world as an efficiently repressive state is no state at all. Therefore, beyond preventing state-based wrongs, human rights require the state to provide certain (civil, political, economic, social, and cultural) goods, services, and opportunities.

This more positive human rights vision of the state also goes back to seventeenth and eighteenth century social contract theories. Contractarians such as Locke, Kant, and Paine emphasized that the rights one possesses naturally, simply as a human being, could not be enjoyed in a state of nature. Society and government are essential to the enjoyment of natural or human rights. In fact, within the contractarian tradition the legitimacy of a state can largely be measured by the extent to which it implements and protects natural rights.

The essential role of the state in securing the enjoyment of human rights is, if anything, even clearer when we turn from theory to practice. The struggle of dispossessed groups has typically been a struggle for full legal and political recognition by the state, and thus inclusion among those whose rights are protected by the state. Opponents of racial, religious, ethnic, and gender discrimination, political persecution, torture, disappearances, and massacre typically have sought not simply to end abuses but to transform the state from a predator into a protector of rights.

The need for an active state has always been especially clear for economic and social human rights. Even early bourgeois arguments emphasizing the natural right to property stressed the importance of active state protection. In fact, the "classic" liberalism of the eighteenth and nineteenth centuries saw the state as, in large measure, a mechanism to give legal form and protection to private property rights. Since the late nineteenth century, as our conceptions of the proper range of economic and social rights have expanded, the politics of economic and social rights has emphasized state provision where market and family mechanisms fail to ensure enjoyment of these rights.

A positive role for the state, however, is no less central to civil and political rights. The effective implementation of the right to nondiscrimination, for example, often requires extensive positive actions to realize the underlying value of equality. Even procedural rights such as due process entail substantial positive endeavors with respect to police, courts, and administrative procedures. And free, fair, and open elections do not happen through state restraint and inaction. The state must not merely refrain from certain harmful actions but create a political environment that fosters the development of active, engaged, autonomous citizens.

Because human rights first emerged in an era of personal, and thus often arbitrary, rule, an initial emphasis on individual liberty and state restraint was understandable. As the intrusive and coercive powers of the state have grown—steadily, and to now frightening dimensions—an emphasis on controlling the state continues to make immense political sense. The language of human rights abuses and violations continues, quite properly, to focus our attention on combating active state threats to human rights.

Nonetheless, a state that does no active harm itself is not enough. The state must also include protecting individuals against abuses by other individuals and private groups. The "classic" right to personal security, for example, is about safety against physical assaults by private actors, not just attacks by agents of the state. The state, although needing to be tamed, is in the contemporary world the principal institution we rely on to tame social forces no less dangerous to the rights, interests, and dignity of individuals, families, and communities.

Other strategies have been tried or proposed to control the destructive capacities of the state and harness its capabilities to realize important human goods and values. The virtue or wisdom of leaders, party members, or clerics, the expertise of technocrats, and the special skills and social position of the military have seemed to many to be attractive alternatives to human rights as bases of political order and legitimacy. But the human rights approach of individual rights and popular empowerment has proved far more effective than any alternative yet tried—or at least that is how I read the remarkably consistent collapse of dictatorships of the left and right alike over the past two decades in Latin America, Central and Eastern Europe, Africa, and Asia (although not [yet?] in most of the Middle East).

Most of the alternatives to human rights treat people as objects rather than as agents, beneficiaries but not right-holders. They rest on an inegalitarian and paternalistic view of the average person as someone to be provided for, a passive recipient of benefits, rather than a creative agent with a right to shape his or her life. Thus even if we overlook their naively benign view of power and the state, they grossly undervalue both autonomy and participation. Or, to use the language that I develop in Chapter 3, they fail to treat citizens with equal concern and respect. This requirement is the substantive core of the Universal Declaration model.

3/ Equal Concern and Respect

Having described the central features of the Universal Declaration model, we can now begin to move toward defending it. This chapter offers a series of increasingly deep and substantive, and thus increasingly controversial, justifications. I will argue that the Universal Declaration model is rooted in an attractive moral vision of human beings as equal and autonomous agents living in states that treat each citizen with equal concern and respect. I will also argue that a certain kind of liberalism provides, if not the best, then at least a good justification for this system of rights.

1. Hegemony and Settled Norms

I begin with a descriptive, empirical claim: human rights have become a hegemonic political discourse, or what Mervyn Frost (1996: 104–111) calls "settled norms" of contemporary international society, principles that are widely accepted as authoritative within the society of states. Both nationally and internationally, political legitimacy is increasingly judged by and expressed in terms of human rights.

The six leading international human rights treaties (on civil and political rights; economic, social, and cultural rights; racial discrimination; discrimination against women; torture; and the rights of the child) had an average of 156 parties at the end of 2001.[1] Even more notable is the penetration of human rights into bilateral, multilateral, and transnational diplomacy. In the 1970s, controversy still raged over whether human rights were even an appropriate concern of foreign policy. As late as 1980, only a handful of states had explicit international human rights policies. Today, however, human rights are a standard subject of bilateral and multilateral diplomacy.

Most national societies are also increasingly penetrated by human rights norms and values. Both governments and their opponents appeal to human

1. http://www.unhchr.ch/pdf/report.pdf

rights much more frequently and more centrally than just a few decades ago. Compare, for example, the terms of debate and the range of political options seriously considered nationally and regionally today in Latin America, Africa, and Asia with those of the 1960s and 1970s.

The collapse of the Soviet Union and its empire, and the retreat of dictatorial regimes in all areas of the world, suggests that, when given a chance, people in the contemporary world usually choose human rights. That choice has been made with varying degrees of enthusiasm and understanding. For many, human rights are a "default option,"[2] accepted only because the leading competitors have been delegitimized. Nonetheless, in contemporary international society there is no widely endorsed alternative.[3] And when given a choice, experience suggests that people rarely choose the alternatives that dictators of various stripes claim that they prefer (but, tellingly, refuse to allow them the opportunity to choose freely).

Even China, where in the 1980s the very use of the term *human rights* could land one in jail, has (reluctantly) come to adopt that language. Such uses, to be sure, are often cynical. The need to appear to be acting on behalf of human rights, however, tells us much about dominant values and aspirations. Even cynical uses pay tribute to the moral imperative of a commitment to human rights. And as the Helsinki process suggests (see §14.5), such norms can take on an independent life of their own, with consequences very different from those intended by cynical endorsers.

Even where citizens do not have a particularly sophisticated sense of what a commitment to human rights means, they respond to the general idea that they and their fellow citizens are equally entitled to certain basic goods, services, protections, and opportunities. The Universal Declaration, I would suggest, offers a good first approximation of the list that they would accept, largely irrespective of civilization, after considerable reflection. More precisely, there is almost nothing in the Universal Declaration that they would not put there, although one might readily imagine a global constitutional convention compiling a somewhat larger list.

The prominence of human rights in contemporary international society is not unrelated to their endorsement by the world's leading power, the United States, and its principal allies. But example has been far more powerful than advocacy—which has often been clumsy, even insulting—or imposition.

2. I take this term from Claus Offe, who used it at a conference on globalization and human rights at Yale University in the spring of 1999.

3. This is perhaps a modest exaggeration. Islamic fundamentalism is perhaps a real challenger in several countries, and one with genuinely universalistic aspirations. Xeonophobic nationalism might also be seen as a recurrent challenger, but one that is fundamentally inegalitarian and rarely capable of universalization (and thus of less interest, for reasons that are discussed in Sections 5.B and 6 later).

Human rights have moral and political authority that goes well beyond their backing by power (force). They dominate contemporary political discussions not only, or even primarily, because of the support of materially dominant powers but rather because they respond to some of the most important social and political aspirations of individuals, families, and groups in most countries of the world. Human rights have become internationally "hegemonic" in a Gramscian sense of the term.[4]

2. An Overlapping Consensus on International Human Rights

My claim that there is an international consensus on the system of human rights rooted in the Universal Declaration is *relatively* uncontroversial—although we will return to several elements of contention in Parts II and IV. My more controversial argument that this consensus is more voluntary then coerced would be substantially strengthened if I could account for how it came about in the face of the considerable, at times profound, philosophical differences that exist between (and within) civilizations, cultures, and societies in the contemporary world. John Rawls's idea of an overlapping consensus offers a descriptively accurate and morally attractive explanation.

Rawls distinguishes "comprehensive religious, philosophical, or moral doctrines" from "political conceptions of justice" (1996: xliii–xlv, 11–15, 174–176; 1999b: 31–32, 172–173). Because the latter address only the political structure of society, defined (as far as possible) independent of any particular comprehensive doctrine, adherents of different comprehensive doctrines may reach an "overlapping consensus" on a political conception of justice (Rawls 1996: 133–172, 385–396). I will argue that there is an international overlapping consensus on the Universal Declaration model.

The idea of overlapping (rather than complete) political (rather than moral or religious) consensus offers a plausible answer to the question: "How is it possible that there can be a stable and just society whose free and equal citizens are deeply divided by conflicting and even incommensurable religious, philosophical, and moral doctrines?" (Rawls 1996: 133). Although formulated initially for domestic societies, this idea has an obvious extension to international society, particularly a culturally and politically diverse pluralist international society.

Human rights can be readily derived from a considerable variety of moral theories; for example, they can be seen as encoded in the natural law, as politi-

4. Gramsci's discussion is scattered through (and can be roughly followed using the index in) Gramsci (1971). For an extended secondary discussion, see Femia (1981: 1–129). Compare also Cox (1996: chap. 6, 7). I use the term here descriptively, and without any necessary implications of class domination (which is essential to Gramsci's own account), but in what I take to be the root sense, namely, ideological power arising from the effective exclusion of viable normative alternatives within the mainstream of a society.

cal means to further human good or utility, or political institutions designed to produce virtuous citizens. The increasing political prominence of human rights over the past few decades has led more and more adherents of a growing range of comprehensive doctrines to endorse human rights—but (only) as a political conception of justice. For example, Muslims of various political persuasions in many parts of the Islamic world have in recent decades developed Islamic doctrines of human rights that are strikingly similar in substance to the Universal Declaration.

Although internationally recognized human rights do not depend on any particular religious or philosophical doctrine, they are *not* compatible with all comprehensive doctrines. The link between human rights and comprehensive doctrines, although loose, is a matter of substance, not just procedural agreement. Claims such as those in the Covenants that "these rights derive from the inherent dignity of the human person" or in the Vienna Declaration that "all human rights derive from the dignity and worth inherent in the human person" set the range of possible comprehensive doctrines within an overlapping consensus. Most important, human rights, because they are held equally by all human beings, are incompatible with fundamentally inegalitarian comprehensive doctrines, which are in principle excluded from the consensus (compare §5.B).

Are inegalitarian comprehensive doctrines predominant, or even prominent, in contemporary African, Asian, Western, or Islamic civilizations? We will return to this question in Part II. For now I will simply assert that they are not.

In their past, *all* major regional civilizations have at times been dominated by views that treated some significant portion of human beings as "outsiders" who not entitled to guarantees that could be taken for granted by "insiders." For example, in few regions of the globe have slavery or similar forms of human bondage never been practiced and widely justified. And for most of their histories all civilizations relied on inegalitarian ascriptive characteristics such as birth, age, or gender to assign social roles, rights, and duties.

Today, however, the basic moral equality of all human beings is not merely accepted but strongly endorsed by all leading comprehensive doctrines in all regions of the world. This convergence on egalitarian comprehensive doctrines, both within and between civilizations, provides the foundation for a convergence on the rights of the Universal Declaration. In principle, a great variety of social practices other than human rights might provide the basis for politically implementing foundational egalitarian values. In practice, for reasons that are explored in the Chapter 4, human rights have become the preferred option.

3. Moral Theory, Political Theory, and Human Rights

This appeal to overlapping consensus suggests that human rights fall more in the domain of political theory (political conceptions of justice) than the domain of moral theory (comprehensive doctrines). This suggestion is reinforced by the place of human rights in modern Western moral theory.

It is conventional to distinguish deontological (duty-based) theories, such as Kant's categorical imperative, from teleological (ends-, goals-, or consequence-based) theories, such as Bentham's utilitarianism or (neo-Aristotelian) virtue-based theories. Deontological and teleological theories posit radically different relationships between the right and the good.[5] Right is the moral primitive for deontological theories. We are required to do what is right (follow our duty), period, independent of the effects, for good or bad, produced by our actions (e.g., "Thou shalt not . . ."). In teleological theories, by contrast, the moral primitive is the good. Duty depends on the consequences of our actions. We are morally required to, within the limits of our skills and resources, increase human happiness, virtue, or some other end (or reduce human suffering, vice, etc.).[6]

This common classification of moral theories, however, tells us little about human rights, which have played a vanishingly small part in the history of (Western) moral theory, even during the modern era. For example, rights play no significant role in Kant's *Grounding for the Metaphysics of Morals*. For utilitarians, rights are only second order rules that save us the (often considerable) task of calculating utilities in particular cases. We might in principle imagine rights-based moral theories, but in practice such a category has historically been largely an empty one.[7] Human rights logically may be, but in fact rarely have been, taken to be a moral primitive.[8]

When we turn to *political* theory, however, (human) rights often become central.[9] For example, in Part I of Kant's "Theory and Practice" (1983: 61–92), which deals with individual morality, rights make no significant appearance. But rights (entitlements) become central in Part II, which treats "political right." In fact, Kant's contractarian political theory is centered on the rights we

5. Within Anglo-American philosophy, Ross (1930) provides a classic discussion.

6. Deontological and teleological theories thus posit different accounts of the relationship between means and ends. Teleologists are concerned primarily with consequences, and thus ends. Actions ("means") are evaluated by their contribution to realizing the defining moral end (e.g., utility maximization). Deontological theories, while recognizing the instrumental value of actions, see the morality of an act as determined by its inherent nature rather than its consequences. For deontologists, moral acts are required because they are right, not because they produce some other effect in the world. They are not means to anything at all. They instantiate rather than cause or bring about the realization of the right.

7. Alan Gewirth (1982; 1996) may be a contemporary exception that proves this rule. I am aware of no pre–twentieth century exceptions.

8. Elsewhere I refer to human rights as providing a moral vision of legitimate governance. "Moral" there is used in a wider, and perhaps looser, sense of the term. My point here is that Western moral theories rely on foundational principles such as duty, virtue, and utility, not rights.

9. Thus Dworkin (1977: 171–172) distinguishes between goal-based, right[s]-based, and duty-based political theories.

have as human beings, as subjects, and as citizens (1983: 72–77). More generally, human rights are at the heart, and a defining feature, of contractarian political theories.

Other political theories may endorse a human rights standard of political legitimacy by other routes. One might even argue that the loose and weak link between human rights and leading moral theories is an attraction rather than a drawback, allowing for a considerable degree of *political* consensus despite moral divergences.[10] By remaining open to many egalitarian moral and political theories, human rights may allow us to handle certain questions of political justice and right while circumventing difficult and usually inconclusive disputes over moral foundations.

This is particularly attractive in a "postmodern" world skeptical of the possibility of finding logically unassailable foundations. Political theorists have increasingly turned their attention to notions such as deliberative consensus (Habermas 1998; 1996; 1993) and recognition (e.g., Gutmann 1994). Human rights may provide a focal point for forging such a consensus or for negotiating mutual recognition. Certainly no other substantive ideal has come even close to such widespread international endorsement by both governments and movements of political opposition across the globe.[11]

Therefore, in the remainder of this chapter, and in most of the rest of this book, I will be concerned with the political, rather than moral, theory of human rights. We will be concerned with questions of *political* rights and obligations, a point already suggested by the special place of states in the Universal Declaration model (see §2.4). To put it in slightly different terms, internationally recognized human rights provide a standard of political legitimacy. In the contemporary world—the world in which there is an overlapping consensus on the Universal Declaration model—states are legitimate largely to the extent that they respect, protect, and implement the rights of their citizens.

4. Equal Concern and Respect

What is the political conception of justice around which this overlapping consensus has formed? I want to suggest that it is something very much like Ronald Dworkin's idea that the state is required to treat each citizen with equal concern and respect.

10. Compare my earlier argument (§1.3.C) for the virtues of an analytic theory.

11. This is only a modest exaggeration. "Peace" and "development" are probably more widely endorsed. But neither—at least in their common senses of absence of war and sustainable economic growth—provides anything like the attractive comprehensive standard of political legitimacy offered by human rights. "Justice" may also be more widely endorsed, but only in a very abstract form. When we get to the level of detail of the Universal Declaration, the differences in conceptions of justice are striking.

A. EQUALITY AND AUTONOMY

> Government must treat those whom it governs with concern, that is, as human beings who are capable of suffering and frustration, and with respect, that is, as human beings who are capable of forming and acting on intelligent conceptions of how their lives should be lived. Government must not only treat people with concern and respect, but with equal concern and respect. It must not distribute goods or opportunities unequally on the ground that some citizens are entitled to more because they are worthy of more concern. It must not constrain liberty on the ground that one citizen's conception of the good life . . . is nobler or superior to another's. (Dworkin 1977: 272–273)

The state must treat each person as a moral and political equal. Inequalities in goods or opportunities that arise directly or indirectly from political decisions must be compatible with a political conception of justice founded on equal concern and respect.

This understanding of the equality of all human beings leads "naturally" to a political emphasis on autonomy. Personal liberty, especially the liberty to choose and pursue one's own life, clearly is entailed by the idea of equal respect. For the state to interfere in matters of personal morality would be to treat the life plans and values of some as superior to those of others. A certain amount of economic liberty is also required, at least to the extent that decisions concerning consumption, investment, and risk reflect free decisions based on personal values that arise from autonomously chosen conceptions of the good life.

Liberty alone, however, cannot serve as the overriding value of social life or the sole end of political association. Unless checked by a fairly expansive, positive conception of the persons in relation to whom it is exercised, individual liberty readily degenerates into license and social atomization. If liberty is to foster dignity it must be not merely equal liberty for all, but liberty exercised within the constraints of the principle of equal concern and respect.

Autonomy (liberty) and equality are less a pair of guiding principles—let alone competing principles—than different manifestations of the central commitment to the equal worth and dignity of each and every person, whatever that person's social utility. To justify denying or severely restricting individual autonomy almost necessarily involves an appeal to inequality.[12] Equal and autonomous rights-bearing individuals are entitled to make fundamental choices about what constitutes the good life (for them), with whom they associate, and how. They have no right to force on one another ideas of what is right and proper, because to do so would treat those others as less than equal moral agents. Regardless of who they are or where they stand, individuals have an in-

12. The obvious exception is the protection of the equal autonomy of others.

herent dignity and worth for which the state must demonstrate an active and equal concern. And everyone is *entitled* to this equal concern and respect (with the political consequences discussed in §1.1).

Human rights simultaneously constitute individuals as equal and autonomous citizens and states as polities fit to govern such rights-bearing citizens. The constructivist theory sketched in §1.3.B is thus beginning to acquire some substance.

B. THE UNIVERSAL DECLARATION AND EQUAL CONCERN AND RESPECT

It is a relatively simple matter to derive the full list of rights in the Universal Declaration from the political principle of equal concern and respect. Other lists of rights can also be derived from this principle. Other political conceptions of justice may be compatible with the Universal Declaration model. I would suggest, however, that the close overlap is much more than a coincidence.

To treat someone with concern and respect, an individual must first be recognized as a moral and legal person. This in turn requires certain basic personal rights. Rights to recognition before the law and to nationality (Universal Declaration, Art. 6, 15) are political prerequisites. In a different vein, the right to life, as well as rights to protection against slavery, torture, and other inhuman or degrading treatment (Art. 3, 4, 5), are essential to recognition and respect as a person.

Such rights as freedom of speech, conscience, religion, and association (Art. 18, 19) protect a sphere of personal autonomy. The right to privacy (Art. 12) even more explicitly aims to guarantee the capacity to realize personal visions of a life worthy of a human being. Personal autonomy also requires economic and social rights, such as the right to education (Art. 26), which makes available the intellectual resources for informed autonomous choices as well as the skills needed to act on them, and the right to participate in the cultural life of the community (Art. 27), which recognizes the social and cultural dimensions of personal development. In its political dimension, equal respect also implies democratic control of the state and therefore rights to political participation and to freedoms of (political) speech, press, assembly, and association (Art. 19, 20, 21).

The principle of equal concern and respect also requires that the government intervene to reduce certain social and economic inequalities. The state must protect those who, as a result of natural or voluntary membership in an unpopular group, are subject to social, political, or economic discrimination that limits their access to a fair share of social resources or opportunities. Such rights as equal protection of the laws and protection against discrimination on such bases as race, color, sex, language, religion, opinion, origin, property, birth, or status (Art. 2, 7) are essential to ensure that all people are treated as fully and equally human.

In the economic sphere, an attachment to a market-based system of production both fosters efficiency (and thus aggregate prosperity) and places minimal restraints on economic liberty, thus augmenting personal autonomy. Market distribution, however, tends to be grossly unequal. Inequality is not necessarily objectionable. The principle of equal concern and respect, however, implies an economic floor; degrading inequalities cannot be permitted (Shue 1980: 19–23). The state thus must act positively to counteract unjustifiable market inequalities, at least to the point that all are assured a minimum share of resources through the implementation of social and economic rights. In human rights terms this implies, for example, rights to food, health care, and social insurance (Art. 22, 25).

Efforts to alleviate degrading or disrespectful deprivation do not exhaust the scope of the economic demands of the principle of equal concern and respect. The right to work (Art. 23), which is essentially a right to economic participation, is of special importance. Work has considerable intrinsic value, as an element of a life of dignity as well as instrumental value in satisfying basic material needs and providing an economic foundation for personal autonomy. A (limited) right to property (Art. 17) can be justified in similar terms.

Finally, the special threat to personal autonomy and equality presented by the modern state requires a set of legal rights, such as the presumption of innocence and rights to due process, fair and public hearings before an independent tribunal, and protection from arbitrary arrest, detention, or exile (Art. 8–11). More broadly, the special threat to dignity posed by the state is reflected in the fact that all human rights are held particularly against the state. Moreover, they hold against all types of states, democratic as much as any other (compare §11.3): if one's government treats one as less than fully human, it matters little how that government came to power. The individual does have social duties (Art. 29), but the discharge of social obligations is not a precondition for having or exercising human rights.

The substantive attractions of this particular "realistic utopia" (Rawls 1999b: 11), I would suggest, go a long way toward explaining the hegemonic power of the Universal Declaration model. This, I believe, largely accounts for the overlapping international consensus on the rights of the Universal Declaration.

5. Toward a Liberal Theory of Human Rights

Equal concern and respect, understood as a political conception of justice, can be endorsed by a variety of comprehensive doctrines. I turn now to one, liberalism. This chapter thus moves from (relatively) descriptive to largely prescriptive argument. Accepting the common association of human rights with

"Western liberalism," both in their historical development and in contemporary political practice, I argue that (a particular type of) liberalism provides a strong and attractive normative foundation for the Universal Declaration model.

A. DEFINING LIBERALISM

"Liberalism" is a complex and contested set of orientations and values. It is *relatively* uncontroversial, however, to say that it is rooted in a commitment to liberty, freedom, or, in the formulation I prefer, autonomy. More precisely, liberals give central political place to *individual* autonomy, rather than to the liberty of society, the state, or other corporate actors. Liberals see individuals as entitled to "govern" their lives, to make important life choices for themselves, within limits connected primarily with the mutual recognition of equal liberties and opportunities for others.

Liberalism also is specially committed to equality[13]—although most liberal (and nonliberal) theories and all liberal (and nonliberal) societies ultimately permit substantial economic, social, or political inequality. Liberty is not a special privilege of the elite but (in principle) ought to be available to all. Equal liberty for all is at the heart of any liberal political vision.[14]

But not all liberals are friends of rights, let alone human rights. And different liberals cash out the commitment to equal liberty in different ways. Figure 3.1 categorizes liberal theories along two dimensions: the extent to which they emphasize rights or the good (or virtue, or some other value) and the substantive "thickness" of their conceptions of those core values.

Locke is the seminal figure in the strand of liberalism that grounds the commitment to equal liberty on natural, or what we today call human, rights. Its roots go back at least to Leveler and Digger arguments during the English Civil War. Kant, Paine, and Rousseau were leading eighteenth century proponents. Rawls and Dworkin are prominent recent (American) representatives.

Liberalism, however, also has a strong historical association, going back at least to Hobbes, with utilitarianism, a good-based theory. The seminal figure is Bentham. Utilitarian liberalism was dominant in Britain in the nineteenth century. A microeconomic version underlies contemporary "neoliberal" market-oriented economic reforms.

My purpose here is to advance a rights-based liberal defense of the Universal Declaration model. Good-based conceptions, however, make human rights at best a second-order or derivative political principle. Therefore, although

13. Dworkin (1985: chap. 9) offers an especially forceful argument for the centrality of equality to liberalism.

14. There are striking analogies with the motto of the High Commissioner for Human Rights in 1998, the year of the fiftieth anniversary of the Universal Declaration: "All human rights for all."

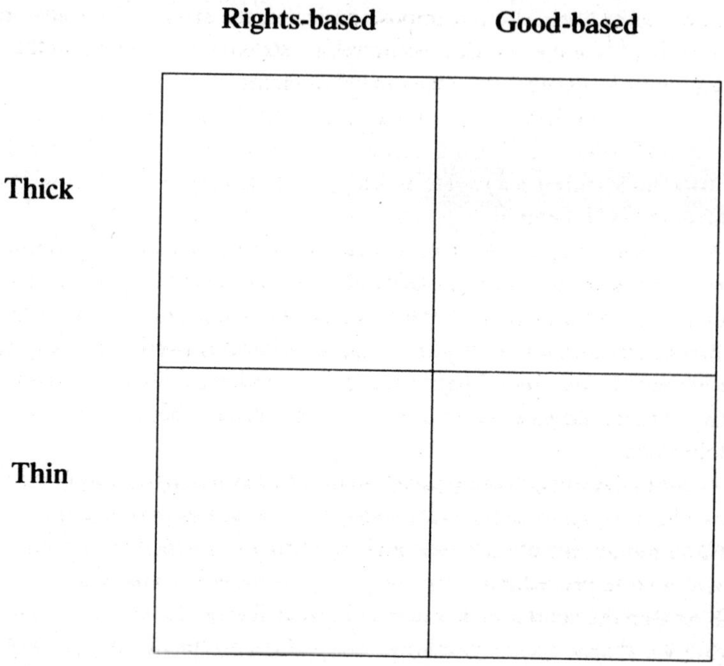

Figure 3.1 A Typology of Liberal Theories

many good-based liberals participate in the overlapping consensus on international human rights, their views are not considered here.

In fact, microeconomic, utilitarian "neoliberalism" is fundamentally opposed to the liberal human rights perspective I defend. As we will see in more detail in §11.7, its logic of efficiency contrasts sharply with the logic of individual human rights. Neoliberal equality involves political indifference to competing preferences—unbiased treatment in the marketplace—rather than guaranteed access to essential goods, services, and opportunities. And neoliberal structural adjustment is *very* different from the welfare states of Europe and North America with which the Universal Declaration model has (rightly) been specially associated.

Turning to the second dimension of our typology, the range of recognized rights, the end points of the continuum are represented by what I label "social democratic" and "minimalist" (or libertarian) liberalism. A liberalism compatible with the Universal Declaration model must be strongly egalitarian, must actively embrace an extensive system of economic and social rights, and must reflect a robust conception of democratic political control (compare §11.3).

The European welfare state is the leading practical exemplar. *All* internationally recognized human rights are seen as entitlements of individuals—social and political claims that impose duties on the state and society—rather than mere liberties. Even with recent welfare state retrenchments, all the states of Western Europe lie toward the top left of Figure 3.1.

At the bottom left lies a minimalist liberalism that emphasizes individual personal liberties and includes only a short list of economic and social rights. In some circles this is referred to as "classical" liberalism. In the United States it is often called "libertarian."

Minimalist liberalism's truncated list of human rights is substantively incompatible with the Universal Declaration model. Whatever its historical pedigree or philosophical merits,[15] it is best seen as a critique of the substance of the Universal Declaration model, despite the considerable overlap on civil and political rights.[16] And for the past half century *no* Western liberal democratic regime, not even Reagan's America or Thatcher's Britain, has pursued libertarian minimalism.

A politically important (although not obviously theoretically coherent) "intermediate" rights-based liberal perspective emphasizes personal and civil liberties, a modest list of economic and social rights provided by a welfare state, and primarily procedural democracy. This "American" vision is much more willing than the libertarian to restrict personal liberties to remedy invidious inequalities. It also is somewhat more sympathetic to the idea of state action to assure minimum access to social and economic goods, services, and opportunities. But the American welfare state is much less robust than those of Europe. In the United States this perspective is usually referred to as "liberal," pejoratively by the right. I would suggest that it is the thinnest plausible liberal conception of the Universal Declaration model.

Both "American" and "social democratic" liberalisms are committed both to a democracy that operates only within the substantive requirements of equal human rights for all and to a welfare state that supplements a market system of production with substantial "welfare state" redistribution. I will use "liberal" without qualification to refer to this shared political ideal based on an underlying vision of equal concern and respect.

B. EQUALITY, AUTONOMY, NEUTRALITY, AND TOLERATION

Liberals often make exaggerated claims for the neutrality of their principles.[17] Although liberals do characteristically defend a limited principle of neutrality

15. §2.3 criticizes minimalism's characteristic attack on economic and social rights.

16. Most minimalists nonetheless participate in the international overlapping consensus on human rights, subordinating their unease with economic and social rights to their overriding (even defining) commitment to civil and political rights.

17. Daniel Bell succinctly but perceptively focuses on this shortcoming of many liberal theories. See 1993: 3–4; 1996: 660–662.

based on the principle of equal concern and respect, liberalism, no less than any other substantive moral or political position, privileges some competing conceptions of the good and marginalize others. Any list of human rights cannot but make substantive judgments about the range of conceptions of the good life that are considered within the pale of reasonable argument. The real issue is not whether certain views are excluded but the grounds for inclusion/exclusion. In this section I want to defend a tolerant liberal "neutrality" toward a wide range of, but not all, competing visions of the good life.

Liberal neutrality—neutrality bounded by liberal principles—is an expression of the core liberal values of equality and autonomy in a world without indubitable moral and political foundations. If we cannot be certain of the substance of the good life, particularly in its details,[18] and if we are committed to the basic moral equality of all human beings, then a stance of at least principled tolerance is required for all conceptions that respect the equal dignity of all human beings. Commitment to individual autonomy provides additional support for a tolerant liberal neutrality: one is entitled to make such determinations, within the bounds set by the equal autonomy of others.

Viewed from the other side, to impose a particular substantive conception of the good life would be to infringe or deny the equality and autonomy of those on whom it is being imposed. And if one might be wrong, the denial cannot even be justified by paternalistic arguments. Liberal political theory thus seems especially attractive in a world that is skeptical of ostensibly secure moral foundations (which, conversely, militate against liberal neutrality).

Liberal neutrality, however, is not—cannot be—neutral with respect to claims that some groups of human beings are categorically superior or inferior to others, and thus have different basic rights. Liberals also are not neutral with respect to theories that deny individuals and groups the right to pursue their own conception of the good (so long as they allow exactly the same right to other individuals and groups).

Of course, liberal "intolerance" toward those who categorically attack equality and autonomy is vulnerable to skeptical external challenge. In practice, however, I do not think that many liberals (or their critics) would be embarrassed to reject out of hand those who claim that some human beings are categorically superior or inferior to others. And I do not believe that liberals (or others) need apologize for rejecting out of hand arguments that some groups are entitled to pursue their conception of the good life at the cost of the good life thus defined of others. Whatever the abstract philosophical interest or power of fundamental challenges to the basic moral equality of all human be-

18. More precisely, if our own certainty is not something that is shared by many of those with whom we interact, and if we have sufficient respect for them, then we cannot impose our vision of the good life.

ings and the recognition of considerable space for them to choose for themselves the good life, in the contemporary world it is those who make such challenges, rather than liberals, who are likely to be embarrassed by such arguments.[19]

Many nonliberals, as well as good-based liberals, are likely to note that most of the real work in the preceding paragraphs is done by the claim of equality. Autonomy provides additional support, but most of the same conclusions can be reached through appeals to equality alone. Therefore, to the extent that my argument is persuasive it supports a cluster of positions that include but is much broader than liberalism. In other words, although explicitly liberal, the argument of this section has strong substantive connections with arguments based on other political or moral theories or perspectives that participate in the overlapping consensus on the Universal Declaration model.

6. Consensus: Overlapping but Bounded

At the risk of some repetition I want to (re-)emphasize the bounded nature of the consensus on the Universal Declaration model. Bhikhu Parekh may be correct in claiming that "some values are embedded in and underpin all human societies" (1999: 135), but that list of values is, at best, short. And because some societies have rejected the very notion that all members of the species *Homo sapiens* are in some morally important sense equally human beings, whatever consensus on values does exist will not help us much with human rights.

The overlapping consensus on the Universal Declaration model is *not* a transhistorical "anthropological" consensus. It does not imply that every person, every society, or even every single government accepts the Universal Declaration. Rather, the claim is that most leading elements in almost all contemporary societies endorse the idea that every human being has certain equal and inalienable rights and is thus entitled to equal concern and respect from the state—and that what holds this otherwise disparate group together is a fundamental commitment to human equality and autonomy.

Participation in the overlapping consensus on the Universal Declaration model is (only) possible for those who see "human being" as a fundamental moral category and who see human beings as in some important sense au-

19. Ken Booth may not be entirely fair in the following quoted passage, but I think he expresses well the underlying moral intuition: "James Der Derian has endorsed a Nietzschean perspective on 'the very necessity of difference,' looking towards a 'practical strategy to celebrate, rather than exacerbate, the anxiety, insecurity and fear of a new world order where radical otherness is ubiquitous and indomitable.' Celebrating anxiety, insecurity and fear, from the comfort of Western academe, on behalf of those anxious about being beaten up or worse, insecure about having any cash to feed their children, or fearing their total dependence on the next rainfall, strikes me as deeply patronising, immoral and unthinking" (1999: 57–58).

tonomous actors. These "foundational" commitments define the range of views that must be taken into account in cross-cultural and cross-philosophical discussions, to which Part II of this book is devoted. Those outside the community thus defined should be listened to and perhaps even sought out—because of our own commitment to respect for all human beings, in an effort to change the minds of those who hold such views, or to sharpen our own views by subjecting them to external critique. But proponents of such views are legitimately treated as in some important sense "unreasonable."

It is not necessarily illogical to claim that some members of the species *Homo sapiens* are born to be slaves or untouchables or subordinated to men. It is not necessarily incoherent to claim that members of one racial or ethnic group ought to be subordinated to another. It is, however, almost by definition *morally* unreasonable *in the contemporary world*. In particular, it is beyond the pale in almost all countries today to advocate social institutions that enforce qualitative differences between groups of human beings, especially when those differences are defined by ascriptive characteristics.[20] Such institutions are not expressions of alternative conceptions of human rights but rather are fundamental challenges to the idea of human rights (compare Chapter 5).

The core commitment to equality and autonomy underlying the Universal Declaration model suggests the importance of uncoerced consensus. But those same principles also require that the range of substantive positions within that consensus be strictly bounded by a shared commitment to equal autonomy for all. This is perhaps the essential insight in Rousseau's distinction between the general will and the will of all:[21] there are some individual wills that simply cannot be allowed to be expressed in the general will if it is to maintain its moral character.

When Rousseau speaks of forcing people to be free,[22] however, he seems to me (as a liberal) to go too far. But he nonetheless points toward an important insight. Some forms of behavior cannot be tolerated in a rights-protective society. Some interests must be excluded from the calculation of the public interest, no matter how deeply their proponents are attached to them.

We may be forced to live with or next to those who hold morally and politically loathsome views. Our commitment to equality and autonomy may compel us not to use force against them to try to change those views. But we have no obligation to tolerate attempts to impose these views on those who are judged inferior. Quite the contrary, we have a moral obligation at least to con-

20. I began making the final revisions on this chapter just as the World Conference on Racism opened in Durban. The debate over including practices such as caste, anti-Semitism, and Zionism (which many argue are not really issues of "race") nicely illustrates the power of the contemporary international desire to delegitimate all forms of group superiority.

21. *The Social Contract*, Book II, Chapter 3.

22. *The Social Contract*, Book I, Chapter 7.

demn those who would act to implement, for example, systems of slavery, caste, or racial domination. And we would seem to have a national political obligation to resist, with force if necessary, nonverbal behavior that seeks to create institutions of domination and subordination.[23]

A system of equal and inalienable rights cannot be sustained in the face of social practices that deny the possibility of each enjoying his or her rights equally. As individuals, proponents of racial domination, for example, have the right to hold, perhaps even to advocate,[24] their views. But efforts to implement them in practice fall outside the international consensus on human rights and may be—must be—resisted with all vigor.

23. Given the current development of international society (see §2.4 and chaps.8, 14), there is no widely accepted parallel international legal or political obligation.

24. I say "perhaps" because although a strong moral case can be made for such a liberty, it is *legally* prohibited in Article 4 of the 1965 International Convention on the Elimination of All Forms of Racial Discrimination.

PART II

Cultural Relativism and International Human Rights

4/ Markets, States, and "The West"

The idea of an overlapping consensus explains how agreement might be possible on a list of human rights despite extensive cultural and moral diversity. Functional, causal, or historical accounts would explain why there has been convergence on the particulars of the Universal Declaration model. I will argue that human rights are centrally linked to "modernity" and have been (and remain) specially connected to the political rise and practices of "the West."

1. The Evolution of Lists of Human Rights

In the most general terms, a list of rights reflects a society's understanding of the principal "standard threats" (Shue 1980: 29–34) to human dignity. A human right to excrete,[1] for example, seems silly because there is no serious threat. But if preventing excretion became a diabolical new tool of torture or repressive social control, recognizing a human right to excrete might make sense.

Consider, by contrast, the internationally recognized right to "rest, leisure and reasonable limitation of working hours and periodic holidays with pay." Here we face not the fantasy of a perverse imagination but a common assault on the dignity of workers, from nineteenth-century factories in Manchester, to twentieth-century sweatshops in New York, to textile and electronics factories across Southeast Asia today.

Not every kind of systematic suffering leads to a recognized right. Politics largely determines whether any particular indignity/threat/right is recognized. Nonetheless, our list of human rights has evolved, and will continue to change, in response to social and technological changes, the emergence of new techniques of repression, changing ideas of human dignity, the rise of new political forces, and even past human rights successes (which allow attention and re-

1. This right actually was advanced by Johan Galtung in a paper circulated in the mid-1970s, although I am no longer able to find the reference.

sources to be shifted to threats that previously were inadequately recognized or insufficiently addressed).

Consider economic and social human rights. Although John Locke's short list of life, liberty, and estates in Thomas Jefferson's hands was expanded to life, liberty, and the pursuit of happiness, economic and social rights began to make substantial headway only with the nineteenth-century rise of the working class as an effective political force. The resulting political struggles led to new understandings of the meaning of and conditions necessary for a life of dignity, rooted in significant measure in the experience of the social and economic devastation of early industrialization. Over the course of more than a century, the right to property gradually was supplemented by, and ultimately largely subordinated to, an extensive set of economic, social, and cultural rights.

Our list of civil and political rights has also changed dramatically. Today in the West we take the right to a free press largely for granted. Two hundred years ago, however, Tom Paine was prosecuted for sedition because of his pamphleteering, and President Adams used the notorious restrictions of the Alien and Sedition Acts against his political adversaries, including Thomas Jefferson. The right to freedom of association has been extended to associations of workers for scarcely more than a century. Genocide was recognized as an international crime only in the aftermath of the Holocaust. "Disappearances" have more recently reshaped our understandings of the rights to life and protection against arbitrary arrest and detention.

Lists of human rights are based only loosely on abstract philosophical reasoning and *a priori* moral principles. They emerge instead from the concrete experiences, especially the sufferings, of real human beings and their political struggles to defend or realize their dignity. Internationally recognized human rights reflect a politically driven process of social learning.[2]

2. Markets, States, and Political Equality

Turning toward a more structural and historical, causal account, in this and the following sections I argue that the idea and practice of human rights arose from two interrelated pairs of changes associated with "modernity": the rise of modern markets and modern states and the rise of political claims of equality and toleration. As a result, a hierarchical world of rulers and subjects was transformed into a more egalitarian world of office holders and citizens.

To reduce half a millennium to a few paragraphs, ever more powerful (capitalist) markets and (sovereign, bureaucratic) states gradually penetrated first Europe and then the globe. In the process, "traditional" communities, and

2. Wellman (1997) offers a thoughtful and balanced look, considering both moral and political issues, at the growth of rights and rights claims in recent years.

their systems of mutual support and obligation, were disrupted, destroyed, or radically transformed, typically with traumatic consequences. These changes created the problems that human rights were "designed" to solve: vast numbers of (relatively) separate families and individuals left to face a growing range of increasingly unbuffered economic and political threats to their interests and dignity.

The absolutist state—increasingly freed from the constraints of cross-cutting feudal obligations, independent religious authorities, and tradition—offered one solution: a society organized around a monarchist hierarchy justified by a state religion. But the newly emergent bourgeoisie, the other principal beneficiary of early modern markets and states, envisioned a society in which the claims of property balanced those of birth. By the late seventeenth century, such claims increasingly were formulated in terms of natural rights.

More or less contemporaneously, the Reformation disrupted the unity of Christendom, with consequences that were often even more violent. By the middle of the seventeenth century, however, states gradually began to stop fighting over religion. (The Westphalia settlement of 1648 is conventionally presented as the start of "modern" international relations.) Although full religious equality was far distant—just as bourgeois calls for "equal" treatment initially fell far short of full political equality even for themselves, let alone for all—religious toleration (at least for many Christians sects) gradually became the European norm.[3]

Add to this the growing possibilities for physical and social mobility and we have the crucible out of which contemporary human rights ideas and practices were formed. Privileged ruling groups faced a growing barrage of demands—first for relief from legal and political disabilities, then for full inclusion on the basis of equality—from an ever widening range of dispossessed groups. Such demands took many forms, including appeals to scripture, church, morality, tradition, justice, natural law, order, social utility, and national strength. But claims of equal and inalienable natural or human rights increasingly came to be preferred.

Modern societies, especially in the twentieth century, have increasingly come to be organized around states guaranteeing to their citizens (rather than subjects), as matters of entitlement, an extensive array of civil, political, economic, social, and cultural goods, services, and opportunities.[4] As we saw in

3. The special place of markets and states is only contingently Western; the structural economic and political logic of transformation was first experienced in the West but has spread, in very similar forms, throughout the globe. The role of religious differences, however, is more essentially a Western story.

4. In recent decades, the hegemony of rights claims has become so pronounced that critics increasingly refer to the "tyranny" or "imperialism" of rights. See, for example, Glendon (1991). Compare Gordon (1998: 698–699, 789).

Chapter 2, there has also been a parallel move toward human rights as a preferred basis for advancing claims of justice in international society.

3. Expanding the Subjects and Substance of Human Rights

Locke's classic formulation strikes most readers today as far too narrow, in both its substance and its subjects.[5] Life, liberty, and estates, even in expansive readings of these terms, fall far short of the substance of the Universal Declaration. And despite the apparent universalism of the language of natural rights, Locke clearly envisioned a political world of propertied Christian men. Women, along with "savages," servants, and wage laborers, were never imagined to be holders of natural rights.

Human rights struggles in the subsequent three centuries have gradually expanded the recognized subjects of human rights, pushing us significantly closer to the ideal of full and equal inclusion of all members of the species *Homo sapiens*. Racist, bourgeois, Christian patriarchs have found the same arguments they used against aristocratic privilege turned against them by members of new social groups seeking full participation in public and private life as autonomous subjects and agents.

Many of the great political struggles of the past two centuries have revolved around expanding the recognized subjects of human rights. The rights of working men led to often violent political conflict in nineteenth- and early twentieth-century Europe and North America. The rights of colonized peoples were a major global political issue during the 1950s, 1960s, and 1970s. Struggles to eliminate discrimination based on race and gender have been prominent in many countries over the past thirty years.

In each case, the essential claim was that however different ("other") we—religious dissenters, the poor, women, nonwhites, ethnic minorities—may be, we are, no less than you, human beings, and as such are entitled to the same basic rights. Members of each disadvantaged or despised group have used the rights they did enjoy to press for legal recognition of rights being denied them. For example, workers used their votes, along with what freedom of the press and freedom of association they were allowed, to press to eliminate legal discrimination based on wealth or property.

The substance of human rights thus expanded in tandem with their subjects. For example, the political left argued that unlimited private property rights were incompatible with true liberty, equality, and security for working men (and, later, women). Intense and often violent political struggles led to the rise of social insurance schemes, regulations on working conditions, and an ex-

5. The issues examined in this section are also considered in §13.2.

tended range of recognized economic, social, and cultural rights, culminating in the welfare state societies of late twentieth-century Europe.

The International Human Rights Covenants both expanded the subjects of human rights to all human beings everywhere on the globe and codified an evolved, shared understanding of the principal systematic public threats to human dignity in the contemporary world (and the rights-based practices necessary to counter them). To oversimplify only slightly, they set out as a hegemonic political model something very much like the liberal democratic welfare state of Western Europe, in which all adult nationals are incorporated as full legal and political equals entitled to an extensive array of social welfare services, social and economic opportunities, and civil and political liberties (compare §2.3, 11.8).

Contemporary liberals may be tempted to see in this history a gradual unfolding of the inherent logic of natural rights, but we must be wary of Whiggish self-satisfaction and comfortable teleological views of moral progress. A list of rights reflects a contingent response to historically specific conditions. For example, Article 11 of the International Covenant on Civil and Political Rights—"No one shall be imprisoned merely on the ground of inability to fulfill a contractual obligation"—responds to the (historically very unusual) practice of debtor prisons. An authoritative list of human rights emerges out of an ongoing series of political struggles that have changed our understanding of human dignity, the major threats (both old and new) to that dignity, and the institutions, practices, and values necessary to protect it.

The historical contingency of international human rights norms, however, in no way diminishes their status or importance. Although conventional, internationally recognized human rights certainly are not arbitrary. And they cannot be changed merely through acts of the will. They are deeply rooted social constructions that shape our lives. Human rights have become a central, perhaps even defining, feature of our social and political reality. The vision of human dignity they reflect and seek to implement is accepted by almost all states as authoritative, whatever their deviations from these norms in practice.

4. Linking "The West" and Human Rights

So far I have shown that human rights, rather than a timeless system of essential moral principles, are a set of social practices that regulate relations between, and help to constitute, citizens and states in "modern" societies. The remainder of this chapter further contextualizes contemporary human rights norms by exploring the special linkage of internationally recognized human rights to "the West" where, as a matter of historical fact, these ideas and practices first emerged.

This historical priority, of course, reflects no special Western virtue or merit. The characteristic indignities and injustices of modern markets and modern states simply happen to have been experienced first in the West. Nonetheless both history and the high degree of development of Western human rights practices[6] have given a special "Western" twist to internationally recognized human rights. The remainder of this chapter seeks to establish this historical fact and to sketch in greater institutional detail the currently "hegemonic" vision of the Universal Declaration model. The remaining chapters of Part II deal with "relativistic" arguments against the Universal Declaration model arising from this special Western role.

It is difficult, perhaps ultimately impossible, to talk intelligently about something as vast and varied as "the West." Politically, "the West" has been classically embodied in Sparta, Athens, and Rome (both the Republic and the Empire); the France of Louis IX, Francis I, Louis XIV, Robespierre, Napoleon, Louis Napoleon, the Third Republic, the Popular Front, Petain, and de Gaulle; the Germany of Emperor Frederick III, the Great Elector Frederick William, Frederick the Great, Kaiser Wilhelm II, Adolf Hitler, Willy Brandt, and Helmut Kohl; the England of Henry VIII, Elizabeth I, Oliver Cromwell, George III, Gladstone, Disraeli, Lloyd George, Chamberlain, Churchill, Thatcher, and Lady/Princess Diana; and the United States of Washington, Jefferson, Jackson, Lincoln, Grant, Wilson, two Roosevelts, two Johnsons, several Kennedys, and various Bushes—not to mention Nixon, Carter, Reagan, and Clinton. And the cultural variation—Strauss and the Sex Pistols, the Arc de Triomphe and the Golden Arches, Don Quixote and Donald Duck—is, if anything, even greater.

Nonetheless, talk of "the West" and its special link to human rights is common, inside and outside the West, among critics and defenders alike. I think that we should take such talk seriously. The West is also historically associated with the Atlantic slave trade, often savage colonialism, religious persecution, virulent racism, absolute monarchy, predatory capitalism, global warfare of almost unthinkable destructiveness, fascism, communist totalitarianism, and a host of other evils and social ills. Many countries, groups, and individuals, both Western and non-Western, have suffered, and continue to suffer, under burdens directly or indirectly created by Western policies and practices. Nonetheless, the association of the West with internationally recognized human rights seems to me, as a matter of historical fact, fundamentally correct.

The West is the only region of the world in which political practice over the past half century has been largely consonant with, and in significant measure

6. This is not to deny the existence of many and often severe human rights violations in Western countries or the role of Western states, especially the United States, in supporting, even creating, human rights violations elsewhere. *All* states everywhere fall short of international human rights standards. Nonetheless, the fact remains that, as a group, Western states, especially the states of the European Union, fall somewhat less short than other regional groups.

guided by, the full set of rights in the Universal Declaration.[7] Additionally, the "Western" vision of political legitimacy has come to largely dominate international discussions—because of the collapse of the leading alternatives; because of Western military, political, and economic power; but also because of the normative power of the Western practice of human rights.

The Western implementation of internationally recognized human rights has emphasized popular sovereignty operating within the rule of law, welfare state provision of economic and social rights, and liberal democratic political legitimacy. The next three sections consider these features of contemporary Western practice at the national level. The following sections briefly examine the Western treatment of human rights in international relations. The chapter concludes with a brief methodological discussion of some of the implications of this historically unique Western role.

To avoid misunderstanding, I want to emphasize that I am presenting an ideal type model at a very high level of abstraction. Although neither "complete" nor "neutral," it is widely used, both internally and externally, for purposes of exposition, defense, and criticism. What follows is an attempt to describe the dominant contemporary institutionalization of the rights of the Universal Declaration model. For better or worse, it began, and is still usefully characterized, as "Western."

My argument is descriptive, dealing with historical genesis and contemporary practice. It is not about "ownership." I do not argue that "human rights are the exclusive heritage of the Western liberal political tradition" (Messer 1997: 310). Although human rights are indeed an important part of the Western heritage, my focus on universality and overlapping consensus clearly indicates that they have also become part of the heritage of every culture, religion, or civilization. I am not claiming that "all human rights imagination [i]s the estate of the West" (Baxi 1999: 134). Over the past several decades it has become the possession of all peoples.

I very clearly am *not* arguing, despite claims to the contrary, that human rights is "the monopoly or the sole prerogative of any one culture or people" (Mutua 1995: 345). The theory and practice of human rights, as a matter of fact, began in the West and have become a central, in many ways politically defining, part of contemporary Western societies. But this says nothing about the broader relevance of these ideas and practices (compare §5.6). Like other things or practices invented or developed in one place, human rights may be adopted or adapted by others elsewhere. My argument is that internationally recognized human rights have been (or are at least are being) and ought to be

7. The United States is a partial exception, although it is easy to exaggerate American reticence toward economic and social rights. For all its failings, the American welfare state is not merely alive but thriving.

adopted, with modest adaptations, by peoples cultures and peoples across the world.[8]

5. States, Citizens, and the Legal Order

Modern politics in the West has been organized around the state. As dynastic regimes and multiethnic empires gave way to parliamentary and popular governments, nineteenth- and twentieth-century Western states increasingly came to be (re)organized in nationalist terms. Although the aspiration for "nation-states" (terminal political entities in which peoples and political boundaries coincide) has always been problematic, it has been a powerful ideal for much of the past two centuries. Consider, for example, understandings of France as the state of the French or Italy as the state of the Italians.

In recent decades, however, citizens in Western countries have increasingly come to be seen in juridical rather than national/ethnic/cultural terms. "The people" are coming to be seen more as those who share a common political life under the jurisdiction of a state than those who share a culture, past, or blood. For example, Germany's new citizenship laws move in the direction of the territorial *jus soli,* in contrast to the traditional genealogical *jus sanguinis* doctrine.

In redefining the people, increasing emphasis has been placed on the rule of law or the related idea of a *Rechtstaat.* Impartial public law, rather than charisma, divine donation, custom, inheritance, power, virtue, or even the will of the people is increasingly seen as the source of legitimate authority. The state thus appears as a juridical entity in which the people are bound together, even defined, by common participation in and subordination to (democratic public) law.

This transition from nationalist to territorial and juridical conceptions of political community has been closely associated with an ideology of human rights. One's rights depend not on who one is (e.g., a well-born English Protestant male property owner) but simply on the fact that one is a human being. In a world of states, this has taken the form of an emphasis on equal rights for all citizens.

6. Economic and Social Rights and the Welfare State

A prominent myth in the human rights literature; especially during the Cold War, has been that the Western approach to human rights rests on a near ex-

8. If origin is irrelevant to applicability, one might ask why devote so much attention to the question. The superficial answer is that there is a lot of bad argument in scholarly, diplomatic, and popular discussions that simply gets the facts wrong. The deeper answer is that these errors concerning historical origins are closely connected with (mis)understandings of human rights (and culture) that are politically dangerous and have been regularly used by dictators to justify their depredations. Chapters 5–7 present the evidence for this claim.

clusive commitment to civil and political rights, plus the right to private property.[9] "In Western capitalist states economic and social rights are perceived as not within the purview of state responsibility" (Pollis and Schwab 1980b: xiii; compare Espiell 1979). "Philosophically the Western doctrine of human rights excludes economic and social rights" (Pollis 1996: 318). "The dominant Western conception of human rights . . . emphasizes only civil and political rights" (Muzaffar 1999: 29). Such claims bear little connection to reality. Quite the contrary, during the Cold War the West was the only region that in practice took seriously the often-repeated assertion of the indivisibility of all internationally recognized human rights.

In the nineteenth century, private property was indeed the only economic right that received extensive state protection in the West. But it boggles the mind that anyone with even a passing acquaintance with the American welfare state, let alone post–World War II Western Europe, could claim that this has been true of the West over the past half century. No Western country seriously debates whether to implement economic and social rights. Discussion instead focuses on the means to achieve this unquestioned end, how massive the commitment of resources should be, and which particular rights should be recognized and given priority.

Robert Goodin and colleagues (1999) usefully identify what they call liberal, social democratic, and corporatist welfare regimes (represented by the United States, the Netherlands, and Germany). The human consequences of the different ways in which these regimes seek to reduce poverty while promoting efficiency, equity, integration, stability, and autonomy are illustrated by the thirty or forty million Americans who are largely excluded from access to most of the health care system. From a broad comparative perspective, however, the similarities between Western welfare regimes are much more striking than their differences.

7. Inside, Outside, and the Society of States

Human rights have an inherently universalizing logic rooted in the fact that all human beings have the same human rights. In their internal legal and political practice, Western states have vigorously endeavored, with some success, to give concrete expression to this moral universality. One might expect, therefore, that these internal human rights commitments would be linked to advocacy of cosmopolitan or solidarist international human rights politics. In fact, however, the state remains the central organizing principle in Western conceptions

9. A more subtle version of this argument, which still is often encountered, presents three "generations" of human rights—civil and political, economic and social, and collective—which are at least loosely associated with the West, socialism, and the Third World. See, for example, Marks (1981); Flinterman (1990); Vasak (1984); Vasak (1991). I develop an extended historical and theoretical critique of this conceptualization in Donnelly (1993b).

of international order and legitimacy. National provision of internationally recognized human rights is the preferred Western strategy in both national and international politics (compare §2.4.A).

This disjunction reflects accommodation to, even unthinking acceptance of, a world of sovereign states. It also helps to protect the privileged position of Western states and societies. And it is rooted in a social contract vision of political society that authorizes, perhaps even encourages, the "choice" of individuals to form political associations that are not global in extent.[10] The balance among these three explanations—the necessities of political order, narrow self-interest, and respect for national autonomy and communal integrity—will largely determine how one evaluates this disjunction.

In any case, the process of growing inclusiveness that I emphasized earlier is largely limited by state boundaries in contemporary Western theory and practice. Sovereignty remains the fundamental principle of international legitimacy (compare Chapter 14). As we will see in Chapter 8, global human rights institutions largely lack coercive power.

As Terry Nardin puts it (1983: chap. 1), borrowing from Michael Oakeshott, the contemporary society of states is more a practical than a purposive association. Its rules seek more to facilitate states' realization of their own purposes than to realize any particular shared substantive purposes. To use a distinction that has become popular within the "English School" of international studies (Bull 1977: 148–149, 156–158, 238–240), the underlying conception of international society is "pluralist" rather than "solidarist."

Martin Wight usefully distinguishes three traditions of international theory (1966; 1992). The "realist" ("Hobbesian") tradition sees the society of states as extraordinarily thin and not very far removed from the constant threat of war. Coexistence is the most that ordinarily can be expected in international society. The "revolutionary" ("Kantian") tradition envisions something much more like a cosmopolitan world society. Solidarity—between states, peoples, and individual human beings—is envisioned as a realistic option in international relations. The "internationalist" ("Grotian") tradition envisions and advocates a relatively thick but still essentially pluralist society of states (rather than a single world society). The contemporary Western approach is, in these terms, internationalist. To return to contractarian language, individuals form societies and states that then interact politically with one another.

Kant's three definitive articles of perpetual peace provide a classic expression of this vision.[11] States should be "republican," or roughly what I have

10. The most direct expression of this contractarian political logic is the principle of national self-determination. Compare §14.3.

11. Wight clearly misreads Kant in placing him in the revolutionary or solidarist camp. He is, instead, an archetypical "Grotian."

called liberal democratic. "International right" should be based on a federation for peace—close to what we would call today a collective security organization—rather than even a federal world government, leaving international relations largely the province of sovereign states (operating in a relatively thick society of states). And, Kant argues, "cosmopolitan right," the international legal and political expression of human moral solidarity, should be limited to freedom of movement and trade, again emphasizing the centrality of states (1983: 112–119).

Part III of this book offers considerable support for the empirical accuracy of this analysis.[12] For the moment the essential point is that although states are no longer (and perhaps never were) the sole important international actors,[13] they remain the central actors in contemporary international relations in general, and in the international politics of human rights in particular.

8. Global Markets

The currently hegemonic (Western) approach to the international dimensions of implementing economic and social human rights is built around global markets. The meager amounts of humanitarian and development aid currently offered amount not even to a down payment on an emaciated global welfare state. Although clearly a reflection of the self-interest of states that are both relatively well-positioned to compete in international markets and unwilling to fund massive international income transfers, self-interest is not the entire explanation of the Western preference for global markets.

Most states, both Western and non-Western, are profoundly disinterested in (if not violently opposed to) creating a central international political authority. States, large and small, in all regions of the world, tend to be extraordinarily sensitive to their sovereign rights and privileges. And sovereignty—at least one's own sovereignty—is widely endorsed by the citizens of most states in all regions.

Most non-Western states would, of course, like to see increased flows of resources from the West to their *states*, preferably without political, economic, or human rights conditions. As was the case during discussions of a New Interna-

12. Chapter 14 explores post–Cold War changes that suggest a more solidarist approach to questions of humanitarian intervention.

13. To select somewhat randomly from the recent literature, Keck and Skikkink (1998) provide an insightful discussion of the role of transnational advocacy networks; Risse, Ropp, and Sikkink (1999) examine the processes by which international human rights norms diffuse into national societies; and Brysk (2000) offers an interesting study of the global dimensions of the struggles for indigenous rights in the Americas. Falk (2000) is the most recent effort of the leading American scholarly advocate of a global approach to human rights issues. More broadly, Lipschutz (1996) provides a provocative (although to me unpersuasive) account of the emergence of a global civil society.

tional Economic Order in the 1970s, however, their approach to welfare remains at least as statist as that of the West. They show no interest in allowing their citizens to establish the links with foreign states and international organizations implied by a cosmopolitan approach to welfare.

Having more or less by consensus (or at least default) rejected a cosmopolitan welfare state in favor of a world of sovereign territorial states, markets—whether relatively "free" or more heavily and directly managed—are an "obvious" choice.[14] In an international society of sovereign states, in which power and authority are radically decentralized, we can expect dominant international norms and institutions to reflect the preferences of leading powers. The result today is often called the neoliberal "Washington consensus."[15]

But contemporary international support for global markets reflects more than raw power. Although the details of "structural adjustment"—greater openness to market forces and their logic of economic efficiency—often are largely imposed, the need for adjustment is increasingly, if reluctantly, acknowledged by a growing number and range of non-Western states. Perhaps the most dramatic illustration is the recent decision of the Chinese Communist party to accept capitalist entrepreneurs—heretofore "exploiters," or worse—as members.

During the Cold War, most non-Western countries argued not only that development could be achieved by relying on state direction but also that this was the best and most efficient route to realizing economic and social rights (see §11.5). Such projects, however, proved unsustainable, when they were not failures from the outset. And the leading dirigiste development successes (excluding the special case of oil-exporting countries) were states, such as Taiwan and Korea, that relied heavily on the economic discipline of international markets.

Today there is a growing (if justifiably grudging) recognition that realizing economic and social rights requires a complex combination of (market-based) efficiency in production and (state-mediated) equity in distribution. Substantial reliance on national and international markets is becoming closer to a hegemonic, rather than simply an imposed, principle. Although little enthusiasm for neoliberal international economic regimes is evident even in the West (outside of the United States), there is no serious challenger, at least at the level of elite interstate debate.

In §11.7 we will return to the (huge) human rights deficiencies of markets. For now I simply want to emphasize that a commitment to international markets (with some rather crude, self-interested interventions to protect national

14. Although not the only choice, the leading historical alternatives at the international level—autarky, mercantilism, and state trading systems—hold few attractions for those interested in economic and social rights. And command economies have consistently proved to have disastrous national welfare consequences in the medium or long run.

15. See, for example, Gore (2000); Naim (2000); Steger (2001: chaps. 1, 2); and Williamson (1993).

labor and firms) is clearly the dominant Western vision of the appropriate international path for realizing economic and social rights—and, not coincidentally, the reigning approach in the contemporary society of states.

9. Historical Analysis and the Genetic Fallacy

In the preceding sections I have tried to present an accurate and fair (although basically sympathetic) account of the central role of Western national and international practice in the social construction of dominant international human rights ideas and practices. Chapter 5 examines challenges to the empirical accuracy of this account. Chapter 6 tries to grapple, in general theoretical terms, with the problems of cultural relativism. Chapter 7 explores the most prominent challenge to universalism in the 1990s, namely, "Asian values," and cultural regionalism more broadly. But before moving on to these inquiries, I want to draw attention to the danger of what logicians call the genetic fallacy.

Let us grant, at least for the sake of argument, that contemporary national and international human rights values and institutions were in significant measure developed in and shaped by the West. This tells us absolutely nothing about the "applicability," "relevance," "appropriateness," or "value" of these ideas, values, and practices—either inside or outside the West. From a causal or historical account analysis of the genesis of a social practice, we cannot conclude anything about its appropriate range of applicability.

Gunpowder was invented in China. Arabic numerals, and much of the mathematics with which they were associated, were developed in the Muslim Near East. Jews in Palestine created Christianity. Yoga is an ancient Indian philosophy, science, or discipline. Submarines, tanks, and fighter jets were invented in the West. Human beings themselves first emerged in Africa. From none of these facts do we conclude that the things or practices in question are of merely local application or validity. Nor should we make such an error in the case of human rights.

This is particularly true if my argument about the standard threats of modern markets and states is correct. We rightly speak of "capitalist," "international," or "global"— not Western—markets (even though global markets are dominated by Western firms and capital). We rightly speak of modern states, an organizational form that has penetrated all areas of the globe. Although Westerners played the decisive role in spreading these institutions across the globe, states have been enthusiastically adopted in all regions of the globe and markets have reshaped all but the most isolated local communities.

It is well worth taking seriously arguments that Western hegemony prevents recognizing certain standard threats.[16] We should also seriously consider argu-

16. Perhaps the most serious such challenge concerns group rights, a subject to which we return in Chapter 12.

ments that particular Western human rights institutions have defensible functional analogs elsewhere. Even the claim that a particular society or culture has a defensible conception of human dignity that is not associated with an idea of equal and inalienable rights deserves careful consideration. But the suggestion that internationally recognized human rights are appropriately rejected outside of the Western world because Westerners played the central role in developing those ideas and practices should be met with derision.

Historical or "genealogical" analysis is important in understanding how contemporary ideas and practices have come to be constructed. It may provide important insights into the limits of dominant practices and highlight needed changes. But human rights are too important to be rejected—or accepted—on the basis of their origins.

Asmarom Legesse argues that "any system of ideas that claims to be universal must contain critical elements in its fabric that are avowedly of African, Latin American or Asian derivation" (1980: 123). But we certainly would not accept something as correct or useful simply because it is Western. Likewise we must not assume that because something is non-Western that it is valuable or that because it is distinctively Western in its origins or contemporary dispersion it is somehow defective.

There is an instrumental reason for trying to root human rights ideas in local cultural traditions—just as in the modern West proponents of natural rights used existing cultural resources, especially the Bible and appeals to natural law, on behalf of these new ideas and practices. There certainly is some truth to Daniel Bell's claim that "if the ultimate aim of human rights diplomacy is to persuade others of the value of human rights, it is more likely that the struggle to promote human rights can be won if it is fought in ways that build on, rather than challenge, local cultural traditions" (1996: 652). But not just any cultural traditions will do.

Some local traditions—both Western and non-Western—are antithetical to human rights and must be approached as such. Furthermore, we must be very clear that we are drawing on cultural resources for the purposes of human rights advocacy, not defining human rights by culture. And, as we will see in some detail in Chapter 5, working ideas and practices of universal human rights into local cultures with different histories, traditions, and foundations involves progressive cultural change, just as it did in the West.

In accepting or rejecting human rights we must demand substantive, not historical, arguments. Part I offered such an argument on behalf of the Universal Declaration model. The remaining chapters of Part II look at a variety of relativist challenges to the contemporary universality of that model.

5/ Non-Western Conceptions of Human Rights

In sharp contrast to Chapter 4, which argues that human rights first emerged in the West in response to the social changes produced by modern markets and states, one regularly encounters claims that "human rights are not a western discovery" (Mangalpus 1978). For example, Adamantia Pollis and Peter Schwab argue that "all societies have human rights notions" (1980b: xiv). Yogindra Khushalani even offers the (patently absurd) claim that "the concept of human rights can be traced to the origin of the human race itself" (1983: 404).

It simply is not true that "all societies cross-culturally and historically manifest conceptions of human rights" (Pollis and Schwab 1980a: 15). Human rights, as we saw in Part I, envision equal citizens endowed with inalienable rights that entitle them to equal concern and respect from the state. Human rights are not just a set of abstract values or objectives (e.g., welfare, liberty, political participation) but, even more important, a distinctive set of social practices (see §1.1–2) tied to particular notions of human dignity (see §1.3, 3.4). In this chapter I argue that non-Western cultural and political traditions, *like the premodern West*, lacked not only the practice of human rights but also the very concept.

"Traditional" societies—Western and non-Western alike—typically have had elaborate systems of duties. Many of those duties even correspond to values and obligations that we associate with human rights today. But such societies had conceptions of justice, political legitimacy, and human flourishing that sought to realize human dignity, flourishing, or well-being entirely independent of human rights. These institutions and practices are alternatives to, rather than different formulations of, human rights.

This chapter examines claims that traditional Islamic, African, Chinese, and Indian societies had well-established indigenous conceptions of human rights. To emphasize the fact that my argument is structural and not cultural, I also briefly examine the premodern West, in the form of medieval Europe.

At the outset let me note that the understanding of "culture" in the following sections is highly problematic. The arguments that I address frequently rest on dubious caricatures, a point addressed in the final section of this chapter. Nonetheless, such arguments have been and remain a regular part of academic, elite, and popular discussions of international human rights. This chapter takes such standard claims about distinctive traditional cultural conceptions of human rights at face value and shows them to be historically mistaken and analytically muddled.

1. Islam and Human Rights

"In almost all contemporary Arab literature on this subject [human rights], we find a listing of the basic rights established by modern conventions and declarations, and then a serious attempt to trace them back to Koranic texts" (Zakaria 1986: 228). Many authors (e.g., Tabandeh 1970: 1, 85) even argue that contemporary human rights doctrines merely replicate 1400-year-old Islamic ideas. The standard argument in this now extensive literature is that "Islam has laid down some universal fundamental rights for humanity as a whole, which are to be observed and respected under all circumstances . . . fundamental rights for every man by virtue of his status as a human being" (Mawdudi 1976: 10). "The basic concepts and principles of human rights [have] from the very beginning been embodied in Islamic law."[1] Such claims, however, are almost entirely baseless.

Khalid M. Ishaque argues that "Muslims are enjoined constantly to seek ways and means to assure to each other what in modern parlance we call 'human rights'" (1974: 32). While he admits that "human rights" cannot be translated into the language of the Islamic holy works, he nevertheless claims that they lie at the core of Islamic doctrine.[2] The fourteen "human rights" that Ishaque claims are recognized and established by Islam (1974: 32–38), however, prove to be only duties of rulers and individuals, not rights held by anyone.[3]

The scriptural passages cited as establishing a "right to protection of life" are in fact divine injunctions not to kill and to consider life inviolable. The "right to justice" proves to be instead a duty of rulers to establish justice. The "right to freedom" is a duty not to enslave unjustly (not even a general duty not to enslave). "Economic rights" turn out to be duties to help to provide for the needy. And the purported "right to freedom of expression" is actually an obli-

1. Mr. Makki, representative of Oman to the Third Committee of the U.N. General Assembly, speech of October 25, 1979. UN document A/C.3/34/SR.27.

2. Unless our concepts are independent of language—a highly implausible notion, especially for a social practice such as rights in which language is so central to its functioning—it is hard to see how this claim could even in principle be true. At most these texts enjoin functional analogues or different practices to produce similar ends—and my argument in the rest of this section suggests that even that is not true.

3. On the conceptual distinctions between rights and duties, and the practical differences this makes, see §1.1 above and §2 below.

gation to speak the truth—that is, not even an obligation of others but an obligation of the alleged right-holder.

Similarly, Abdul Aziz Said claims "to identify precepts that establish human rights in the Islamic tradition" (1979: 64) and argues that in Islam "human beings have certain God granted rights" (1980: 92). But not only does he present no evidence in direct support of this claim, but the discussion he does offer demonstrates once more the absence of the concept of human rights in Islam. All of the nine basic regulating precepts of an Islamic political system that Said lists (1979: 65–68) involve either a rights-less duty or are rights held because one has a certain legal or spiritual status, not simply because one is a human being.[4]

Muslims are indeed regularly and forcefully called upon—by scripture, tradition, religious leaders, and ordinary believers—to treat others with respect and dignity. They are enjoined, in the strongest possible terms, to pursue both personal well-being and social justice. These injunctions clearly call to mind the *values* of the Universal Declaration of Human Rights, but they appeal to divine commands that establish duties, not (human) rights. The *practices* traditionally established to realize these values simply did not include equal and inalienable rights held by all human beings.

Consider Majid Khadduri's claim that "human rights in Islam are the privilege of Allah (God), because authority ultimately belongs to Him" (1946: 78). This is, quite literally, incoherent: "human rights" that are not rights of human beings but privileges of God. But this is not an idiosyncratic conception. Mahmood Monshipouri also argues that "in Islamic tradtions human rights are entirely owned by God" (1998: 72).

"Human rights in Islam, as prescribed by the divine law, are the privilege only of persons of full legal status. A person with full legal capacity is a living human being of mature age, free, and of Moslem faith" (Khadduri 1946: 79). This makes "human rights" the privileges of (only) free adult Muslims. Infidels receive only guarantees of life, property, and freedom of religion; slaves only a right to life.[5] And women enjoy still another set of rights and duties.

> The essential characteristic of human rights in Islam is that they constitute obligations connected with the Divine and derive their force from

4. In a similar fashion, Majid Khadduri (1946: 77–78) lists five rights held by men according to Islam—rights to personal safety, respect of personal reputation, equality, brotherhood, and justice—but his supporting evidence in fact shows that Islam treated these subjects entirely in terms of duties that are not correlative to rights. Likewise, Ahmad Moussalli identifies human rights with the "five necessities" (*al-darruyiyyat al-khams*), the duties to preserve religion, self, reason, the family, and money (2001: 126). See also Mawdudi (1976: 17–24); Tabandeh (1970).

5. Similarly, Monshipouri claims that individuals can enjoy human rights only "in their relationship with God" (1998: 72). Those without the religiously specified relationship to God thus would not have human rights—an obviously untenable conception of human rights, unless we are to say infidels are not human (which poses its own, equally serious, problems).

> this connection. . . . Individuals possess certain obligations towards God, fellow humans and nature, all of which are defined by Shariah. When individuals meet these obligations they acquire certain rights and freedoms which are again prescribed by the Shariah. (Said 1979: 63,73–74)

In Islam, in the realm of "human rights" (read "human dignity"), what matters is duty rather than rights, and the rights that one does hold are a consequence of one's status or actions, not the moral fact of being human. If the rights we are discussing are indeed "duty based and interdependent on duties one owes to God and the community" (Ali 2000: 25), they are not human rights.

Sultanhussein Tabendeh even claims that the preferential treatment of Muslims in certain criminal cases is "quite free of difficulty" from a human rights perspective, because "people who have not put their reliance in conviction and faith, nor had that basic abiding-place nor believed in the one Invisible God, are reckoned as outside the pale of humanity" (1970: 17). "Human rights" thus are supposed to be based on a conception that sees the majority of the population of the world as "outside of the pale of humanity."[6]

The Holy Qur'an certainly does not require Muslims to accept such legal ideas and their associated practices. Many contemporary Muslims (entirely justifiably) reject such views. Nonetheless, this accurately represents the historically dominant practice of most Muslim societies—much as most Christian societies throughout most of their histories treated non-Christians as inferior, despite the apparently universalistic egalitarianism of the New Testament.

The issue at the moment is not how Muslim (or any other) holy texts might or ought to be read, today or in the past, but rather how those texts were in fact read and acted on by "traditional" Muslim societies. As in most other "traditional" societies, rights and duties were largely dependent on community membership. The "universe of obligation," to use Helen Fein's apt term (1979: 33), was largely that of all believers[7]—Dar al Islam—not humanity.

6. Somewhat less starkly, but with a similar implication, Norani Othman describes the rights recognized in Islam as "open to all faithful believers" (1999: 72), which would seem to exclude the unfaithful and unbelievers from the enjoyment of human rights. Consider also Ahmad Moussalli's claim that "human rights in Islam are creedal rights" (2001: 126). Whatever these may be, precisely because they rest on adherence to a particular religious creed, they are not human rights in the ordinary sense of that term.

7. This is both too broad—within the *umma,* the community of believers, there were slaves—and too narrow—Christians and Jews living in Muslim communities often enjoyed both freedom of religion and limited rights of self-government, despite being treated as legally, politically, socially, and morally inferior to Muslims.

Islam does teach that "it is the state's duty to enhance human dignity and alleviate conditions that hinder individuals in their efforts to achieve happiness" (Said 1980: 87). It may be true that "there is no aspect of human need but Islam, in its ethical, social and liturgical precepts, has made provision for it" (Tabandeh 1970: 10). The social and political precepts of Islam do reflect a strong concern for human good and human dignity, which may even be a prerequisite for human rights. Central to Muslim traditions is "a profound affirmation of human freedom, dignity, and autonomy" (Othman 1999: 189). But none of this is equivalent to a concern for, or a recognition of, human rights.

The substantive similarities, at the level of basic values, between classical Islam and the Universal Declaration model—for example, "the *Qur'anic* notion of a common human ontology (*fitna*) and . . . an Islamic idiom of moral universalism" (Othman 1999: 173)—explain why devout Muslims might choose to participate in the contemporary overlapping international consensus on human rights (see §3.2, 3.6). Traditional Muslim societies, however, simply did not pursue human dignity or flourishing through the practice of equal and inalienable rights held by all human beings. Such differences in fundamental legal and political institutions and practices made these societies very different from (modern) human rights–based societies of *any* culture, religion, or civilization.

To avoid misunderstanding, let me state clearly and emphatically that none of this suggests that Islam is in any way inherently hostile to or fundamentally incompatible with human rights. I readily agree that "the notions of democracy, pluralism, and human rights are . . . in harmony with Islamic thought" (Moussalli 2001: 2)—if by that we mean that Islam (like Christianity) can, and even ought to be, read in this way. My point is that traditionally, as with Christianity throughout most of its history, it has not been read in that way.

Shaheen Sardar Ali seriously understates the analytical and historical problem when she notes, almost in passing, that "the extent and application of human rights in Islam, *equally, and to all human beings*, poses a number of problems." But she is clearly correct when she later claims that support for human rights today can be found in the canonical Islamic "sources and accompanying juristic techniques, namely the *Qur'an, Haddith, Ijma, Qiyas Itjihad*" (2000: 16, 19). And relying on these resources in advocating respect for internationally recognized human rights makes immense practical sense.

Rooting contemporary human rights ideas and practice in such sources and resources will, for many Muslims, give them a depth, meaning, and impact they could not otherwise attain—just as rooting the rights of the Universal Declaration in the Bible gives them a special meaning and force to many Christians. My point, however, is that none of this tells us anything about how life was organized in Baghdad in the fourth century after the Hijra, in the Ottoman Empire six hundred years later, or in Syria when Western colonial domination was imposed. And unless we appreciate these differences in social practices—that is, the sharp break with traditional ways implicit in the idea and practice of equal and inalienable rights held by all human beings—we delude ourselves about the past and obscure central elements of the meaning and importance of human rights today.

2. The Premodern West

Despite my protestations in the three previous paragraphs, many readers will see the preceding discussion as reflecting cultural arrogance, or worse. My argument, however, is structural not cultural. And it is analytical rather than normative. To underscore this point, I want to turn immediately to the premodern West, where it is equally clear that the idea and practice of human rights were utterly foreign.[8]

One searches in vain for human rights in (Western) classical or medieval political theory or practice. For example, the Greeks distinguished between Hellenes and barbarians (non-Greeks), whom they considered congenitally inferior. The Romans recognized rights based on birth, citizenship, and achievement, not on mere humanity. In the millennium following the fall of Rome, Christian theorists and rulers allotted dramatically different political treatment to believers and nonbelievers. And within Christendom, the spiritual equality of all believers most definitely did not extend to political equality.

In the premodern West, the duty of rulers to further the common good arose from divine commandment, natural law, tradition, or contingent political arrangements rather than rights (entitlements) of all human beings to be ruled justly. Although the people were expected to benefit from the political obligations of their rulers, they had no (natural or human) rights that could be exercised against unjust rulers. The reigning idea was natural right (in the sense of rectitude), not natural rights (entitlement).

Consider Thomas Aquinas, whose political theory is widely considered to be representative the high medieval period. Right (*ius*) for Aquinas is the good at which justice aims and law (*lex*) is the written expression of right or justice. Right and law are thus two ways of stating a duty under which one is placed by right in the sense of "what is right." Right (*ius*) does not necessarily include the

8. It happens that I first developed my general argument, and the conceptual distinctions on which it is based, while grappling with the differences between medieval and modern Western conceptions of "natural right." See Donnelly (1980), which provides detailed support for the (exceedingly brief) discussion of Aquinas in this section.

English notion of right in the sense entitlement.[9] And Thomist natural law does not give rise to natural rights; rather, it states what is right.[10]

The practical differences this makes can be illustrated by Aquinas's treatment of tyranny. A tyrant is, like every human being, obliged to obey the natural law. In ruling tyrannically, he violates the substance of the natural law as well as his special obligation to rule justly. These obligations, however, are owed to God, not the people. Although the tyrant is guilty of great crimes against the people, it is against God and God's law that he has sinned, and only God is entitled to demand redress.

Lacking explicit authority to change their rulers—which was *not* something that people were thought to have naturally—the people might legitimately point out to the tyrant the error of his ways, call on him to conform to the natural law, or pray for divine assistance. But the natural law gave them no right to change their rulers. They were not entitled to demand redress.

Medieval writers thus regularly appealed to Paul's claim that all power is from God and that resistance to rulers will bring damnation (Romans 13:1–2). The Augustinian notion of misrule as a punishment for evil was widely accepted: "It is by divine permission that wicked men receive power as a punishment for sin. . . . Sin must therefore be done away with in order that the scourge of tyrants may cease."[11]

The demands of natural law may be considerable, but the position of a people in a political system based on natural law without natural rights is quite different from that of modern citizens endowed with human rights. Natural law and human rights both serve as standards of political legitimacy. But unlike Aquinas's natural law, human rights also provide citizens with grounds for political action—in extreme cases, even revolution—against tyrants.

9. The tendency to read modern rights notions back into a premodern past is not restricted to non-Western contexts. My favorite example involves Aquinas's treatment of "private property." In the well-known D'Entreves anthology (D'Entreves 1959) several passages are grouped under the heading of "The Right to Private Property." But this heading is to be found nowhere in Aquinas's text. Most of the passages instead come from a discussion of "the vices opposed to justice" (*Summa Theologicae* 2a.2ae.63–79) and under the particular heading *de furto et rapina* (of theft and rapine). And the particular questions Aquinas actually investigates are *utrum naturalis sit homini posessio exteriorum rerum* (whether it is natural for man to possess external things ["property"]) and *utrum liceat alicui rem aliquam quasi propriam possidere* (whether it is lawful or legitimate to possess anything as one's own). The issue, clearly, is not one of rights (entitlement) but rectitude and legality. In the medieval world, people certainly did have possessions. But if there was anything like what we would understand as a system of "property rights," it was very limited. For example, land, the central productive resource of these societies, rarely was held as private property, even by princes. And possessions regularly were not fully alienable, in sharp contrast to modern private property.

10. My point is not that (neo-)Thomist theory cannot find a place for human rights. See, for example, Maritain (1943) and especially Finnis (1980). During the medieval era, however, no such space was made. The issue in this chapter, to repeat, is how actual (in this case Western) societies treated issues that we now treat as matters of human rights.

11. *De Regimine Principum* I.vi.52.

My argument, in both this and especially in Chapter 4, thus is about Western culture only accidentally and in so far as it has been shaped by modern markets and states (and the associated ideas and practices of human rights). Social structure, not "culture," does the explanatory work. When the West was filled with "traditional societies," it had social and political ideas and practices strikingly similar to those of traditional Asia, Africa, and the Near East. Conversely, as those regions and civilizations have been similarly penetrated by modern markets and states, the social conditions that demand human rights have been created. This is the foundation of the overlapping consensus on and the contemporary moral universality of human rights.

The historical connection of human rights with the West is more accident or effect than cause. Westerners had no special cultural proclivity that led them to human rights. Rather, the West had the (good or bad) fortune to suffer the indignities of modern markets and states before other regions. By necessity rather than superior virtue they got a jump on the rest of the world in developing the response of human rights.

3. Traditional Africa

"The African conception of human rights was an essential aspect of African humanism" (Asante 1969: 75). "It is not often remembered that traditional African societies supported and practiced human rights" (Wai 1980: 116). Such assertions, much as in the case of Islam (and the premodern West), prove to be not only unsupported but actually undercut by the evidence presented on their behalf.

Dunstan Wai, author of the second quoted passage, continues: "Traditional African attitudes, beliefs, institutions, and experiences sustained the 'view that certain rights should be upheld against alleged necessities of state'" (1980: 116). This confuses human rights with limited government.[12] There are many other bases on which a government might be limited, including divine commandment, legal rights, and extralegal checks such as a balance of power or the threat of popular revolt. Even having a right to limited government does not mean that one recognizes or has human rights.

"There is no point in belaboring the concern for rights, democratic institutions, and rule of law in traditional African politics" (Wai 1980: 117). To this we can add only that it is particularly pointless in a discussion of human rights, given the form such concerns took. Even where Africans had personal rights

12. "This chapter will argue that authoritarianism in modern Africa is not at all in accord with the spirit and practice of traditional political systems" (Wai 1980: 115). Compare Legesse (1980: 125–127) and Busia (1994: 231). For non-African examples of a similar confusion, see Said (1979: 65); Magalpus (1978); and Pollis and Schwab (1980b: xiv).

against their government,[13] those rights were based not on one's humanity but on such criteria as age, sex, lineage, achievement, or community membership.

Asmarom Legesse argues along similar lines that "many studies . . . suggest that distributive justice, in the economic and political spheres, is the cardinal ethical principle that is shared by most Africans" (1980: 127; compare Fernyhough 1993: 61). This is quite true, but once again irrelevant. Distributive justice and human rights are different concepts. Plato, Burke, and Bentham all had theories of distributive justice, but no one would ever think to suggest that they advocated human rights. Although giving to each his own—distributive justice—typically involves respecting the rights of others, unless "one's own" is defined in terms of that to which one is entitled simply as a human being, the rights in question will not be human rights. In African societies, rights typically were assigned on the basis of social roles and status within the community.

In a similar vein, Timothy Fernyhough argues that "many precolonial societies were distinguished by their respect for judicial and political procedure" (1993: 61). This is even more obviously irrelevant. The question, of course, is the nature of the procedures, in particular whether they were based on universal rights. They were not.

We again see an attempt to establish that the differences with the modern ("Western") practices are merely a matter of verbal labels. "Different societies formulate their conception of human rights in diverse cultural idioms" (Legesse 1980: 124). In fact the differences are matters of concept and practice. African societies had concepts and practices of human dignity that simply did not involve human rights. "Many African traditional societies did respect many of the basic values that underlie human rights" (Penna and Campbell 1998: 21). The ways in which they were valued, however, and the practices established to implement them were quite different. Recognition of human rights simply was not the way of traditional Africa, with obvious and important consequences for political practice (compare Howard 1986: chap. 2).

4. Traditional Confucian China

"The protection of human rights is an integral part" of the traditions of Asian societies (Anwar 1994: 2). "All the countries of the region would agree that 'human rights' as a concept existed in their tradition" (Coomaraswamy 1980: 224). "The idea of human rights developed very early in China" (Lo 1949: 186), "as early as 2,000 years ago" (Han 1996: 93). In arguing against such claims, I will focus on traditional (Confucian) China.

Consider the following representative argument:

13. Fernyhough (1993: 55ff.) offers several examples of personal rights enjoyed in precolonial African societies. See also Mutua (1995: 348–351).

> Human rights under the traditional Chinese political culture were conceived to be part of a larger body of morally prescribed norms of collective human conduct. . . . The Confucian code of ethics recognized each individual's right to personal dignity and worth, but this right was "not considered innate within each human soul as in the West, but had to be acquired" by his living up to the code. (Tai 1985: 88; quoting Fairbank 1972: 119)

Such a right clearly is not a *human* right. It had to be earned. It could be lost. The ground of the right was not the fact that one was a human being. The dignity and worth in question were not seen to be inalienable and inherent in the person.

"In a broad sense, the concept of human rights concerns the relationship between the individual and the state; it involves the status, claims, and duties of the former in the jurisdiction of the latter. As such, it is a subject as old as politics, and every nation has to grapple with it" (Tai 1985: 79). But not all institutionalized relationships between individuals and the state are governed by, related to, or even consistent with, human rights.

What the state owes to those it rules is indeed a perennial question of politics. Human rights, however, provide but one answer. Divine right monarchy is another. The dictatorship of the proletariat, the principle of utility, aristocracy, theocracy, democracy, and plutocracy are still different answers.

The traditional Chinese theory of the Mandate of Heaven viewed political power as a heavenly grant to ensure order, harmony, justice, and prosperity. This required the Emperor to discharge properly the duties of his office. If he systematically failed to do so, Confucian civil servants, as the authorized representatives of society, were obliged to remonstrate the ruler. If he proved recalcitrant and unusually vicious, popular resistance was authorized. In fact, widespread resistance was evidence that the ruler had lost his mandate.

Limited government, however, should not be confused with government limited by the human rights of its citizens. Irregular political participation in cases of extreme tyranny should not be confused with a (human) right to political participation.

Individuals may have held rights as members of families, villages, and other groups. But the purpose of political rights "was not to protect the individual against the state but to enable the individual to function more effectively to strengthen the state" (Nathan 1986: 148). Whatever the value or importance of such rights, they are not human rights as that term is ordinarily used.

Many commentators seem uncomfortable with this fact. For example, Lo Chung-Sho notes that "there was no open declaration of human rights in China, either by individual thinkers or by political constitutions, until this concept was introduced from the West. In fact, the early translators of Western political thought found it difficult to arrive at a Chinese equivalent for the term 'rights'" (1949: 186). But, Lo continues, "this of course does not mean that the Chinese never claimed human rights or enjoyed the basic rights of man" (1949: 186).

I cannot imagine how the Chinese managed to claim human rights without the language to make such claims, and Lo presents no evidence that they actually asserted or otherwise exercised such rights. Quite the contrary, his examples show only a divinely imposed duty of the ruler to govern for the common good, not rights of the people.

This is not a "different approach to human rights" (Lo 1949: 188). It is an approach to human dignity, well-being, or flourishing that does not rely on human rights. Lo fails to draw the crucial conceptual distinction between having a right and enjoying a benefit. As a result, he confuses making claims of (in)justice with claiming a (human) right. Simply because acts that we would say involved violations of human rights were considered impermissible does not mean that people were seen as having, let alone that they could claim or enjoy, human rights.

"Different civilizations or societies have different conceptions of human well-being. Hence, they have a different attitude toward human rights issues" (Lee 1985: 131). Even this is significantly misleading. Other societies may have (similar or different) attitudes toward issues that *we* consider in terms of human rights, but unless they possess a concept of human rights they are unlikely to have *any* attitude toward human rights. To fail to respect this important conceptual distinction is not to show cultural sensitivity, respect, or tolerance but rather to misunderstand the social and ethical foundations and functioning of a society as a result of anachronistically imposing an alien analytical framework.

5. Caste and Human Rights

India is a partial exception to the tendency to argue that all major civilizations or cultures have traditional conceptions of human rights. Even during the Cold War many authors recognized that human rights did not exist in traditional Hindu India.[14] Nonetheless, a surprising number of authors do argue that human rights ideas are present in traditional Indian (Hindu) ideas and practice. Yougindra Khushalani claims that "Hindu civilization had a well-developed system which guaranteed both civil and political as well as the economic, social and cultural rights of the human being" (Khushalani 1983: 408; compare Saksena 1967: 360–361). Ralph Buultjens speaks of caste as India's "traditional, multidimensional views of human rights" (1980: 113). Max Stackhouse devotes

14. See, for example, Thapar (1966) and Mitra (1982). More recently see Elder (1996: 70, 81).

two chapters of *Creeds, Society, and Human Rights* (1984) to Hinduism, taking it for granted that there is a Hindu concept of human rights.[15]

In fact, though, "Indians . . . base their social structure on duties and obligations rather than on rights."[16] Whatever rights one had rested on the discharge of status-based duties. In traditional Indian (Hindu) society, "people's duties and rights are specified not in terms of their humanity but in terms of specific caste, age and sex" (Mitra 1982: 79). And the caste system made the ascriptive hierarchy so rigid that for all intents and purposes one's duties and rights were defined by birth.

> The caste system divides the whole society into a large number of hereditary groups, distinguished from one another and connected by three characteristics: *separation* in matters of marriage and contact, whether direct or indirect (food); *division* of labor, each group having, in theory or by tradition, a profession from which their members can depart only within certain limits; and finally *hierarchy,* which ranks the groups as relatively superior or inferior to one another. (Dumont 1980: 21; compare Beteille 1965: 46)

All societies have social hierarchies, with a tendency for different groups to separate from one another. Hereditary occupational specialization is common. But the combination of separation, division, and hierarchy in the intensity characteristic of India makes the caste system largely unique to South Asia.

Ancient formulas recognize four castes (*varnas*), Brahman, Kshatriya, Vaishya, and Shudra, which roughly correspond to priests, warriors/rulers, the landed and mercantile classes, and the servile classes. Below these were Chandalas, "untouchables." By the third or fourth century A.D., however, a much more complex system of caste segmentation existed, based on the *jati*, a smaller descent group. Today "there are so many [castes] that it is virtually impossible to determine their exact number."[17]

The boundaries between castes are maintained by detailed rules of ritual purity: contact with, in some instances even sight of, lower castes is viewed as polluting; intimate contact, especially in marriage or at meals, is especially defiling. These rules of purity are embedded in a kin-based social system of "rigid

15. Perhaps the oddest argument is the claim that "the ancient Indian concept of human rights . . . was based on wars and regulated humanitarian laws to be adopted before, during and after war" (Raj 2000: 2). The suggestion that human rights has to do with relations between political communities, rather than within them, is bizarre.

16. Saksena (1967: 372). Compare Pandeya (1986: 271); Mitra (1982: 78–79); and Thapar (1966: 35).

17. Beteille (1965: 230). Hutton gives a rough estimate of more than three thousand (1963: 67). Sharma found 16 separate castes in a village of only 144 households (1985: 68 and table 7).

boundaries and collective or corporate rank" (Bayly 1999: 10). "In the world of caste, virtually every aspect of behavior is regulated by kin—not only major decisions such as marriage, occupation, and place of residence, but everyday activities such as what one eats and who with, or the forms of address one employs for different categories of people" (Quigley 1993: 87).

Birth, according to the Hindu theory of reincarnation, is a reflection of moral justice and order. "One is born where one belongs by reason of his acts over many incarnations" (Organ 1974: 194). "The body or family in which a person is born, the society in which he lives, and the position or station in life which he occupies, are all determined by his past conduct and behaviour" (Chatterjee 1950: 78). Caste hierarchy thus "is the expression of a secret justice" (Bougle 1971 [1908]: 76). Social status was seen as not accidental or even conventional but as part of the natural fabric of the universe.

Caste and human rights are clearly radically incompatible. Human rights "derive from the inherent dignity of the human person," to quote the International Human Rights Covenants once again. Each person has an inherent dignity and worth that arises simply from being human. Thus each person has the *same* basic dignity, and human rights are held equally by all. Furthermore, human beings, in their worth and dignity, are radically distinguished from the rest of creation.

The caste system, by contrast, denies the equal worth of all human beings. The "secret justice" of caste, the intimate link between and mutual reinforcement of the type of life one leads and one's natural worth, gives social inequality a special moral significance. Equal and inalienable human rights held by all members of the species *Homo sapiens,* far from being a "foundational" moral assumption, would be a moral outrage, an affront to and attack on natural order and justice. "The principal criterion on which the caste system is based is the principal of *natural superiority*" (Gupta 1992: 2).

"Human nature"—if we can even use that term without gross anachronism—differs in traditional India from person to person, or, rather, from group to group. "The essential feature of caste was the assumption that there are fundamental and unchangeable differences in the status and nature of human beings" (Buultjens 1980: 112). "In Indian thought, the caste is a *species* of mankind" (Kolenda 1978: 150).

Traditional Indian thought does not draw a qualitative distinction between human beings and other creatures. The human soul is only a somewhat more evolved (self-aware) incarnation of the soul of other animals and even plants. In fact, in many ways the distance between high castes and low castes is greater than that between lower castes and animals. For example, the *Law of Manu* prescribes the same penance whether a Brahman kills a cat, a mongoose, a blue jay, a frog, dog, iguana, owl, crow, or Shudra (11.132). "Dying, without the expectation of a reward, for the sake of Brahmans and of cows" will secure beatitude for Chandalas (untouchables) (10.62; 11.80) To take a modern example, Beteille reports that Brahmans in the village he studied did not even include people of other castes in their count of the village's population and that members of non-Brahman castes likewise did not count untouchables (1965: 25).

Whatever one may think of my arguments about Asia, Africa, and Islam, the Indian case makes it painfully clear that it simply is not true, to quote Pollis and Schwab again, that "all societies cross-culturally and historically manifest conceptions of human rights" (1980a: 15). It is not true that there is a "notion, common to all societies, that human beings are special and worthy of protection that distinguishes humans from animals" (Mutua 1995: 358). And it certainly is not the case that people in every region and culture "share certain beliefs with all humanity by virtue of their humanity" (Penna and Campbell 1998: 21).

6. The Relevance of Human Rights

A very different culturalist argument uses the Western origin of human rights to argue that the Universal Declaration model is inappropriate or irrelevant to contemporary Third World problems and needs. For example, Pollis and Schwab contend that because in most countries "human rights as defined by the West are rejected or, more accurately, are meaningless," the Western concept is "inapplicable," "of limited validity," and "irrelevant" (1980a: 13, 8, 9). These are strong claims that do not necessarily rest on the genetic fallacy (see §4.9). For the most part, however, they are unjustified.

There are no objective standards of relevance or applicability. Even demonstrating that most people in a country have been and continue to be unaware of the concept, or that they have adopted alternative mechanisms to realize human dignity, will not establish that human rights are objectively irrelevant (compare Barnhart 2001). And subjective senses of "irrelevant" raise a variety of difficult issues.

Our problems arise, it seems to me, because we face competing intuitions. We want to recognize the importance of traditional values and institutions[18] as well as the rights of modern nations, states, communities, and individuals to choose their own destiny. At the same time, though, we feel a need to reject an

18. Michael Barnhart notes that in earlier work I have not explicitly argued why we should respect cultural variety (2001: 53). I had assumed that it was sufficiently obvious that it need not be stated—an assumption that any good philosopher will rightly challenge. Cultural diversity deserves our respect (within a human rights framework) not because it is different, or because it is characteristic, but to the extent that it reflects the autonomous choices of the rights-holding individuals who participate in the practices in question (compare §12.6). Although by no means a nontrivial assumption, it seems to me pretty unproblematic once we have accepted the existence of universal human rights.

"anything goes" attitude. This dilemma is the central concern of Chapter 6. A few brief comments, however, are in order here.

Certainly Louis XVI found the revolutionary rights of man to be inappropriate, and today's historians seem to be not altogether certain that the majority of his subjects, especially those outside of Paris, disagreed. In the 1970s and 1980s, Idi Amin and "Emperor" Bokassa found human rights concerns to be irrelevant, while both Pol Pot and his Vietnamese-backed successors determined that human rights were inappropriate to Cambodia's needs and interests. In the 1990s, Saddam Hussein and the *genocidaires* in Rwanda also saw human rights as irrelevant (or worse) and did their best to render them meaningless in local political practice. There is widespread agreement that these men were (morally) wrong. Elucidating the bases for such a conclusion and then applying the resulting principles to less extreme cases, however, raises serious difficulties.

Human rights are, among other things, means to realize human dignity. To the extent that they have instrumental value we can (in principle at least) assess their merits empirically. I contend that for most of the goals of non-Western countries, as defined by these countries themselves, human rights are as effective as, or more effective than, either traditional approaches or modern strategies not based on human rights.

If our concern is with the realization of human dignity, one could argue (along the lines suggested in §4.2-3) that the conditions created by modernization render the individual too vulnerable in the absence of human rights. If the concern is with development and social justice, a strong case might be made that recognizing and protecting human rights would increase participation (and therefore popular support and productivity), open up lines of communication between people and government (thus providing greater efficiency and important checks against corruption and mismanagement), spur the provision of basic services through the recognition of economic and social rights, and provide dispossessed groups with regular and important channels for demanding redress. If one is concerned with stability, an argument might be advanced that a regime that systematically violates human rights engenders destabilizing opposition. It is essential that we move beyond simply demonstrating differences in values (which is the level of most current discussions) to assessing the relative merits of competing approaches.

James C. Hsiung, like many other culturalists, advocates an effort "to develop a definition of human rights that is compatible with a country's cultural legacy" (1985: 20). To a certain extent this is both morally appropriate and instrumentally prudent, but there must be limits.

Some cultural legacies are incompatible with any plausible idea of human rights. For example, racism, sexism, and anti-Semitism were for many centuries—many would argue still are—deeply entrenched elements of the cultural and political legacy of the West. One of its principal political achievements has been precisely to challenge, in theory and in practice, this legacy, and, through the mechanism of human rights, help to create another. Human rights are not, and should not be, neutral with respect to political forms or cultural traditions.

Whether the political vision of the Universal Declaration model is in all its details best for every contemporary society is a matter of legitimate debate, to which we return in the next two chapters. But unless the distinctive nature of the human rights approach is recognized, that debate will be, at best, vacuous or misguided.

It may be desirable to reduce or minimize the place of human rights in political doctrine and practice, or even to replace human rights entirely. But such arguments rarely are made today. Instead, "human rights" is too often used as roughly equivalent to "our approach to human dignity"—or, even worse, whatever oppressive rulers say it is. Such ways of thinking and speaking insidiously erode the distinctive and distinctly valuable aspects of a human rights approach.

7. Culture and Human Rights

Ann-Belinda Preis, in what I consider the most important article on culture and human rights published in the 1990s, shows that anthropology has largely abandoned the understanding of culture as "a homogenous, integral, and coherent unity" that underlies most of the literature on non-Western conceptions of human rights (1996: 288–289)—my own contributions included. In this literature, Preis continues, " 'culture' is implicitly or explicitly conceptualized as a static, homogenous, and bounded entity, defined by its specific 'traits.' " (1996: 289) In fact, however, cultures are complex, variable, multivocal, and above all contested. Rather than static things, "cultures" are fluid complexes of intersubjective meanings and practices.[19]

Preis is certainly correct to criticize the resulting "fallacious reductionism" (1996: 296). "Culture" is used in much of the human rights literature in ways that too often lead to spurious explanation based on false essentialism and excessive aggregation.

In partial self-defense, however, I would reply that my work is a response to an argument that has been widespread for over half a century[20] and that still dominates the literature. The ultimate solution is the one Preis proposes,

19. Andrew Nathan (2001), in what I think is the best piece on the topic of the current decade (so far at least), develops a similar argument.

20. For the classic statements within anthropology, see Preis (1996: 285–286).

namely, for anthropologists and others who seriously study culture to demonstrate the flawed nature of the underlying conception of culture in this literature. But there is also a place, I believe, for my kind of argument, which accepts, *arguendo*, the understanding of culture advanced in this literature but shows that the conclusions typically drawn from it simply do not follow.[21]

I am all in favor of a cross-cultural dialogue that "will allow the incorporation of non-Western symbolism into the international human rights discourse, and make support for human rights more powerful in non-Western societies" (Penna and Campbell 1998: 9). But that dialogue must be based on an clear and accurate understanding of the nature of internationally recognized human rights and a reading of the historical record that can bear empirical scrutiny. The literature I have critiqued here is theoretically muddled or historically inaccurate (and often both).

Nothing is gained by confusing human rights with justice, fairness, limited government, or any other values or practices. Quite the contrary, human rights will be threatened if we do not see that the human rights approach to, say, fairness is very different from other approaches. Even the Indian caste system reflects conceptions of justice and fairness, of giving each his own. Thus I continue to insist that the claims that I address in this chapter merit the most vigorous rebuttal.

It simply is not true that all peoples at all times have had human rights ideas and practices, if by "human rights" we mean equal and inalienable paramount moral rights held by all members of the species. Most traditional legal and political practices are not just human rights practices dressed up in different clothing. And those who insist that they are, whatever their intention may be, make an argument that not only can be but regularly has been used by repressive regimes to support denying their citizens internationally recognized human rights (compare §6.6). In a world in which dictators regularly try to hide behind the cloak of indigenous "culture," even the limited sort of unmasking that my work represents may be of some value.

In any case, it is the only contribution I have to make. My fields are political theory and international relations. My strength is conceptual analysis. And I think that the sort of conceptual clarity for which I strive in this chapter, and in this book more generally, is of both intellectual and political value. I would also point out that anthropologists, right through the Cold War, consistently failed to enter this debate with a more sophisticated critique. In fact, their work both

21. Preis is also correct that the resulting literature, including my own interventions in it, is excessively adversarial. This is particularly clear from our current historical vantage. In my view, the most promising and productive work in this field explores the indigenous "cultural" resources that may be used to support internationally recognized human rights. The work of Abdullahi An-Na'im is particularly important here. See, for example, 1987; 1990; 1992; 2001. For other work in this same general vein, see, for example, Bell (2000); Ali (2000); Lindholt (1997); Monshipour (1998).

directly and indirectly supported the kind of false essentialism that I have tried, however inadequately, to argue against for twenty years now.

I also think that it is important to resist the argument that internationally recognized human rights are a Western artifact that is irrelevant and meaningless in most of the rest of the world. Ideas and social practices move no less readily than, say, noodles and gunpowder. If human rights are irrelevant in a particular place, it is not because of where they were invented or when they were introduced into that place. Culture is *not* destiny.

Preis is probably correct that the ultimate remedy to this mistaken view lies in the sort of detailed, local analysis that she provides in her article (the empirical portions of which look at contemporary Botswana). But work at a high level of abstraction can have some value—especially when it directly addresses arguments that are prevalent in both academic and policy discussions.

Having said all of this, though, I readily admit that there are undeniable differences between, say, Tokyo, Tehran, and Texas and the "cultures" of which they are exemplars. How ought we to deal with these differences? That is the question of the next chapter.

6/ Human Rights and Cultural Relativism

Cultural relativity is an undeniable fact; moral rules and social institutions evidence astonishing cultural and historical variability. The doctrine of cultural relativism holds that some such variations cannot be legitimately criticized by outsiders. I argue, instead, for a fundamentally universalistic approach to internationally recognized human rights.

In most recent discussions of cultures or civilizations[1]—whether they are seen as clashing, converging, or conversing—the emphasis has been on differences, especially differences between the West and the rest. From a broad cross-cultural or intercivilizational perspective, however, the most striking fact about human rights in the contemporary world is the extensive overlapping consensus on the Universal Declaration of Human Rights (compare §3.2). Real conflicts do indeed exist over a few internationally recognized human rights. There are numerous variations in interpretations and modes of implementing internationally recognized human rights. Nonetheless, I argue that culture[2] poses only a modest challenge to the contemporary normative universality of human rights.

1. Defining Cultural Relativism

When internal and external judgments of a practice diverge, cultural relativists give priority to the internal judgments of a society. In its most extreme form, what we can call *radical cultural relativism* holds that culture is the sole source

1. Civilizations seems to be emerging as the term of choice in UN-based discussions. 2001 was designated the United Nations Year of Dialogue Among Civilizations. For a sampling of Unesco sources, see http://www.unesco.org/dialogue2001/en/culture1.htm. I use "culture" and "civilization" more or less interchangeably, although I think that a useful convention would be to treat civilizations as larger or broader: for example, French culture but Western civilization.

2. As in the preceding chapter, I begin by taking at face value the common understanding of culture as static, unitary, and integral. See, however, §5.7 and §6.

of the validity of a moral right or rule.[3] *Radical universalism,* by contrast, would hold that culture is irrelevant to the (universal) validity of moral rights and rules. The body of the continuum defined by these end points can be roughly divided into what we can call strong and weak cultural relativism.

Strong cultural relativism holds that culture is the principal source of the validity of a right or rule. At its furthest extreme, strong cultural relativism accepts a few basic rights with virtually universal application but allows such a wide range of variation that two entirely justifiable sets of rights might overlap only slightly.

Weak cultural relativism, which might also be called strong universalism, considers culture a secondary source of the validity of a right or rule. Universality is initially presumed, but the relativity of human nature, communities, and rules checks potential excesses of universalism. At its furthest extreme, weak cultural relativism recognizes a comprehensive set of prima facie universal human rights but allows limited local variations.

We can also distinguish a qualitative dimension to relativist claims. Legitimate cultural divergences from international human rights norms might be advocated concerning the *substance* of lists of human rights, the *interpretation* of particular rights, and the *form* in which those rights are implemented (see §4). I will defend a weak cultural relativist (strong universalist) position that permits deviations from international human rights norms primarily at the level of form or implementation.

2. Relativity and Universality: A Necessary Tension

Beyond the obvious dangers of moral imperialism, radical universalism requires a rigid hierarchical ordering of the multiple moral communities to which we belong. The radical universalist would give absolute priority to the demands of the cosmopolitan moral community over other ("lower") communities. Such a complete denial of national and subnational ethical autonomy, however, is rare and implausible. There is no compelling moral reason why peoples cannot accept, say, the nation-state, as a major locus of extrafamilial moral and political commitments. And at least certain choices of a variety of moral communities demand respect from outsiders—not uncritical acceptance, let alone emulation, but, in some cases at least, tolerance.

But if human rights are based in human nature, on the fact that one is a human being, how can human rights be relative in any fundamental way? The simple answer is that human nature is itself relative (see §1.3). There is a sense in which this is true even biologically. For example, if marriage partners are

3. I am concerned here only with cultural relativist views as they apply to human rights, although my argument probably has applicability to other relativist claims.

chosen on the basis of cultural preferences for certain physical attributes, the gene pool in a community may be altered. More important, culture can significantly influence the presence and expression of many aspects of human nature by encouraging or discouraging the development or perpetuation of certain personality traits and types. Whether we stress the "unalterable" core or the variability around it—and however we judge their relative size and importance—"human nature," the realized nature of real human beings, is as much a social project as a natural given.

But if human nature were infinitely variable, or if all moral values were determined solely by culture (as radical cultural relativism holds), there could be no human rights (rights that one has "simply as a human being") because the concept "human being" would have no specificity or moral significance. As we saw in the case of Hindu India (§5.5), some societies have not even recognized "human being" as a descriptive category. The very names of many cultures mean simply "the people" (e.g., Hopi, Arapahoe), and their origin myths define them as separate from outsiders, who are somehow "not-human."

Such views, however, are almost universally rejected in the contemporary world. For example, chattel slavery and caste-based legal and political systems, which implicitly deny the existence of a morally significant common humanity, are almost universally condemned, even in the most rigid class societies.

The radical relativist response that consensus is morally irrelevant is logically impeccable. But many people do believe that such consensus strengthens a rule, and most think that it increases the justifiability of certain sorts of international action. In effect, a moral analogue to customary international law seems to operate. If a practice is nearly universal and generally perceived as obligatory, it is required of all members of the community. Even a weak cosmopolitan moral community imposes substantive limitations on the range of permissible moral variation.

Notice, however, that I contend only that there are a few cross-culturally valid moral *values*. This still leaves open the possibility of a radical cultural relativist denial of human *rights*. Plausible arguments can be (and have been) advanced to justify alternative mechanisms to guarantee human dignity. But few states today attempt such an argument. In all regions of the world, a strong commitment to human *rights* is almost universally proclaimed. Even where practice throws that commitment into question, such a widespread rhetorical "fashion" must have some substantive basis.

That basis, as I argued in Chapter 4, lies in the hazards to human dignity posed by modern markets and states. The political power of traditional rulers usually was substantially limited by customs and laws that were entirely independent of human rights. The relative technological and administrative weakness of traditional political institutions further restrained abuses of power. In such a world, inalienable entitlements of individuals held against state and society might plausibly be held to be superfluous (because dignity was guaranteed by alternative mechanisms), if not positively dangerous to important and well-established values and practices.

Such a world, however, exists today only in a relatively small number of isolated areas. The modern state, even in the Third World, not only has been freed from many of the moral constraints of custom but also has a far greater administrative and technological reach. It thus represents a serious threat to basic human dignity, whether that dignity is defined in "traditional" or "modern" terms. In such circumstances, human rights seem necessary rather than optional. Radical or unrestricted relativism thus is as inappropriate as radical universalism.[4] Some kind of intermediate position is required.

3. Internal Versus External Judgments

Respect for autonomous moral communities would seem to demand a certain deference to a society's internal evaluations of its practices, but to commit ourselves to acting on the basis of the moral judgments of others would abrogate our own moral responsibilities. The choice between internal and external evaluations is a moral one, and whatever choice we make will be problematic.

Where internal and external judgments conflict, assessing the relative importance attached to those judgments may be a reasonable place to start in seeking to resolve them. Figure 6.1 offers a simple typology.

Case 1—morally unimportant both externally and internally—is uninteresting. Whether or not one maintains one's initial external condemnation is of little intrinsic interest to anyone. Case 2—externally unimportant, internally very important—is probably best handled by refusing to press the negative external judgment. To press a negative external judgment that one feels is relatively unimportant when the issue is of great importance internally usually will be, at best, insensitive. By the same token, Case 3—externally very important, internally unimportant—presents the best occasion to press an external judgment (with some tact).

Case 4, in which the practice is of great moral importance to both sides, is the most difficult to handle, but even here we may have good reasons to press a negative external judgment. Consider, for example, slavery. Most people today would agree that no matter how ancient and well established the practice may be, to turn one's back on the enslavement of human beings in the name of cultural relativity would reflect moral obtuseness, not sensitivity. Human sacri-

4. We can also note that radical relativism is descriptively inaccurate. Few people anywhere believe that their moral beliefs rest on nothing more than tradition. The radical relativist insistence that they do offers an implausible (and unattractive) account of the nature and meaning of morality.

		Internal judgment of practice	
		Morally unimportant	Morally very important
External judgment of practice	Morally unimportant	Case 1	Case 2
	Morally very important	Case 3	Case 4

Figure 6.1 Type Conflicts over Culturally Relative Practices

fice, trial by ordeal, extrajudicial execution, and female infanticide are other cultural practices that are (in my view rightly) condemned by almost all external observers today.

Underlying such judgments is the inherent universality of basic moral precepts, at least as we understand morality in the West. We simply do not believe that our moral precepts are for us and us alone. This is most evident in Kant's deontological universalism. But it is no less true of the principle of utility. And, of course, human rights are also inherently universal.

In any case, our moral precepts are *our* moral precepts. As such, they demand our obedience. To abandon them simply because others reject them is to fail to give proper weight to our own moral beliefs (at least where they involve central moral precepts such as the equality of all human beings and the protection of innocents).

Finally, no matter how firmly someone else, or even a whole culture, believes differently, at some point—slavery and untouchability come to mind—we simply must say that those contrary beliefs are wrong. Negative external judgments may be problematic. In some cases, however, they are not merely permissible but demanded.

4. Concepts, Interpretations, Implementations

In evaluating arguments of cultural relativism, we must distinguish between variations in substance, interpretation, and form. Even very weak cultural relativists—that is, strong universalists—are likely to allow considerable variation in the form in which rights are implemented. For example, whether free legal assistance is required by the right to equal protection of the laws usually will best be viewed as largely beyond the legitimate reach of universal standards.

Important differences between strong and weak relativists are likely to arise, however, at the levels of interpretation and, especially, substance.

A. SUBSTANCE OR CONCEPT

The Universal Declaration generally formulates rights at the level of what I will call the *concept,* an abstract, general statement of an orienting value. "Everyone has the right to work, to free choice of employment, to just and favorable conditions of work and to protection against unemployment" (Art. 23). *Only* at this level do I claim that there is a consensus on the rights of the Universal Declaration, and at this level, most appeals to cultural relativism fail.

It is difficult to imagine arguments against recognizing the rights of Articles 3–12, which include life, liberty, and security of the person; the guarantee of legal personality, equality before the law, and privacy; and protections against slavery, arbitrary arrest, detention, or exile, and inhuman or degrading treatment. These are so clearly connected to basic requirements of human dignity, and are stated in sufficiently general terms, that virtually every morally defensible contemporary form of social organization must recognize them (although perhaps not necessarily as inalienable rights). I am even tempted to say that conceptions of human nature or society that are incompatible with such rights are almost by definition indefensible in contemporary international society.

Civil rights such as freedom of conscience, speech, and association may be a bit more relative. Because they assume the existence and positive evaluation of relatively autonomous individuals, they may be of questionable applicability in strong, thriving traditional communities. In such communities, however, they would rarely be at issue. If traditional practices truly are based on and protect culturally accepted conceptions of human dignity, then members of such a community will not have the desire or the need to claim such rights. In the more typical contemporary case, however, in which relatively autonomous individuals face modern states, it is hard for me to imagine a defensible conception of human dignity that does not include almost all of these rights. A similar argument can be made for the economic and social rights of the Universal Declaration.

In twenty years of working with issues of cultural relativism, I have developed a simple test that I pose to skeptical audiences. Which rights in the Universal Declaration, I ask, does your society or culture reject? Rarely has a single full right (other than the right to private property) been rejected. Never has it been suggested to me that as many as four should be eliminated.

Typical was the experience I had in Iran in early 2001, where I posed this question to three different audiences. In each case, discussion moved quickly to freedom of religion, and in particular atheism and apostasy by Muslims (which the Universal Declaration permits but Iran prohibits).[5] Given the continuing repression of Iranian Bahais—although, for the moment at least, the apparent end to executions—this was quite a sensitive issue. Even here, though, the challenge was not to the principle, or even the right, of freedom of religion (which almost all Muslims support) but to competing "Western" and "Muslim" conceptions of its limits. And we must remember that *every* society places some limits on religious liberty. In the United States, for example, recent court cases have dealt with forced medical treatment for the children of Christian Scientists, live animal sacrifice by practitioners of santaria, and the rights of Jehovah's Witnesses to evangelize at private residences.

We must be careful, however, not to read too much into this consensus at the level of the concept, which may obscure important disagreements concerning definitions and implicit limitations. Consider Article 5 of the Universal Declaration: "No one shall be subjected to torture or to cruel, inhuman or degrading treatment or punishment." The real controversy comes over definitions of terms such as "cruel." Is the death penalty cruel, inhuman, or degrading? Most European states consider it to be. The United States does not. We must recognize and address such differences without overstating their importance or misrepresenting their character.

Implicit limits on rights may also pose challenges to universalist arguments. Most of the rights in the Universal Declaration are formulated in categorical terms. For example, Article 19 begins: "Everyone has the right to freedom of opinion and expression." To use the hackneyed American example, this does not mean that one can scream "Fire!" in a crowded theater. All rights have limits.[6] But if these limits differ widely and systematically across civilizations, the resulting differences in human rights practices might indeed be considerable.

Are there systematic differences in definitions of terms across civilizations? Do cultures differ systematically in the standard limits they put on the exercises of rights? And if these differences are systematic, how significant are they? I have suggested that the answers to these questions are largely negative. For reasons of space—as well as the fact that such negative arguments cannot be conclusively established—I leave this claim as a challenge. Critics may refute my argument with several well-chosen examples of substantial cultural variation either at the level of concepts or in systematic variations at the level of interpretation that undermine the apparent conceptual consensus. So far, at least, I

5. Gender equality, perhaps surprisingly, did not come up (although these were elite, English-speaking audiences, and Iran has, self-consciously, made considerable progress on women's rights issues in recent years). But even when it does, dispute usually focuses on the meaning of nondiscrimination or on particular practices, such as equal rights in marriage.

6. Logically, there can be at most one absolute right (unless we implausibly assume that rights never conflict with one another).

have not encountered anyone capable of presenting such a pattern of contradictory evidence, except in the case of small and relatively isolated communities.[7]

B. INTERPRETATIONS

What ought to count, for example, as adequate protection against unemployment? Does it mean a guaranteed job, or is it enough to provide compensation to those who are unemployed? Both seem to me plausible interpretations. Some such variations in interpreting rights seem not merely defensible but desirable, and even necessary.

Particular human rights are like "essentially contested concepts," in which there is a substantial but rather general consensus on basic meaning coupled with no less important, systematic, and apparently irresolvable conflicts of interpretations (Gallie 1968). In such circumstances, culture provides one plausible and defensible mechanism for selecting interpretations (and forms).

We should also note that the Universal Declaration lists some rights that are best viewed as interpretations. For example, the right of free and full consent of intending spouses reflects an interpretation of marriage over which legitimate controversy is possible. Notice, however, that the right (as stated in Sec. 2 of Art. 16) is subordinate to the right to marry and to found a family (over which, at this highest level of generality, there is little international dispute). Furthermore, some traditional customs, such as bride price, provide alternative protections for women that address at least some of the underlying concerns that gave rise to the norm of free and full consent.

I would suggest, however, that defensible variations in interpretations are likely to be relatively modest in number. And not all "interpretations" are equally plausible or defensible. They are *interpretations*, not free associations or arbitrary, let alone self-interested, stipulations. The meaning of, for example, "the right to political participation" is controversial, but an election in which a people were allowed to choose an absolute dictator for life ("one man, one vote, once," as a West African quip put it) is simply indefensible.

We must also note that considerable divergences in interpretation exist not only between but also *within* cultures or civilizations. Consider, for example, differences within the West between Europe and the United States on the death penalty and the welfare state. Japan and Vietnam have rather different interpretations of the rights to freedom of speech and association, despite being East Asians.

7. The general similarity of regional human rights instruments underscores this argument. Even the African Charter of Human and Peoples' Rights, the most heterodox regional treaty, differs largely at the level of interpretation and, in substance or concept, by addition (of peoples' rights) rather than by subtraction.

Even where there are variations between two cultures, we still need to ask whether culture in fact is the source of cause of these differences. I doubt that we are actually saying much of interest or importance when we talk of, say, Japan as Asian. Consider the common claim that Asian societies are communitarian and consensual and Western societies are individualistic and competitive. What exactly is this supposed to explain, or even refer to, in any particular Asian or Western country? Dutch or Norwegian politics is at least as consensual as Thai politics. The Dutch welfare state is in its own way as caring and paternalistic as the most traditional of Japanese employers. Such examples, which are easily multiplied, suggest that even where variations in practice exist, culture does much less explanatory work than most relativists suggest—or at least that the "culture" in question is more local or national rather than regional or a matter of civilization.

C. IMPLEMENTATION OR FORM

Just as concepts need to be interpreted, interpretations need to be implemented in law and political practice. To continue with the example of the right to work, what rate of unemployment compensation should be provided, for how long, in what circumstances? The range of actual and defensible variation here is considerable—although limited by the governing concept and interpretation.

Even a number of rights in the International Human Rights Covenants involve specifications at the level of form. For example, Article 10(2)(b) of the International Covenant on Civil and Political Rights requires the segregation of juvenile defendants. In some cultures the very notion of a juvenile criminal defendant (or a penitentiary system) does not exist. Although there are good reasons to suggest such rules, to demand them in the face of strong reasoned opposition seems to me to make little sense—so long as the underlying objectives are realized in some other fashion.

Differences in implementations, however, often seem to have little to do with culture. And even where they do, it is not obvious that cultural differences deserve more (or less) respect than differing implementations attributable to other causes (e.g., levels of economic development or unique national historical experiences).

I stress this three-level scheme to avoid a common misconception. My argument is for universality only at the level of the concept. The Universal Declaration insists that all states share a limited but important range of obligations. It is, in its own words, "a common standard of achievement for all peoples and all nations." The ways in which these rights are implemented, however, so long as they fall within the range of variation consistent with the overarching concept, are matters of legitimate variation (compare §7.7).

This is particularly important because most of the "hot button" issues in recent discussions have occurred at the level of implementation. For example, debates about pornography are about the limits—interpretation or implementation—of freedom of expression. Most Western countries permit the graphic depiction of virtually any sex act (so long as it does not involve and is not shown to children). Many others countries punish those who produce, distribute, or consume such material. This dispute, however, does not suggest a rejection of human rights, the idea of personal autonomy, or even the right to freedom of speech.

We should also note that controversy over pornography rages internally in many countries. Every country criminalizes some forms of pornography, and most countries—Taliban Afghanistan being the exception that proves the rule—permit some depictions of sexual behavior or the display of erotic images that another country has within living memory banned as pornographic. Wherever one draws the line, it leaves intact both the basic internationally recognized human right to freedom of speech and the underlying value of personal autonomy.

D. UNIVERSALITY WITHIN DIVERSITY

There are at least three ways in which rights that vary in form and interpretation can still be plausibly described as "universal." First, and most important, there may be an overlapping consensus (see §3.2) on the substance of the list, despite diversity in interpretations and implementations. Second, even where there are differences at the level of substance or concept, a large common core may exist with relatively few differences "around the edges." Third, even where substantial substantive disagreements occur, we might still be justified in speaking of universal rights if there are strong statistical regularities and the outliers are few and clearly overshadowed by the central tendency.

In contemporary international society, I think that we can say that there are few far outliers (e.g., North Korea) at least at the level of agreed-on concepts. I would admit that overlapping conceptual consensus often is thin. Nonetheless, I think that we can fairly (although not without controversy) say that variations at the level of concepts are infrequent. Somewhat more contentious is the claim that I would also advance that the range of diversity in standard interpretations is modest and poses relatively few serious international political disputes.

We do not face an either-or choice between cultural relativism and universal human rights. Rather, we need to recognize both the universality of human rights and their particularity and thus accept a certain *limited* relativity, especially with respect to forms of implementation. We must take seriously the initially paradoxical idea of the relative universality of internationally recognized human rights.[8]

8. Coming at a similar perspective from the other end of the spectrum, Richard Wilson notes that human rights, and struggles over their implementation, "are embedded in local normative orders and yet are caught within webs of power and meaning which extend beyond the local" (1997: 23). Andrew Nathan has recently described this orientation as "tempered universalism" (2001).

5. Explaining the Persistence of Culturalist Arguments

If my argument for relative universality is even close to correct, how can we explain the persistence of foundational appeals to culture? If we could explain this puzzle, both for the relativist arguments considered in this chapter and for the claims about human rights in traditional societies considered in Chapter 5, the plausibility of a universalist perspective would be enhanced. At least six explanations come to mind.

First, it is surprisingly common for even otherwise sophisticated individuals to take the particular institutions associated with the realization of a right in their country or culture to be essential to that right. Americans, in particular, seem to have unusually great difficulty in realizing that the way we do things here is not necessarily what international human rights norms require.

Second, narrow-minded and ham-handed (Western, and especially American) international human rights policies and statements exacerbate these confusions. Consider Michael Fay, an American teenager who vandalized hundreds of thousands of dollars worth of property in Singapore. When he was sentenced to be publicly caned, there was a furor in the United States. President Clinton argued, with apparently genuine indignation, that it was abominable to cane someone, but he failed to find it even notable that in his own country people are being fried in the electric chair. If this indeed is what universalism means—and I hasten to repeat that it is not—then of course relativism looks far more attractive.

The legacy of colonialism provides a third important explanation for the popularity of relativist arguments. African, Asian, and Muslim (as well as Latin American) leaders and citizens have vivid, sometimes personal, recollections of their sufferings under colonial masters. Even when the statements and actions of great powers stay within the range of the overlapping consensus on the Universal Declaration, there is understandable (although not necessarily justifiable) sensitivity to external pressure. (Compare the sensitivity of the United States to external criticism even in the absence of such a historical legacy.) When international pressures exceed the bounds of the overlapping consensus, that sensitivity often becomes (justifiably) very intense.

Fourth, arguments of relativism are often rooted in a desire to express and foster national, regional, cultural, or civilizational pride. It is no coincidence that the "Asian values" debate (see Chapter 7) took off in the wake of the Asian economic miracle—and dramatically subsided after the 1977 financial crisis.

The belief that such arguments have instrumental efficacy in promoting internationally recognized human rights is a fifth important reason. For example, Daniel Bell plausibly argues that building human rights implementation strategies on local traditions (1) is "more likely to lead to long term commitment to human rights"; (2) "may shed light on the groups most likely to bring about desirable social and political change"; (3) "allows the human rights activist to draw on the most compelling justifications"; (4) "may shed light on the appropriate attitude to be employed by human rights activists"; and (5) "may also make one more sensitive to the possibility of alternative" mechanisms for protecting rights (1996: 657–659). I would insist only that we be clear that this is a practical, not a theoretical, argument; that we operate with a plausible theory of culture and an accurate understanding of the culture in question; and that we not assume that culture trumps international norms. "To realize greater social justice on an international scale, activists and intellectuals must take culture seriously, but not in the totalizing, undifferentiated way in which some leaders of non-Western nations have used it as a trump card" (L. Bell 2001: 21).

This leads to the sixth, and perhaps the most important, explanation for the prevalence of culturalist arguments, namely, that they are used by vicious elites as a way to attempt to deflect attention from their repressive policies. And well-meaning Westerners with a well-developed sense of the legacy of Western colonialism indirectly support such arguments when they shy away from criticizing arguments advanced by non-Westerners even when they are empirically inaccurate or morally absurd.

6. Culture and Politics

So far I have proceeded, in line with the standard assumption of cultural relativists, by treating "cultures" as homogenous, static, all-encompassing, and voluntarily accepted "things," the substance of which can be relatively easily and uncontroversially determined. None of these assumptions is defensible.

A. IDENTIFYING A "CULTURE"

Cultures are anything but homogenous. In fact, differences *within* civilizations often are as striking and as important as those between civilizations. "The Western tradition," for example, includes both Caligula and Marcus Aurelius, Francis of Assisi and Torquemada, Leopold II of Belgium and Albert Schweitzer, Jesus and Hitler—and just about everything in between.

We thus face a difficult problem even in determining what is to count as evidence for a claim of the form "civilization *x* holds belief *y*." Political authorities are but one (very problematic) source of evidence of the views and practices of a civilization. Nor can we rely on authoritative texts. For example, the Christian Bible has significantly shaped Western civilization. But even when particular practices do not diverge from what one might expect from reading this "foundational" text—and setting aside the fact that such expectations change with time, place, and reader—few Western practices are adequately explained in terms of, let alone reducible to, those texts.[9]

Even the long-established practice of leading states may diverge significantly from the norms and values of the civilization of which they are a part. The United States, for example, is in many ways a very *atypical* Western country in its approach to economic and social rights. In characterizing and comparing civilizations, we must not mistake some particular expressions, however characteristic, for the whole. For example, Christianity and secularism are arguably equally important to modern Western civilization. And the balance between secular and religious forces, values, and orientations varies dramatically with time, place, and issue in "the West."

Such cautions are especially important because culturalist arguments regularly rely on appeals to a distant past, such as the precolonial African village, Native American tribes, and traditional Islamic societies. The traditional culture advanced to justify cultural relativism far too often no longer exists—if it ever did in the idealized form in which it is typically presented. In the Third World today we usually see not the persistence of "traditional" culture in the face of "modern" intrusions, or even the development of syncretic cultures and values, but rather disruptive "Westernization," rapid cultural change, or people enthusiastically embracing "modern" practices and values.[10] And the modern nation-states and contemporary nationalist regimes that have replaced traditional communities and practices cannot be judged by standards of a bygone era.

We must also be careful to distinguish "civilization" or "culture" from religion and politics. The United States is a state, a political entity, not a civilization. Islam is not a civilization but a religion, or, as many believers would put it, a true and comprehensive way of life that transcends culture or civilization. An "Islamic civilization"—centered on Mecca and running, say, from the Maghreb to the Indus—does not include all Muslims, or even all majority Muslim countries. The broader Muslim world, running from Dakar to Jakarta, may be an international political unit of growing interest or importance, but it certainly is not a culture or civilization. And tens of millions of Muslims live outside of even this community.

9. To cite one example of misplaced textualism, Roger Ames (1997) manages to devote an entire article to "the conversation on Chinese human rights" that manages to make only a few passing, exceedingly delicate, mentions of events since 1949. China and its culture would seem to have been unaffected by such forces as decades of brutal party dictatorship or the impact of both socialism and capitalism on land tenure and residence patterns. In fact, although he cites a number of passages from Confucius, Ames does not even attempt to show how traditional Confucian ideas express themselves in contemporary Chinese human rights debates.

10. None of this should be surprising when we compare the legal, political, and cultural practices of the contemporary West with those of ancient Athens, medieval Paris, Renaissance Florence, or even Victorian London.

B. THE POLITICS OF CULTURAL RELATIVISM

Cultures are not merely diverse but are contested. In fact, contemporary anthropologists increasingly depict "cultures" not as "things" but as sites of contestation. "Rather than simply a domain of sharing and commonality, culture figures here more as a site of difference and contestation, simultaneously ground and stake of a rich field of cultural-political practices" (Gupta and Ferguson 1997: 5).

> Culture is usually viewed by the new cultural theorists as contested—a social context in which power struggles are constantly waged over the meaning and control of what Pierre Bourdieu has called "symbolic capital" as well as over more overtly material forms of wealth and power. In short, culture is not a given, but rather a congeries of ways of thinking, believing, and acting that are constantly in the state of being produced; it is contingent and always unstable, especially as the forces of "modernity" have barreled down upon most people throughout the world over the course of the twentieth century. (Bell, Nathan, and Peleg 2001: 11)

> All forms of cultural relativism fundamentally fail to recognize culture as an ongoing historic and institutional process where the existence of a given custom does not mean that the custom is either adaptive, optimal, or consented to by a majority of its adherents. Culture is far more effectively characterized as an ongoing adaptation to a changing environment rather than as a static superorganic entity. In a changing environment, cultural practices routinely outlive their usefulness, and cultural values change either through internal dialogue within the cultural group or through cross-cultural influences. (Zechenter 1997: 332–333)

"Culture" is constructed through selective appropriations from a diverse and contested past and present. Those appropriations are rarely neutral in process, intent, or consequences. Cultural relativist arguments thus regularly obscure often troubling realities of power and politics.

Arguments of cultural relativism are far too often made by (or on behalf of) economic and political elites that have long since left traditional culture behind. Even when this represents an admirable effort to retain or recapture cherished traditional values, it is at least ironic to see "Westernized" elites warning against the values and practices they have adopted. There is also more than a hint of a troubling, even tragic, paternalism. For example, "villagization" in Tanzania, which was supposed to reflect traditional African conceptions, was accomplished only by force, against the strong opposition of much of the population.

Even such troubling sincerity is unfortunately rare. Government officials denounce the corrosive individualism of Western values—while they line their pockets with the proceeds of massive corruption, drive imported luxury automobiles, and plan European or American vacations. Leaders sing the praises of traditional communities—while they wield arbitrary power antithetical to traditional values, pursue development policies that systematically undermine traditional communities, and replace traditional leaders with corrupt cronies and party hacks. Rigged elections, military dictatorships, and malnutrition caused by government incentives to produce cash crops rather than food are just a few of the widespread abuses of internationally recognized human rights that do not express, but rather infringe, indigenous cultural values.

In traditional cultures—at least the kinds of traditional cultures that might justify deviations from international human rights standards—people are not victims of the arbitrary decisions of rulers whose principal claim to power is their control of modern instruments of force and administration. Traditional customs and practices usually provide each person with a place in society and a certain amount of dignity and protection. Furthermore, rulers and ruled (and rich and poor) usually are linked by reciprocal bonds. The human rights violations of most Third World regimes are as antithetical to such cultural traditions as they are to "Western" human rights conceptions.

Relativist arguments became particularly perverse when they support a small elite that has arrogated to itself the "right" to speak for "its" culture or civilization, and then imposes its own self-interested views and practices on the broader society—invoking cultural relativism abroad while ruthlessly trampling on local customs. Consider, for example, Suharto and his cronies in Indonesia, who sought to cloak their version of modern state-based repression and crony capitalism in the aura of traditional culture. In Zaire, President Mobutu created the practice of *salongo*, a form of communal labor with a supposedly traditional basis, which was in fact essentially a revival of the colonial practice of corvee labor (Callaghy 1980: 490). Macias Nguema of Equatorial Guinea, perhaps the most vicious ruler independent black Africa has seen, called himself "Grand Master of Popular Education, Science, and Traditional Culture," a title that might be comical were the situation not so tragic.

7. Dialogue over Real Differences

The above discussion is intentionally one-sided. I have drawn attention to commonalities and minimized (real) differences. But even if I am correct about the extent of those differences, we must not confuse overlapping consensus with homogeneity.

Furthermore, the fact that differences are *relatively* minor, in the context of the full body of internationally recognized human rights, does not mean that they are unimportant, especially at the level of day-to-day politics. Questions about such issues as capital and corporal punishment, the limits of religious liberty, and the dimensions of gender equality merit intensive discussions both within and between states and civilizations.

Should traditional notions of "family values" and gender roles be emphasized in the interest of children and society, or should families be conceived in more individualistic and egalitarian terms? What is the proper balance between rewarding individual economic initiative and redistributive taxation in the interest of social harmony and support for disadvantaged individuals and groups? At what point should the words or behaviors of deviant or dissident individuals be forced to give way the interests or desires of society?

Questions such as these, which in my terminology involve conflicting interpretations, involve vital issues of political controversy in virtually all societies. In discussing them we must often walk the difficult line between respect for the other and respect for one's own values. A number of examples of how this might be done in contemporary Asia are found in §7.7. Here I want to consider a relatively easy case—slavery—in an unconventional way.

Suppose that in contemporary Saudi Arabia a group were to emerge arguing that because slavery was accepted in the early Muslim world it should be reinstituted in contemporary Saudi Arabia. I am certain that almost all Saudis, from the most learned clerics to the most ordinary citizens, would reject this view. But how should these individuals be dealt with?

Dialogue seems to me the appropriate route, so long as they do not attempt to *practice* slavery. Those in the majority who would remonstrate these individuals for their despicable views have, I think, an obligation to use precisely such forceful moral terms. Nonetheless, freedom of belief and speech requires the majority to tolerate these views, in the minimal sense of not imposing legal liabilities on those who hold or express them. Should they attempt to practice slavery, however, the force of the law is appropriately applied to suppress and punish this practice. Condemnation by outsiders also seems appropriate, although so long as the problem is restricted to expressions of beliefs only in Saudi Arabia there probably will be few occasions for such condemnations.

But suppose that the unthinkable were to occur and the practice of slavery were reintroduced in Saudi Arabia—not, let us imagine, as a matter of law, but rather through the state refusing to prosecute slave-holders. Here we run up against the state system and the fact that international human rights law gives states near total discretion to implement internationally recognized human rights within their own territories.

One might argue that slavery is legally prohibited as a matter of *jus cogens*, general principles of law, and customary (as well as treaty) law. But coercive international enforcement is extraordinarily contentious and without much legal precedent. Outsiders, however, remain bound by their own moral principles (as well as by international human rights norms) to condemn such practices in the strongest possible terms. And foreign states would be entirely justified in putting whatever pressure, short of force, they could mobilize on Saudi Arabia to halt the practice.

This hypothetical example illustrates the fact that *some* cultural practices, rather that deserve our respect, demand our condemnation. It also indicates, though, that some beliefs, however despicable, demand our toleration—because freedom of opinion and belief is an internationally recognized human right. So long as one stays within the limits of internationally recognized human rights, one is entitled to at least a limited and grudging toleration and the personal space that comes with that. But such individuals are *owed* nothing more.

Many cases, however, are not so easy. This is especially true where cultures are undergoing substantial or unusually rapid transformation. In much of the Third World we regularly face the problem of "modern" individuals or groups who reject traditional practices. Should we give priority to the idea of community self-determination and permit the enforcement of customary practices against modern "deviants" even if this violates "universal" human rights? Or should individual self-determination prevail, thus sanctioning claims of universal human rights against traditional society?

In discussing women's rights in Africa, Rhoda Howard suggests an attractive and widely applicable compromise strategy (1984: 66–68). On a combination of practical and moral grounds, she argues against an outright ban on such practices as child betrothal and widow inheritance, but she also argues strongly for national legislation that permits women (and the families of female children) to "opt out" of traditional practices. This would permit individuals and families to, in effect, choose the terms on which they participate in the cultures that are of value to their lives. Unless we think of culture as an oppressive external force, this seems entirely appropriate.

Conflicting practices, however, may sometimes be irreconcilable. For example, a right to private ownership of the means of production is incompatible with the maintenance of a village society in which families hold only rights of use to communally owned land. Allowing individuals to opt out and fully own their land would destroy the traditional system. Even such conflicts, however, may sometimes be resolved, or at least minimized, by the physical or legal separation of adherents of old and new values, particularly with practices that are not material to the maintenance or integrity of either culture.

Nevertheless, a choice must sometimes be made, at least by default, between irreconcilable practices. Such cases take us out of the realm in which useful general guidelines are possible. Fortunately, though, they are the exception rather than the rule—although no easier for that fact to deal with when they do arise.

It would be dangerous either to deny differences between civilizations where they do exist or to exaggerate their extent or practical importance. Whatever the situation in other issue areas, in the case of human rights, for all the undeniable differences, it is the similarities across civilizations that are more striking and important. Whatever our differences, now or in the past, all contemporary civilizations are linked by the growing recognition of the Universal Declaration as, in its own words, "a common standard of achievement for all peoples and all nations." Or, as I prefer to put it, human rights are relatively universal.

7/ Human Rights and "Asian Values"

The debate over culture and human rights in the 1970s and 1980s was dominated by discussions of so-called nonwestern conceptions of human rights, which I discussed critically in Chapter 5. In the 1990s, discussions took on a more combative tone, especially in the debate over "Asian values."[1] Asian leaders and (often politically well-connected) intellectuals began to assert claims of legitimate, culturally based differences that justified substantial deviations from standard international interpretations of human rights norms.[2] Articles in prominent Western journals began appearing with titles such as "Asia's Different Standard" (Kausikan 1993), "Culture is Destiny" (Zakaria 1994), and "Can Asians Think?" (Mahbubani 1998). Regional figures, such as Singapore's Lee Kwan Yew and Malaysia's Mahathir bin Mohamad emerged onto a wider international stage. And the "East Asian Economic Miracle"—which even after the crisis of 1997 remains impressive—increased interest in such arguments in other regions.

The first six sections of this chapter present a critical reading of these arguments. The final section, however, steps back and seeks to illustrate the space for local variation in an Asian context; that is, the relative universality of internationally recognized human rights.

1. Langlois (2001) provides an excellent recent discussion. Chapter 1 offers a fine overview and Chapters 2 and 3 usefully seek to separate politics and cant from legitimate concerns and insights. For good collections of essays provoked by and participating in the Asian values debate, see Bauer and Bell (1999), Van Ness and Aziz (1999), van Hoof et al. (1996), Cauquelin, Lim, and Mayer-Konig (1998), and Jacobsen and Bruun (2000).

2. A focal point for this discussion was the Regional Meeting for Asia of the World Conference on Human Rights, held March 29–April 2, 1993 in Bangkok, and relativist arguments advanced that summer at the Vienna Conference. This discussion was also fostered by the decision of China to move from denial of the relevance of international human rights standards (and of its own human rights problems) to acceptance, but with a strong relativist twist, as symbolized in its 1991 White Paper (China 1991).

1. Sovereignty and International Human Rights

Sovereignty is one standard ground for rejecting international human rights standards.[3] Chinese officials and scholars in particular have insisted that "sovereignty is the foundation and basic guarantee of human rights" (Xie and Niu 1994; compare China 1991: 1). "The rights of each country to formulate its own policies on human rights protection in light of its own conditions should . . . be respected and guaranteed" (China 1993: 5; compare Cooper 1994: 69).

Taken at face value, this amounts to a claim that whatever a country does with respect to human rights is its business alone. Rather than a defensible conception of human rights, this would subordinate human rights to the competing rights and values of sovereignty. And, of course, there is nothing distinctively Asian about a commitment to sovereignty.

The record of Western (and Japanese) colonial rule certainly suggests that sovereignty is a necessary condition for a rights-protective regime. But it is by no means a sufficient condition. Sovereignty removes some international impediments to implementing internationally recognized human rights. It does little to address issues of *internal* human rights protection and violation. In fact, sovereignty is typically the mantle behind which rights-abusive regimes hide when faced with international human rights criticism.

Mahathir complains that "it would seem that Asians have no right to define and practice their own set of values about human rights" (1994: 9). This is to a considerable extent true, not just for Asians, but for all countries. Authoritative international human rights norms govern internationally defensible definitions of human rights. The Bangkok Declaration on Human Rights, adopted at the Asia and Pacific regional preparatory meeting for the Vienna Conference, reiterates the indisputable international legal right of all countries "to determine their political system." But there is also a substantial body of international human rights law—the authority of the Universal Declaration and the Covenants is reaffirmed by both the Bangkok Declaration and the Vienna Final Document—that severely restricts the range of internationally defensible definitions of human rights.

"Imposing the human rights standard of one's own country or region on other countries or regions is an infringement upon other countries' sovereignty and interference into other countries' internal affairs" (Xie and Niu 1994: 1; compare China 1991: 61). The standards being "imposed," however, are simply those of the Universal Declaration of Human Rights. These are not distinctively Western, as even many critics of the West emphasize. "All the countries of the

3. For a complementary discussion of sovereignty and human rights, see Inoue (1999: 30–34). Xin (1996: 54–56) provides an unusually open attempt by a Chinese scholar to address the competing claims of sovereignty and human rights.

region are party to the U.N. Charter. None has rejected the Universal Declaration" (Kausikan 1993: 25).

"They threaten sanctions, withdrawal of aid, stoppage of loans, economic and trade boycotts and actual military strikes against those they accuse of violating human rights" (Mahathir 1994: 7). Military strikes by one state in response to human rights violations in another would almost certainly violate sovereignty and territorial integrity. But Mahathir conveniently neglects to mention even a single example. In fact, he criticizes the West for *failing* to use force on behalf of the Iraqi Kurds and Bosnian Muslims (1994: 5, 6, 8). And the other activities of which he complains are entirely legitimate.

Why shouldn't a country withdraw aid if it objects to a recipient's human rights practices? Why must it loan money to tyrants? Were a state or group of states to claim "a right to impose their system of government" or "[arrogate] to themselves the right to intervene anywhere where human rights are violated" (Mahathir 1994: 4, 8) they would indeed be guilty of serious international offenses. But it is completely legitimate for a country to use its financial and political resources on behalf of internationally recognized human rights.

Human rights are a legitimate and well-established international concern. Sovereignty requires only that states refrain from the threat or use of force in trying to influence the human rights practices of other states. Short of force, states are free to use most ordinary means of foreign policy on behalf of internationally recognized human rights.

2. The Demands of Development

In Asia, as elsewhere, it is often argued that systematic infringements of internationally recognized human rights are necessary, and thus justifiable or even desirable, to achieve rapid economic development. §11.5 criticizes standard arguments for development-rights trade-offs. Here I restrict myself to questioning their plausibility and relevance to cross-cultural discussions of human rights.

We can begin by noting that there is nothing distinctively Asian to such arguments. The sacrifice of civil and political rights to economic development has been a mainstay of dictatorships of various stripes in all regions. The (short-run) sacrifice of economic and social rights to development has been a staple of capitalist development strategies and is part of the new orthodoxy preached (and imposed) by the International Monetary Fund and other (Western-dominated) international financial institutions. Rather than rely on culturally relative Asian values, trade-off arguments appeal to a universal developmental imperative that overrides both culture and human rights.

Furthermore, at most they justify only temporary human rights infringements. It is perhaps true that "when poverty and lack of adequate food are commonplace and people's basic needs are not guaranteed, priority should be given to economic development" (China 1993: 3). But this is at best a short-run excuse. Regimes that sacrifice either civil and political rights or economic, social, and cultural rights to development do not represent a desirable form of government. Such sacrifices ought to be a matter of profound regret and discomfort. They are to be endured, in the hope of a better life for one's children, not celebrated.

We must be especially wary of arguments for categorical sacrifices of human rights. For example, U.S.-style interest group politics may inappropriately favor certain special interests over the general welfare or introduce unacceptable political and administrative inefficiencies.[4] But this does not justify wholesale denial of freedom of speech, assembly, and association, let alone practices such as arbitrary arrest and detention or outlawing opposition political movements and parties.

We also need to be skeptical of the empirical basis of trade-off arguments. In Japan, Taiwan, and South Korea, extraordinary growth brought improved satisfaction of basic needs for the poor and did not create a wildly unequal income distribution. Although no state has launched sustained, rapid development at an early stage of growth under a rights-protective government, the necessity of repression—as opposed to its convenience for the wealthy and powerful—is hardly clear. And "authoritarian rule more often than not has been used as a masquerade for kleptocracies, bureaucratic incompetence, and worst of all, for unbridled nepotism and corruption" (Anwar 1994: 4).

Particular infringements of internationally recognized human rights may be justified in the pursuit of rapid economic development. But the burden of proof lies on those who would resort to the prima facie evil of denying rights. And even when trade-offs are justified, governments must be forcefully reminded that such sacrifices are tragic necessities that must be kept to an absolute minimum in number, duration, and severity.

3. Economic and Social Rights

"The central issue in the contemporary discourse on human rights is not so much whether it is Western or Eastern in origin but rather the balance between civil and political rights on the one hand, and societal[5] and economic rights on the other" (Anwar 1994: 2). Critics (e.g., Kausikan 1993: 35) typically argue that

4. Asian "soft authoritarianism," however, seems at least equally prone to the corrupting influences of special interests, but with a much narrower range of interests able to participate in the process.

5. I am unsure how to read "societal" here. I am taking it as an alternative verbal formula for "social" rights, as in economic and social rights. If it means instead the rights of society, it raises issues of group human rights that I address in Chapter 12.

in the West civil and political rights are overemphasized while economic, social, and cultural rights are systematically denigrated. But as I argued in §4.6, it is hard to imagine that anyone looking at the welfare states of Western Europe could make such claims seriously.

In any case, it simply is not clear that contemporary Asian societies give unusual emphasis to economic and social human rights. Many Asian governments seem willing, even anxious, to sacrifice (the short- and medium-term enjoyment of) economic and social rights to the pursuit of rapid growth. This certainly has been the case in China over the past decade. Too often in Asia—as in other regions—an alleged concern for economic and social rights is in fact a concern for growth/development irrespective of its distributional/rights consequences.

As I argue in more detail in §11.7, a developmental perspective is aggregate and focuses on production. Economic and social rights, by contrast, are concerned with *distributions* of goods, services, and opportunities, which must be guaranteed to every person even when pursuing the most noble social goals.

Consider Singaporean social welfare policy.

> It is the PAP government's policy not to provide direct funds to individuals in its "welfare" programs. Instead, much is spent on education, public housing, health care and infrastructure build-up as human capital investments to enable the individual and the nation as a whole to become economically competitive in a capitalist world. . . . For those who fall through the economic net . . . public assistance is marginal and difficult to obtain. . . . The government's position is that "helping the needy" is a moral responsibility of the community itself and not just of the state. So construed, the recipients of the moral largesse of the community are to consider themselves privileged and bear the appropriate sense of gratitude (Chua 1992: 95).

Whatever the merits of this approach, it clearly does not emphasize economic and social human rights. A system based on "moral largesse" that sees assistance as a privilege has little to do with human rights.

Setting aside issues of comparative practice, I want to argue against calls emanating from Asia for an overriding emphasis on economic and social rights. For example, at the Vienna Conference China argued that "the major criteria for judging the human rights situation in a developing country should be whether its policies and measures help to promote economic and social progress" (China 1993: 3). Even if we assume that this progress is equally distributed (which in the absence of civil and political rights it rarely will be), such claims reflect a sadly impoverished view of human dignity. A life constantly subject to arbitrary power is one that human beings may learn to settle for, not one to which they do or ought to aspire.

Jiang Zemin's argument that the "right of survival of China's population is more important than political rights" (quoted in Cooper 1994: 56) may have some attractions in extraordinarily poor societies. If the denial of political rights will bring physical survival, a free people may choose survival (although even this is not obvious). But to reduce human rights to a guarantee of mere survival is a perverse betrayal of any plausible conception of human dignity. A state forced to make such a choice acts under a tragic necessity. Its policies represent, at best, triage. And if after more than forty years in power a regime must still rely on arguments of mere survival it is hard not to conclude that the poor are being forced to suffer doubly for the poverty to which their government has condemned them.

Such judgments do not reflect Western romanticism or ethnocentrism. The Bangkok Declaration reaffirms "the interdependence and indivisibility of economic, social, cultural, civil and political rights, and the need to give equal emphasis to all categories of human rights." At Vienna, Korea's Minister of Foreign Affairs argued that "it is neither justifiable nor appropriate to deny some human rights in order to guarantee others." And the Ad Hoc Coalition of Asian NGO Participants at Vienna strongly rejected suggestions "that the enjoyment of civil and political rights be deferred until economic development has been achieved."

Whatever the cultural differences between East and West, I am aware of no evidence that Asians value protection from arbitrary government any less than their Western counterparts, or that Asians do not highly value the opportunity for families and individuals to make important choices about their lives and futures. "Tyranny and injustice are repugnant to civil society wherever they may occur, and to cite cultural differences or Asian values in order to deflect from ourselves criticism against human rights violations is an affront to our moral sense" (Anwar 1994: 1–2).

4. Individuals and Society

Another cluster of arguments centers on the claim that Western human rights practices reflect a corrosive, hedonistic individualism that gives inadequate attention to social duties and is incompatible not only with traditional values but with any plausible conception of human dignity and decency (compare §12.1). At the end of this chapter I will argue that international human rights norms are sufficiently broad to accommodate most Asian desires for more communitarian practices. Here I will focus on extreme communitarian arguments that amount to denials of human rights.

For example, Mahathir argues that "governments, according to the liberal democrats, cannot in any way act against the personal wishes of the individual in society. . . . incest to them is not wrong . . . if that is what is desired by the individuals" (1994: 6). This obviously, even ludicrously, misdescribes practice in the West. Rhoda Howard describes such arguments as examples of "The Central Park Thesis:" human rights have returned the western world to an anomic, Hobbesian state of nature best represented by New York's Central Park at night (Howard 1995a: 23). They reflect what she aptly labels "Occidentalism," a caricature of a static, monolithic, Western "other" (Howard 1995b).

Beneath this caricature lies a common misunderstanding of human rights as absolute rights. "There are no absolute rights and freedoms in the world. The individual rights and freedoms must be subjected to the requirement and provisions of the law" (Xie and Niu 1994: 4). One function of law is indeed to delimit the range of rights. But a central function of human rights is to set limits on the state and its laws. Legally sanctioned racial discrimination, for example, is especially reprehensible, not permissible.

Many internationally recognized human rights do require the state not to interfere with the pursuit of individual desires, for example, to speak one's mind, choose and practice a religion, associate with whomever one pleases, and raise a family. But none of these rights is absolute. Freedom of religion does not extend to human sacrifice. Freedom of association does not cover conspiracy to commit ordinary crimes. Family relations are constrained by rules to protect the health and safety of children.

What is at stake here is a society's understanding of the proper balance between individual and community rights and interests.

> The view of society as an organic whole whose collective rights prevail over the individual, the idea that man exists for the state rather than vice versa and that rights, rather than having any absolute value, derive from the state, have been themes prevailing in old as well as new China. . . . The idea of the individual was not absent: but it was of an order of importance secondary to a family-based community system which differentiated between roles and abilities (Kent 1993: 30–31).

To the extent that this description is correct—"man exists for the state rather than vice versa"—this comes close to denying the very idea of human rights.

> Any emphasis on individual human rights, apart from the rights of the community in which this individual lives, is sheer nonsense. In real history, human rights for the community come first, and human rights for any individual are conditioned by a healthy social environment and appropriate social institutions (Hussein 1994: 1).

This too amounts to a denial of human rights. The rights of the community, whatever priority we give to them, are not human rights (any more than the sovereign rights of states are human rights). *Enjoyment* of individual human rights will be greatly fostered by a healthy social environment and supportive social institutions. But if society is the source of all individual rights, such an individual has no *human* rights.

The Chinese claim at Vienna that "individuals must put the state's rights before their own" (quoted in Cooper 1994: 69) is incompatible with *any* plausible conception of human rights. An individual may often be legitimately asked, even required, to sacrifice or defer the exercise or enjoyment of her rights. But there have been many states whose rights merited little respect from individuals. And sometimes it is society that must give way to the basic rights of individuals.

"No one is entitled to put his individual right above the interest of the state, society, and others. This is the universal principle of all civilized society" (Xie and Niu 1994: 4). This is roughly equivalent to having no rights at all.[6] And a society in which self must always be categorically subordinated to other simply cannot be considered "civilized" in the twenty-first century.

There is no doubt that human rights are more individualistic than many other social and political practices. But to rail against it in the absence of an alternative solution to the very real problems of protecting the individual and human dignity in the face of modern markets and states is, at best, utopian or shortsighted.

5. Rights and Duties

As we saw in §5.4, not only were traditional Asian societies structured around duties, not rights, but any rights held by individuals, families, or communities were largely dependent on the discharge of duties.[7] Essential to any plausible conception of human rights, however, is the claim that all human beings have certain rights prior to and irrespective of their discharge of social duties.

"The rights and obligations of the citizens are indivisible and interrelated"

6. This is a common argument outside Asia as well. For example, Asmarom Legesse suggests that "if Africans were the sole authors of the Universal Declaration of Human Rights, they might have ranked the rights of communities above those of individuals" (1980: 128). Whether desirable or not, such a change would render human rights little more than an irrelevant formality. If an extensive set of social rights and duties were to take priority over individual "human rights," in those instances in which one would be inclined to assert or claim it (i.e., where the right is threatened, challenged, violated, or frustrated), the "right" would be largely useless because it would be easily overridden by the rights of society.

7. This, of course, is hardly a distinctively Asian view. Consider, for example, the claim by the Soviet commentator A. G. Egorov: "the significance and worth of each person are determined by the way he exercises his rights and performs his duties" (1979: 36).

(Xie and Niu 1994: 4). This commonly expressed view[8] is either false or merely trivially true. Rights do have correlative duties. Many (but not all) duties have correlative rights. But particular rights and duties may stand in a great variety of relations to one another. And many rights are held independent of the discharge of duties. Anne has a right to being repaid the ten dollars that Bob borrowed simply because he borrowed it. One has human rights simply because one is a human being.

It is not true that "freedom of speech entails a corresponding duty not to disseminate lies, not to incite communal and religious hatred, and generally not to undermine the moral fabric of society" (Anwar 1994: 5). A right to free speech has no logical connection to an obligation not to disseminate lies. Society and the state may legitimately punish me for spreading vicious lies that harm others. Those penalties, however, rest on the rights or interests of those who I harm, not on my right to free speech. If I slander someone, I do not lose my right to freedom of speech—if we conceive of it as a human right. Incitement to communal or religious hatred may be legitimately prohibited and punished, but even the most vocal hate monger still has a right to express his views on other subjects—if free speech is a human right.

Defensible limits on the exercise of a right should not be confused with duties inherent in the possession of a right. When irresponsible exercises of a recognized right threaten interests that are legitimate matters of social or political regulation, they may be appropriately prohibited. These restrictions, however, are separate from the right—unless the right in question is contingent on accepting those restrictions, in which case it is not a human right.

6. Traditional Order and Human Rights

Arguments against individualism and in favor of duty feed into a broader critique stressing social order and harmony. Traditional China provides a frequent point of reference.

The Confucian tradition stresses the pursuit of harmony (*he*) at all levels,

8. Again, this argument is in no way distinctively Asian. For example, from an Islamic perspective, Khalifa Abdul Hakim argues that "rights and duties are two facets of the same picture. Whoever demands a right to liberty has to respect a similar right in others, which circumscribes his right to personal liberty very considerably. If an individual thinks it his right to be fed and clothed and maintained in proper health and if he has a right to work, it is also his duty to work according to his energies and skill and accept the work which the welfare of the community demands from him" (1955). It was also a central theme in Soviet discussions of human rights. For example, Article 59 of the 1977 Soviet constitution states: "The exercise of rights and liberties is inseparable from the performance by citizens of their duties." This same characterization was common in semiofficial accounts. "The linkage of rights and duties [is] the special quality of socialist law" (Sawczuk 1979: 88). "The most important feature of the Soviet citizen's legal status is the organic unity between their rights and their obligations" (Chkhidvadze 1980: 18).

from the cosmic to the personal (Kent, 1993: 31–40; Fenton et al. 1983: ch. 14–16). The path to harmony is *li.* Although often translated as "propriety," that term, in contemporary American English at least, is far too weak to encompass *li*'s force, range, or depth. *Li* prescribes a complex set of interlocking, hierarchical social roles and relations centered on filial piety (*xiao*) and loyalty (*zhong*). Deference and mutual accommodation were the ideal. Personal ethics emphasized self-cultivation in the pursuit of *ren* (humanness), achieved by self-mastery under the guidance of *li.*

This system of values and social relations is incompatible with the vision of equal and autonomous individuals that underlies international human rights norms. In fact, the "Western" emphasis on individual rights is likely to seem little short of moral inversion.

Asian critics of demands for "Western" (internationally recognized) human rights argue that they have developed alternative political ideals and practices that preserve the values of family, community, decorum, and devotion to duty. And they are committed to avoiding the excesses of the rights-obsessed West: "guns, drugs, violent crime, vagrancy, unbecoming behavior in public—in sum, the breakdown of civil society" (Zakaria 1994: 111).

The most interesting arguments for an Asian third way, however, advocate a selective appropriation of "Western" values and practices to produce an Asian version of modernity. For example, Singapore's senior minister Lee Kwan Yew advocates a dynamic (if cautious) melding of the indigenous and the exotic. "Let me be frank; if we did not have the good points of the West to guide us, we wouldn't have got out of our backwardness. We would have been a backward economy and a backward society. But we do not want all of the West" (Zakaria 1994: 125).

Consider Chandra Muzaffar's call to move "from Western human rights to universal human dignity" (1994: 4).

> Mainstream human rights ideas . . . have contributed significantly to human civilization in at least four ways. *One,* they have endowed the individual with certain basic rights such as the right of free speech, the right of association, the right to a fair trial and so on. *Two,* they have strengthened the position of the ordinary citizen against the arbitrariness of power. *Three,* they have expanded the space and scope for individual participation in public decision-making. *Four,* they have forced the State and authority in general to be accountable to the public (Muzaffar 1994: 1; compare 1999: 25–26).

Implicit in this list of contributions is a powerful critique of traditional society for inadequate attention to individual equality and autonomy. But Muzaffar sees human rights (and democracy), particularly in their characteristic Western implementations, as inadequate to achieve the broader and higher goal of human dignity.

Such arguments cannot be rejected out of hand. It is for the people of Asia, individually and collectively, to resolve these issues as they see fit. Within certain fairly broad limits, a free people is free to order its life as it sees fit. This is the fundamental implication of the rights to self-determination and political participation. Nonetheless, I am skeptical of projects for an Asian third way.

Many are politically naive. For example, Muzaffar argues that the remedy to "the crass individualism and self-centredness which both capitalism and democracy (as it is practised) tend to encourage" lies in the "much cherished ideal in all religious traditions" of "sacrificing one's own personal interests for the well-being of others." "Religion integrates the individual with society in a much more harmonious way" (Muzaffar 1994: 10, 11). This borders on a utopian denial of the notorious problems of linking religion and politics. Critics of the destructive unintended consequences of Western practices must confront the problems of implementing their alternative visions. To compare existing Western practices with a vague, never-yet-implemented ideal is unfair and unilluminating—as is underscored by the deviation between Western ideals and practice on which so much Asian criticism rests.

A different form of political naiveté can be seen in the assumption of the continuing relevance of traditional practices in modern conditions. Is an authoritarian leader backed by the coercive capabilities of the modern state really all that similar to traditional leaders? What has happened to traditional local autonomy in the face of economic and political integration in a modern nation state? How relevant to modern urban life are practices developed for rural societies with little social mobility or demographic change? Can consensual community decision-making and dispute resolution through nonlegal means really work in the absence of relatively closed and close-knit communities? What would they even look like in sprawling urban centers inhabited by strangers and migrants? These are only rhetorical questions, not arguments. But they are the sorts of questions that need to be answered before we can accept denying internationally recognized human rights in the name of traditional culture.

I am especially skeptical of such claims because most of the arguments being made about Asian differences could have been made equally well in eighteenth century Europe.[9] Although Asians need not follow the same path of development, I think it is legitimate to ask why they are likely to respond to similar conditions in very different ways.

Arguments for an Asian alternative rest on the claim that Asian peoples do not want to live in a liberal democratic welfare state. "Popular pressures against

9. In a recent conversation, Ken Booth commented that when he hears talk about Asian values all he can think is "That's my grandfather!" (a Welchman).

East and Southeast Asian governments may not be so much for 'human rights' or 'democracy' but for good government: effective, efficient, and honest administrations able to provide security and basic needs with good opportunities for an improved standard of living" (Kausikan 1993: 37). But even granting that this is true—and in fact I think this is a description of the minimum people are willing to tolerate rather than that to which they aspire—I would suggest that good government is unlikely in the absence of human rights.

Even if a country is fortunate enough to get an efficient and relatively benevolent and incorruptible despot or ruling elite, I am skeptical that Asians will prove more successful than Westerners in keeping the successor generation from succumbing to corruption without reliance on human rights—especially with the immense wealth made available by economic growth. The spread of money politics throughout the region, which increasingly distances people from rulers and makes politics not merely venal but predatory, raises serious questions about the future of even minimal good government in regimes that do not open themselves to the often adversarial popular scrutiny of "Western" human rights. Asian authoritarianism, like its Western counterpart, lacks the powerful internal mechanisms of self-correction and continued rededication to the common good provided by human rights.

Human rights, in contrast to traditional (Eastern and Western) political practices, provide clear and powerful mechanisms for ascertaining whether rulers' claims about popular preferences are true. For all their shortcomings, free, fair, and open periodic elections carried out in an environment with few restrictions on freedoms of speech, press, assembly, and association do provide a relatively reliable gauge of popular political preferences. Alternative schemes based on duty, deference, or hierarchy rarely do.

Consider, for example, the argument of Indonesia's Foreign Minister at the Vienna Conference. "When it comes to a decision by a Head of State upon a matter involving its [the State's] life, the ordinary rights of individuals must yield to what he deems the necessities of the moment" (quoted in van Hoof 1996: 6). Setting aside the fact that decisions involving the state's very existence are rare, how should we deal with cases in which the people disagree with their ruler's judgment of the necessities of the moment? Electoral accountability provides at least some sort of test once the (alleged) crisis has passed. Individual rights to freedom of political speech provide a mechanism for immediate dissent. Traditional mechanisms of remonstrance, by contrast, have little relevance in a world of powerful, intrusive, centralized states and modern political parties. Party cadres are hardly analogous to traditional Confucian bureaucrats.

If the problem in the West is that too many people and institutions are guarding the guardians, the problem with "traditional" Asian alternatives, at least as they operate in their contemporary variants, is that too few are guarding, and they have inadequate power. Not surprisingly, I suggest that if we must err it should be on the side of human rights. I say this, however, not simply as a Westerner who is comfortable with liberal democracy, but as a believer in universal human rights who is convinced that if the differences between East and West truly are as claimed, Asians can be trusted to exercise internationally recognized human rights in responsible ways that make the proper allowances for their cultural values. Asian autocrats, it seems, think much less of the inclinations and capabilities of their people.

7. Human Rights and "Asian Values"

None of the above is meant to suggest that Asian societies ought to follow "Western" models blindly. Quite the contrary, internationally recognized human rights leave considerable space for distinctively Asian implementations of these rights.

In the preceding chapter I described this approach to human rights as "weak cultural relativism." Andrew Nathan speaks of "tempered universalism" (2001). Human rights are treated as fundamentally universal, but substantial space is allowed for variations in implementing these universal norms.

Core rights "concepts" laid down in authoritative international documents, such as equal protection and social security, should be considered largely invariant. But they are subject to differing "interpretations," within the range laid down by the concept. And concrete "implementations" of these interpretations have a wide range of legitimate variation.

Consider, for example, Article 10 of the Universal Declaration of Human Rights: "Everyone is entitled in full equality to a fair and public hearing by an independent and impartial tribunal." (Art. 10) "Independent" and "impartial" certainly are subject to a variety of legitimate (and illegitimate) interpretations. And while "full equality" would seem to require some sort of right to competent legal advice, the particular form may vary with differing national conceptions of fairness (as well as differing levels of available resources).

Internationally recognized human rights concepts may be interpreted and implemented in significantly divergent ways. But legitimate variations are limited to the (relatively narrow) range specified by the core concept of the right in question. And countries cannot legitimately just pick and choose among internationally recognized human rights.

Consider a few Asian examples. James C. Hsiung presents the Northeast Asian practice of permanent employment as a distinctively Asian style of implementing economic and social rights (1985: 20–21). Likewise, families in Asia often bear social welfare obligations that in the West today fall more on the state. (This would seem to be central to Japan's remarkable social stability after a decade of recession.) International human rights standards leave Asians entirely free to follow these preferences, so long as the state assures that people who are not adequately cared for by these preferred mechanisms have another recourse.[10]

Deference to seniority and hierarchy, which is often presented as characteristic of Asian societies, may, as Lawrence Beer notes of Japan, "stifle the free expression of individual thought" (1976: 105). But this deference is not very problematic (from a human rights perspective) when it is enforced largely through informal social sanction rather than government policy. This is how people in Japan typically choose to interact with one another, how they choose to exercise their rights of free speech—which are legally guaranteed. As Beer emphasizes, despite such cultural differences in standard patterns of verbal interaction, "freedom of expression is viable and protected in Japan" (1976: 99).

"Rulers in Korea have always been father figures. A super-father figure like Kim Il-sung . . . is not an accidental phenomenon, for the principles of hierarchy and deference to superiors remain deeply ingrained in the behavior of all Koreans" (Lée 1985: 136). Citizens may exercise their political rights to select and defer to a patriarchal leader—although this is a highly problematic reading of the situation in North Korea. It is entirely defensible for free and equal citizens to consent and defer to paternalistic political authorities, as happened, for example, in many immigrant wards of large American cities for much of this century.

The Asian preference for consensual decision making is likely to have a major impact on party politics. Consider, for example, Japan's system of de facto one party rule. So long as peaceful political activity by opposition parties and groups is unhindered and the rules by which elections are contested are generally perceived as fair and impartially executed, the choice of voters to return candidates predominantly from a single party cannot be legitimately questioned or denied.

Gender equality is often a particularly sensitive matter in cross-cultural discussions. International standards do require that all human rights be available to men and women without discrimination. But that does not require the elimination of differential gender roles. For example, women cannot be denied the right to run for political office. They do, however, remain free to choose not to see that as their role, and voters of both sexes are at liberty to treat sex as a relevant consideration in selecting candidates. Everyone has the right to work and to free choice of employment. Therefore, women cannot legitimately be prevented from working outside the home. They are, however, free to choose not

10. Where the state does not provide a safety net, however, it is guilty of human rights violations. And if huge numbers of people "fall through the cracks," as happens, for example, in the United States, the basic strategy would appear problematic.

to. Similarly, women cannot be prevented from speaking in public, although they remain free to keep a deferential silence.

I realize that this talk of freedom to choose is somewhat forced. Women are under immense social pressure to conform to traditional gender roles in Asia (as in all other regions of the world). But that is precisely why insisting on the right to choose is so crucial. The right to nondiscrimination not only precludes the state from sanctioning or imposing gender discrimination, it requires the state to protect those who flout convention. "Free" choice rarely is without costs. But so long as the choice is a matter of human rights, those costs must not be imposed by the state.

The right to nondiscrimination allows women to determine—in conjunction with those with whom they associate, intimately as well as casually, in a great variety of circumstances—the extent to which they will conform to, reject, or modify traditional gender roles. If they choose traditional roles, that choice is protected, no less (but no more) than the choice to challenge conventional definitions of what they ought to be and how they ought to act. Human rights simply seek to assure that no group of human beings is authorized to use the apparatus of the state to impose on any other group of human beings standards, rules, or roles that they do not also impose on themselves.[11]

Human rights empower those individuals and groups who will bear the consequences to decide, within certain limits, how they will lead their lives. Some differences in implementing international human rights therefore are not merely justifiable but desirable. For example, rural Thai children might be expected to give greater weight to the views and interests of their families in decisions to marry than urban Norwegian children. Confrontational political tactics will be less common (and less effective). There will be greater social constraints on deviant public speech and behavior of all sorts.

These examples, however, illustrate individuals exercising their internationally recognized human rights in a particular fashion, not a fundamentally different conception of human rights. And they do not suggest the legitimacy, let alone the necessity, of coercively prohibiting the "Western" style of exercising these rights. If Asians choose to exercise their rights in "Western" ways, that too is their right.

Children cannot be legally prohibited from marrying the partner of their

11. This is obviously an exaggeration. Any system of law involves imposing social values. Nonetheless, human rights seek to specify domains of personal autonomy in which the values of others are legitimately held at bay, no matter how widely or deeply they are shared by the mainstream of society. The idea of human rights rests on the claim that there are important and substantial areas in the lives of individuals from which the state and society are legitimately excluded. Debates over lists of human rights, and their interpretations and implementations, are about how to define these protected domains.

choice—unless we are to deny the human right to marry and found a family. Families may sanction their choices in a variety of ways, but it is not the role of the state to enforce family preferences on adult children. Members of minority religious communities may (not il)legitimately suffer social sanctions or even ostracism. But unless we deny the human right to freedom of religion, the state has no business punishing or discriminating against people for their religious beliefs or practices. If individuals and groups that make unpopular choices are willing to accept the social sanctions associated with "deviant" behavior, their decisions, whatever their relation to cultural tradition, must be not merely tolerated but protected by the state—or we must abandon the idea of human rights.

A human rights approach assumes that people probably are best suited, and in any case are entitled, to choose the good life for themselves. If Asians truly do value family over self, they will exercise their personal rights with the consequences for their family in mind. If they value harmony and order, they will exercise their civil liberties in a harmonious and orderly fashion. International human rights norms do not require or even encourage Asians to give up their culture—any more than Locke, Paine, or Jefferson asked their contemporaries to give up their culture.

But human rights also empower people to modify or reject parts of their traditional culture. Cultural traditions are socially created legacies. Some are good. Others are bad. Still others are simply irrelevant. And which is considered which varies among individuals and changes with time. Tradition legitimately governs and limits fundamental life choices covered by human rights guarantees only to the extent that individuals and groups choose to follow, and thus reproduce, that tradition.

To the extent that traditions continue to have valued meanings, they are likely to be reproduced. If people choose not to conform to tradition, however, so much the worse for tradition. In particular, so much the worse for those who hold political power who insist that tradition must be followed. For example, the fact that the Chinese tolerated, accepted, or even embraced often arbitrary imperial rule for centuries is no reason why they should embrace repressive party rule today. The people, not their rulers, must decide what they value.

So long as individual and group choices are protected by and within the limits laid out by international human rights standards, they must be respected—by both foreigners and Asian governments and elites. Anyone, anywhere, who denies these choices, must be opposed. And once we recognize that Asian values need not be sacrificed in the name of human rights, many of the arguments I have considered above appear in their true light, namely, as efforts by rapacious ruling elites to manipulate public fear and understandable resentment against an often arrogant and overbearing West in order to shore up their predatory rule and to deflect attention from their own responsibility for the sufferings of their fellow citizens.

One of the things that makes us human is our capacity to create and change our culture. Nonetheless, the essential insight of human rights is that the worlds we make for ourselves, intentionally and unintentionally, must conform to relatively universal requirements that rest on our common humanity and seek to guarantee each person equal concern and respect from the state.

Human rights, as specified in the Universal Declaration and the Covenants, represent the international community's best effort to define the social and political parameters of our common humanity. Within these limits, all is possible. Outside of them, little should be allowed.

PART III

Human Rights and International Action

8/ International Human Rights Regimes

Although human rights have hardly replaced considerations of power, security, ideology, and economic interests in international relations, they have, as we have seen, become a significant international concern. This chapter examines the multilateral machinery that has been developed to implement internationally recognized human rights. Chapter 9 considers human rights in bilateral foreign policy.

1. International Regimes

Students of international relations often speak of "international regimes," systems of norms and decision-making procedures accepted by states as binding in a particular issue area.[1] Regime norms, standards, or rules (I use the terms interchangeably here) may run from fully international to entirely national. International human rights norms are widely accepted by states as authoritative. In May 2002, the six leading international human rights treaties had an average of 157 parties.[2]

Decision-making procedures in international regimes can be roughly grouped into enforcement, implementation, and promotional activities. International enforcement involves binding international decision making (and perhaps also very strong forms of international monitoring of national compliance with international norms). International implementation includes monitoring procedures and policy coordination, in which states make regular use of an international forum to coordinate policies that ultimately remain under national control. International promotion involves encouraging or assisting national implementation of international norms.

1. The standard discussion introductory discussion is Krasner (1982). See also Haggard and Simmons (1987), Rittberger and Mayer (1993), Hasenclever, Mayer, and Rittberger (1997), and Hasenclever, Mayer, and Rittberger (2000).
2. See http://www.unhchr.ch/pdf/report.pdf

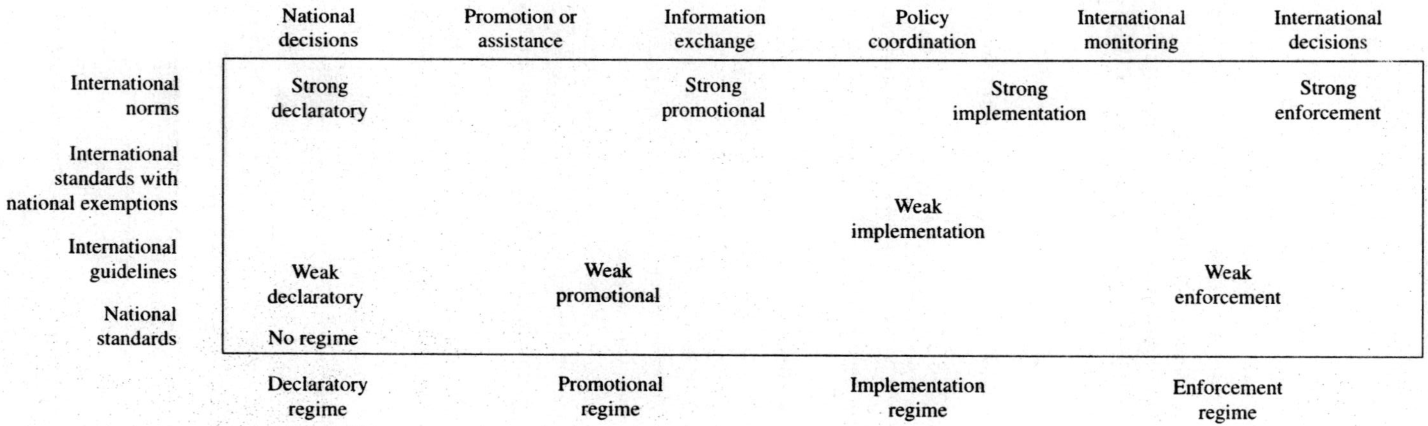

Figure 8.1 Types of International Regimes

Based on these procedures we can classify international regimes as promotional, implementation, and enforcement regimes, each of which can be further classified as relatively strong or weak. To this, we can add declaratory regimes, which involve international norms but no international decision making (except in the creation of norms). Figure 8.1 diagrams this typology. Table 8.1 in §6 applies the typology to the major international and regional human rights regimes.

2. The Global Human Rights Regime

The Universal Declaration and the Covenants provide the norms of what we can call "the global human rights regime," a system of rules and implementation procedures centered on the United Nations. Its principal organs are the UN Commission on Human Rights, the Human Rights Committee, and the High Commissioner for Human Rights.

A. THE UN COMMISSION ON HUMAN RIGHTS

The most important body in the global human rights regime is the United Nations Commission on Human Rights.[3] Since 1946 it has been the principal forum for negotiating international human rights norms (including the Universal Declaration and the Covenants). Over the past three decades it has also acquired some modest monitoring powers.

Economic and Social Council (ECOSOC) resolution 1503 (1970) authorizes the Commission to investigate communications (complaints) that "appear to reveal a consistent pattern of gross and reliably attested violations of human rights." ECOSOC resolution 2000/3 recently reorganized procedures for handling communications. A new Working Group on Communications, may refer a country's practices to the (also newly created) Working Group on Situations, which may in turn refer the case to the full Commission.

Stringent criteria of admissibility[4] limit the cases considered. Only situations of gross and systematic violations are covered; particular abuses and individual cases cannot be examined. The entire procedure is confidential until a final report is made to ECOCOC.[5] Although confidentiality may encourage cooperation by states, it can dramatically slow an already cumbersome pro-

3. Although somewhat out of date, Tolley (1987) remains the best single work on the Commission. On recent developments, see Dennis (2002, 2001, 2000).

4. See Zuijdwijk (1982: 30–39) and, more briefly, http://www.unhchr.ch/html/menu2/8/1503.htm.

5. The Commission has circumvented some of the strictures of confidentiality by, beginning in 1978, publicly announcing a "black list" of countries being studied. We thus know that practices of more than fifty countries have been examined under the procedure. Given the hurdles involved in reaching this stage, appearance on the blacklist is typically "interpreted as at least demonstrating that the allegations in a communication have some merit" Shelton (1984: 65).

TABLE 8.1 Change in International Human Rights Regimes, 1945–2000

	1945	1960	1975	1990	2000
GLOBAL REGIME	**NONE**	**DECLARATORY**	**PROMOTIONAL**	**STRONG PROMOTIONAL**	**STRONG PROMOTIONAL**
Norms	None	Guidelines	Standards with exemptions	Global norms with exemptions	Authoritative global norms
Procedures	None	Weak promotion	Promotion	Strong promotion/monitoring	Strong promotion/monitoring
			REGIONAL HUMAN RIGHTS REGIMES		
European Regime	None	Promotional/ Implementation	Implementation/ Enforcement	Enforcement	Strong Enforcement
Norms	None	Guidelines/ regional norms	Regional norms	Authoritative regional norms	Authoritative regional norms
Procedures	None	Promotion/ monitoring	Regional decisions with exemptions	Regional decisions	Binding regional decisions
Inter-American Regime	None	Declaratory	Promotional	Strong Promotional	Strong Promotional
Norms	None	Guidelines	Standards with exemptions	Regional norms	Authoritative regional norms
Procedures	None	None	Promotion/monitoring	Monitoring/very limited regional decisions	Monitoring/very limited regional decisions
African Regime	None	None	None	Declaratory	Declaratory
Norms	None	None	None	Guidelines	Weak standards with exemptions
Procedures	None	None	None	Weak promotion	Weak promotion
Asia	None	None	None	None	None
Middle East	None	None	None	None	None

SINGLE-ISSUE REGIMES

Worker's Rights	Promotional	Strong Promotional	Strong Promotional	Strong Promotional	Strong Promotional
Norms	Limited guidelines	Standards with exemptions	Strong standards with exemptions	Strong standards with exemptions	Strong standards with exemptions
Procedures	Promotion/monitoring	Promotion/monitoring	Promotion/monitoring	Promotion/monitoring	Promotion/monitoring
Racial Discrimination	None	None	Promotional	Strong Promotional	Strong Promotional
Norms	None	None	Standards with exemptions	Strong standards with exemptions	Strong standards with exemptions
Procedures	None	None	Promotion/weak monitoring	Promotion/weak monitoring	Promotion/weak monitoring
Women's Rights	None	None/Very Weak Declaratory	Declaratory	Strong Promotional	Strong Promotional
Norms	None	None/Limited guidelines	Guidelines	Standards with exemptions	Standards with exemptions
Procedures	None	None	Weak promotion	Promotion/weak monitoring	Promotion/weak monitoring
Torture	None	None	Declaratory	Strong Promotional	Strong Promotional
Norms	None	None	Guidelines	Strong standards with exemptions	Global norms
Procedures	None	None	None	Promotion/monitoring	Promotion/monitoring
Genocide	None	Very Weak Declaratory	Very Weak Declaratory	Very Weak Declaratory	Declaratory/Ad hoc Enforcement
Norms	None	Guidelines	Guidelines	Guidelines	Authoritative global norms
Procedures	None	None	None	None	None/Ad hoc Enforcement
Children	None	None	None	Declaratory/Promotional	Promotional
Norms	None	None	None	Guidelines	Standards with exemptions
Procedure	None	None	None	None	Promotion/weak monitoring

cess.[6] In the end, "enforcement" means making publicly available the evidence that has been acquired, along with the Commission's views on it. Only a handful of cases have even reached this stage.

The 1503 procedure is thus largely a promotional device involving weak, sporadic, and limited monitoring. In addition, it is at best semi-independent: the Commission is composed of state representatives, not independent experts. Given the sensitivity of human rights questions, even this may be of real practical value, especially where a government cares about its international reputation. The limitations of the procedure, however, deserve at least as much emphasis as its achievements.

Much the same is true of the Commission's other activities. For example, the 26-member Sub-Commission on the Promotion and Protection of Human Rights (known until 1999 as the Sub-Commission on the Prevention of Discrimination and Protection of Minorities) has undertaken a number of useful studies. Together with the Commission, it has helped to focus international public opinion on conditions in at least a few countries (e.g., South Africa, Chile) and on selected violations and issues such as disappearances, torture, religious liberty, human rights defenders, migrant workers, and indigenous peoples.

Particularly important in this regard are the Commission's "global" or "thematic" procedures involving working groups and special rapporteurs on a wide range of topics, including disappearances, torture, summary or arbitrary executions, and, most recently, human rights defenders, food, housing, and indigenous peoples. In recent years, about twenty separate thematic initiatives have been taking place at any given time.[7] The Commission has also given considerable attention to particular vulnerable groups, especially women, children, indigenous people, minorities, displaced persons, migrant workers, and human rights defenders.

The Commission also addresses human rights situations in individual countries, both in public during its annual session—situations in more than two dozen countries are discussed each year—and through the activities of country rapporteurs and representatives, who have examined situations even in high-profile countries such as Guatemala, Iran, Iraq, occupied Palestinian

6. The 1503 procedure rarely can be brought fully into play in less than two or three years after complaints are received (which may be well after serious violations began). A state can usually delay at least a year by pretending to cooperate, as Argentina did in 1979 and 1980. Political considerations often stretch a case out even longer. For example, genocide against Paraguayan Indians remained under scrutiny for nine years without any action. A decision on Uruguay, after seven years of scrutiny, came only after the guilty government had been removed from office. Things have improved a bit since the end of the Cold War, but the procedure still could never be called efficient or timely.

7. For a list of currently operating thematic procedures, see http://www.unhchr.ch/html/menu2/7/b/tm.htm.

territories, and Burma.[8] Like their thematic counterparts, the country rapporteurs are individual experts who report to the Commission, rather than the voice of the Commission as a whole. Thus not only do they operate with fewer diplomatic and political constraints, but their narrow mandate also allows them to maintain sustained, focused attention and in some cases even develop a constructive exchange of views with a government.

The limitations of all of these procedures, however, are tragically illustrated by the case of Rwanda. Rwanda was discussed confidentially under the 1503 procedure in 1992 and 1993. In addition, the report of the special rapporteur on extrajudicial executions was discussed in the spring of 1994, just before the outbreak of the genocide. In it, the special rapporteur confirmed reports of official involvement in the massacre of civilians and explicitly suggested that genocidal acts were already occurring. Nonetheless, it was not until May 25—seven weeks after the genocide began, almost a month after the Secretary-General called for Security Council action, and even a week after the Security Council (belatedly) authorized a new peacekeeping force—that the Commission even appointed a country rapporteur.

This example, however, is in many ways unfair. The Commission was never intended to have enforcement powers, let alone the capacity to stop human rights violations before they occurred. In the area of promotion, it does serve a variety of useful roles, particularly as a source of authoritative information and publicity about human rights practices in any country of the world. Furthermore—and I think most important—its role in developing international human rights norms has been, and remains, vital and irreplaceable. For all its limitations, the United Nations Commission on Human Rights is in many ways the heart of the global human rights regime.

B. THE HUMAN RIGHTS COMMITTEE

The second principal body of the global human rights regime is the Human Rights Committee, a body of eighteen independent experts established to monitor compliance with the International Covenant on Civil and Political Rights.[9] The primary function of the Committee is to review periodic reports on compliance submitted by parties.[10]

8. In 2001, special rapporteurs, representatives, and experts examined situations in Afghanistan, Bosnia and Yugoslavia, Burundi, Cambodia, Democratic Republic of the Congo, Equatorial Guinea, Haiti, Iran, Iraq, Myanmar (Burma), occupied Palestinian territories, Somalia, and Sudan. See http://www.unhchr.ch/html/menu2/7/a/cm.htm for links to reports, documents, and related materials.

9. McGoldrick (1991) is the standard study of the Committee. See also Joseph, Schultz, and Castan (2000). More briefly see Steiner (2000).

10. The International Covenant on Economic, Social, and Cultural Rights also requires periodic reports. These reports were reviewed by a Sessional Working Group of ECOSOC until 1986, when the Committee on Economic, Social, and Cultural Rights, a body of experts roughly analo-

The committee does not formally judge or evaluate state practices. Reports are discussed in a public session, however, often lasting a full day, in which state representatives are questioned in an environment that is relatively free of posturing and, by diplomatic standards at least, neither excessively deferential nor merely pro forma. In many instances, state representatives are responsive, occasionally even thoughtful. In such cases the result is a genuine exchange of views that provides a real element of international monitoring. The procedure has even provoked minor changes in national law, and a number of parties use their dealings with the Committee to review and reexamine national laws, policies, and practices (on Canada, see Nolan 1988).

The reporting procedure thus has provided a fairly widely accepted promotional mechanism,[11] but it involves only information exchange and the weakest monitoring. Even the information exchange is flawed. The reports of many countries are thorough and revealing, but others are farces.[12] Some are not submitted.[13] Furthermore, only parties to the Covenant must report—although with three quarter's of the world's countries now parties (148 in May 2002), this is less of a drawback than in the past.

The Committee also considers individual petitions under the (first) Optional Protocol.[14] Through November 13, 2001, 1026 communications had been registered concerning 69 countries. Approximately half of these cases were either found to be inadmissible or discontinued. Substantive determinations, however, had been reached on 377 communications, and another 206 were still within the system. The procedure seems to be relatively open and highly independent, providing genuine (if extremely limited) international monitoring, which in at least a few cases has altered state practice.

The procedure, however, covers only parties to the Optional Protocol, which in May 2002 numbered 103. Furthermore, almost half of the violations exam-

---

gous to the Human Rights Committee, was created. On the operation of the Committee, see Leckie (2000) and Dandan (2000).

11. On reporting procedures in general and in other treaty bodies, see Bayefsky (2000: Part I), especially Connors (2000), and Clapham (2000).

12. For example, many reports consist principally of extracts from national constitutions and statutes. A significant number are simply evasive. For example, Guinea has claimed that "citizens of Guinea felt no need to invoke the Covenant because national legislation was at a more advanced stage" (A/39/40 par. 139). The Mongolian representative, in response to a question by a member of the Committee, proudly claimed that there had never been a complaint about torture or cruel or inhuman treatment made in his country (A/35/40 par. 108).

13. Zaire (Congo) presents an extreme case. Its initial report, due in 1978, was not submitted until 1987, despite ten reminders. Its second report was submitted essentially on time two years later. But as of August 2001 no further reports had been submitted. On the general problem of absent or tardy reports to supervisory committees, see Crawford (2000: 4–5).

14. Steiner (2000) provides a good overview and evaluation of the process. On individual complaint mechanisms more broadly and in other bodies, see Bayefsky (2000: Part III), and especially Byrnes (2000).

ined have been in two countries, Jamaica and Uruguay. Relatively strong procedures thus apply primarily where they are not most needed. Unfortunately, this is only to be expected, given that participation is entirely voluntary.

C. THE HIGH COMMISSIONER FOR HUMAN RIGHTS

The office of United Nations High Commissioner for Human Rights, created in 1993, generalizes this investigation-advocacy approach. The High Commissioner has the global reach of the Commission, without its cumbersome procedures. Like the special rapporteurs, the High Commissioner may deal directly with governments to seek improved respect for internationally recognized human rights—but with the added advantage of an explicit mandate to deal with all governments on all issues. Additionally, the High Commissioner holds the office in her personal capacity, not as a representative of any state.[15]

The initial appointee, José Ayala Lasso, who served from 1994 to 1997, showed little enthusiasm for public action. The current incumbent, Mary Robinson, has done much to increase the profile of the High Commissioner and has tried, with some success, to expand her authority and reach. If the Commission on Human Rights is the heart of the global human rights regime, Mrs. Robinson has gone a long way toward making the High Commissioner its public face.[16] Considerable progress has also been made in improving the office's capacity to disseminate information, especially through its admirable website (http://www.unhchr.ch). A fairly extensive system of technical assistance and cooperation has also become institutionalized (see http://www.unhchr.ch/html/menu2/techcoop.htm).

3. Political Foundations of the Global Regime

The global human rights regime involves widely accepted substantive norms, authoritative multilateral standard-setting procedures, considerable promotional activity, but very limited international implementation that rarely goes beyond mandatory reporting procedures. There is no international enforcement. Such normative strength and procedural weakness is not accidental but the result of conscious political decisions.

Regimes are political creations set up to overcome perceived problems arising from inadequately regulated or insufficiently coordinated national action. Robert Keohane (1982) offers a useful market analogy: regimes arise when sufficient international "demand" is met by a state or group of states willing and

15. For the mandate and mission statement of the High Commissioner, see http://www.unhchr.ch/html/hchr.htm;ew and ;owhttp://www.unhchr.ch/html/ohchrmission.htm.

16. For a good, brief official overview of the various dimensions of the United Nations Human Rights Programme, see http://www.unhchr.ch/html/abo-intr.htm.

able to "supply" international norms and decision-making procedures. In each issue area there are makers, breakers, and takers of (potential) international regimes. Understanding the structure of a regime (or its absence) requires that we know who has played which roles, when and why, and what agreements they reached.

World War II marks a decisive break not just in international politics but in international human rights as well: the defeat of Germany ushered in the global human rights regime. Revulsion at the array of human rights abuses that came to be summarized in the term *Nazi* engendered a brief period of enthusiastic international action. Hitler's actions shocked the conscience of the international community, but they did not clearly contravene well-established explicit international norms. It was therefore *relatively* easy to agree on a set of international principles against gross and persistent systematic violations of basic rights—namely, the Universal Declaration and the Convention on Genocide, which was even more clearly a direct legacy of Hitler.

It is perhaps surprising that this moral "demand" should have produced even this much in a world in which more material national interests usually prevail. Immediately following World War II, however, there were willing and able makers, numerous takers, and no breakers of the regime. The moral and emotional demands ran both wide and deep, and, prior to the emergence of the Cold War, countervailing concerns and interests were largely subordinated.

A cynic might suggest that these postwar "achievements" simply reflect the minimal international constraints and very low costs of a declaratory regime: implementation and decision making under the Universal Declaration remained entirely national, and it would be nearly thirty years before even the rudimentary promotion and monitoring procedures of the Covenants came into effect. Yet before the war, even a declaratory regime had rarely been contemplated.

Moving much beyond a declaratory regime, however, has proved difficult. It is in this relative constancy of the regime (critics and frustrated optimists are likely to say "stagnation") that the weakness of the demand is most evident. A strong global human rights regime simply does not reflect the perceived interests of a state or coalition willing and able to supply it.

States typically participate in an international regime only to achieve national objectives in an environment of perceived international interdependence. Even then they usually participate only when independent national action has failed and when participation appears "safe," all things considered—a very serious constraint, given states' notorious jealousy of their sovereign prerogatives. Few states today see a stronger global regime as a safe source of important but otherwise unattainable national benefits.

Moral interests such as human rights are no less "real" than material interests. They are, however, less tangible, and national policy, for better or worse, tends to be made in response to relatively tangible national objectives.

In addition, the extreme sensitivity of human rights practices makes the very subject intensely threatening to many states. National human rights practices often would be a matter for considerable embarrassment should they be subject to full international scrutiny. In a number of cases, such as Iraq, North Korea, Zimbabwe, and Cuba, compliance with international human rights standards would mean removal of those in power.

Finally, human rights—at least in the Universal Declaration model—are ultimately a profoundly national, not international, issue. As I will argue in Chapter 10, international action usually can be, at best, an impetus toward and support for national action to implement and enforce human rights.

If international regimes arise primarily because of international interdependence—the inability to achieve important national objectives by independent national action—how can we account for the creation, and even modest growth, of the global human rights regime? First and foremost, by the persisting relevance of the "moral" concerns that brought it into being in the first place. Butchers such as Pol Pot and the *genocidaires* of Rwanda still shock the popular conscience and provoke a desire to reject them as not merely reprehensible but also prohibited by clear, public, authoritative international norms. Even governments with dismal human rights records seem to feel compelled to join in condemning the abuses of such rulers.

Although cynics might interpret such condemnations as craven abuse of the rhetoric of human rights, they are just as easily seen as expressions of a sense of *moral* interdependence. States—not only governments, but frequently citizens as well—often are unwilling to translate this perceived moral interdependence into action, let alone into an international regime with strong decision-making powers. But they also are unwilling (or at least politically unable) to return to treating national human rights practices as properly beyond international scrutiny and evaluation.

A weak global human rights regime also may contribute, in a way acceptable to states, to improved national practice. For example, new governments with a commitment to human rights may find it helpful to be able to draw on and point to the constraints of authoritative international standards. We can see this, perhaps, in the case of the Alfonsin government, which took power after the Dirty War in Argentina, and in post-Soviet regimes in Central Europe. Likewise, established regimes may find the additional check provided by an international regime a salutary supplement to national efforts, as seems to be the case for many smaller Western powers. And most states, even if only for considerations of image and prestige, are likely to be willing to accept regime norms and procedures that do not appear immediately threatening.

An international regime reflects states' collective vision of a problem and its solutions and their willingness to "fund" those solutions. In the area of human rights, this vision does not extend much beyond a politically weak moral interdependence. States are willing to "pay" very little in diminished national sovereignty to realize the benefits of cooperation. The result is a regime with extensive, coherent, and widely accepted norms but extremely limited international decision-making powers—that is, a strong promotional regime.

4. Regional Human Rights Regimes

Adopting a metaphor from Vinod Aggarwal, Keohane notes that international regimes "are 'nested' within more comprehensive agreements . . . that constitute a complex and interlinked pattern of relations" (1982: 334). Although "nesting" may imply too neat and hierarchical an arrangement, some regional and single-issue human rights regimes can usefully be seen as autonomous but relatively coherently nested international human rights (sub) regimes. This section considers regional regimes. The following section takes up single-issue human rights regimes.

A. EUROPE

A strong regional regime exists among the (primarily Western European) members of the Council of Europe. Personal, legal, civil, and political rights are guaranteed by the (European) Convention for the Protection of Human Rights and Fundamental Freedoms (1950) and its Protocols, and economic and social rights are laid down in the European Social Charter (1961, revised 1996).[17] The lists of rights in these documents are very similar to those of the Universal Declaration and the Covenants. The decision-making procedures of the European regime, however, are of special interest, especially the authoritative decision-making powers of the European Court of Human Rights.

A two-tier system was initially created. The European Commission of Human Rights, an independent body of experts (one from each member state),

17. I shall restrict the term "European human rights regime" to the norms and procedures established in these documents. For a brief introduction see O'Boyle (2000). For extended legal analyses, see Dijk and Hoof (1998), Harris, O'Boyle, and Warbrick (2001), and Mowbray (2001). The official website (http://www.echr.coe.int/) is excellent. Although the international human rights activities of the European Union have become increasingly significant (see Alston 1999), for reasons of space they are not considered here. Of particular symbolic importance was the adoption in 2000 of the Charter of Fundamental Rights of the European Union. Space also precludes considering the Organization for Security and Cooperation in Europe (OSCE), which has a historically important place in the process leading to the end of the Cold War and which has undertaken some important human rights initiatives through its Office for Democratic Institutions and Human Rights (see http://www.osce.org/odihr/overview/), especially in the area of minority rights (see Kemp 2001).

reviewed "applications" (complaints) from persons, groups of individuals, nongovernmental organizations (NGOs), and states alleging violations of the rights guaranteed by the Convention. If friendly settlement could not be reached, the Commission was authorized to report formally its opinion on the state's compliance with the Convention. Although these reports were not legally binding, they usually were accepted by states. If not, either the Commission or the state involved could refer the case to the Court for binding enforcement action.

Not only are these procedures, which have been implemented with scrupulous impartiality, of unmatched formal strength and completeness, they also have been almost completely accepted in practice. Decisions of the European Commission and Court have had a considerable impact on law and practice in a number of states (Blackburn 1996). For example, detention practices have been altered in Belgium, Germany, Greece, and Italy. The treatment of aliens has been changed in the Netherlands and Switzerland. Press freedom legislation was altered in Britain. Wiretapping regulations have been changed in Switzerland. Legal aid practices have been revised in Italy and Denmark. Procedures to speed trials have been implemented in Italy, the Netherlands, and Sweden. Privacy legislation was revamped in Italy.

The impact of the Court has been especially strong and important because of its adoption of the principle of "evolutive interpretation." The Court interprets the European Convention not according to the conditions and understandings that existed in 1950 when it was drafted but in light of the current regional practices. This has resulted in a slowly but steadily rising bar and considerable pressure on states that lag behind European norms. Examples include restrictions on corporal punishment in schools in the United Kingdom and eliminating discrimination against unmarried mothers and children born outside of marriage in Belgium.

The growing success of the system and the post–Cold War expansion of membership, however, led to a crushing administrative burden. In 1981 the Commission registered 404 applications. By 1993 this had increased to 2037, and by 1997 the number had jumped to 4750 (with nearly 8000 additional files opened that did not lead to registered applications). Cases referred to the Court in those years rose from 7 to 52 to 119.

A complete restructuring was proposed in 1994 in Protocol No. 11, which was ratified in 1997 and came into effect the following year. In late 1999, the Commission was merged into a completely restructured European Court of Human Rights. In addition, jurisdiction of the Court was made compulsory (previously states had the option to participate in only the Commission and not the Court).

The Parliamentary Assembly of the Council of Europe elects one judge for each member state (currently forty-one) for a six-year term. The Court is divided into four Sections, with attention to geographical and gender balance and representation of different legal systems. Each Section includes a committee of three judges that performs much of the filtering work previously assigned to the Commission. Seven member Chambers in each Section (including the Section President and a judge representing the state in question) hear cases. There is also a seventeen-member Grand Chamber representing all the Sections.

Another notable post–Cold War innovation has been the creation of a Council of Europe Commissioner for Human Rights in 1999 (see http://www.commissioner.coe.int/). This entirely independent institution aims to promote education and awareness of human rights issues, improve the enjoyment of recognized rights, and identify possible shortcomings in national law and practice. Other than the requirement that he or she not deal with individual complaints, the Commissioner may look into any aspect of human rights in Europe, deal directly with governments, and issue opinions, reports, and recommendations. Member states even have a positive obligation to facilitate the independent and effective functioning of the Commissioner. On paper at least, these powers are of unprecedented strength and scope, and there seems every reason to believe that they will be utilized, especially as the Commissioner—Alvaro Gil-Robles of Spain was elected in 1999— and his staff become settled in their work.

The system for dealing with economic, social, and cultural rights has also changed significantly. The substance of the 1961 European Social Charter was substantially expanded by protocols in 1988, 1991, and 1995. In 1996 these changes, and some others, were consolidated into a Revised Charter of Social Rights, which entered into force in 1999. The net result was not only to expand the rights covered but also to strengthen the supervisory system and open it more fully to NGOs and so-called social partners such as workers' organizations. Rather than judicial settlement, however, supervision is through a system of reporting and collective complaints to an Independent Committee of Experts, which reports to the Council of Ministers for further action (see Harris 2000).

The Council of Europe system also includes a European Committee for Equality Between Women and Men, a Human Rights Documentation Center, and a Steering Committee for Human Rights (with three expert committees, dealing with the further development of human rights norms, improving procedures, and promotion, education, and information, respectively). There are also well-developed procedures for NGO participation.

The real strength of the European regime lies in voluntary acceptance of the regime by its participating states. The machinery of even the strongest international regime primarily checks backsliding, applies pressure for further progress, provides authoritative interpretations in controversial cases, and remedies occasional deviations (compare Chayes and Chayes 1995). These are hardly negligible functions; they are precisely what is lacking in the global regime. Strong international procedures, however, rest ultimately on national commitment, which is both wide and deep in Europe. Strong procedures are less a cause than a reflection of the regime's strength.

A regime's shape and strength, as I argued in §3, usually can be explained by perceptions of interdependence, of benefits to be received (including burdens avoided), and of the risks of turning over authority to an international agency. The strong national commitment of the European states to human rights greatly increases the perceived value of the "moral" benefits that states can expect to achieve, suggesting that moral interdependence can occasionally rival material interdependence in political force. Furthermore, relatively good national human rights records reduce the political risks of strong international procedures. The European regime is also "safe," because it operates within a relatively homogeneous and close sociocultural community, which greatly reduces both the likelihood of radical differences in interpreting regime norms and the risk of partisan abuse or manipulation of the regime. Perceived community also helps to increase the perception of moral interdependence.

Although voluntary compliance is the heart of the regime's success, we should not belittle either the strength or the significance of the European regime's enforcement measures. Not only is completely voluntary compliance a utopian ideal, but the European case also suggests a process of mutual reinforcement between national commitment and international procedures. A strong regime is a device to increase the chances that states will enjoy the best that they "deserve" in that issue area—that is, the best to which they will commit themselves to aspire, and then struggle to achieve.

B. THE AMERICAS

The American Declaration of the Rights and Duties of Man (1948) presents a list of human rights very similar to that of the Universal Declaration. The American Convention on Human Rights (1969) recognizes personal, legal, civil, and political rights, plus the right to property. The 1988 "Protocol of San Salvador," which deals with economic, social, and cultural rights, came into force in 1999. As in the European case, though, the procedures rather than the norms are of most interest.[18]

The Inter-American Court of Human Rights, established in 1979 and sitting in San Jose, Costa Rica, may take binding enforcement action, although its ad-

18. Medina Quiroga (1988), although often dry and technical, is excellent on the Cold War era. Harris and Livingstone (1998) is probably the best single source today.

judicatory jurisdiction is optional.[19] The Court may also issue advisory opinions requested by members of the Organization of American States (OAS). The Court, however, has handled far fewer cases, with much less impact, than the European Court, despite an apparently much greater potential caseload.

The procedural heart of the regime lies instead in the Inter-American Commission of Human Rights. It is empowered to develop awareness of human rights, make recommendations to governments, respond to inquiries of states, prepare studies and reports, request information from and make recommendations to governments, and conduct on-site investigations (with the consent of the government). The Commission also may receive communications (complaints) from individuals and groups concerning the practice of any member of the OAS, whether a party to the Convention or not.

An "autonomous entity" within the Organization of American States (OAS), established twenty years before the Inter-American Court, the Commission has vigorously exploited this autonomy, especially in the 1970s and 1980s, in the face of strongly resistant states. It has adopted decisions and resolutions arising from individual communications from more than twenty countries in the region, including the United States. Country Reports documenting particularly serious human rights situations in more than a dozen countries have been issued, usually to be followed up by renewed and intensified monitoring. The Commission has also adopted special resolutions on major regional problems, such as states of siege.

The wide-ranging nonpartisan activism of the Commission can be attributed largely to the fact that its members serve in their personal capacity; it is more a technical, quasi-judicial body than a political body. But how are we to explain the fact that the American states, many of which have not been notably solicitous toward human rights (especially during the Cold War), have allowed the Commission to be so forceful and so active? A large part of the explanation lies in the dominant power of the United States.

The literature on international economic regimes suggests that the power of a hegemonic state typically is crucial to establishing (although not necessarily to maintaining) strong, stable regimes (Keohane 1984). Although hegemonic power had virtually nothing to do with the European regime, it has been central to the genesis and operation of the Inter-American regime. The United States, for whatever reasons, has often used its hegemonic power to support the Inter-American regime, which has also been strongly supported by some of the more democratic regimes of the region.

Consensual commitment and hegemonic power are, to a certain extent,

19. By 2000, twenty states had accepted the Court's jurisdiction. On the functioning of the Court, see Davidson (1992) and Travieso (1996) and the relevant portions of Buergenthal and Shelton (1995), Davidson (1997), and Harris and Livingstone (1998).

functional equivalents for establishing state acceptance. Voluntary compliance is, of course, the ideal, both for its own sake and because of the limited ability of even hegemonic power to overcome persistent national resistance. Coercion, however, may produce a certain level of limited participation. Consider, for example, the grudging participation of military dictatorships in Chile and Argentina during the 1970s.

Nevertheless, the relative mix of coercion and consensus does influence the nature and functioning of a regime. Coerced participation is sure to be marked by constant and often effective national resistance, and regime procedures are likely to be more adversarial. Hegemony may ensure a certain degree of international monitoring, but even a hegemon can impose only a limited range of changes.

Democratization in the region over the past two decades has led to voluntary acceptance largely replacing external coercion. It has also created a much more genuinely regional commitment to human rights. Nevertheless, only very modest incremental growth has occurred in the regime. Consent has largely replaced coercion without any significant increases in regime strength.

Both the Court and the Commission have modestly increased their levels of activity. New conventions, on torture (1985), disappearances (1994), violence against women (1994), and disabled persons (1999, not yet entered into force), have been adopted. The OAS General Assembly, the Inter-American system's principal political organ, has become much more sympathetic to human rights (in sharp contrast to its stance in the 1970s, when it was often an active impediment to the Commission). Democracy promotion activities have increased dramatically. States have even adopted much less adversarial attitudes toward the Commission. They have not, however, shown any enthusiasm for strengthening regional institutions (compare King-Hopkins 2000).

C. AFRICA, ASIA, AND THE MIDDLE EAST

In 1981 the Organization of African Unity (OAU) adopted The African Charter on Human and Peoples' Rights, drafted in Banjul, Gambia.[20] There are some interesting normative innovations in the African (Banjul) Charter, most notably the addition of and emphasis on collective or "peoples'" rights (Art. 19–24), such as the rights to peace and development, and the particularly prominent place the Charter gives individual duties (Art. 27–29). Typically, however, the substantive guarantees are narrower or more subject to state discretion than in other international human rights regimes.

20. Evans and Murray (2002) provide the first comprehensive scholarly evaluation of the operation of the African Charter system. Murray (2000) adopts a feminist perspective that leads to some unusual but often interesting assessments. On the issue of the relationship between the African Charter and national law and practice in the region, see Lindholt (1997).

The Banjul Charter creates an African Commission on Human and Peoples' Rights that may receive interstate complaints and individual communications. The activities of the Commission, however, are severely hampered by woefully inadequate administrative resources[21] and a requirement of complete confidentiality until an investigation has been completed. Little of substance seems to have emerged from its proceedings, although it has played a significant role in fostering the development and improving the functioning of local and regional human rights NGOs (Welch 1995; International Commission of Jurists 1996).

The regional organizational environment in Africa is extremely unpromising for any substantial strengthening of the regime. Previous efforts at regional and even subregional cooperation in other issue areas have not been very successful. The OAU is not only highly politicized but extremely deferential to sovereignty. Although this is understandable, given the weak states and strong subnational loyalties in most of black Africa, there is no reason to expect the OAU to deviate from its standard practice in an area as sensitive as human rights.

The prospects are no better when we took at national practice. During the Cold War, the human rights record of the typical African country was about average for the Third World, despite lurid and relatively overreported aberrations such as occurred under the rule of Idi Amin and "Emperor" Bokassa. Today, only the Middle East has a worse regional record. In the absence of strong pressure by a regional hegemon, the national human rights record of the typical African government suggests a high degree of aversion to international monitoring. Furthermore, the low level of autonomous economic, social, and political organization in most African states suggests that this situation is unlikely to be changed soon through mass popular action.

Even the weak procedures of the African regime, though, are far more developed than those in Asia and the Middle East. In Asia there are neither regional norms nor decision-making procedures.[22] The Association of South East Asian Nations (ASEAN) is perhaps the most promising subregional organization, but even there deference to sovereignty is high and regional cooperation low (compare Thio 1999).

The League of Arab States established a Permanent Arab Commission on Human Rights in 1968, but it has been notably inactive, except for publicizing

21. On the broad issue of resource shortages, which are a serious problem in all international human rights (with the possible but only partial exception of Europe), see Evatt (2000) and Schmidt (2000).

22. The 1996 Asian Human Rights Charter is an interesting effort by Asian NGOs to forge a regional document, but it clearly reflects NGO perspectives. See http://www.ahrchk.net/charter/final_content.html. For a report on the most recent official discussions of a regional system, see United Nations (1996).

the human rights situation in the Israeli-occupied territories. Even the regional normative environment is weak. The Arab Charter of Human Rights languished largely ignored from its drafting in 1971 until it was finally adopted by the Council of the League in 1994.[23] There currently is no basis for even the weakest of regional regimes, which is not surprising given the generally dismal state of national human rights practices in the region.[24]

5. Single-Issue Human Rights Regimes

A different type of "nested" human rights (sub)regime is represented by universal membership organizations with a limited functional competence and by less institution-bound single-issue regimes. Single-issue regimes establish a place for themselves in the network of interdependence by restricting their activities to a limited range of issues—for example, workers' or women's rights—to induce widespread participation in a single area of mutual interest.

A. WORKERS' RIGHTS

The first international human rights regime of any sort was the functional regime of the International Labor Organization (ILO),[25] established by the Treaty of Versailles. Most of the regime's substantive norms were developed after World War II, including important conventions on freedom of association, the right to organize and bargain collectively, discrimination in employment, equality of remuneration, forced labor, migrant workers, workers' representatives, and basic aims and standards of social policy. Although developed autonomously, these rules supplement and extend parallel substantive norms of the global regime.

Because regime norms are formulated in individual Conventions and Recommendations, which states adopt or not as they see fit, there is neither universality nor uniformity of coverage. Nevertheless, states are required to submit all Conventions and Recommendations to competent national authorities to be considered for adoption, and they may be required to submit reports on their practice even with respect to Conventions they have not ratified.

23. For the text, see http://www1.umn.edu/humanrts/instree/arabhrcharter.html. I can find no evidence that it has had any appreciable effect. The Cairo Declaration on Human Rights in Islam may also be of some normative interest. See http://www1.umn.edu/humanrts/instree/cairodeclaration.html.

24. On the general regional situation, see Magnarella (1999), Dwyer (1991), and Strawson (1997). See also Waltz (1995), which provides a careful and still largely accurate overview of the opportunities for and limits on human rights activism in the region.

25. The classic study of human rights in the ILO is Haas (1970). See also Wolf (1984) and Bartolomei de la Cruz, Potobsky, and Swepston (1996).

Periodic reports are required on compliance with ratified Conventions.[26] The highly professional Committee of Experts on the Application of Conventions and Recommendations reviews reports. Although it may only make "observations," it does so with vigor and considerable impartiality, and Committee observations have often induced changes in national practice.

Much of the success of this reporting-monitoring system lies in the ILO's "tripartite" structure, in which workers' and employers' delegates from each member state are voting members of the organization, along with government representatives. Because "victims" are represented by national trade union representatives, it is relatively difficult for states to cover up their failure to discharge their obligations, especially if some national workers' representatives adopt an internationalist perspective and question practices in countries where labor has less freedom to organize and advocate.

The issue of workers' rights has also been important to the strength and success of the ILO regime, providing considerable ideological homogeneity across a universal membership. During the Cold War, Western, Soviet bloc, and "socialist" Third World regimes certainly had different interpretations of the meaning of "freedom of association" and other relevant norms, but all faced serious internal and ideological constraints on overt noncompliance.

In a reversal of the usual pattern, however, post-Cold War changes have not been favorable for workers' rights. Globalization and neo-liberal structural adjustment have not been kind to organized labor and its advocates. Furthermore, the Cold War era's warm ideological embrace of workers pretty much across the mainstream of the political spectrum has turned tepid, and in some cases downright chilly.

To the extent that organizational structure and ideological appeal explain the success of the ILO's functional human rights regime, the prospects for other single-issue regimes seem dim. Direct voting representation for victims has not been, and almost certainly will not be, replicated in other organizations and only a handful of other human rights issues have near-universal ideological appeal.

B. RACIAL DISCRIMINATION

Racial discrimination, however, is one such issue.[27] The 1965 International Convention on the Elimination of All Forms of Racial Discrimination provides a clear and powerful extension and elaboration of the global regime's norms

26. There is a procedure for interstate complaints, but it is rarely used. Of more importance is the special complaint procedure for freedom-of-association cases arising under Conventions 87 and 98, which works through national and international trade union complaints, reviewed by the Governing Body's Standing Committee on Freedom of Association.

27. See Alston and Fredman (2001), Banton (1996), and more briefly Banton (2000) on the racial discrimination regime.

against racial discrimination, but its implementation provisions are fairly weak. The Committee on the Elimination of Racial Discrimination (CERD), a body of experts established under the Convention, has very narrowly interpreted its powers to "make suggestions and general recommendations based on the examination of the reports and information received from the States Parties" (Art. 9[2]). The interstate complaint procedure has never been utilized and fewer than two dozen individual communications have been considered. Even the information-exchange elements of the reporting procedure are not without flaws; the public examination of reports, although sometimes critical, often is less penetrating than in the Human Rights Committee.

Much of the explanation of this weakness lies in the very different institutional environments of the ILO and CERD. Most of the hundreds of ILO Conventions and recommendations are technical instruments regulating working conditions: for example, hours of work, minimum age, weekly rest and holidays with pay, seafarers' identity documents, radiation protection, fishermen's medical examinations, and exposure to benzene. Much of the work of the Committee of Experts thus deals with relatively uncontroversial technical matters. In the course of this work, expectations of neutrality are established and reconfirmed, so that when human rights issues are considered they are examined in a relatively depoliticized context as only one part of the work of an essentially technical body of experts. In addition, the wide range and great number of ILO activities tie states into a web of interstate, transgovernmental, and transnational relationships centered on the organization. CERD enjoys none of these advantages.

C. TORTURE

Another human rights issue with nearly universal appeal is torture. The 1984 Convention against Torture and Other Cruel, Inhuman or Degrading Treatment or Punishment contains a strong elaboration of norms against torture, providing a good illustration of the contribution of additional treaties to the progressive development of substantive international human rights law. "No exceptional circumstances whatsoever, whether a state of war or threat of war, internal political instability or any other public emergency, may be invoked as a justification of torture" (Art. 2[2]). Orders from superiors are explicitly excluded as a defense. Special obligations are established for training law enforcement personnel and reviewing interrogation regulations and methods. To reduce incentives for torture, statements obtained through torture must be made inadmissible in all legal proceedings. The convention also requires that wherever the alleged torture occurred, and whatever the nationality of the torturer or victim, parties must either prosecute alleged torturers or extradite them to a country that will.

A Committee against Torture receives and reviews periodic reports from states parties every four years. The Convention also contains optional provisions that allow the Committee to receive communications analogous to those permitted under the 1503 procedure, as well as interstate complaints and individual communications.[28]

Although the Convention and the Committee stand at the core of the international regime against torture, other actors are important participants. The Special Rapporteur on Torture of the UN Commission on Human Rights has played a prominent role, especially in the 1980s. We should also note the very strong European regional regime against torture (Evans and Morgan 1998; Morgan and Evans 1999), which has unprecedented on-site investigatory powers. The weaker 1985 Inter-American Convention to Prevent and Punish Torture is also of some note, especially in the context of the history of the region.

Ongoing promotional activities should also be noted. For example, the UN Voluntary Fund for Victims of Torture, established in 1982, makes grants to groups throughout the world. In 2000 and 2001, it disbursed about $7 million to approximately 150 NGOs in 65 countries.

Finally, the NGO dimension is particularly significant in the area of torture (as well as in women's rights, considered immediately below).[29] The campaigns of Amnesty International contributed greatly to the creation of both the Convention and the Special Rapporteur and have been extremely important in continuing to publicize the issue, thus increasing the impact of the regime. In a very different vein, Copenhagen is the home of an international Rehabilitation and Research Center for Torture Victims, a location that reflects the leading role of Denmark in international action against torture. Similar centers operate in Canada, Norway, and other countries.

D. WOMEN'S RIGHTS

Women's rights was until recently something of a stepchild in the field of human rights.[30] Although racial discrimination is considered in the UN Commission on Human Rights and throughout the UN-centered regime, gender discrimination was largely segregated in the UN Commission on the Status of Women. In past two decades, though, there have been a substantial normative and procedural changes in the women's rights regime and the language of

28. On the Committee against Torture, see United Nations (1992), Bank (2000), and Burns (2000).

29. For a good introduction to the role of NGOs in UN treaty bodies, see Bayefsky (2000: Part IV) and especially Grant (2000).

30. Among the substantial literature on women's human rights, see, for example, Askin and Koenig (1999), Grimshaw, Holmes, and Lake (2[illegible]), Wallace (1997: chap. 2), and Cook (1994). On the particularly important issue of national legal implementation, see Byrnes, Connors, and Bik (1997), Adams and Byrnes (1999), and United Nations (2000).

"women's human rights"—as opposed to classic "women's rights"—has entered the mainstream of discussions.[31]

The Commission on the Status of Women, a subsidiary body of ECOSOC established in 1947, has played a role in norm creation very similar to that played by the Commission on Human Rights, having drafted a variety of specialized treaties, such as the 1952 Convention on the Political Rights of Women, as well as the major general treaty in this area, the 1979 Convention on the Elimination of All Forms of Discrimination against Women. The Commission has also undertaken various promotional activities and studied individual communications between 1984 and 2000.

The Optional Protocol to the Convention, which entered into force at the end of 2000, has moved the consideration of communications to the Committee on the Elimination of Discrimination against Women (CEDAW). CEDAW, which meets annually, has examined reports of states parties since its inception in 1982 (see Shalev 2000). It now has an array of powers roughly comparable to that of the Human Rights Committee. Although the symbolism of this change was very important to a number of activists, it is much too early to say whether it will have much impact on the functioning of the regime.[32]

The strengthening of the women's rights regime can be traced primarily to the changing international awareness of women's issues centered around the designation of 1975 as International Women's Year and the associated World Conference in Mexico City. In conjunction with political and "consciousness-raising" activities of national women's movements, a major international constituency for women's rights was created; a growing set of regime makers and takers emerged, while potential breakers were deterred from active opposition either by domestic ideological stands or by the emerging international normative consensus. Follow-up conferences in Nairobi in 1985 and Beijing in 1995 have helped to solidify and deepen this international consensus. They have also provided striking illustrations of the important role of NGOs, and their dramatic proliferation, especially in the non-Western world.

E. CHILDREN

Children are perhaps the only group with more universal appeal than victims of racial or gender discrimination and torture.[33] Nonetheless, the speed with

31. For a useful discussion of these linguistic issues and some of their implications, see Peach (2001).

32. For a thoughtful assessment of the opportunities and constraints facing the Committee, see Bustelo (2000).

33. Alston, Parker, and Seymour (1992), Asquith and Hill (1994), Wallace (1997: chap. 5), Van Beuren (1998), Fottrell (2000), and Detrick (2000) provide good general overviews of the children's rights regime. For a more philosophical approach, see Freeman (1997). On the Convention on the

which the 1989 Convention on the Rights of the Child came into force was stunning: it took less than a year to obtain the twenty required parties (in contrast to two and a half years for the Convention against Torture) and barely more than two years to reach 100 parties. In May 2002 it had 191 parties, by far the most of any international human rights treaties.

The Committee on the Rights of the Child is structured and functions much like other treaty-based supervisory committees (Lansdown, 2000; Karp, 2000). It does not have the power to receive individual communications.

F. GENOCIDE

The 1948 Convention on the Prevention and Punishment of the Crime of Genocide was a central part of the first wave of post–World War II international human rights action.[34] It was the most direct international response to the Holocaust, which played a decisive role in moving human rights onto international agendas. In the ensuing decades, however, the genocide regime remained purely declaratory and of little or no practical effect.

The Genocide Convention envisions enforcement solely through national and international courts; it establishes no supervisory machinery. The UN Commission on Human Rights and its Sub-Commission, which might have had the authority to explore issues of genocide, were notably silent on this important class of violations. In fact, genocide until very recently has been treated largely outside the framework of international human rights law and institutions.[35]

One of the major changes in the post–Cold War politics of international human rights has been the development of a practice of multilateral armed intervention against genocide (see Chapter 14). At the same time, and through closely related political processes, a system of individual criminal responsibility has been established through ad hoc tribunals for Rwanda and the former Yugoslavia and the creation of the International Criminal Court.

The interesting, although very odd, result has been the development of a regime with real powers of international judicial punishment and even the capacity to intervene with military force. Yet the regime still lacks a clear institutional focus or any multilateral supervisory mechanism. Furthermore, international

---

Rights of the Child in particular, see Detrick, Doek, and Cantwell (1992) and LeBlanc (1995). The important issue of integrating international standards with traditional values and practices, which provides an interesting context for exploring some of the issues we considered in Part II, is considered in Alston and Gilmour-Walsh (1996) and Douglas and Sebba (1998).

34. The standard international legal discussion is now Schabas (2000). On the rather tortured relationship of the United States to the Genocide Convention, see LeBlanc (1991) and Ronayne (2001).

35. During the Cold War in particular it was much more likely to have been addressed in the context of international humanitarian law or even the law of war. On the relationship between human rights and humanitarian law, see Provost (2002) and Meron (2000).

efforts remain largely focused on punishing violators rather than on the promotional and preventive activities characteristic of most other international human rights regimes.

G. MINORITIES

The final international human rights regime I want to consider here is the emerging one on minority rights.[36] Although racial discrimination has been a central international human rights concern at least since the 1960s—the racial discrimination convention was adopted even before the Covenants—discrimination against other minorities was largely ignored until well into the 1980s. In 1992, however, the UN General Assembly adopted the Declaration on the Rights of Persons belonging to National, or Ethnic, Religious and Linguistic Minorities. The Working Group on Minorities and Indigenous Peoples of the UN Sub-Commission has done important promotional work in recent years.

The most interesting work, however, is being done in Europe, where the issue of minority rights first received significant multilateral attention (during the interwar period) and where the aftermath of the breakups of Yugoslavia and the Soviet Union have given the issue immense topic significance (Jackson Preece 1998). Both the Council of Europe and the Organization for Security and Cooperation in Europe have active and innovative promotional programs that involve working with both states and civil society at local, national, and regional levels (see Cumper and Wheatley 1999).

6. The Evolution of Human Rights Regimes

What, if anything, can we say in general about the nature, creation, and evolution of international human rights regimes? Table 8.1 presents a summary overview of the regimes discussed in this chapter, viewed at several intervals since 1945. The most striking pattern is the near-complete absence of international human rights regimes in 1945, in contrast to the presence of several in all the later periods. We can also note the gradual strengthening of most international human rights regimes over the last thirty years. Even today, though, promotional regimes remain the rule.

Once states accept norms stronger than nonbinding guidelines, declaratory

36. The literature on minority rights has exploded in recent years. Perhaps the best places to start are Jackson Preece (1998), which despite its focus on Europe has wide general applicability, Wallace (1997: chap. 3), and Alfredsson and Ferrer (1999). Claude (1955) still merits consideration, despite being obviously dated. Among other sources, I would single out Phillips and Rosas (1995), Henrard (2000), Rehman (2000), and Skurbaty (2000). In large part as a result of the work and influence of Will Kymlicka, an excellent theoretical literature, with direct practical application, is available. See especially Kymlicka (1995) and Kymlicka and Norman (2000). The issue of group human rights for minorities is addressed in §12.5.

regimes readily evolve into promotional regimes. If the regime's norms are important or appealing enough for states to commit themselves to them, then it is difficult to argue against promoting their further spread and implementation. The move to implementation or enforcement, however, involves a major qualitative jump that most states resist, with considerable vigor when necessary, and usually with success.[37]

Regime evolution may be gradual and largely incremental within declaratory and promotional regimes (and perhaps within implementation and enforcement regimes as well), but there seems to be a profound discontinuity in the emergence of implementation and enforcement activities. Promotional regimes require a relatively low level of commitment. The move to an implementation or enforcement regime requires a major qualitative increase in the commitment of states that rarely is forthcoming. Most of the growth in international human rights regimes has therefore been "easy" growth that does not naturally lead to further expansion. This would seem to explain the merely incremental growth of almost all international human rights regimes in the post–Cold War era, despite the substantially improved international human rights climate.

We have already considered some of the central factors that explain this pattern of limited growth, emphasizing both awareness and power, which usually are created or mobilized by conceptual changes in response to domestic political action (e.g., women's rights) or international moral shock (e.g., the global regime or torture). By galvanizing support for the creation or growth of a regime and delegitimizing opposition, human rights advocates may make moral interdependence more difficult for states to resist. National commitment, cultural community, and hegemony are of significant importance in the processes of change.

National commitment is the single most important contributor to a strong regime; it usually is the source of the often mentioned "political will" that underlies strong regimes. If a state has a good human rights record, then not only will a strong regime appear relatively unthreatening but also the additional support it provides for national efforts is likely to be welcomed. The European regime's unprecedented strength provides the most striking example of the power of national commitment.

The importance of cultural community is suggested by the fact that the only enforcement regimes are regional. In the absence of sociocultural and ideological consensus, strong procedures are likely to appear too subject to partisan use or abuse to be accepted even by states with good records and strong na-

37. For an interesting recent attempt to theorize the national adoption of international human rights norms, based on carefully designed and executed case studies, see Risse, Ropp, and Sikkink (1999).

tional commitments.[38] For example, opponents of stronger procedures in the global human rights regime and in single-issue regimes include major countries from all regions with good, mediocre, and poor national human rights records alike. The broad membership of all but the regional regimes undercuts the relative homogeneity that seems almost necessary for movement beyond a promotional regime.

Finally, we must stress the importance of dominant power and hegemony, which should be kept analytically distinct. Beyond mere dominant power, hegemonic leadership requires substantial ideological resources, a crucial element in the acceptance of, or at least acquiescence in, the authority of the hegemon. The effective exercise of even hegemonic power usually requires not merely dominating material and organizational resources, but also an ideological justification sufficiently powerful to win at least acquiescence from nonhegemonic powers.

Leaders require followers; regime makers need takers. The reasons for taking a regime may be largely accidental or external to the issue, but sometimes the reasons for taking a regime are connected with the ideological hegemony of the proposed project.[39] The seemingly inescapable normative appeal of human rights over the past half century, even during the ideological rivalry of the Cold War, thus is an important element in the rise of international human rights regimes. Power, in the sense that the term traditionally has had in the study of international politics, still is important, but true hegemony often is based on ideological "power" as well. We might even argue that the ideological hegemony of human rights is more important than dominant material power.

A hegemonic idea such as human rights may actually draw power to itself; power may coalesce around, rather than create, hegemonic ideas, such as human rights and the regimes that emerge from them. For example, the overriding ideological appeal of the idea of workers' rights has been crucial to the success of the ILO. In Europe, the "hegemonic" power behind the very strong European regime came not from any single dominant state but from a coalition built around the ideological dominance of the idea of human rights. The ideological hegemony of human rights is essential to explaining the creation of an African human rights regime in the face of the OAU's notorious respect for even the tiniest trappings of sovereignty. The emergence of the global human rights regime cannot be understood without taking account of this impulse, discussed earlier in terms of perceived moral interdependence.

38. The United States presents an exaggerated version of such fears, most strikingly in the U.S. Senate's extended resistance to, for example, the Genocide Convention and the International Covenant on Civil and Political Rights, with which U.S. law and practice already conformed in almost all particulars. These fears, in a less extreme form, are common and widespread.

39. Ruggie's (1982) account of "embedded liberalism" and the importance of the ideology of the welfare state in the creation of postwar economic regimes might be read in this way.

Hegemonic power, however, does ultimately require material power, and even hegemonic ideas have a limited ability to attract such power. Hegemonic ideas can be expected to facilitate states accepting relatively weak regimes, but beyond promotional activities (that is, once significant sacrifices of sovereignty are required) something more is needed. In other words, hegemony too points to the pattern of limited growth noted earlier.

The evolution toward strong promotional procedures can be expected to continue, but we should expect states to resist, usually successfully, efforts to cross over to implementation and enforcement. We have little reason to expect that the 2010 column of Table 8.1 will show many significant changes from 2000.[40] We must not forget, though, how far we have come since 1945.

40. Over the coming decade, I would expect only the development of weak declaratory regimes for the rights of indigenous peoples (see §12.7) and of the disabled (see Degener and Koster-Dreese [1995] and Wallace [1997: chap. 6]). In the dozen years between the first and second editions of this book, the only significant changes were (a) in the genocide regime, which was sufficiently weak and moribund that I did not even include it in the table, and (b) the creation of a weak declaratory minority rights regime.

9/ Human Rights and Foreign Policy

In addition to the activities in the multilateral forums discussed in Chapter 8, human rights have become increasingly important in the bilateral policies of many states. Few states, however, make more than occasional, modest sacrifices of other foreign policy interests in the name of human rights. In this chapter I try to draw attention to both the reality and the limits of states' concern with international human rights.

1. Human Rights: A Legitimate Concern of Foreign Policy?

I want to begin, however, with debates over incorporating human rights concerns into national foreign policies. As John Vincent put it at the outset of *Foreign Policy and Human Rights*, "there is no obvious connection between human rights and foreign policy" (1986: 1). In fact, there are at least three standard arguments against making the connection.

The realist rejects a concern for international human rights because foreign policy ought to be about the national interest defined in terms of power. The statist (or legalist) considers an active concern for the human rights practices of other states inconsistent with the fundamental principle of state sovereignty. The relativist (or pluralist) views international human rights policies as moral imperialism.

These arguments point to problems in overemphasizing human rights in foreign policy. They do not, however, establish that the human rights practices of other states are or ought to be an illegitimate concern of foreign policy.

A. THE REALIST ARGUMENT

Realists see international politics as a struggle between self-aggrandizing states in an environment of anarchy. Faced with a world of (potential or real) enemies and no government to turn to for protection, a concern for power must override just about everything else. To act in any other way—for example, to pursue justice or act out of compassion—would leave one's state open to, even invite, attack. Foreign policy, to use Hans Morgenthau's famous formulation, is (must be) about the "[national] interest defined in terms of power" (1954: 5). An intrinsic concern for human rights in foreign policy, as opposed to using human rights instrumentally to further the national interest, would be a dangerous mistake.

The statesman, because of the nature of his office and the realities of international politics, cannot afford to act on the basis of moral considerations; morality is appropriate to individual relations but not to the relations of states.[1] Thus Reinhold Niebuhr's *Moral Man and Immoral Society* emphasizes the disjunction between the individual world of moral relations and the world of collective action, which is dominated by power. The tragic necessity of amorality, even immorality, is for the realist an enduring, almost a defining, fact of international relations.

> The interests of the national society for which government has to concern itself are basically those of its military security, the integrity of its political life and the well being of its people. These needs have no moral quality. They are the unavoidable necessities of national existence and therefore are subject to classification neither as "good" or "bad." (Kennan 1985/86: 206)

Both academic realists and their brethren in foreign offices have therefore attempted to exclude moral concerns from foreign policy—or, where they have been excised, keep them excluded.

But power is (at most) only the cardinal, not the exclusive, concern of foreign policy. Whether the pursuit of other concerns is in fact compatible with the pursuit of power is an empirical question. Realism, if true, reveals the danger of overemphasizing human rights, but that is quite a different matter from excluding them altogether on principle.

Morgenthau argues that "the principle of the defense of human rights cannot be consistently applied in foreign policy because it can and must come in conflict with other interests that may be more important than the defense of human rights in a particular circumstance" (1979: 7). Although this is true of most objectives of foreign policy, realists (rightly) do not rail against pursuing economic interests, friendly diplomatic relations, cultural contacts, or the principle of *pacta sunt servanda* because they sometimes conflict with the pursuit of power. We should not accept such arguments with respect to human rights.

George Kennan, in drawing the contrast between the national interest and

1. "I stick to the fundamental principle that lying is immoral. But I realize that when you are dealing in the context of foreign policy, lying is inevitable. In private affairs, however, you do not deceive others, especially friends" (Morgenthau 1979: 10–11).

morality, speaks of "our interest rather than just our sensibilities" and contrasts the national interest with "the moral impulses that individual elements of that society may experience" (1985/86: 209, 206). Such arguments rest on unsupported stipulations about the national interest (and the character of morality) rather than theoretical, let alone empirical, arguments.

Interests are *not* reducible to power. As the term suggests, they are a function of what states are interested in, what they value—which in all cases is much more than power. As we have seen in a variety of ways in earlier chapters, most states are in fact interested in international human rights.

In certain (contingent) circumstances it may be unwise to pursue human rights. That, however, must be determined empirically, case by case. Realists simply are not entitled to categorically exclude human rights (or any other concern) as a legitimate goal of foreign policy.

B. THE STATIST (LEGALIST) ARGUMENT

International relations is structured around the principle of sovereignty, which grants a state exclusive jurisdiction over its own territory and resources, including its population. Sovereignty in turn implies nonintervention in the internal affairs of other states. The statist or legalist argues that human rights must be excluded from foreign policy because what a state does with respect to its own nationals on its own territory—which is what we usually are concerned with when we discuss human rights violations—is on its face an archetypal matter of sovereign national jurisdiction and thus of no legitimate concern to other states.

Where the realist is concerned with the realities of power in an environment of anarchy, the statist stresses the principal widely accepted limits on the pursuit of power, namely, sovereignty and the traditional body of international law that flows from it. Where the realist argues that it is unwise to pursue human rights in foreign policy, the statist argues that it contravenes the fundamental structural and normative principles of international politics.

Statists, like realists, begin from an important insight. For all the talk of globalization, states remain the primary actors in contemporary international relations. However much we may talk of world public order, international law is at its core a law of sovereignty, and virtually all states in every region regularly insist on the primacy of sovereignty, especially when their own sovereign rights are at stake.

Sovereignty, however, is the starting point of international law, not its end point. In fact, international law can be seen as the body of restrictions on sovereignty that have been accepted by states through the mechanisms of custom and treaty. Over the past half century an extensive body of international human rights law has been developed. Human rights thus have become a legitimate subject in international relations even from a strict legalist position—because sovereign states have chosen to make them so.

The weakness of existing international implementation and enforcement mechanisms (see Chapter 8) might allow the statist to argue that incorporating human rights into foreign policy still contravenes the fundamental principle of nonintervention. In practice, many states whose human rights practices are called into question make precisely such an argument, even when they are willing to raise human rights issues elsewhere. But numerous instrumentalities of foreign policy—for example, diplomatic representations and granting (or withdrawing) preferential trade agreements—do not involve intervention. Such means may be used on behalf of human rights as legitimately as they may be used on behalf of other goals of foreign policy. Illegitimate intervention occurs only when influence is exercised through strongly coercive, essentially dictatorial means. So long as such means are avoided, statism provides no ground for excluding human rights concerns from foreign policy.

C. THE RELATIVIST (PLURALIST) ARGUMENT

Viewed as a way to protect one's own state from outside interference, statism fits nicely with realism. Many proponents of a strong principle of nonintervention, however, advance a relativist argument that emphasizes the principle of self-determination or a commitment to international pluralism (compare §14.3.B). A country's social and political order should be, on its face, entirely a matter of domestic jurisdiction. In human rights terms, it reflects (or at least ought to reflect) the exercise of basic human rights, such as the right to political participation (compare §14.3.A).

Each society, acting collectively and independent of external coercion, ought to be allowed to choose its own form of government. Within a certain range of freedom, the autonomous choices of a free people should be respected. A similar conclusion can be reached by stressing the positive value of cultural diversity or respect for the values of other peoples and cultures.

Realists often make similar relativist arguments. For example, Morgenthau speaks of "the issue of what is now called human rights—that is, to what extent is a nation entitled and obliged to impose its moral principles upon other nations?" (1979: 4). Kennan argues that "there are no internationally accepted standards of morality to which the U.S. government could appeal if it wished to act in the name of moral principles" (1985/86: 207). This simply is not true in the case of human rights.

Virtually all states regularly and explicitly proclaim their commitment to the human rights enumerated in the Universal Declaration and the Covenants. To act on behalf of internationally recognized human rights is not to impose one's own values on other countries. It involves an effort to bring the practice of other governments more into line with their own professed values (which we share).

There *are* authoritative international human rights norms. So long as human rights policy is based on these norms, it does not reflect moral imperialism. In fact, failure to insist on compliance with internationally recognized human rights norms perversely risks reverse racism or elitism. The standards of internationally recognized human rights are minimal standards of decency, not luxuries of the West:

> It is not by chance that the most important international instrument in this field is entitled the Universal Declaration of Human Rights, and was adopted without a single dissentient vote. The assertion was that the standards laid down could and should be attained in any country. It was never expected that any state is too small, too remote or too poor to be expected to attain them. (Luard 1981: 21)

We cannot stand by idly and watch torture, disappearances, arbitrary arrest and detention, racism, anti-Semitism, repression of trade unions and churches, debilitating poverty, illiteracy, and disease in the name of diversity or respect for cultural traditions. None of these practices deserves our respect, even if they are traditional—which they usually are not (compare §5.7, 6.6). What Arthur Schlesinger said of civil and political rights holds true for almost all internationally recognized human rights: it is "hard to believe that the instinct for political and civil freedom is confined to the happy few in the North Atlantic littoral" (1979: 521).

The relativist argument usefully reminds us that universal standards need to be tailored in their implementation to reflect particular cultural and historical circumstances.[2] It does not show pursuing human rights in foreign policy to be inappropriate.

2. International Human Rights and National Identity

States choose to pursue human rights in their foreign policy for a variety of reasons. Often, though, a significant reason is that human rights are important to national identity. This is particularly clear in the case of the United States, where a combination of moral, historical, political, and national interest concerns have led to a relatively strong and assertive international human rights policy.

Human rights are the rights all human beings, whether they are citizens of

2. This "weak relativism" is defended in Chapter 6 and §7.7.

the United States or not. National governments may have the primary responsibility for implementing internationally recognized human rights in their own countries, but if human rights are paramount moral rights, they impose some sort of obligation on all people and not just on fellow nationals.

The legal realities of sovereignty may limit legitimate action on behalf of the human rights of foreigners to means short of intervention. The political realities of competing national interests further restrict the international human rights policies of the United States and all other states. However, the moral realities of the pervasive violation of universal human rights demand, and regularly have received, at least some active response, especially in the past twenty-five years.

Historical considerations focus on the central place of human rights in the American political tradition:

> The United States was founded on the proclamation of "unalienable" rights, and human rights ever since have had a peculiar resonance in the American tradition. Nor was the application of this idea to foreign policy an innovation of the Carter Administration. Americans have agreed since 1776 that the United States must be a beacon of human rights to an unregenerate world. The question has always been how America is to execute this mission. (Schlesinger 1979: 505)

William F. Buckley is (typically) more acerbic, and a bit more accurate, in noting America's "cyclical romances with the notion of responsibility for the rights of extranationals" (1980: 776).

This responsibility has been expressed in two principal forms, implying very different international human rights strategies. On the one hand, America has been seen as a beacon, the proverbial city on the hill, whose human rights mission was to set an example for a corrupt world. This strand of the American diplomatic tradition can be traced back at least to Washington's Farewell Address (Gilbert 1961). In its extreme forms this leads to neutralism and isolationism. On the other hand, the American mission has been seen to require positive action abroad. The United States must teach not simply by its domestic example but by active international involvement on behalf of human rights. This equally venerable strand of the American tradition has been predominant in the contemporary revival of concern for human rights.[3]

The combination of these moral and historical considerations provides a political case for linking human rights and American foreign policy. Given

3. The cyclical American commitment to international action on behalf of human rights abroad that Buckley identifies can perhaps best be seen as an oscillation between these two conceptions of the American mission.

these characteristic self-understandings, it is difficult for an American government to ignore the concern of its citizens for the human rights impact of U.S. foreign policy. We can also make a national interest argument that focuses on the long-run costs of too close an association with rights-abusive regimes.

Although the first country to place natural or human rights at the heart of its national self-definition, the United States is hardly unique. Human rights were also part of the founding self-image of the states of Central and South America when they threw off Spanish (and Portuguese) colonial rule. But the tortured fate of human rights in most of Latin America since independence—Costa Rica over the past half century has been the exception that proves the rule—makes India a much more interesting case. Indian independence in 1947 gave considerable additional impetus to the post–World War II surge of decolonization. India's identification with the human rights values of self-determination and racial equality was (along with its relatively great power) central to its leadership efforts in the Third World during the Cold War era (Banerjee 2000).

Countries without human rights in their founding myths have in recent decades increasingly incorporated human rights into their national self-conceptions. In South Africa, for example, human rights became a central part of the national self-image through a revolutionary (although not especially violent) political transformation that brought the end of apartheid.

The United Kingdom and the Netherlands illustrate the path of evolutionary transformation. By the end of World War II, both countries had come to identify themselves with the cause of universal human rights—at home. Once they had dismantled their colonial empires, in part through the influence of human rights ideas (in both metropolitan and colonized political communities), human rights emerged as an increasingly prominent part of both national identity and foreign policy.

Immediately after World War II, the Netherlands fought to maintain colonial rule over Indonesia. In the 1960s, massive Indonesian human rights violations were met by little more than muted verbal condemnation. By the early 1990s, however, the Netherlands was willing to accept modest but real economic and political costs, and face the stinging charge of neocolonialism, to press concerns over Indonesian human rights violations.[4]

In all these cases, and many others, national and international ideas and values interacted dynamically. The international dimension has been perhaps most striking in cases of revolutionary transformation, going back at least to Tom Paine's pamphleteering on behalf of the American and French revolutions. In India, Gandhi learned from his earlier South African experiences and, like many later nationalist leaders in Asia and Africa, effectively used the "Western" language of self-determination and equal rights against colonialism.

4. (Baehr 2000a: 71–72). Compare and Baehr (1997).

The struggle against apartheid in South Africa had an important international dimension that ultimately changed the foreign policies of most Western countries, turning even American conservatives such as Newt Gingrich against support for continued white rule. Beyond any material costs associated with economic sanctions, this weakened the sense of legitimacy and resolve of many white South Africans. In the Soviet bloc, the Helsinki Final Act and the follow-up meetings of the Council on Security and Cooperation in Europe (CSCE) provided important support for human rights activists, especially in Russia and Czechoslovakia and contributed subtly but significantly to the delegitimation of totalitarian rule (Thomas 2001).

The international dimension is also clear where human rights have been incorporated into national self-images by more evolutionary means. In most of Western Europe, participation in the Council of Europe's regional human rights regime has placed national rights in a broader international perspective. Britain's decision in 1997 to incorporate the European Convention directly into British law is a striking example of the interpenetration of national and international rights conceptions. A very different kind of international impetus was provided, in Europe and elsewhere, by Jimmy Carter's 1977 decision to make human rights an explicit priority in American foreign policy. It is no coincidence, for example, that the seminal 1979 Dutch White Paper followed closely on the U.S. example.

Independent human rights activists with prominent transnational connections—for example, Aun Song Su Ky in Burma and Jose Ramos-Horta in East Timor—are an increasingly prominent feature of the political landscape. In addition, ordinary citizens have increasingly come to frame their political and economic aspirations in terms of respect for human rights. Such individuals, and the groups they represent and participate in, are nodes for an increasingly transnational process of normative transformation that is reshaping notions of political legitimacy and national identity—and, through these, national foreign policies.

3. Trade-offs

International human rights policies are (at most) one part of national foreign policies, which all states consider to be appropriately driven primarily by the pursuit of the *national* interest. Therefore, unless we implausibly assume that international human rights take priority over all other national interests, human rights must sometimes be sacrificed to other interests and values. How often and in what circumstances are states characteristically willing to subordinate international human rights concerns? *How much* do states value international human rights?

A state might in principle put international human rights at the bottom of its priorities (unwilling to sacrifice any other interest in the pursuit of international human rights objectives) or at the very top (willing to subordinate all other interests that conflict with its international human rights concerns). Most if not all contemporary states lie toward the minimalist edge of this continuum. Human rights typically (but not always) lose out in conflicts with most (but not all) competing foreign policy objectives.

Imagine a simple foreign policy model with four interests: security, economic, human rights, and other. I can think of no prominent example of a state sacrificing a major perceived national security interest for human rights. As security conflicts have somewhat moderated in number and intensity in most (but not all) parts of the globe in the post–Cold War era, human rights may be less often "trumped" by national security. This, however, is a change in the frequency of conflicts, not in the relative rankings between international human rights and national security.[5]

States do, however, occasionally give human rights priority over economic interests. For example, Dutch aid sanctions against Indonesia in the early 1990s involved modest but real economic (and political) costs. Such behavior, however, is exceptional rather than regular, even for the Dutch (Baehr 2000b).

International responses to the 1989 Tiananmen massacre illustrate the range of responses characteristic even in high-profile cases (see Foot 2000). Most states that had substantial economic relations with China did adopt aid, trade, or investment sanctions. Japan did so with considerable reluctance, great inconsistency, and for the briefest possible period—yet with real costs to Japanese firms. The United States, by contrast, responded with sufficient vigor that economic sanctions were the central issue in U.S.-Chinese relations until 1994 and a major irritant into 1997. Most European states took a middle course.

India, however, remained largely silent and thus indirectly, but intentionally, supportive of China. Russia, which also shares a border with China, largely restricted itself to verbal criticism. Japan's reluctance to pursue sanctions had important security as well as economic dimensions. Even the United States never consistently applied the military and political sanctions it announced. Tiananmen thus illustrates both the characteristic subordination of human rights to national security and the occasional willingness of states to subordinate economic interests to human rights.

Although "other interests" is so broad a category that little of general interest can be said, it is worth noting that human rights could be usefully separated from the "other" category only relatively recently. In most countries today

5. This assessment may be too harsh and static as a result of assuming a fairly conventional definition of national security. For example, an emphasis on personal security for citizens would make human rights and national security in many instances complementary rather than competing concerns. On conceptualizing the relationship between human rights and security, see Forsythe (1993). Compare §14.5.

more interests are in the "other" category, with which human rights (at least occasionally) can compete successfully, than twenty-five, or even ten, years ago.

4. Choice of Means

The intensity of commitment can also be measured by the direct costs a state is willing to bear. When other interests do not override international human rights, how far are states willing to go? What are the means characteristically used in support of international human rights objectives?

Although the higher the ranking, the more likely a state is to use strong means to realize it, the analytical distinction between these two measures of intensity of commitment is sometimes useful. For example, even if human rights remain below security concerns, we still will want to know which means a state is typically willing to use when security interests do not preclude action. To take an example from a different issue area, over the past century the willingness of states to use force on behalf of economic interests has declined substantially despite economic interests having been downgraded on the foreign policy agendas of few if any states.

Evan Luard provides a fairly broad list of means that have been used in the pursuit of human rights objectives: confidential representations, joint representations with other governments, public statements, support for calls for international investigation, initiation of calls for investigation, cancellation or postponement of ministerial visits, restrictions on cultural and sporting contacts, embargoes on arms sales, reductions in aid, withdrawal of ambassadors, cessation of aid, breaking diplomatic relations, and trade sanctions (1981: 26–27). To this list we should add support for civil society groups, aiding legal opposition groups, aiding illegal nonviolent opposition movements, aiding armed opposition movements, and invasion.

International human rights interests, however, are almost never pursued with military force. Only when faced with genocide or severe humanitarian emergencies (see Chapter 14) have states used force to pursue international human rights bilaterally (e.g., India in East Pakistan [Bangladesh]) or multilaterally (e.g., Somalia, Bosnia, and East Timor).[6] During the Cold War, comparably severe emergencies did not mobilize international armed force, and in the post–Cold War era forceful responses have not been universal. Consider, for example, the tragically tardy international response to Rwanda and the

6. Some might want to add the inclusion of human rights into UN peacekeeping missions in countries such as Guatemala and Angola. In such cases, however, the use of force was modest and entirely within a broader international peace and security mandate. The same is even more clearly true of humanitarian operations in northern and southern Iraq; the human rights of the Kurds were an afterthought, and those of Iraq's southern Shiites an even later (and even more modestly felt) thought.

continuing refusal to use force to halt the genocidal civil war in Sudan. We should also note the reluctance of states to risk the lives of their own nationals, which was especially striking in Kosovo, in peacekeeping and armed humanitarian operations.

Moving down the ladder of strength of means we find occasional uses of trade and investment sanctions, most notably in the international campaign against apartheid in South Africa in the 1980s. But strong economic sanctions remain exceptional. States sometimes will pay more in money than in lives, but not very often.

Aid is more regularly used to pursue international human rights objectives. Although aggregate data show at best a modest relationship between foreign aid allocations and the level of respect for human rights in recipient countries,[7] human rights concerns have altered aid allocations in many particular instances. Even Japan, which has historically been extremely reticent to link aid and human rights, has included human rights considerations (at least formally) in allocating development assistance since 1992.

We should note, however, that aid and (especially) trade have been used primarily punitively. Countries such as the Netherlands, Sweden, Norway, and Canada have made fairly concerted efforts over the past two decades to direct aid to rights-protective regimes, not just away from rights-abusive regimes (Stokke 1989). In recent years, other countries have begun to give greater consideration to aid as a positive inducement or reward.[8] Nonetheless, states often are more willing to withdraw or withhold aid to punish bad human rights performance—and even then with little consistency—than to reward good performance with additional aid.[9]

Verbal rather than material sanctions and inducements provide the heart of most international human rights initiatives. Condemnations of violations and

7. There is a fairly substantial quantitative literature on aid and human rights in U.S. foreign policy. Carleton and Stohl (1985) present a classic finding of no linkage. Cingranelli and Pasquarello (1985) find more of a link. Steven Poe and his associates have done especially good work. See, for example, Poe (1990), Poe and Sirirangsi (1994), and Poe, Pilatovsky, and Miller (1994). The latest and most comprehensive study, undertaken by Apodaca and Stohl (1999), finds a modest relationship in the case of economic assistance but not for military aid.

8. Proposals to establish trade preferences for rights-protective regimes, however, have not been seriously considered, at least in the United States, GATT, and the WTO. For one interesting academic proposal, focusing especially on labor rights, see DeMartino (1996: 28–34).

9. The rationale for this approach might be that respect for internationally recognized human rights should be routinely expected from all states, rather than treated as an achievement deserving reward. Although I have considerable sympathy toward this view, it ignores the political realities of achieving progress in implementing human rights, especially when starting from a record of systematic violations. Working positively to support governments making human rights progress may be far more effective than using aid punitively, if only because systematic violators are unlikely to be swayed by the modest amounts typically involved in aid sanctions. International financial support for governments making real progress is not only powerful symbolism but may in some cases also have a real political impact.

praise for good or improved performance are the most common means used by all states to further their international human rights objectives. Although words may be cheap, rarely are they free, especially in the world of diplomacy. In any case, verbal policy is an important and appropriate means for pursuing human rights, like other, interests. Furthermore, verbal policy may have an impact on the international normative environment within which states act, and thus indirectly on future state behavior.

States also regularly take symbolic actions such as recalling ambassadors, suspending cultural or sporting exchanges, endorsing international investigations, and voting for condemnatory resolutions in international organizations. Even aid sanctions often are largely symbolic. For example, Dutch aid to Indonesia in the early 1990s was less than two percent of the world total, and Japan responded to Holland's cuts by increasing its own assistance to Indonesia.

An increasing number of states also support local human rights activists and nongovernmental organizations. Such support may cross over from symbolic to material action. Nonetheless, it is relatively indirect, involving support for local human rights advocates rather than direct bilateral or multilateral action against another state.

In summary, we can say that international human rights initiatives, although always subordinated to security interests and usually subordinated to economic interests as well, are a regular and increasingly common part of the foreign policy of many states. When human rights concerns coordinate rather than compete with other foreign policy interests—for example, in India's opposition to genocidal massacres in East Pakistan (Bangladesh) or U.S. policy toward post-Tiananmen China—relatively forceful responses become possible. East Timor and Kosovo suggest that in a few cases some states will use even force to protect internationally recognized human rights in the absence of major security or economic interests.[10]

5. The Purposes of International Human Rights Policies

Most states in the contemporary world are more concerned with human rights at home than abroad. Liberal democratic regimes in particular regularly tolerate international human rights practices they would not even consider accepting nationally (compare §4.7, 4.8). Although cosmopolitan moralists may condemn this "inconsistency," it is deeply rooted in the world of sovereign states, which have a special legal and political responsibility for the rights and interests

10. The case of Timor is especially interesting because Western and Australian economic and security interests lay with Indonesia but were overridden by humanitarian concerns for (poor and weak) East Timor.

of their own nationals. National foreign policies are *supposed* to treat the interests of nationals and foreigners differently.

An initially more troubling inconsistency involves treating comparable human rights violations differently in different places or at different times. Before we can say much about the consistency, or even the efficacy, of states' international human rights policies, however, we need to know what they are attempting to achieve.

The "obvious" goal of altering the behavior of the country targeted by a particular initiative requires little comment. Many, perhaps most, international human rights initiatives, however, have other purposes as well. Therefore, they cannot be evaluated simply—perhaps not even primarily—by success in altering the human rights practices of targeted states.

India did not expect to change South African policy by supporting UN resolutions condemning apartheid. When Holland suspended aid to Indonesia, it had no real expectation of changing the policies of the Suharto regime. No reasonable American expected that sanctions imposed after the Tiananmen massacre had any prospect of establishing democracy in China or even returning the country to the level of political openness it had reached in the late spring of 1989.

In these examples there was some hope of contributing to eventual changes. Deterring similar violations in the future may justify pursuing initiatives for which a state expects no tangible impact in the target country. This may be especially important in relations with weaker or more dependent countries. Even in the immediate target, "unsuccessful" action may reduce or forestall future abuses. One might read this as a lesson of international pressures on Chile and Argentina in the 1970s and El Salvador and Guatemala in the 1980s.

Even where there is no long-run expectation of altering behavior in the target state, international human rights initiatives may be reasonably undertaken. For example, the aim may be punishment rather than remedy or reform. Even if competing interests or limited resources preclude a realistic possibility of altering behavior in the target, states may reasonably chose to impose costs on those who violate internationally recognized human rights. However modest, imposing some costs on rights-abusive regimes often will be preferable to imposing none.

A more diffuse objective may be to contribute to maintaining or transforming the international normative environment, especially dominant conceptions of political legitimacy. The fact that postcommunist governments in Hungary, Poland, and Czechoslovakia saw themselves as beneficiaries of such a normative transformation explains much of their enthusiasm for strengthening the OSCE. American and European pressures for multiparty elections, especially since the end of the Cold War, have often been directed at influencing broader standards of legitimacy, beyond any impact they may (or may not) have in the immediate target country.

The "precedents" of international human rights policies, however, may have an internal rather than an external target. Their aim may be to establish or support a pattern, or future stream, of foreign policy initiatives. When the Carter administration suspended U.S. aid to Guatemala in 1977, the purpose was at least as much to set a new precedent for American policy as it was to alter Guatemalan human rights practices. Peter Baehr suggests that the precedent established by strong sanctions against Suriname in the 1980s helped to tip the balance in favor of Dutch sanctions against Indonesia in the 1990s (2000). Sanctions that had little discernible short- or medium-term effect in Paramaribo seem to have had a significant medium- and long-term impact in The Hague.

Finally, irrespective of any immediate or long-term impact—direct, indirect or diffuse, internal or external—states may undertake international human rights initiatives because they are legally, politically, or morally demanded. The U.S. Congress has required the president to impose sanctions for certain human rights violations, perhaps most notably in the Jackson-Vanik Amendment's requirement that trade preferences be denied to countries that restrict emigration. Internal (and even international) political pressure may leave foreign policy decision makers little choice but to act, as illustrated by both American and Japanese sanctions against China after the Tiananmen tragedy. Occasionally, a response to international human rights violations is even seen by states as morally demanded, irrespective of legal or political pressure.

States sometimes find it important to stand up for what they value, independent of any other pressures or expected impact, at home or abroad. Such symbolic acts of "witness"—acting out of respect for and to give voice to one's values—may influence the international normative environment. They may have a long-run impact on the target (or another) state's human rights practices. They may sustain a desirable pattern of foreign policy practice. Even if they do not, though, they may be demanded, for their own sake.

States are much more likely to "do the right thing" when costs are low or other interests provide additional incentives. Nonetheless, international human rights initiatives occasionally are undertaken primarily because they are right, and often they do reflect a solidaristic identification with the rights or well-being of foreigners.

6. Selectivity and Consistency

If human rights are moral values, though, how can they be appropriately or "consistently" sacrificed to nonmoral interests? Such a question rests on a contentious conception of morality. For example, utilitarianism and other consequentialist moral theories see morality as centrally concerned with calculating relative costs and benefits, rather than rigidly following a moral law. But even if we conceive of morality as a matter of categorical imperatives, challenges to the "consistency" of international human rights policies often confuse foreign policy and moral decision making.

Realists rightly remind us that foreign policy decision makers are required by their office to take into account the national interest, which is (at most) only partly defined by morality. Moral perfectionism is an inappropriate standard for foreign policy, but the national interest may—and today for many states does—include a moral dimension. Moral interests are no crazier an idea than economic or security interests. The task of the statesman is to balance competing national interests, whatever their substance or character.

Nonetheless, the differences between human rights and, say, national security do seem to be matters of quality, not mere quantity. How then are we to treat like cases alike—consistently—in the absence of a common metric? To pursue the balancing metaphor, how much does one unit of national security (whatever that might mean) weigh relative to a unit of human rights?

Although a serious problem, it is not obviously more difficult in the case of human rights than for other foreign policy objectives. Consider trade with and investment in political adversaries such as China, Iran, or Iraq. Debates over their limits involve fundamental disagreements about the relative weights that ought to be assigned to security and economic interests. For example, the controversy over Chinese launches of American commercial satellites a few years ago raised issues strikingly similar to those in the debate over the place of human rights in Sino-American relations.

Consider also the choice of means. How many American (or Pakistani or Canadian) lives was it worth to save hundreds of thousands of Somalis from starvation in 1992? To save a smaller number of Somalis from factional warfare among their leaders in 1993? There is no apparent qualitative difference between such calculations and those involved in, for example, the Gulf War. How many foreign soldiers' lives was it worth to expel Iraq from Kuwait? To overthrow Saddam Hussein? The problem of competing incommensurable interests is a general problem of foreign policy, not one restricted to human rights or moral interests.

Issues of consistency do have a special force in moral reasoning. The Golden Rule of doing unto others as one would have done to oneself underscores the fact that morality in significant measure means not making an exception for oneself (or those to whom one has a special relation). But even from a purely moral point of view, only comparable human rights violations require comparable responses. Human rights may be "interdependent and indivisible," but that does not require an identical response to every violation of every right.

Furthermore, considerations of cost may be relevant even in purely moral reasoning. Few would consider the United States to be morally bound, all things considered, to risk nuclear war to remedy human rights violations in China simply because we acted strongly to remedy similar violations in some other country. Conversely, the fact that no state is willing to threaten the use of force to free Tibet from Chinese domination does not mean that considerations of moral consistency ought to have precluded the use of force in, say, East Timor. Balancing competing values *requires* taking account of all the values involved. And consistency requires treating like cases alike *all things considered*, not just looking at one dimension.

In any case, to address only moral (in)consistency is to address but one part of the relevant foreign policy. In addition to the authoritative international human rights standards of the Universal Declaration and the Covenants, which can be taken as a rough approximation of an international moral standard, states must consider their own, often much more limited, international human rights objectives, as well as other aspects of the national interest. Even if a state's actions or policies are morally inconsistent, they may be consistent from a foreign policy point of view.

For example, George Bush extended most favored nation trading status to China in 1990 but denied it to the Soviet Union. Looking solely at human rights—Tiananmen versus perestroika, glasnost, new thinking, and the collapse of the Soviet empire—this seems wildly inconsistent. But considering all the interests involved, it is plausible, if controversial, to find no *foreign policy* inconsistency. Bush argued, not implausibly, that he properly balanced a complex set of competing security, economic, and human rights interests.

Consider again the "precedent" of Suriname for Dutch policy toward Indonesia. Would it have been "inconsistent" not to have suspended aid? Perhaps. But it might instead have reflected a reasonable and consistent calculation that the economic and security costs in Indonesia were sufficiently great to justify, perhaps even require, subordinating Dutch international human rights concerns.

We can only know whether different responses to comparable human rights violations represent inconsistent foreign policy if we know the values (weights) attached to all relevant interests. Alleged inconsistencies in international human rights policies may be—and I would suggest most often are—consistent policies based on a relatively low weighting of international human rights interests. It may be inconsistent, from an abstract human rights point of view, for Hungary to undertake international initiatives on behalf of the Hungarian minority in Romania, but not Russian minorities in Lithuania or Ukraine, or the Tamil minority in Sri Lanka, but there is no obvious conflict with the Hungarian national interest.

Hypocrisy, error, and inattention are no less common in foreign policy than in other human endeavors. In considering the issue of consistency, however, we must not confuse the standards of international human rights norms, nationally defined international human rights objectives, and the national interest more broadly conceived. Furthermore, all three must be distinguished from foreign policy actions that reflect a relatively low evaluation of a state's international human rights interests. Because human rights policies are at best a part—most often, a rather modest part—of the foreign policy of most states, it is unavoidable that even well-designed foreign policies will treat comparable human rights violations differently.

7. Towards More Effective International Human Rights Policies

Much of the real and remediable (more than moral) inconsistency in the international human rights policies arises not from miscalculation or conscious choice but from inattention and lack of coordination. Foreign policy, whether addressing human rights or other interests, tends to be made on a case-by-case basis, with relatively little coordination or strategic vision. Balances are struck not by omniscient rational actors but in more or less intuitive ways by decision makers grappling with competing demands and multiple pressures without much time for deep reflection.

Bureaucratic politics also plays a role. The frequent conflicts between human rights and national security officials are well known. Regional branches within the foreign ministry may operate with very different baseline assumptions and expectations. Those working with international financial institutions may come to the table with a very different perspective from that of those working on human rights. Bureaucratic organization thus may be significant to the success of a state's international human rights policy. For example, during the Carter administration, human rights concerns were infused more broadly through the foreign policy bureaucracy by devices such as the creation of a Bureau of Human Rights and Humanitarian Affairs within the U.S. State Department and the interagency "Christopher group," as well as by Congressionally mandated reporting (which required local embassies to give greater attention to human rights issues).

The other principal source of inconsistency, I suggest, is a tendency to overly grand policy pronouncements. Perhaps the classic example is Jimmy Carter's claim that human rights were the "heart" of American foreign policy. Having raised unrealistic expectations, it is not surprising that many observers came to judge American actions as heartless and inconsistent.

Both of these kinds of inconsistency are related to a relatively low valuation of international human rights. Excessively grand rhetoric is a sign of an interest having a lower value in practice than policy pronouncements suggest. And the higher an interest is valued, the more a state is likely to struggle against the tendency toward bureaucratic fragmentation. The biggest "problem" is that foreign policy decision makers often value human rights less than human rights advocates would like them to. In most countries, the single greatest contributor to more effective international human rights policies would be to increase the priority of human rights relative to other foreign policy objectives.

Talk of balancing human rights against other concerns suggests "putting a price" on human dignity and suffering, but this is necessarily done when foreign policy decisions are made. The real issue is whether it is done explicitly or implicitly, thoughtfully or casually, effectively or ineffectively.

Consistency is a matter of correctly adding up the various "prices" and values already assigned to foreign policy interests. Sometimes just calculating correctly will be enough to get "better" human rights policies (judged from the standpoint of human rights advocates). This is especially true in foreign ministries where realist rhetoric has special force or in countries where national security or economics ministries dominate the decision-making process. An even greater contribution (again, measured from the perspective of human rights advocates) could be made, though, by "getting the prices right," by increasing what states are willing to pay to achieve their international human rights objectives.

Human rights have a greater prominence in the contemporary foreign policy of more states than at any other time. The end of the Cold War has removed, or at least moderated, many impediments to more effective international human rights policies. But while international human rights are working their way up the foreign policy agendas of a growing number of states, in few if any have they gotten even close to the top.

10/ The Priority of National Action

What has been the practical impact of the multilateral and bilateral instruments and actions considered in the preceding chapters? International action, especially the creation of authoritative international human rights norms, has had, and continues to have, an impact on the fate of human rights. Its role, however, is ultimately subsidiary. The fate of human rights—their implementation, abridgement, protection, violation, enforcement, denial, or enjoyment—is largely a matter of national, not international, action. This implies a further particularity to universal human rights, a national particularity in the way international norms are put into practice.

1. The Limits of Multilateral Action

As we saw in Chapter 8, multilateral machinery, with the exception of the strong European regional regime, is largely restricted to promotional activities with limited monitoring powers. Complaint systems have very limited coverage and in the end do not (except in Europe) lead to enforceable judgments against states. Reporting systems, although on paper apparently "weaker," because of their wider coverage and their recognition that monitoring power is rooted primarily in information, actually may be of more significance. More generally, the nonjudicial and noncoercive aspects of international human rights are those that produce the greatest impact.

A. INTERNATIONAL REPORTING PROCEDURES

Reporting procedures are at the heart of multilateral implementation systems. In the end, however, reporting is "based essentially on self-criticism and good faith efforts" (Crawford 2000: 7). Without underestimating the importance of good faith and self-criticism, especially in a context of conscientious oversight by the supervisory committee, the limits of such a mechanism are obvious, particularly in cases of severe and systematic violations.

Committees cannot always even ensure that the required reports are submitted. Should a state submit even the most pro forma of reports, including little more than pious generalities and extracts from its constitution and statutes, it will have formally discharged its reporting obligation. States need not respond to particular questions asked during the public review of the report, let alone provide responses that the questioner or even the committee as a whole considers adequate. There is no formal follow-up procedure (other than review of the next scheduled report) unless the state initiates it with some form of supplemental report or information, which is likely to be reviewed on an ad hoc or informal basis.

The international human rights obligations of states are implemented, if at all, through national action. Like most obligations in international law, international human rights obligations ultimately rest on the more or less voluntary willingness of states to discharge their obligations. To pretend otherwise is to confuse aspiration with action, legal rules with practice. Reporting does not even provide a strong system of international monitoring: no organized system exists for acquiring independent information; reports are considered according to a predefined schedule, rather than as the circumstances of state behavior require; no effective follow-up procedures are provided; and the committees may only raise questions, not make even unenforceable judgments of compliance.

Whatever pressure a supervisory committee can exert rests on its ability to either appeal to the good will and shared concerns of the state or to (threaten to) embarrass it by drawing international attention to apparent violations or inadequacies in reports that might seem to be attempts to cover up questionable or culpable practices. Such subtle pressure may in some cases have an effect: for both domestic and international reasons, most states are concerned with how their human rights practices are perceived internationally. Even shame, however, is ultimately dependent on a sort of good faith on the part of the violator. Reporting-questioning procedures in the field of human rights are therefore likely to have even a marginal impact only as a supplement to sincere and dedicated national efforts. But they can serve both as a spur to and a check on national efforts.

Perhaps the most important contribution of mandatory periodic reporting is the occasion that drafting the report provides for a periodic national review of a state's own practice. If a country is serious about its reporting obligation, such reviews should help to guard against complacency and resultant shortcomings in practice. Inadequacies and areas for improvement may be uncovered, and the occasion of the next report may serve as a target for remedial action. A purely national reporting system might in theory accomplish all of these purposes, but independent international scrutiny offers one more level of checks and is likely to provide an additional spur to action.

Periodic national reviews of practice in the course of preparing a report also may serve to strengthen the force of particular substantive provisions. For example, the systematic review of interrogation and detention procedures and practices required by Article 11 of the Torture Convention should be placed on nothing less than a four-year cycle, corresponding to the reporting cycle. Similarly, the training procedures required by Article 10 will be placed under a cycle of periodic review if the reporting obligation is undertaken with full seriousness. In general, whenever states are required to look carefully at their practices, as they must in the course of conscientiously preparing a report, the relevant treaty provisions may play a constructive role in furthering the cause of human rights.

Periodic reporting may also provide the occasion for national improvements in information gathering and processing that then serve as the basis for policy reforms—for example, by highlighting local problems or fostering the spread of knowledge about innovative or particularly effective local efforts. Furthermore, the review process itself is likely to increase the awareness and attention of responsible public officials, which should produce even more and better information. Reporting may even further *international* information exchange, allowing states to learn from one another's experiences. This could be greatly encouraged if monitoring bodies were to use their authority to make general comments on reports to highlight points of broader international interest in innovative national practices or commonly encountered difficulties.

The way supervisory committees exercise their limited powers of review can also have an impact on national practice. The more thorough the questioning, the less likely it is that a state will be able to hide its shortcomings. In at least some instances we can even expect that practices that cannot be covered up will be reformed. Furthermore, the more impartial the committee, the more likely it is to receive open and honest reports; even states with good records and strong national commitments are less likely to participate in or cooperate with procedures and committees that are perceived as biased. The need to induce and maintain state participation and cooperation limits the extent to which a committee can push states: an overaggressive committee may alienate some states and thus lose its opportunity to have any impact at all in these countries, but an efficient, well-respected, and savvy committee may be able, at least occasionally, to tip the scales in national policies. Such an impact may prove impossible to pinpoint or disaggregate, but we should expect it to be there in some instances.

In certain circumstances, international reporting systems can have a minor impact on human rights practices. Conversely, the absence of reporting systems may make it slightly easier for states to get away with violating human rights. In the end, though; reports are just that: reports, on national practice. National practice is the key, and that practice usually can be only marginally influenced by even the strongest international reporting system.

B. COMMUNICATIONS (COMPLAINT) PROCEDURES

Complaint/communication procedures also depend very heavily on the good intentions of states. In most instances, the emphasis is on achieving a cooperative resolution of the dispute. Confidentiality and direct state participation is the norm. In the end the only real sanction available to most supervisory committees is whatever additional publicity its report may provide.

As in the case of reporting procedures, the less serious (and the more isolated; that is, less systematic) the violation, the more likely it is that the international complaint procedures will have an impact. Most complaint procedures are optional; parties to the treaty need to opt in. States contemplating or engaging in questionable practices thus usually exempt themselves. This is perhaps the single most significant limitation of multilateral human rights procedures: the states most likely to commit violations that most cry out for international action are precisely the states least likely to participate in strong international procedures.

We also should be wary of the excessive individualism implicit in an overemphasis on individual complaint proceedings. Such procedures are completely dependent on the receipt of admissible communications, which in turn depend not only on a state's formal participation in the procedure but also on the ability of victims (or their advocates) to get information into the hands of the relevant committee. As a result, there is "no correlation between the general level of complaints (or for that matter their complete absence) and the state of human rights compliance in a given country" (Crawford 2000: 8).

Certainly every individual who is helped is a valuable success story for international procedures. A person whose rights are violated in a relatively open country, or even in a country that has a generally exemplary human rights record, is not any less deserving of international protection. Nonetheless, individual complaint procedures can be expected to help directly only a relative handful of individuals.

Furthermore, even a large number of individual complaints to even the most impartial and aggressive international monitoring bodies will not address the real problem of human rights violations. Action on individual complaints can, at best, address only the symptoms of the underlying problem. Protecting people against abuses is not so much a matter of providing international remedies as it is a matter of altering national practices that allow or even encourage human rights violations. True protection against human rights violations rests on fundamental *national* political changes. International monitoring is almost certain to be a largely peripheral factor in bringing about such changes.

Excessive judicialism is the other pitfall of an overemphasis on individual complaint procedures. In fact, the quasi-judicial nature of such proceedings actually obscures their real impact. The review of individual complaints is essentially a mechanism to encourage national cooperation and action—that is, an effort to try to convince, or perhaps shame, a state to mend its ways. Recalcitrant states can ignore international committees with impunity, and they regularly do.

2. The Limits of Bilateral Action

When considering international action on behalf of human rights, one reason to begin with multilateral activity is that the normative consensus worked out in the United Nations provides a context for bilateral action. Another, no less important reason is that although we can trace intensive multilateral activity back over half a century to the very beginning of the United Nations, human rights has been an active concern of the national foreign policies of most countries for scarcely half that time. For example, U.S. legislation, which has focused on linking foreign aid and arms sales to human rights practices in recipient countries, goes back only to 1973. Even such countries as Norway and the Netherlands, which have gone the furthest in their efforts to pursue human rights concerns in their foreign policies, can trace these endeavors back not much more than two decades.

Given this history, we might be tempted to say that until recently the human rights impact of bilateral action has been nil. This is true if we look at actions directly undertaken in the name of human rights. Policies undertaken for other reasons, however, often have significant human rights consequences. For example, efforts to foster "democracy" and "development," which have been a part of the foreign policies of most developed countries over the past fifty years, may in some cases have helped to increase the enjoyment of both civil and political rights and economic and social rights. Actions by the United States to protect the "free world" from "communism," however, had a devastating impact on human rights in such countries as Guatemala, Chile, South Korea, Indonesia, Zaire, and South Africa. Likewise, aid programs in the 1950s and 1960s that focused on aggregate growth and "modernization" in many instances actually impeded the enjoyment of economic, social, and cultural rights in recipient countries.

Bilateral relations seem to provide a much greater range of opportunities—and dangers—for international action on behalf of human rights. It is very difficult to produce examples (outside of Europe) in which multilateral action has had a similar influence, whether for good or for evil, on human rights conditions. States, particularly powerful states, have more resources at their disposal than international organizations do. States control, and thus can manipulate for the purpose of their human rights policies, access to markets, resources, and foreign aid. At least some states can make use of the desire of other countries for cordial diplomatic relations or political cooperation to exert pressure on behalf of human rights. In addition, the scrupulous concern for sovereignty characteristic of virtually all international organizations and supervisory bodies is less pronounced in the bilateral foreign policy of some states. Although intervention is no less illegal in bilateral relations, states much more frequently choose to ignore or override the prohibition in their bilateral policies.

Like most moral considerations, human rights are rarely the bases for positive foreign policy action, except when that action is otherwise beneficial or, at the very least, not contradicted by other interests. By contrast, security, economic, political, and ideological considerations are the principal bases of foreign policy in almost all countries. When human rights goals conflict with these objectives, human rights usually lose out. States ignore human rights violations or act in ways that harm human rights much more often than they act strongly on behalf of human rights abroad, because it is more often in their security, economic, political, or ideological interest to do so.

Even more troubling is the relatively great capacity of external action to harm the human rights situation in another country. This was especially evident during the Cold War era. There seems to be a profound and troubling asymmetry in the relative efficacy of bilateral international action on behalf of and against human rights: it is much easier to produce great harm than to provide major help. Over and over again we have seen dictatorships propped up by foreign support (at least in the medium run)—for example, in Poland, Zaire, the Shah's Iran, and Marcos's Philippines—but there are few examples of regimes that respect the full range of internationally recognized human rights that owe their start, let alone their continued existence, to external support.[1]

Democratic rule requires popular support and participation and thus can rarely be established through external action. Dictatorship requires only sufficient force to repress opposition. As the fates of countries such as Chile, Guatemala, Poland, and Hungary so sadly illustrate, such force is much easier to acquire as the result of foreign support or intervention. A government that respects human rights must be principally the result of internal political action. A government that violates human rights can owe its existence in significant measure to external forces.

The theoretical potential in bilateral action should not be ignored. Bilateral actors have more resources at their disposal, and operate with fewer constraints, than almost all multilateral organizations. If they choose, countries can exercise a considerable range of foreign policy resources on behalf of human rights. This is especially true of relatively powerful regional actors, such as the United States in Latin America. There is a real possibility for a small but still significant impact on human rights abroad, especially where the target state has a certain degree of sympathy with the objective. Typically, however, foreign policy resources have been exercised on behalf of human rights only

1. The only striking counterexamples are countries that were decisively defeated in war, such as Japan and Germany, or countries such as El Salvador where a regime change was part of an internationally negotiated settlement to end an internationalized civil war.

sporadically, if that. And there is a great potential for powerful nations to use their power to undermine human rights in foreign countries.

This suggests that the most significant foreign policy contribution of great powers to human rights might lie in self-restraint, in avoiding actions that actively support or encourage rights-violating regimes. If all countries, and particularly all major powers, were to avoid support for and complicity with repressive regimes, bilateral action could have a more than marginal impact on human rights abroad. At the very least, this would return the fate of human rights to a national struggle between dictators and their citizens, which is where the issue really belongs and where any lasting success must ultimately rest.

3. The Limits of International Action

Human rights are ultimately a profoundly *national*, not international, issue. In an international system where government is national rather than global, human rights are by definition principally a national matter. States are the principal violators of human rights and the principal actors governed by international norms. Thus the probable impact of international action is limited.

The likelihood of international implementation and enforcement is also reduced because international action on behalf of human rights rests on perceived moral (rather than material) interdependence. Other states are not directly harmed by a government's failure to respect human rights; the immediate victims are that government's own citizens. Therefore, the self-interested incentives of other states to retaliate are low, or at least intangible.

In addition, "retaliation" is particularly difficult. The only leverage available, beyond moral suasion, must be imported from other issue areas, such as trade or aid. This makes retaliation relatively costly and increases the risk of escalation. In addition, because the means of retaliation are not clearly and directly tied to the violations, its legitimacy is likely to be seen as more questionable.

Even in the best of circumstances, respecting human rights is extremely inconvenient for a government, and the less pure the motives of those in power, the more irksome human rights appear. Who is to prevent a government from succumbing to the temptations and arrogance of position and power? Who can force a government to respect human rights? The only plausible candidate is the people whose rights are at stake.

Foreign pressure may help to remove a repressive government. With luck and skill, foreign actors may even be able to place good people in charge of finely crafted institutions based on the best of principles. They may provide tutelage, supervision, and monitoring; moral and material support; and protection against enemies. All this is extremely unlikely. Even if we do attribute such unrealistically pure motives and unbelievable skill and dedication to external powers, however, a regime's ultimate success—its persistence in respecting, implementing, and enforcing human rights—will depend principally on *internal* political factors.

A government that respects human rights is almost always the legacy of persistent national political struggles against human rights violations. Most governments that respect human rights have been created not from the top down but from the bottom up. Paternalism, whether national or international, is unlikely to produce respect for human rights. The struggle for international human rights is, in the end, a series of national struggles. International action can support these struggles, or it can frustrate and sometimes even prevent them. International action is thus an important factor in the fate of human rights, but not the most important factor.

Despite the foregoing, we should not give up on international action. Few states press at the limits of the possibilities of international action either in their bilateral relations or in their activities in international organizations. We must recognize, nevertheless, that there *are* major limits to international action and turn our attention to realistic international objectives.

It is also important to emphasize the limits of international action because the academic study of human rights has been, and still remains, dominated by students of international law and politics. In addition, policy-oriented discussions of human rights in North America, and to a lesser extent in Europe, have focused predominantly on human rights practices abroad and on the ability of Western governments to influence them. If my arguments above are correct, such scholarly efforts have been misdirected, at least in part. The study of human rights must in the final analysis rest most heavily on the study of *comparative* politics, not international politics.

There are a variety of historical and sociological reasons for this misdirection. The international normative consensus was worked out in the United Nations, which is studied almost exclusively by students of international law and organization, gave those working in these disciplines an advantage over their colleagues in other fields. International lawyers have played a major role in drafting the legal instruments, giving them a similar advantage. The distressing tendency toward disciplinary exclusivity and interdisciplinary blindness in much academic work then played a major role in keeping the study of human rights rather narrowly confined—until politics, largely in the person of Jimmy Carter, brought it to the forefront of attention. Because the Carter human rights campaign was almost exclusively international, not national, the relative overemphasis on international action was actually strengthened.[2] Further-

2. We might also add that, in the United States, deep-seated attitudes of American exceptionalism, combined with a belief that what occurs in the United States is almost by definition respect of human rights, also plays a significant role. Most Americans apparently believe that "human rights" problems exist only in places that must be reached by flying over large bodies of salt water.

more, students of comparative politics, law, and sociology could go about their work quite adequately without ever making explicit reference to internationally recognized human rights. Much of that work is indeed of central importance to the study of human rights, but because it has not been cast in such terms it has not been widely drawn on by those who dominate the scholarly community in the field of human rights (principally internationalists, not comparativists).

I do not suggest that the international dimensions of human rights have been overstudied. It is clear, however, that the national dimensions have been woefully understudied. We should not stop studying the international dimensions of human rights, let alone give up pursuing human rights goals in national foreign policies and through international and regional regimes, but we must not forget that international mechanisms are, at best, supplemental to national endeavors. Furthermore, even specialists in international relations cannot successfully carry out studies of human rights independent of the work of students of national or comparative politics. Even when the focus of our work is on the international dimensions of human rights, we must pay greater attention to the interaction of national and international factors in the success or failure of international initiatives. International factors are but a small and subsidiary part of the picture.

Thus Part III ends, appropriately, by once more emphasizing the interaction between the universality and the particularity of human rights. The moral universality of human rights, which has been codified in a strong set of authoritative international norms, must be realized through the particularities of national action.

PART IV

Essays on Contemporary Theory and Practice

11/ Human Rights, Democracy, and Development

Human rights has become a hegemonic political idea in contemporary international society, a widely accepted standard of international political legitimacy (see Chapter 3). Development and democracy also have a comparable status. Regimes that do not at least claim to pursue rapid and sustained economic growth ("development"), popular political participation ("democracy"), and respect for the rights of their citizens ("human rights") place their national and international legitimacy at risk.[1]

The relationship between these goals, however, is complex and problematic. This chapter challenges the comfortable contemporary assumption that, as the Declaration and Program of Action of the 1993 Vienna World Conference on Human Rights put it, "democracy, development and respect for human rights and fundamental freedoms are interdependent and mutually reinforcing."[2] Without disparaging the important practical and theoretical linkages, I focus on tensions between the logics of human rights, democracy, and development.[3]

The struggle for human rights certainly has been fostered by an awareness that many Cold War era claims of conflicts between human rights, democracy, and development were misguided. The first edition of this book

1. Exceptions such as North Korea or Taliban Afghanistan typically advocate an ostensibly counter-hegemonic revolutionary ideal and are (self-consciously) isolated from an international society that tends to ostracize them. Consider the current debate within Iran in which openness to both human rights and international society are associated with the forces of reform.

2. This formulation has been regularly repeated. See, for example, General Assembly resolutions 52/148 (ninth preliminary paragraph) and 55/108 (fourth operative paragraph) and Commission on Human Rights resolutions 1998/72 (fourth operative paragraph) and 2000/5 (fourth operative paragraph).

3. I do not pursue relations between democracy and development for reasons for space, interest, and the focus of this book. For a sampling of more or less mainstream views, see the symposiums in the October 1994 and April 1995 issues of *Journal of Democracy*. Przeworski and Limongi (1997) argue, through cross-national analysis, that economic development does not facilitate transitions to democracy, but that it does strengthen established democracies. Londregan and Poole (1996), however, find a more generally positive relationship between development and democracy.

devoted two chapters to criticizing then-standard arguments for the necessity of development-rights trade-offs. Today, however, it is at least as important to challenge assumptions and arguments that human rights and development are necessarily or automatically linked. These two seemingly very different lines of argument are linked by the insistence that there is no automatic relationship, either positive or negative, between the struggles for human rights and for development. The consequences of development for human rights, and of human rights for development, are in large measure political and they vary considerably with time, place, and policy. The same is true of democracy and human rights. Unless democracy and development are understood and pursued in very particular ways, their pursuit may place human rights at risk.

1. The Contemporary Language of Legitimacy

The link between legitimacy and prosperity (which today we regularly speak of in terms of development) is close to a universal, cross-cultural political law. Whatever a ruling regime's sociological and ideological bases, sustained or severe inability to deliver prosperity, however that may be understood locally, typically leads to serious political challenge.

Democracy has much less regularly been a ground for legitimacy. Most polities throughout history have rested authority on a divine grant, natural order, or tradition that legitimated hierarchical rule by those with superior virtue (defined by birth, age, gender, wealth, skill, or power). For the past half century, however, most regimes have appealed to bottom-up authorization from "the people," rather than to a "higher" source.

Political legitimacy has been held to rest on the defense of natural or human rights at least since the seventeenth century. Human rights, however, emerged as a ground of *international* legitimacy only after World War II. It has been a regular, if controversial, issue in bilateral and multilateral politics since the 1970s. In the past decade human rights has joined democracy and development to complete a legitimating triumvirate.

Democracy, development, and human rights do have important conceptual and practical affinities. Most obviously, international human rights norms require democratic government. As Article 21 of the Universal Declaration puts it, "The will of the people shall be the basis of the authority of government." Democracy, although not necessary for development (especially in the short and medium runs) may restrict predatory misrule that undermines development. Civil and political rights provide accountability and transparency that can help to channel economic growth into national development rather than private enrichment. The redistributions required by economic and social rights similarly seek to ensure that prosperity is diffused throughout society. Conversely, those living on the economic edge, or with no realistic prospect of a better life for their children, are less likely to be willing to accommodate the interests or respect the rights of others.

Realizing such affinities, however, is neither automatic nor inevitable; it depends on context, institutional design, and political practice. People often want to do extremely nasty things to (some of) their "fellow" citizens. Vast inequalities in countries such as Brazil and the United States underscore the central role of politics in translating "development" (aggregate national prosperity) into the enjoyment of internationally recognized economic and social rights. South Korea and Taiwan, not to mention western Europe in the nineteenth century, show that development can be sustained for decades despite systematic denials of civil and political rights.

Twenty-five years ago, most states justified systematic sacrifices of human rights not only by appeals to national security (as opposed to personal security) and cultural relativism (as opposed to universal human rights) but also by appeals to the "higher" imperatives of development and democracy. Appeals to development imperatives still are a feature of contemporary international discussions (see §7.2), but in post–Cold War international society, arguments of interdependence have become the norm, as in a recent United Nations Development Program (UNDP) policy statement asserting that "human rights and sustainable human development are interdependent and mutually reinforcing" (1998).

The power of this new vision of international legitimacy is evident in the surprisingly rapid demise of most of the standard regime types of the Cold War era. Peoples' democracies—which sacrificed the rights of class enemies to a greater (party-specified) collective good—passed rapidly from the scene wherever the people were offered a choice. National security states—which sacrificed whatever and whoever they deemed necessary in the struggle against communism—have also become discredited. The fall of Kaunda in Zambia and Suharto in Indonesia are striking examples of the declining appeal of paternalism. Military rule is in decline even in sub-Saharan Africa, where it has been the most common form of government since independence.

We should not overemphasize the power of the idea of human rights. Economic failure has been central to the collapse of most of these regimes. Popular demands for democracy and human rights have often been naive. Official policy statements are often disingenuous. Appeals to cultural relativism and national particularities, as we saw in Chapter 7, have hardly disappeared from discussions of human rights. Nonetheless, the strong endorsement of the universality of internationally recognized human rights at the World Human Rights Conference in Vienna in 1993, despite the substantial efforts of China and its allies on behalf of a strong cultural relativism, illustrates the dramatic change in dominant international attitudes.[4] Whatever the gap between theory and practice, most states today prominently feature appeals to human rights, democracy, and development in their efforts to establish national and international legitimacy.

It is a helpful oversimplification to say that this hegemonic international ideology rests on the success of Western liberal democratic (and social democratic) welfare states. They are very well off economically, yet they remain deeply committed to an extensive, redistributive welfare state. Politically, they enjoy vigorous and open competitive electoral systems—along with an unusually strong consensus on basic political values and structures—and nowhere else has so much progress been made in ensuring that close to the full population enjoys most internationally recognized civil, political, economic, and social rights. This particular fusion of development, democracy, and human rights, however, reflects a distinctive and contingent balancing of markets (development), elections (democracy), and individual human rights.

2. Defining Democracy

"Democracy is based on the freely expressed will of the people to determine their own political, economic, social and cultural systems and their full participation in all aspects of their lives." This statement from the Vienna Declaration is as good a place as any to begin. Like all plausible definitions, it is rooted in the etymology of the term: the Greek *demokratia,* literally, rule or power (*kratos*) of the people (*demos*).

The *demos* was not the whole population, but rather a particular social class: the masses, or *hoi polloi*—literally, the many, but with the same social connotations as the transliterated term in Victorian England. Athenian democracy, even in its "Golden Age," was class rule by ordinary citizens, a class (of free males) that typically saw their interests as opposed to their aristocratic (literally, rule of the best), oligarchic (rule of the few), or plutocratic (rule of the wealthy) "betters."

Throughout most of its history, the theory and practice of democracy has focused on opposing claims to authority by competing social classes. Thus David Held begins *Models of Democracy* by defining democracy as "a form of government in which, in contradistinction to monarchies and aristocracies, the people rule" (1987: 2).

Democracy as a result has had, until relatively recently, a bad name—con-

4. The Vienna Declaration asserts that "the universal nature of these rights and freedoms is beyond question." "All human rights are universal, indivisible and interdependent and interrelated. The international community must treat human rights globally in a fair and equal manner, on the same footing, and with the same emphasis. . . . it is the duty of States, regardless of their political, economic and cultural systems, to promote and protect all human rights and fundamental freedoms."

sider, for example, the negative connotations even today of "demagogue," a leader of (speaker for) the people—and not just because democrats until the late eighteenth century almost always lost. Unless we assume, as few societies have, that reason or virtue is more or less randomly distributed among citizens or subjects, the claims of ordinary citizens to rule rest on "mere numbers." Thus from Plato and Aristotle through Kant and Hegel, democracy was disparaged as incompatible with good rule. Even advocates of mixed or "republican" regimes—from Aristotle, to Machiavelli, to Madison and Kant—recognized the interests and claims of the many but counterbalanced them by the claims of the few to superior wisdom or virtue.[5] Only over the past two centuries—and especially the past half century—have liberal, socialist, and anticolonial struggles transformed dominant conceptions of "the people," and thus delegitimated nondemocratic rule.[6]

What, though, does it mean for the people to rule? Held offers a partial list of common meanings:

> 1. That all should govern, in the sense that all should be involved in legislating, in deciding on general policy, in applying laws and in governmental administration.
> 2. That all should be personally involved in crucial decision making, that is to say in deciding general laws and matters of general policy.
> 3. That rulers should be accountable to the ruled; they should, in other words, be obliged to justify their actions to the ruled and be removable by the ruled.
> 4. That rulers should be accountable to the representatives of the ruled.
> 5. That rulers should be chosen by the ruled.
> 6. That rulers should be chosen by the representatives of the ruled.
> 7. That rulers should act in the interests of the ruled. (1987: 3)

The last of these senses, although often encountered, is not a defensible conception of democracy. Bourbon kings, Chinese emperors, and Ottoman sultans all (contentiously yet plausibly) claimed to rule in the interests of the people. Government *for* the people may or may not be democratic. Democracy, if that term is to mean more than the absence of systematic misrule by a nar-

5. Even the American Revolution was more "republican" than "democratic": the leading political parties in the early republic styled themselves Republicans and Federalists; "Democrats" did not become a major force for forty years. Likewise, the strong democrats of the French Revolution were largely defeated. The term democracy did not gain widespread political currency in France until 1848 (Rosanvallon 1995: 140).

6. Democracy has also been advocated on instrumental grounds: for example, as a device to limit abuses of power or to balance competing class interests. I am interested here, however, only in arguments for democracy as an intrinsically desirable form of rule.

row segment of society, must be government *of* or *by* the people. Beyond benefiting from good governance, the people in a democracy must be the source of the government's authority to rule.[7]

Held's six other senses, however, encompass an immense variety of political forms that can plausibly be called democratic, and all are extremely open. What does it mean to "be involved" in decision making? What are the mechanisms and measures of "accountable" government? How should the ruled "choose" their rulers? To return to the Vienna formulation, the issue is to determine "the freely expressed will of the people."

Democratic theories often are distinguished by their reliance on "substantive" or "procedural" tests. Rousseau provides a good illustration of the difference. The will of the people might be determined by consulting them, directly or through representatives. Rousseau, however, disparages this (procedural) "will of all," which often expresses only particular individual and group interests. Instead he advocates following "the general will," the reflective, rational interest of the whole people, which frequently is *not* the same as the aggregated preferences of individuals and groups.[8]

Substantive conceptions, however, tend to lose the link to the idea of the people *ruling*, rather than just benefiting. "Democratic" thus easily slides into a superfluous synonym for "egalitarian." Substantive conceptions are also subject to a variety of practical problems and abuses, ranging from overestimates of the goodness of real people to a paternalism that sees the people as needing to be directed by those with the virtue or insight required to know their "true" interests.

The tendency in recent discussions to stress procedural democracy is thus in my view generally justified. Although popular and policy discussions, especially in the United States, often overemphasize multiparty elections, leading procedural conceptions in the theoretical literature also stress mechanisms to ensure an open and unfettered electoral process. For example, Robert Dahl's "polyarchy," a common reference point in scholarly discussions, requires not only free and fair elections based on an inclusive franchise but also extensive political freedom to ensure truly open elections, including the right of all to run for office, freedom of expression, access to alternative sources of information, and freedom of association (1971; 1989).

Elections, however, no matter how free and open, are merely mechanisms for ascertaining the will of the people. Pure procedural democracy can degen-

7. There is an interesting parallel here with the distinction between having a right and being a right-less beneficiary of someone else's obligation.

8. *Social Contract*, Book II, chapter 3. Rousseau even argues that "while it is not impossible for a private will to be in accord on some point with the general will, it is impossible at least for this accord to be durable and constant. For by its nature the private will tends toward having preferences, and the general will tends toward equality." (Book II, chapter 1.)

erate into empty formalism. Substantive conceptions rightly insist that we not lose sight of the core values of popular authority and effective control over government.

Rather than extend this discussion of forms and types of democracy,[9] I want to bring it to a close by noting the important role of adjectives (e.g., substantive, procedural, electoral, direct, representative, liberal, guided, people's) in most discussions of democracy. I will argue that the human rights work of most contemporary "democracies" is rooted in substantive adjectives such as "liberal." And electoral democracy, even in a broad polyarchic sense of the term, falls far short of the demands of internationally recognized human rights.

3. Democracy and Human Rights

Democracy and human rights share a commitment to the ideal of equal political dignity for all. Furthermore, international human rights norms, as we have already noted, require democratic government. The link, however, need not run in the other direction. Democracy contributes only contingently to the realization of most human rights. Even where democracy and human rights are not in direct conflict, they often point in significantly different directions.

A. EMPOWERMENT: OF WHOM? FOR WHAT?

Democracy aims to empower the people, to ensure that they, rather than some other group in society, rule. Democracy allocates sovereign authority to the people who, because they are sovereign, are free, as the Vienna Declaration put it, "to determine their own political, economic, social and cultural systems."

Human rights, by contrast, aim to empower individuals, thus *limiting* the sovereign people and their government. The acceptable range of political, economic, social, and cultural systems and practices is severely restricted by the requirement that every person receive certain goods, services, and opportunities. Beyond who ought to rule—which is indeed given a democratic answer—human rights are concerned with what rulers do, with how the people (or any other group) rule.

Democracies as a group may on average have a better human rights record than nondemocratic regimes. Some nondemocratic states, however, perform better concerning some rights than do some democratic states. Furthermore, human rights practices among democracies vary dramatically.

Only if a sovereign people wills respect for human rights, and thus constrains its own interests and actions, will democracy contribute to realizing

9. Those interested in pursuing the diversity of definitions should begin with Collier and Levitsky (1997), which is close to exhaustive with respect to recent procedural accounts. See also Schmitter and Karl (1991).

human rights. In practice, however, the will of the people, no matter how it is ascertained, often diverges from the rights of individual citizens.[10] Electoral democracies often serve the particular interests of key constituencies. Direct democracy, as Athens dramatically illustrates, can be remarkably intolerant.

Marxist "peoples' democracies" provide a striking example of the differences in the political projects implied by "All human rights for all" and "All power to the people." The dictatorship of the proletariat, whatever the practical problems of real-world Stalinist regimes, was rooted in the classical democratic ideal, updated with a deeply egalitarian vision of the proletariat as a universal class.[11] Those claiming human rights who insisted on pursuing class (or other selfish) interests inconsistent with the interests of the people/proletariat were, in the name of democracy, to be coerced into compliance with the good of all. Any other alternative would be, in an important sense, antidemocratic.

Human rights advocates would respond, "So much the worse for democracy." In fact, human rights are in an important sense profoundly antidemocratic. For example, the U.S. Supreme Court is often criticized as being antidemocratic, because it regularly frustrates the will of the people. It does so by design. A central purpose of constitutional review is to ensure that the people, through their elected representatives, do not exercise their sovereignty in ways that violate basic rights.

At this point, if not earlier, a frustrated reader might respond that people today have in mind not ancient Greece or theorists such as Kant and Madison, let alone Marx. History and etymology inform but do not determine contemporary conceptions of democracy, which have as their standard referent governments such as those in Britain, France, Germany, India, Japan, and the United States. Fair enough. But what form of government is this?

B. LIBERAL VERSUS ELECTORAL DEMOCRACY

The standard answer from comparative politics is "liberal democracy," a very specific kind of government in which the morally and politically prior rights of citizens (and the requirement of the rule of law[12]) limit the range of democratic decision making. Democracy and human rights are mutually reinforcing in contemporary liberal democracies because the competing claims of democracy and human rights are resolved in favor of human rights.

In liberal democracies, some rights-abusive choices are denied to the people

10. One may stipulate that the people don't *really* will anything inconsistent with internationally recognized human rights. For example, Rousseau claims that the general will is always perfect and incorruptible. (*Social Contract*, Book I, chapter 3) In such a case, however, either democracy or human rights becomes superfluous.

11. For a defense of Marx's democratic credentials, see Miller (1986).

12. There is no necessary connection, however, between democracy and the rule of law. The people may choose to rule through standing, neutral laws or through some other mechanism. Conversely, non-democratic regimes in principle may (although in practice rarely do) respect the rule of law.

("Congress shall make no law . . .") and some rights-protective choices are mandated ("Everyone has the right . . ."). Democratic or popular rule operates only within the constraints set by individual human rights. The liberal commitment to individual rights, more than the democratic commitment to popular empowerment, makes contemporary liberal democracies rights-protective. The adjective "liberal"[13] rather than the noun "democracy" does most of the human rights work.

The adjective also does the human rights work in consociational democracy (Lijphart 1975). The consociational entrenchment of special rights for established social groups—for example, Catholics and Protestants in Holland, or Walloons and Flemish in Belgium—may facilitate guaranteeing human rights for all in plural societies. But, once more, the democratic logic of empowering the people is subordinated to a logic that limits what the people or their representatives may legitimately do.[14]

The struggle for liberal democracy is a struggle for human rights only because human rights have been built into the definition through the adjective. The link between electoral democracy (or democracy without adjectives) and human rights is much more tenuous. Although (electoral) democracy may remove old sources of violations, it need not take us very far toward implementing or enforcing many human rights. Establishing secure electoral democracy in, say, Indonesia or Nigeria, will only be a small (if valuable) step toward establishing rights-protective regimes.

The "democratic revolutions" of the 1980s and 1990s have undoubtedly benefited human rights. But even where antidemocratic forces have not reasserted themselves, numerous internationally recognized human rights continue to be violated systematically in a number of new but illiberal democracies. Those not part of the majority—or whatever group exercises the power of the people—still need the protection of human rights against democratic governments.

This is *not* a matter of "immature" (electoral) versus "mature" (liberal) democracies. Liberal democracy is tempered or constrained, not matured (fully developed), electoral democracy. Similar difficulties beset efforts to talk about liberal democracy as thick, full, or robust, in contrast to a thin electoral democracy. The differences are qualitative not quantitative. Rather than completing or realizing the full logic of popular rule, liberal democracy puts popular rule in its "proper" place: subordinate to human rights.

Such distinctions are of more than theoretical interest. The struggle for

13. As elsewhere in this volume, I use "liberal" to refer to theories and supporters of rights-based political systems (pretty much across the conventional left-right spectrum). See §3.5 and Dworkin (1985: ch. 8).

14. Much the same is true of corporatist regimes in which labor, residents of a particular region, or other social groups are given special status in political decision making. See, for example, Lehmbruch and Schmitter (1982).

human rights can be subtly yet significantly eroded if merely electoral democracies are treated, even implicitly, as reasonable approximations to, or a step toward the more or less automatic achievement of, liberal democracy. This is an especially important caution for American foreign policy, which grossly overemphasizes the mechanism of elections.

4. Defining Development

Definitions of development are almost as diverse as, and perhaps even more contentious than, definitions of democracy.[15] I will distinguish between conceptions that emphasize either *economic* development, understood largely in terms of growth in national productive capabilities, and those that stress *human* development, often very broadly understood.

Defining development as growth in per capita gross domestic product (GDP),[16] despite decades of criticism, continues to dominate the economic, political, and popular mainstreams. The renaissance of market-oriented economic strategies in the past two decades has increased the grip of growth conceptions of development: markets are social institutions tuned to maximize growth (aggregate output).

The most forceful and influential critics of the 1970s and early 1980s emphasized dependency. Dependency theorists argued that underdevelopment, rather than a natural, preindustrial state, is a condition of maldevelopment.[17] Although theoretically moribund today, the dependency perspective usefully focused attention on the dark distributional underside of standard growth strategies (compare James 1997).

One major mainstream response has been to emphasize long-run or sustainable growth. In addition to a broader time frame, sustainable development perspectives give attention to environmental and other "externalities" excluded from neoclassical accounts.[18] Nonetheless, this richer and more holistic understanding of economic processes still sees the capacity for autonomous increases in productive capability, and thus per capita GDP, as what is to be sustained.

More radical alternatives to growth-based understandings of development

15. A good standard textbook introduction can be found in Todaro (1994: ch. 3). Dickson (1997: Part I), although a basic introductory undergraduate text, is useful. See also Weiner (1987). Much more heterodox are Escobar (1995) and Sachs (1992). See also Grillo and Stirrat (1997), Marglin and Marglin (1990), and Hobart (1993).

16. Classic examples include Rostow (1960) and Chenery and Syrquin (1975). Roxborough (1979) provides a standard critical overview.

17. Cardoso and Faletto (1979) are often considered to provide the most subtle and powerful statement of the perspective. The best brief analytical overview remains Palma (1977).

18. See, for example, United Nations Conference on Environment and Development (1993), Faucheux, O'Connor, and Staaten (1998), Kirkpatrick and Lee (1997), Taylor and Pieper (1996), and Lemons and Brown (1995).

have emphasized equity or social justice rather than narrowly "economic" processes. UNDP's vision of "sustainable human development" provides the current culmination of this movement:

> We define human development as expanding the choices for all people in society. . . . There are five aspects to sustainable human development—all affecting the lives of the poor and vulnerable:
>
> Empowerment—The expansion of men and women's capabilities and choices increases their ability to exercise those choices free of hunger, want and deprivation. It also increases their opportunity to participate in, or endorse, decision-making affecting their lives.
>
> Co-operation—With a sense of belonging important for personal fulfillment, well-being and a sense of purpose and meaning, human development is concerned with the ways in which people work together and interact.
>
> Equity—The expansion of capabilities and opportunities means more than income—it also means equity, such as an educational system to which everybody should have access.
>
> Sustainability—The needs of this generation must be met without compromising the right of future generations to be free of poverty and deprivation and to exercise their basic capabilities.
>
> Security—Particularly the security of livelihood. People need to be freed from threats, such as disease or repression and from sudden harmful disruptions in their lives. (1997: chap. 1; compare Anand and Sen [1996]; Nussbaum [1996])

Although I have considerable sympathy with the motives behind such efforts, I reject them for my purposes here on analytic grounds. "Human rights and sustainable human development are inextricably linked" (UNDP 1998) only by definitional legerdemain. "Sustainable human development" simply redefines human rights, along with democracy, peace, and justice, as subsets of development. Aside from the fact that few ordinary people or governments use the term in this way, such a definition leaves unaddressed the relationship between human rights and *economic* development, an important domain of contemporary social action and aspiration. Real tensions between these objectives cannot be evaded by stipulative definitions.

Less radical equity-oriented conceptions face similar problems.[19] For ex-

19. For example, UNDP's annual *Human Development Report* uses a measure that combines per capita GDP with life expectancy and literacy. Although better than GDP alone, it fails to address the relationship between the social and economic indicators of "human development," which reflect very different political logics.

ample, "redistribution with growth" is indeed a desirable objective, but it involves two processes, redistribution and growth, that sometimes support and sometimes conflict with each another. As with liberal democracy, two fundamentally different social and political logics are combined. Although I endorse this combination no less heartily than I endorse liberal democracy, there are analytical and political reasons to draw attention to the differences between the logics of growth and redistribution. Thus by "development" I will mean sustainable growth of per capita GDP.[20]

5. Development-Rights Trade-offs

The contemporary tendency to conflate all good things—reflected not only in discussions of sustainable human development but in some of the more extravagant recent accounts of human security (see §14.5)—stands in sharp contrast to the conventional wisdom of the Cold War era. Human rights advocates then regularly faced the argument, advanced with considerable vigor from both ends of the political spectrum, that

> the necessity of development . . . supersedes all other legitimate claims and prior rights" (Ruffin 1982: 122).
>
> Impressive economic performance . . . in the modern period has depended upon massive poverty and political repression, and it would not have been possible under democratic governments pursuing egalitarian economic policies. (Hewlett 1980: 4)
>
> The tough political systems associated with successes (in satisfying basic needs) . . . have not so far had a good record in terms of liberal virtues. . . . a more liberal political system may be incapable of producing and sustaining the reorientation in the economy necessary for these types of success. (Stewart 1985)

Development was regularly held to conflict with human rights, at least in the short-and medium-run time frames within which politicians and development planners operate.

20. One final definitional issue should be noted. The 1986 Declaration on the Right to Development (General Assembly resolution 41/128) rests on a conception of development that is as broad as "sustainable human development," and poses similar analytical drawbacks. Elsewhere (Donnelly 1985; 1993) I have argued, at length, against the moral, political, legal, and analytical wisdom of recognizing such a human right. Here I simply note that the human right to development fails to address the relationship between *economic* development and the human rights specified in the Universal Declaration and the Covenants.

Such arguments have not disappeared from national and international discussions. As we saw in §7.2, they remain a staple in the self-justifications of rights-abusive Asian regimes. They are also an implicit element of the standard structural adjustment package imposed by the International Monetary Fund. Trade-off arguments therefore continue to deserve (critical) attention, which I offer in this section.

Three trade-offs have been widely advocated:

1. *The needs trade-off.*[21] Rather than devote scarce resources to social programs to satisfy basic human needs (and associated human rights to, for example, food and health care), relatively high levels of absolute poverty (need deprivation) must be accepted to maximize investment. This forgone consumption, however, will be returned with interest in the additional production purchased, thereby minimizing the total economic and human cost of overcoming mass poverty. A "strong" needs trade-off attempts to constrain and control consumption to capture the largest possible share of total resources for investment. A "weak" needs trade-off simply excludes consumption-oriented human rights from development planning.
2. *The equality trade-off.*[22] A "weak" equality trade-off is based on the so-called Kuznets (1955) or (inverted) U hypothesis. Both average incomes and income inequality tend to be lower in the "traditional" sector than in the "modern" sector. Therefore, during the transition to a modern economy, inequality in the size distribution of income will first increase, then be maintained at a high level, and finally recede at moderately high levels of national income, thus producing a U-shaped curve when inequality is plotted against the GNP.
   A "strong" equality trade-off sees inequality as a contributor to, not just an unavoidable consequence of, development. Because only the relatively well-to-do can afford to save and invest, and because investment is the key to rapid growth, inequality is often held to be in the long-run best interest of the poor. Inequality is also often justified as an incentive or reward for superior economic performance.

21. "An autonomous reduction in consumption . . . is the human price that must be paid for a rapidly growing domestic national product" (Enke 1963: 181). "A conscious effort must be made to increase savings, either from existing incomes or by capturing a major share of the rising incomes that result from inducing greater effort and productivity" (Morriss 1967: 306).

22. "Equality, in other words, is a luxury of rich countries. If a poor society is to achieve anything at all it must develop a high degree of inequality—the small economic surplus must be concentrated in a few hands if any high-level achievements are to be made" (Boulding 1958). "There is likely to be a conflict between rapid growth and an equitable distribution of income; and a poor country anxious to develop would probably be well advised not to worry too much about the distribution of income" (Johnson 1962: 153).

3. *The liberty trade-off.*[23] The exercise of civil and political rights may disrupt or threaten to destroy even the best-laid development plan. Elected officials may feel pressured to select policies based on short-run political expediency rather than insist on economically essential but politically unpopular sacrifices; freedoms of speech, press, and assembly may be exercised so as to create or inflame social division, which an already fragile polity may be unable to endure; free trade unions may merely seek additional special benefits for a labor aristocracy; elaborate and punctilious legal systems on the Western model may seem to be extravagant anachronisms; and so forth. Civil and political liberties, it is therefore argued, must be (temporarily) suspended.

All three trade-offs have been widely held to be not only necessary but also temporary and self-correcting. The trickle-down theory of growth is a theory of eventual automatic returns to the poor. The U hypothesis envisions an automatic return to greater equality. And growth and development have been widely held to be crucial to establishing, maintaining, and expanding liberty in the Third World. So long as rapid growth was achieved, it was expected that everything else would take care of itself. Each of these trade-offs thus implies "growth first" development strategies.

Over the past three decades there has been a growing awareness that this "conventional wisdom" was (and remains) tragically misguided. Particular sacrifices of human rights may contribute to development, but categorical trade-offs are almost always unnecessary and often positively harmful. Human rights trade-offs, except perhaps at the very early stages of the move from a "traditional" to a "modern" economy,[24] are not development imperatives but policy choices undertaken for largely political, not technical economic, reasons.

It is relatively easy to make such an argument in the case of the needs and equality trade-offs on the basis of the so-called East Asian model of development.[25] South Korea and Taiwan—which, it must be remembered, in the 1950s were generally seen as relatively *un*likely cases for development success—achieved extremely rapid growth and substantial structural transformation of their economies without gross income inequality (as measured by international comparisons) and with steadily improving basic needs satisfaction

23. See, e.g., Lipset (1959), Bayley (1964), Apter (1965), Bhagwati (1966), Huntington (1968), and Huntington and Nelson (1976).

24. I canvassed such an argument, not entirely unsympathetically, in sections 2 and 3 of Chapter 10 of the first edition of this book.

25. Much of Chapter 9 of the first edition was devoted to developing just such an argument, in some detail, in the case of South Korea.

pretty much across the entire income distribution.[26] There is considerable, often vociferous, debate over the sources and causes of this performance and the extent to which it may be replicable elsewhere. Nonetheless, it is clear that in at least certain circumstances, aggressive policy interventions[27] are able to harmonize the pursuit of growth and economic and social rights.

6. Development and Civil and Political Rights

The liberty trade-off is more problematic (for my argument). There is a strong historical correlation between repression and the early stages of rapid economic growth and structural economic transformation. It is unclear, however, whether the relationship is causal. And I think that it is very difficult to argue convincingly that repression has been necessary for development, rather than convenient for those in charge of the state and the economy. (Let me immediately add, however, that it is no less difficult to argue convincingly that it is not necessary.)

It would appear to be extremely difficult, perhaps impossible, to avoid some repression. I would suggest, however, that this may be due as much as anything to the fact that peaceful structural change of any sort is difficult (especially when it cannot be buffered by the side payments to disadvantaged groups that a high level of development makes possible). Although often functional for *particular* "development" strategies, most repression, rather than an economic necessity, appears to be rooted instead in contingent local political opportunities, problems, and challenges and the particular interests of those doing the repressing.

Development strategies involve both repression, inequality, and needs deprivation and liberty, equality, and needs satisfaction only contingently. Sustainable industrial growth has been achieved by repressive regimes in South Korea, Taiwan, Singapore, and China in recent decades, replicating the earlier experience of Western Europe. Most developmental dictatorships, however, have been dismal failures. In sub-Saharan Africa, even short-term growth rarely was

26. On the East Asian combination of growth, needs satisfaction, and relative income equality see, for example, Leipziger and Thomas (1997), Campos and Root (1996), Rowen (1998), and Goodman, White, and Kwon (1998).

27. Although these countries followed an outward-looking export-oriented development strategy that explicitly incorporated certain international market signals into the planning process, internal markets were not even close to "free" and the relationship to international markets was highly managed. Furthermore, the equity benefits were substantially dependent on relatively aggressive policy interventions to redistribute resources to rural areas. It is crucial to recognize "the strategic role of states in directing a process of economic development with distributive as well as growth objectives, resulting in a relatively egalitarian pattern of income distribution compared with other industrializing regions such as Latin America" (White and Goodman 1998: 13).

achieved. In socialist party-state dictatorships, along with most Latin American and Asian military dictatorships and civilian oligarchies, short-and medium-run growth proved unsustainable. Those forced to sacrifice personal rights and liberties usually have not received development (sustainable growth) in return.

In large measure because of this experience, blanket advocacy of the liberty trade-off—a staple of the 1960s and 1970s—is rarely encountered today.[28] "Soft" authoritarianism still receives some respect, especially when, as in Singapore, promised economic goods are delivered. The growing tendency, however, is to emphasize compatibilities between civil and political rights and development. For example, international financial institutions since the 1990s have increasingly emphasized the economic contributions of "good governance."[29]

Even where sustained economic development has been achieved by highly repressive regimes, there is little evidence that repression has been *necessary* for, rather than not incompatible with, development. Therefore, because the liberty trade-off is intrinsically undesirable, it is entirely appropriate to emphasize, and explore the conditions that allow for or encourage, the compatibility between civil and political rights and economic development.

If this is even close to correct, we need to turn our attention—for the liberty trade-off no less than the needs and equality trade-offs—away from general arguments toward detailed empirical studies of the conditions in which human rights and development are and are not competing goals. That, however, is work for economists and country specialists, not human rights theorists. What I can offer instead is a critique of contemporary mirror-image arguments that suggest a necessarily positive relationship between human rights and development.

7. Markets and Economic and Social Rights

The relationship between development and economic and social rights is complex, especially when we consider the role of markets. Markets are social institutions designed to produce economic efficiency. Countries such as Cuba and Sri Lanka, which achieved short- and medium-run success but long-run failure under development plans emphasizing state-based (re)distribution, suggest that a considerable degree of economic efficiency (and thus reliance on markets) is necessary for *sustainable* progress in implementing economic and social rights.

28. China is the major exception that proves the rule. When the rhetoric is repeated in places like North Korea, Burma, and Belarus, few take it seriously, either inside or outside the country.

29. Perhaps the most important multilateral statement is World Bank (1992). See also Stiefel and Wolfe (1994) and Ginter, Denters, and Waart (1995).

Nonetheless, the contemporary enthusiasm for markets, especially in the United States, is extremely problematic from a human rights perspective. Like (pure) democracy, (free) markets are justified by arguments for collective good and aggregate benefit, not individual human rights. Markets foster efficiency, but not social equity or the enjoyment of individual rights *for all.* Rather than ensure that people are treated with equal concern and respect, markets systematically disadvantage some individuals to achieve the collective benefits of efficiency.

Markets, by design, distribute growth without regard for individual needs and rights (other than property rights). Market distributions reflect economic value added, which varies systematically across social groups (as well as between individuals). The poor tend to be "less efficient"; as a class, they have fewer of the skills valued highly by markets. Their plight is exacerbated when political disadvantage reinforces a vicious rights-abusive cycle of exclusion.

Market advocates typically argue that in return for such short-run disadvantages for the few, everyone benefits from the greater supply of goods and services made available through growth. "Everyone," however, does not mean each (every) person. The referent instead is the *average* "individual," an abstract collective entity. And even "he" is assured gain only in the future. In the here and now, and well into the future, many human beings and families suffer.

Efficient markets improve the lot of some—ideally even the many—at the cost of (relative and perhaps even absolute) deprivation of others. And that suffering is concentrated among society's most vulnerable elements. Even worse, because markets distribute the benefits of growth without regard to short-term deprivations, those who suffer "adjustment costs"—lost jobs, higher food prices, inferior health care—acquire no special claim to a share of the collective benefits of efficient markets. One's "fair share" is measured solely in terms of efficiency, of monetary value added. The human value of suffering, the human costs of deprivation, and the claims they justify are outside the accounting of markets.

All existing liberal democracies use the welfare state to compensate (some of) those who fare less well in the market. Individuals who are harmed by the operation of social institutions (markets and private property rights) that benefit the whole are entitled to a fair share of the social product their participation has helped to produce. The collectivity that benefits in the aggregate has an obligation to look after individual members who are disadvantaged in or harmed by markets. The welfare state guarantees *all* individuals certain economic and social goods, services, and opportunities irrespective of the market value of their labor.

Assuaging short-term suffering and ensuring long-term recompense—which are matters of justice, rights, and obligations, not efficiency—are the work of the (welfare) state, not the market. They raise issues of individual rights that markets simply cannot address them—because they are not designed to do so.

Free markets are an economic analog to a political system of majority rule without minority rights. Like pure democracy, free markets sacrifice individuals and their rights to a "higher" collective good. The welfare state, from this perspective, is a device to ensure that a minority that is disadvantaged in or deprived by markets is treated with minimum economic concern and respect. Because this minority is shifting and indeterminate—much like the minority that would engage in unpopular political speech or be subject to arbitrary arrest—these "minority rights" are defined as individual rights for all.

Human rights are required to civilize both democracy and markets by restricting their operation to a limited, rights-defined domain. Only when the pursuit of prosperity is tamed by economic and social rights—when markets are embedded in a welfare state—does a political economy merit our respect.

8. The Liberal Democratic Welfare State

The liberal democratic welfare states of Western Europe, Japan, and North America are attractive models for much of the rest of the world because of the particular balance they strike among the competing demands of democratic participation, market efficiency, and internationally recognized human rights. But democracy and development, in the absence of a prior commitment to the full range of internationally recognized human rights, lose much of their attraction.

Democracy is almost always preferable to authoritarian rule.[30] Liberal democracy, however, is preferable to (merely) electoral democracy. Markets are preferable to command economies. Welfare states, however, are preferable to free markets. In both cases, a logic of universal individual rights constrains an essentially collectivist, utilitarian logic of aggregate benefits in order to ensure that the common good or good of all is pursued in ways that are consistent with the rights of each.

All actual liberal democratic welfare states fall short of realizing all human rights even for all their own nationals. Nonetheless, only such states are systematically committed to the full range of internationally recognized human rights. Only in such states do robust markets and democracies operate within systematic limits set by human rights. And only (or at least primarily) because of such limits are their markets and democracies worthy of emulation.

If the deepest and broadest attractions of the regimes we most admire arise

30. A free people may reasonably choose an efficient benevolent autocrat over a corrupt incompetent democratic regime. Rarely, however, will such a choice actually be faced (or even available).

from their commitment and contribution to human rights, we need to keep that in the forefront of the language by which we speak of them. If we are really interested in regimes that protect the full range of internationally recognized human rights—which is what I think most well-meaning Western advocates of "democracy" have in mind—why not just say that? Why take the risk of being misread, or glossing over the crucial qualifying adjectives, by talking about democracy? My argument might then be reformulated as a plea for a focus on the creation of rights-protective regimes, as defined by the Universal Declaration of Human Rights.

Those regimes will be democratic. They are desirable, however, because we think that we have good reason to believe that empowering the people is the best political mechanism we have yet devised to secure all human rights for all. Rights-protective regimes will also pursue economic development. But development is desirable as much for the resources it makes available to provide economic and social rights for members of disadvantaged groups as for the intrinsic value of the goods produced.

Countless people over hundreds of years have struggled and suffered for democracy and development. Usually, though, they have seen them not as ends but as means to a life of dignity. Contemporary international society has in substantial measure defined such a life of dignity in terms of respect for internationally recognized human rights. My plea is to keep human rights, and thus this particular understanding of the substantive commitment to human dignity, explicitly central in our political language.

In (over)emphasizing tensions between human rights and democracy and development I have tried to underscore the dangers of what I have suggested amounts to a confusion of means (markets and elections) with ends (human rights, and through them human dignity). Unless we keep human rights explicitly at the center of the discussion, we will place needless conceptual and practical hurdles in the pursuit of such policies that seek equal concern and respect for all.

12/ Group Rights and Human Rights

A standard complaint about human rights, and about liberal visions of human rights in particular, is that they are excessively individualistic (see, e.g., §7.4). Group (human) rights are a frequently advanced solution. I will argue, however, that neither liberal theory nor Western liberal practice is characterized by extreme or corrosive individualism. Furthermore, group human rights are fraught with theoretical and practical difficulties. Liberal human rights approaches usually are capable of accommodating the legitimate interests of even oppressed groups—and where they are not, group human rights rarely are more likely to provide an effective remedy.

1. Individual and Community

"Since the late eighteenth century it has become a commonplace in liberal societies to assert that individuals possess rights . . . that are inalienable and unconditional" (Brown 1999: 104). Modern natural rights theories have made "the individual, the ego, . . . the center and origin of the moral world" (Strauss 1953: 248). Such claims are, at best, grossly misleading caricatures.

A world of unconditional rights and unchecked egoism would indeed be horrible. Such a world, however, is not properly associated, in theory or practice, with either social contract liberalism or the Universal Declaration model (see §3.3-5). It certainly does not flow inevitably from a commitment to individual human rights, and it is not, in practice, the world of liberal rights-protective regimes in the contemporary West.

As we saw in Chapter 1, rights are a social practice that creates systems of obligations between people and groups. It is precisely because Hobbes's state of nature includes no obligations[1] that life is solitary, poor, nasty, brutish, and short. Systems of rights are a solution to, rather than a cause of, atomistic egoism.

1. Hobbes's right of everyone to everything (*Leviathan*, chap. 13) is equivalent to no one having a right to anything, because this "natural right" imposes no obligations on others (who *also* have a right to everything).

Liberal human rights are not "unconditional" rights. For there to be such things, either all human rights would have to be lexically ordered, which they clearly are not, or there must be (even more implausibly) but one human right.

Human rights are not "considerations overriding all other considerations" or "absolutes to be defended in all circumstances" (Brown 1999: 109, 110). Rights, even understood as "trumps" (see §1.1.A), have (only) a *prima facie* priority over utility, social policy, and other considerations. They themselves are sometimes, in the end, "trumped."[2] To repeat the standard example from American constitutional jurisprudence, the right to free speech does not extend to yelling "Fire!" in a crowded theater. The International Covenant on Civil and Political Rights permits derogations from most enumerated rights. The International Covenant on Economic, Social, and Cultural Rights requires that the rights recognized therein be implemented progressively rather than immediately.

Rights-based societies can be, have been, and are societies, not aggregates of possessive, egoistic atoms.[3] However one evaluates the balance struck by particular liberal theories or regimes between the claims of individual rights and the rights and interests of society or other social groups, it is clear that all liberal theories and states balance the competing claims of individuals and communities. Liberal individual rights no more require possessive individualism and atomistic egoism than communitarianism requires that individuals be seen as ciphers or cells that have no value apart from the organic whole of society.

2. Liberal Approaches to Group Difference

Although most liberals, and the Universal Declaration model, do deny human rights to groups, they assume that individuals will exercise many rights as members of "natural" and voluntary groups. Many internationally recognized human rights are of special interest and value to marginalized or despised groups. Freedoms of thought, conscience, religion, opinion, and expression protect group, as well as individual, differences. Family rights protect the transmission of group beliefs and practices. I will argue that a liberal individual-rights approach offers the most effective general strategy in the contemporary world for remedying the sufferings of members of despised, oppressed, or disadvantaged groups.

Communitarians see individuals, and the rights and other social options

2. This is not to "abdicate at the outset" against relativist arguments (Morris 2001: 69), but rather to understand clearly how (human) rights function. To insist on human rights being absolute or unconditional is at best misinformed.

3. For a detailed argument against Macpherson's "possessive individualist" (1962) reading of Locke, perhaps the most influential recent effort to depict liberalism as committed to something very much like a single unconditional right (to private property), see Donnelly (1989: chap. 5).

available to them, as in some significant measure appropriately defined by their group membership. Liberal visions of human rights, by contrast, see group affiliations as largely irrelevant to the rights and opportunities that ought to be available to individuals. This general prohibition of discrimination is powerfully supplemented by rights, such as freedom of expression, belief, and assembly, that specify particularly important activities where the state must respect individual autonomy, whether it is exercised in private or in public or alone or in association with others.

A. NONDISCRIMINATION

We can distinguish three ideal type interpretations of the requirement of nondiscrimination, which I will call toleration, equal protection, and multiculturalism. Toleration requires not imposing disabilities on individuals based on (voluntary, ascriptive, or imposed) group membership or disapproved behavior associated with a group. Toleration involves a principled political decision not to impose special burdens on (members of) despised groups, but they may still be marginalized and socially excluded.

Equal protection requires active efforts to ensure that members of all groups enjoy the (equal) rights that they formally hold. At minimum this requires efforts to ensure that people are not excluded from goods, services, and opportunities that would be available to them were they not members of despised or disadvantaged groups. In its stronger forms—"affirmative action" and certain kinds of "reverse discrimination"—equal protection seeks to ensure that members of targeted groups achieve full legal and political incorporation into society.

Equal protection, however, allows a neutral, even negative, evaluation of diversity. "Multiculturalism" positively values diversity, implying policies that recognize, celebrate, preserve, or foster group differences. Rather than attempt to abstract from group differences, as in toleration and equal treatment, those differences are highlighted and positively valued, within a general context of equal concern and respect.

B. NEUTRALITY AND DIFFERENCE

The legitimacy of the liberal state is defined by its respect for, and endeavors to ensure the realization of, the human rights of its citizens. The (other) purposes of the state thus ordinarily are subordinated to the rights of its citizens. This subordination is often expressed in the claim that the liberal state must be neutral with respect to the values, interests, and life plans of its citizens, in so far as they are rooted in protected autonomous exercises of human rights (see §3.5.B).

Such respect for individual autonomy reflects not indifference to the decisions of citizens but rather an active commitment to fostering their enjoyment of their rights. And liberal neutrality operates only within the boundaries of human rights. To require identical treatment of *all* individual or group differences—consider, for example, pedophiles, violent racists, those who derive pleasure from kidnapping and torturing strangers, and religious missionaries committed to killing those they cannot convert—would be perverse.

The overlapping consensus on the Universal Declaration model does not (and should not) imply neutrality toward all possible views and practices. "Liberalism is not a possible meeting ground for all cultures, but is the political expression of one range of cultures, and quite incompatible with other ranges" (Taylor 1994: 62). Neutrality must be interpreted as an expression of the core value of equal concern and respect.

The liberal state—and the rights-protective regime envisioned in the Universal Declaration model—is required to be neutral with respect to (that is, not discriminate against) exercises of human rights. It is required *not* to be neutral toward activities that infringe or violate human rights, and it is at liberty to be neutral or not, as it sees fit, toward activities that are neither protected nor prohibited by human rights.

A (liberal) state must not discriminate, for example, against any religion, but it need not be neutral toward (show equal concern and respect for) all conceptions of the purpose of sport (which are not ordinarily understood to be protected by internationally recognized human rights). Equal concern and respect is required for all political beliefs but not for all beliefs about the origin of life. Creationism based on a literal reading of *Genesis,* for example, must be protected in so far as it reflects an exercise of human rights to freedoms of religion and speech. It need not—probably should not—be treated equally in science classes or natural history museums.

Each state/society has considerable latitude in how it treats, for example, particular minority religions. It would be completely consistent with international human rights standards to (merely) tolerate minority religion A while actively supporting the majority religion and minority religion B. Such decisions fall within the margin of appreciation left to states by the broadly stated norms of the Universal Declaration (see §6.4). States may choose to treat all religions identically—for example, no state support for any, as in the United States—but that is not required by the Universal Declaration model.

As Michael Walzer nicely puts it, liberalism is "permissive, not determinative." It

> allows for a state committed to the survival and flourishing of a particular nation, culture, or religion, or of a (limited) set of nations, cultures, and religions—so long as the basic rights of citizens who have different commitments or no such commitments at all are protected (1994: 99–100).

There is not merely a place for difference within a liberal approach to human rights, the protection of (many forms of) difference is one of the most important political objectives of a liberal state—because, and to the extent that, its citizens value and seek to create for themselves lives that produce such diversity.

C. FREEDOM OF ASSOCIATION AND GUARANTEED PARTICIPATION

Nondiscrimination, however, is only one part of the liberal approach to difference. Remedying systematic discrimination usually requires collective action, which in the Universal Declaration model is enabled by rights to freedom of association and to economic, social, cultural, and political participation. Freedom of association and rights of participation entitle individuals to act, alone or with others of their own choosing, to realize their visions of the good life. Taken together with rights to nondiscrimination, these rights provide a wide-ranging and coherent set of protections for groups and individuals rooted in the core (liberal and human rights) values of equality and autonomy.

Freedom of association, because it is a right of individuals, models group membership as a "voluntary" exercise of the protected autonomy of its members. Descriptively, this is obviously inaccurate for groups whose identity is in significant measure externally imposed. It may also be problematic for groups marked by biological signs such as skin color or sex—although, it must be emphasized, race and gender are social constructs and not natural categories. Nonetheless, a liberal rights approach has considerable leverage even in such cases.

When individuals are subjected to suffering without any voluntary association with the group in question, nondiscrimination often provides the appropriate remedy. When victims of discrimination begin to act collectively to realize their interests or protect their rights, freedom of association usually moves to the forefront of the struggle for equality and social justice. For all its problems, a vision of group membership as a voluntary exercise of protected individual autonomy challenges coercively imposed ascriptive identities, denies the naturalness of difference, and insists that group membership ought to be irrelevant to the concern and respect one receives from the state.

3. Group Human Rights: A Skeptical View

Even granting that a liberal human rights approach has much to offer to oppressed groups, one might still argue for augmenting it with group human rights. Group human rights thus understood would supplement, perhaps even complete, the Universal Declaration model by providing a more adequate vision of and protections for human dignity in the contemporary world. In this section I pose seven questions that I think should lead us to be extremely wary of such a move.[4]

1. How do we identify the groups that (ought to) hold human rights? This question has a practical dimension. Unless we can restrict the range of collective right-holders, we are likely to be swamped in a wild proliferation of human rights that would devalue the practical force of claims of human rights. In any case, not *all* groups ought to have human rights. Consider, for example, states, multinational corporations, gangs, and barbershop quartets. Suppose that we were to agree that it would be desirable for, say, minorities to have group human rights. By what criteria could we legitimately grant rights to minorities but not to other groups? Although not necessarily an intractable problem, it is an important one that advocates of group rights have largely ignored.

   The most obvious criterion, namely, a long history of ongoing, systematic suffering, would yield group human rights for women, (racial, ethnic, religious, and linguistic) minorities, indigenous peoples, homosexuals, the disabled, the aged, children, and the poor, to mention just some of the more prominent groups. Pretty much everyone except prosperous white Western males—and many of them as well—would have group human rights. Such a radical expansion of right-holders and associated claims of rights seem to me extremely problematic.
2. Having identified group *x* as a potential holder of human rights, what particular substantive rights does/should *x* have? Certainly it is not enough that *x* wants *r* in order to establish a (human) right of *x* to *r* (compare Galenkamp 1996). On what grounds can we say that others do or do not owe *r* to *x as a matter of (human) rights*? This is another problem to which advocates of group human rights have given shockingly little attention.

   The most limited move would be to recognize those rights needed to enjoy already recognized human rights. These, however, would be only temporary, remedial measures and thus probably best seen as practical measures to achieve nondiscrimination. A more interesting class of group rights would appeal instead to the particular character of the group or to values or attributes not already recognized. Such claims need to be evaluated on a case-by-case basis. But, once more, to avoid debasing the currency of

4. To be as clear as possible at the outset, I want to emphasize that I do not argue that we should treat any of the issues raised "on a purely individual basis" (Henrard 2000: 241). An individual rights strategy is still a social strategy. I argue only against groups as holders of human rights. I am not even arguing against recognizing legal (rather than human) rights for groups.

human rights with a flood of new, unregulated coinage, it seems appropriate to place a substantial burden of proof on advocates of such rights.

3. Who exercises group rights? As we saw in §1.1.B, rights work not simply by being voluntarily respected by duty-bearers but, most important, by being exercised by right-holders. The rights of states are exercised by governments and the rights of business corporations, by shareholders, directors, and managers. Who ought—and is able—to exercise, for example, minority rights, understood as rights of a group?

The problems of group agency may be modest for small, concentrated, and homogenous groups with a strong tradition of collective action. (Indigenous peoples come readily to mind.) When the group is largely voluntary (e.g., some religious minorities) the officers of the association (e.g., a clerical hierarchy) may be a plausible agent. Where the group is "natural," ascribed, or coercively defined and maintained, however, agency is likely to be highly problematic, especially when the group is large or heterogeneous.[5] The "solution" of having group rights exercised by individuals or associations of group members, beyond its irony, raises serious questions as to whether such rights really are *group* rights, rather than collective exercises of individual rights.

4. How do we handle conflicts of rights? Although all rights conflict with at least some other rights or important social interests, group rights would not only increase the number of conflicts but also create unusually intense competition between qualitatively different kinds of rights. How should we respond, for example, to a native North American tribe that denies equal treatment to women if women challenge this discrimination? Related issues may be raised by defining who is (and is not) in the group. Especially problematic from a human rights perspective are efforts to block or punish exit from the group.

5. Are the purported group rights necessary? Is the problem a lack of group rights or, rather, inadequate efforts to implement individual human rights? Most often, it seems to me, it is the latter. Once more, the burden of proof ought to lie with advocates of group rights.

6. Why should we expect group rights to succeed where individual rights have failed? If a government refuses to respect the individual rights of a despised minority, it will usually (although perhaps not always) be hard to imagine it being convinced to treat those people better as members of a group. In fact, if the difference between "us" and "them" is emphasized by group rights, might this not lead to even worse treatment?

5. For a thoughtful and balanced philosophical discussion of the problem of group agency in the context of rights, see Nickel (1997).

7. Are group *rights* the best way to protect or realize the interests, values, or desires of a group? "Proponents of collective rights . . . often seem to move in a rather cursory way from the claim that communities are good things to the claim that communities have rights" (Hartney 1995: 203). We must demand an argument for protecting the values in question through the mechanism of rights. In particular, we must ask whether recognizing a new group *human* right—which by definition would hold against all states for all groups of the designated type—is either necessary or desirable.

None of these problems is fatal. Many are largely matters of "negative externalities," undesirable unintended consequences, where the calculus of costs and benefits may vary dramatically with circumstances. Some claims for group human rights may overcome all of these problems. (In §7 I suggest that may be true for at least some indigenous peoples.) Nonetheless, the above discussion does caution *prima facie* skepticism toward (although not automatic rejection of) most (but not necessarily all) group human rights claims. At the very least, we should insist on clarity in specifying the "gap" in the Universal Declaration model that is being addressed and pay careful attention to unintended consequences of the proposed remedy.

4. Women

This section and the following one briefly examine group human rights claims for two typically oppressed groups: women[6] and minorities. In each case I argue that such rights are unnecessary, unworkable, or even counterproductive.

Although women have a sad history of near-universal, systematic suffering in virtually every area of the globe, the idea of group human rights for women is fatally undermined by problems of collective agency for a diverse group that includes half of humanity.[7] It is also unclear what rights women as

6. I do not mean to suggest by what follows any critique of the movement for women's human rights. I consider this example because it seems that if any group has suffered consistently throughout history it is women, and thus they would seem to be strong candidates for group rights. That they are not ordinarily treated in this way—this section considers some of the reasons—seems to me to cut strongly against most standard arguments for group rights.

7. Groups of women in particular localities or concerned with particular issues may have the necessary collective personality, but nondiscrimination and freedom of association usually will allow such groups to act effectively.

a group might be held to possess. Unless we accept gender roles that postulate qualitative differences between men and women, the obvious candidates for special women's rights seem to me best formulated in gender-neutral terms.[8]

For example, family rights, reproductive rights, and protection against domestic violence are not special rights of women. Although the majority of adult victims of violence in the home are women, this no more makes protection against domestic violence a (group) right of women than the fact that the majority of those exercising or suffering violations of trade union rights are men makes the right to bargain collectively a (group) right of men. The principle in each case is independent of sex or gender. No one should be subject to violent assault by anyone, including a domestic partner. Everyone is entitled to bargain collectively.

In practice, of course, women in all countries continue to suffer (more or less severe) deprivations and indignities *as women*. But this simply does not entail the appropriateness, let alone the necessity, of group human rights. Compare workers who suffer as workers and political dissidents who suffer as dissidents.

Suppose, though, that we were to grant women as a group special collective human rights. Why should we expect these rights to be better implemented than already established rights? Especially in light of the insurmountable problems of collective agency, such rights would most likely turn out to be, at best, irrelevant abstractions—when they were not used by patriarchal forces to divert attention and resources away from efforts to establish true nondiscrimination and equal participation for women in all aspects of society.

5. Minorities[9]

Internationally recognized individual human rights can contribute greatly to maintaining and transmitting minority identities. For example, freedoms of religion, expression, and association greatly facilitate expressing and developing religious identity, particularly where families control education. Linguistic

8. This is true even of childbearing: not all women choose to or are capable of bearing children. And the needs of pregnant or potentially pregnant women, it seems to me, can be handled largely within the existing framework of the Universal Declaration.

9. To evade controversy over the term "minorities" (see Henrard 2000: 16–55), I will follow Article 27 of the International Covenant on Civil and Political Rights, which restricts minority rights to "ethnic, religious or linguistic minorities." Racial minorities have been treated in international human rights law separately and with a greater sense of importance and urgency (see §9.5.B), and other minority groups have been largely excluded. On homosexuals, see Chapter 13. In international human rights law, it is decidedly *not* the case that all "minorities," in the broad sense of that term, are treated equally.

minorities can readily argue that it is discriminatory to provide access to public services—including schooling—only in a dominant language.

Advocates of group rights for minorities, however, typically envision much more extensive protections for group identity. Consider Jacob Levy's typology of cultural rights: exemptions, assistance, self-government, external rules restricting nonmembers, internal rules controlling members, recognition or enforcement of traditional rules, minority representation in government bodies, and symbolic acknowledgement of worth or status (1997: 25). Nondiscrimination and freedom of association principally encompass measures involving exemptions, assistance, symbolic acknowledgment, and some forms of external rules on outsiders. Group rights claims, by contrast, are most likely to lie in the other categories.

Are *all* minorities, as a matter of human rights, entitled to, for example, self-government or guaranteed group representation in governmental bodies? A just society may legitimately choose to grant some form of self-government to particular minorities, but is it required to do so (for every minority)? Is the failure of a society to provide minority self-government really appropriately seen as a human rights violation? I think that the answer is clearly no. I can see no reason that minorities, or any other group, should be universally entitled to self-government, or even guaranteed group political representation. Nor am I aware of any morally attractive principle that would grant such rights to minorities that does not also grant them to an impractically large number of other groups as well.

Should minority communities have guaranteed legal rights to discipline members? Because we are dealing with a putative human right, the issue is not whether it is permissible or desirable in particular cases to recognize such legal rights, but whether all minorities everywhere are entitled to such powers over their members. The answer seems to me clear: they are not.

Particular groups that function as free associations of individuals might legitimately have such a right (although not a *human* right). Voluntary membership is readily conceived as implying acceptance of discipline by the group, and by allowing effective exit options, conflicts between the human rights of individuals and the group rights of minorities could be moderated to perhaps acceptable levels. Under any other interpretation, however, individual rights would be subordinated to the group rights of the minority. I can see no reason that minorities should have such superior rights—which are, I think rightly, denied to other groups.

I am not, let me repeat, challenging the idea of minority rights as they are already established in the major international human rights instruments (i.e., as individual rights that provide special protections to members of minority groups). I am not even challenging group rights for minorities. For example, the Singaporean practice of reserving legislative seats for representatives of Hindu and Malay communities clearly is (and ought to remain) defensible on human rights grounds. Rather, I am questioning the idea of group *human* rights for minorities, the requirement that all states must recognize group rights for all minorities.

Singapore's system of reserved legislative seats, or India's more extensive system of reservations for (members of) scheduled castes and tribes, falls within the realm of discretion allowed states in discharging their human rights obligations and coordinating them with the pursuit of other important social purposes. Although controversial, such practices are not prohibited by the Universal Declaration model, but neither are they required. It would be a serious error to view the absence of such reservations—or any other group rights of minorities—as necessarily a violation of human rights.

6. Protecting Group Identity

This liberal approach to difference may, it must be acknowledged, lead to the weakening, even the demise, of some minority (and other group) identities. Group identities, however, are not now, and I think ought not become, subjects of international human rights protection. Only individual autonomy gives rise, and value, to identities that must be respected by others. Neither individually nor collectively do others have a right to impose any particular identity on a resistant individual or group.

Identity is entitled to protection only where it is an autonomous expression of the rights and values of those who carry it. Others may choose to value difference for its own sake or for the social benefits that diversity provides. They are required, as a matter of human rights, only to respect the decisions that people choose to act on for themselves, within the limits of their rights.

Almost all adults have multiple identities. It is for such real, and realistically complex, human beings to balance the varied roles and histories that shape their lives.[10] Such choices are, of course, conditioned, and thus in some (relatively uninteresting) sense not "free." But if equal treatment and freedom of association are fully realized, those choices can appropriately be seen as autonomous exercises of internationally recognized human rights.

In such a social and political environment, groups of all sorts have a "fair" opportunity to compete in shaping the identities of "their" members. If a par-

10. As Jeremy Waldron (1995: 105–108) notes, many advocates of group rights and minority cultures instead assume that individuals are (if not exclusively, at least primarily) members of a single, coherent, even homogenous "culture." This particular construction combines a bad account of the nature of individual identity with an equally bad and dangerous account of culture (see §6.6).

ticular identity is valued sufficiently, it will survive, perhaps even thrive. If that identity is not highly valued, then it will not. And that is the way it should be.[11] The alternative is a frightening paternalism that denies others rights that we take for granted on the ground that these rights are not good for them, an insistence that people in such groups *must* define themselves principally as members of the group whether they want to or not.

People should be—and, through the rights of nondiscrimination, freedom of association, and a variety of other internationally recognized human rights, are—entitled to develop, express, and modify their identities, acting both individually and collectively. I find particularly attractive Jeremy Waldron's suggestion that we think of personal identity "not in terms of hierarchical management, but in terms of democratic self-government of a pluralistic population" (1995: 112). No particular identity ought to be entitled to special protection *as a matter of human rights* beyond that which derives from the (individual and collective) choices of its members.

Having said all this, I must admit that there may be no viable alternative to minority self-government where equal treatment and effective freedom of association are systematically violated. In such cases, minority self-government may indeed be the best human rights strategy. But this does not make minority self-government a human right. Rather, it is a local political decision about means of implementing internationally recognized human rights, within the margin of discretion allowed by international human rights norms.

7. Indigenous Peoples

Indigenous peoples may present an exception to this general argument against group human rights. If indigenous communities are more or less globally subject to threats to their autonomy, equality, and dignity that cannot be countered by existing rights to nondiscrimination and freedom of association, it may make sense to recognize international human rights of indigenous peoples. In other words, a plausible case can be made that this is a standard threat to human dignity that deserves recognition and protection through internationally recognized human rights.

But even such rights, I would argue, should be seen as rights of members of indigenous communities. Special circumstances that justify recognizing indigenous peoples' rights merit emphasis. Internationally recognized human rights for indigenous people should be seen as an exception that proves the rule, rather than as a model for a new general approach to group rights.

11. This does not preclude active state support for the group in question. But such support should be seen as an expression of the values and choices of the society, operating through established political practices, rather than as a matter of group human rights.

To simplify the discussion, let us imagine an indigenous community that is small and, if not a face-to-face society, at least one in which the lineages of most members are known to most other members. It is geographically and culturally separate from the mainstream society. Mainstream institutions thus appear alien to most members of the community. In particular, the individualism of modern institutions contrasts with the typical self-identification as a group member. Because there are also regular contacts with the "outside" world, though, we can think of those who reside in the community as having chosen to stay. Finally, imagine that the indigenous community is fragile in the sense that well-established mainstream institutions would *as an unintended consequence* radically alter the community's way of life in a fashion that most members would reject if given a choice. The principal threat to the survival of the group, in other words, comes not from internal defection or dissidence but from external pressure or assault.

The most serious assaults on native peoples and indigenous societies have typically come through the destruction of the material basis of the community's way of life. Particularly important has been the introduction of private property rights in land, especially by expropriating communally held native lands (as occurred on a massive scale in North America) or allowing outsiders to claim and register such land as private property (as is occurring today in the Brazilian Amazon). The modern state and its economic counterpart of fully alienable property rights in land typically pose the most serious threat to traditional communities and to the collective rights of aboriginal peoples. The plight of indigenous people is thus surprisingly similar in its structure, however different it may be in it particulars, to that of "modern" individuals. As a result, the rights of the Universal Declaration model can provide considerable support and protection.

But I think an expansive understanding of the logic of individual rights requires (or at least authorizes) us to go further. The choice by an indigenous community of a particular way of life that is specially vulnerable to outside attack demands not merely respect from mainstream society and institutions but accommodation and protection as well.

Individual human rights guarantee the autonomy of individuals to choose a way of life. In the case of persons who define themselves not principally as members of a traditional community, that choice of a way of life must be guaranteed—in the name of individual human rights.

The best institutional mechanism, however, may indeed be group rights involving both considerable self-government—which would be facilitated by the group's small size, geographical concentration, and cultural history—and restrictions on the activities of nonmembers (in light of the fragility of the indigenous community). Recognizing such rights is further facilitated by the fact that they would impose severe burdens on relatively few outsiders in return for immense benefits to the group and its members.[12]

The broader significance of this "exception" bears noting. Even if most claims for group human rights are profoundly defective, no particular claim can be rejected without examining its merits. Even where skepticism is the appropriate general attitude, claims for recognizing new human rights, whether held by individuals or by groups, deserves careful scrutiny.

Systematic threats to human dignity change over time. In addition, our understandings of the nature of the life worthy of a human being, and of the practical meaning of equal concern and respect, may change. Therefore, we must always be willing, even eager, to explore gaps in and needed additions to the Universal Declaration model. The Universal Declaration and the Covenants may be (for us, now) authoritative, even definitive. They are not, however, likely to be the last word on international human rights.

8. Group Rights in a Human Rights Framework

Membership and participation in a variety of social groups is an essential part of a life of dignity. Many groups appropriately have a variety of rights. My argument against group *human* rights should not obscure these important points.

Even in the modern West, where individualism seems to have reached the pinnacle of its historical development, few (if any) people define themselves entirely as individuals. Most Westerners see themselves as part of a family; many even see the family as their most important locus of personal identity. Many define themselves in significant measure by their religion. Most blacks see race as an important facet of both their self-definition and their definition by others in society. Gender functions similarly for many women. Most Westerners also have at least a weak sense of "national" pride that is in some cases a significant element of their self-definition. Outside the West, such group self-identifications are widely held to be even more important. And in almost all contemporary societies, a wide range of collective groups—for example, families, private clubs, professional associations, charitable organizations, business corporations, religious communities, and states—hold legal and moral rights.

12. It must be admitted, though, that indigenous people—rather small minority groups within societies that have a more or less coherent dominant culture—present a relatively "easy" case compared to, say, highly divided societies such as in Lebanon. Nevertheless, precisely because individuals see their identity as fundamentally tied to the group and choose to shape their own lives with their compatriots according to their shared understandings and desires, the individual human rights approach (extended as I have suggested above) is at least a plausible—and I would argue the best—way to protect not only individual but group rights as well.

Group rights and individual human rights, however, do sometimes conflict. For example, many societies have denied women an existence and an identity outside the male-dominated family. A number of religious sects (including, in the United States, the Amish, Hasidic Jews, the Nation of Islam, and the Unification Church) regulate contacts with those outside the community. The Indian caste system and South African apartheid are extreme examples of coercively defining personal identity through group membership. Such cases force us to choose between individual human rights and group rights.

I would argue that the strong presumption ought to be in favor of individual human rights, even where their exercise threatens the integrity of the community. So long as a group is transformed or eroded by the free exercise of the human rights of its members, such an outcome is likely to be morally and politically acceptable, often even desirable. For example, if young Amish men and women choose to retain their distinctive style of life, their communities are likely to be preserved. If not, the demise of the group will be their decision, and it is a decision that (only) they have a right to make. The alternative would be to force group membership on those who see it not as a means to creative self-fulfillment but as an oppressive limitation of their existence and identity.

There is a real loss when a community dies out, but if its members freely choose another way of life, we must be prepared to accept that loss. If a group is dissolving or collapsing from within, rarely will it make sense to require that it be kept alive from outside.[13] If a group's survival requires the systematic denial of the internationally recognized human rights of its members, it is unlikely to deserve even our toleration, let alone our support.

9. Cultural Rights

The discussion of group rights provides an occasion for considering cultural rights, which usually receive far less attention than the other principal categories of internationally recognized human rights. This is perhaps most strikingly in the common tendency to elide "and cultural" in discussions of the conventional dichotomy between civil and political rights and economic, social, and cultural rights. Cultural rights protect a communal way of life, which typically has significant value for most members of the community. Participation in "culture" is usually seen as essential to a life of dignity.

People may exercise their human rights both as separate individuals and as members of a community. Cultural rights are the one standard class of rights

13. Where communities can be protected against incursions by the dominant culture, or where state-sponsored social programs can encourage (without coercing) members to remain in the community, these may be attractive options. But they are best seen as a choice that the broader society is at liberty to make (or not), rather than an obligation imposed by the rights of the group.

that refer principally to individuals as members of a community. Furthermore, although the community referred to by most other human rights is the political community (especially as expressed in the state) cultural rights refer to cultural communities, which typically are smaller than and exist within (or across) the confines of a state (from which both individuals and the cultural community are seen as separate).

Cultural rights are especially important because they protect individuals in minority cultural communities against the state and the majority community. All human rights provide protections against incursions of the state in areas that are essential to a life of full human dignity. Cultural rights protect those essential aspects of personal dignity that are based on membership in a cultural community, much as political and economic rights protect those aspects that rest on membership in political and economic communities.

All human rights protect individuals in their choice or pursuit of a way of life (within certain limits). Some human rights focus on minimum standards that are required for the pursuit of any autonomous way of life. Others, especially civil liberties, emphasize the idea that the state cannot be allowed to impose a particular substantive conception of the "good life." Cultural rights as well seek to allow those in a community to defend a way of life against the incursions of other communities, especially the state.

Cultural rights may require more than just tolerant nondiscrimination, however. Protecting a way of life may require not simply the guarantee of formal equality, but special policies of support as well. In fact, the social homogenization of formal equality may be the most serious threat to cultural rights.

Many people do see certain "natural" or acquired characteristics as essential to their definition of their lives and persons. Such defining choices often place a person in a distinctive community. Cultural rights protect the choices of those who see themselves as, in an important way, part of communities of shared culture. As human rights, they protect those choices in distinctive ways.

Consider a relatively simple case, such as Hispanic minorities in the United States. Because language is an important feature of Hispanic culture, bilingual education often has been seen as an issue of cultural rights. Protecting these rights has required considerable positive efforts on the part of school districts, often in the face of resistant majority communities. In other generations and for other groups, the public schools were a principal mechanism by which the children of immigrants lost their cultural, and especially linguistic, distinctiveness. Bilingual education makes the schools an instrument for preserving, rather than overcoming, cultural differences. Internationally recognized cultural rights at the very least allow, and perhaps even require, this change in the socializing function of American public schools.

Bilingual education may "disadvantage" Hispanic children from a cultural viewpoint, but it does little to reduce the force of cultural rights arguments.

The issue is one of cultural choice and not external judgments of what would be better for others. The value of culture may not be easily quantified, but it is no less real than any economic or social costs of bilingual education. So long as Hispanic families and communities are willing to pay the costs of preserving their distinctive cultural identity, cultural rights require that their choice be protected.

10. A Right to Cultural Identity?

This special emphasis on group membership implied by cultural rights, along with the value we place on human (and thus cultural) diversity in our increasingly multicultural world, might suggest the desirability of recognizing a right to cultural identity. Such an idea has received considerable international attention, especially in UNESCO circles.[14] Even setting aside the collective human rights dimensions of a purported right to cultural identity, however, recognizing such a right seems to me at best unnecessary and perhaps even dangerous.

Cultural identity certainly is something that can be attacked by the state or other groups or institutions, resulting in serious affronts to human dignity. Protecting autonomously chosen cultural identity from such attacks is an admirable aim but does not require, and may not even be facilitated by, recognizing a human right to cultural identity.

Such attacks almost always involve discrimination on the basis of the already prohibited grounds of "race, color, sex, language, religion, political or other opinion, national or social origin, property, birth or other status." They also typically involve denials of equal protection of the law; infringements of rights to freedom of thought, conscience, religion, speech, press, assembly, and association; and violations of the cultural rights explicitly recognized in the Universal Declaration and the Covenants.

One might argue in response that, rather than being superfluous or redundant, a right to cultural identity is an implicit right that now deserves to be made explicit. But I cannot see that much could be done with a right to cultural identity that cannot now be done with already recognized rights. One already has a right to participate in cultural life and to choose freely one's beliefs and opinions. Minority cultures, whose cultural identity is most likely to be subject to attack, are already specially protected. Other civil and political rights allow public action on behalf of distinctive cultural practices. And states already have international legal obligations to conserve and develop culture.[15] A right to cul-

14. See, for example, Symonides (2000: 189), Hughes (2000: 8), Shyllon (1998), and Article 6 of the Asian Human Rights Charter (*http://www.ahrchk.net/charter/finalcontent.html*).

15. This is, strictly speaking, true only of parties to the International Covenant on Economic, Social, and Cultural Rights. A new convention on the right to cultural identity, however, would have few parties that are not already parties to the Covenant.

tural identity might add a new layer of rhetoric, but that is hardly a major benefit.

There are, however, a variety of costs, beginning with the costs of the proliferation of human rights. As circumstances change—as standard threats to human dignity evolve—we will need to recognize new rights, but the needless proliferation of human rights only risks devaluing the very idea of human rights and thus subtly weakening all human rights (compare Alston 1984).

We must also ask how states are likely to use such a right to cultural identity. In a large number of states it is certain to be used to facilitate discriminatory infringements of other human rights. Although few proponents of a human right to cultural identity have such uses in mind, they are easy to anticipate. In the absence of readily apparent positive uses, this would seem more than enough to preclude recognizing such a right.

So long as the individual more or less freely chooses cultural identity, it is a valuable goal. It is also a goal closely connected with both the protection and the exercise of human rights. But not every good thing—not even everything essentially connected with human rights—is itself a human right. We do not need a human right to cultural identity.

The principal problem we face is not that our lists of human rights are defective, but rather that states regularly and systematically violate internationally recognized human rights. Our attention and effort ought to be focused on implementing and protecting already recognized human rights, not on conjuring up new ones of dubious utility. Nearly all contemporary human rights problems lie not in defects in authoritative international human rights norms or in the cultural insensitivity of such norms but rather arise in deviations from these norms.

11. Appendix: People's Rights and the Right to Self-Determination

The International Human Rights Covenants do recognize a right of peoples to self-determination:

> Article 1. (1) All peoples have the right to self-determination. By virtue of the right they freely determine their political status and freely pursue their economic, social and cultural development.
>
> (2) All peoples may, for their own ends, freely dispose of their natural wealth and resources. . . . in no case may a people be deprived of its own means of subsistence.

Therefore, whatever the merits of the arguments against collective human rights offered in this chapter, it is clear that the language of peoples' rights is here to stay.[16] In line with the argument developed here, I want to suggest that they are best seen as rights of individuals acting as members of social groups. For the purposes of illustration, let us consider the right to self-determination, the one unambiguously well-established peoples' right.

Reflecting the fact that lists of human rights evolve in reaction to new or newly recognized threats to human dignity (§4.1), we can see a right to self-determination as an appropriate response to imperialism, which usually denied its victims the full range of human rights. The threat to human dignity posed by imperialism is foreign in origin and affects the human rights of entire peoples. Therefore, the emphasis is on the collective dimension of the right to self-determination, and that right is formulated as a right of peoples.

Nonetheless, there is substantial overlap with well-established individual human rights. For example, the right of a people to determine its political status and path of development can be seen as a collective expression of the right to political participation, which under imperial rule was systematically denied to entire peoples. Likewise, the right of a people to its natural wealth and resources can be seen as a guarantee that the material means to satisfy a wide range of rights will not be subject to continued plunder by foreign states or corporations.

Because of this overlap, we can say that respecting the right to self-determination involves something very much like respecting all other human rights and, in particular, the rights to political participation and freedom of speech, press, assembly, and association. If these rights are fully respected, it is difficult to see how the right to self-determination could be denied. Conversely, denial of the right to self-determination takes place principally through the denial of these individual human rights. Little or nothing can be done with the right to self-determination that cannot be accomplished through the exercise of other human rights.

Redundancy, however, is the least of the problems raised by the right to self-determination as it is ordinarily conceived today. Peoples obviously can be denied self-determination by fellow nationals as well as by foreigners. Furthermore, peoples within or spread across established national boundaries (e.g., Ibos in Nigeria, Somalis in the Horn of Africa) would seem to have the same right. However, contemporary political practice restricts the right to self-determination largely to peoples who have been or are subject to Western imperial domination (Pomerance 1982; Buchheit 1978).[17] For example, Kurds in Iraq

16. Elsewhere (Donnelly 1993b) I have presented an extended argument against "third-generation," solidarity, or peoples' rights considered as human rights. For a somewhat more balanced set of views, see Alston (2001).

17. Hannum (1996) provides an excellent and extended discussion of the conflicting claims of sovereignty and self-determination. Other good discussions of self-determination in international law and politics include Danspeckgruber (2002), McCorquodale (2000), Cassese (1998), and Tomuschat (1993).

and Iran and Tamils in Sri Lanka have been almost universally held not to be entitled to self-determination (in the international legal sense of a right to a state).

In practice, then, the internationally recognized right to self-determination, despite its seeming breadth, has been treated as an extremely narrow right.[18] States' fears of secession and governments' fears of revolution have combined to restrict the right to self-determination to little more than a right to sovereignty for those states (and colonies) that currently exist. Given that the right to self-determination emerged as part of the struggle against Western imperialism, this is not surprising. Precisely because of this history, it seems to me best to consider self-determination as an exception that proves the rule, rather than as a model for other new rights. This is especially true because of the statist character of the Universal Declaration model (see §2.4).

As we have seen, states are the principal mechanism by which internationally recognized human rights are protected and implemented. Theoretically, benevolent imperialists might provide protection. In practice, however, they never have. Therefore, a right to self-determination is practically necessary in a statist world. But this necessity is largely a function of that statism, which gives self-determination a very unusual politicolegal status, paralleled only by the individual right to nationality (which is similarly rooted in the statism of contemporary international society).

I would suggest that other peoples' rights, to the extent that they are conceptualized in human rights terms, should also be treated as, at best, summary statements of the collective dimensions of the struggle against widespread and systematic violations or impediments to the realization of already recognized individual human rights. As such they are conceptually redundant. They are also probably politically redundant. I find it difficult to conceive of individuals, states, or organizations that are unmoved by rights to, say, food, health care, social security, education, or work being moved by an appeal to the abstract and disembodied idea of a collective right to development. Collective human rights provide little new leverage in the struggle for human dignity.[19]

For all the talk of excessive individualism, the problem in the world today is not too many individual rights but that individual human rights are not sufficiently respected. States and societies have a variety of claims on individuals, and modern states have awesome powers to bring individuals to their knees; if

18. One possible further attraction of indigenous peoples' rights is that they might provide an international legal model for pushing the discussion of self-determination beyond its current narrow anticolonial understanding. On the issue of indigenous peoples and self-determination, see Lam (2000), Alfredsson (1993), and Sanders (1993).

19. Even the struggle for decolonization could have been, and in considerable measure was, carried out using arguments that the rights of individuals were being denied, especially the rights to democratic political participation and freedoms of speech, press, assembly, and association.

necessary, to break their minds as well as their bodies. Human rights, and parallel legal rights, are among the few resources of individuals in the face of the modern state. The balance is already (always?) tilted against the individual. The only likely result of advocating collective human rights, let alone the so-called human rights of states, is a further strengthening of the forces of repression.

Every day we see individuals crushed by society. Rarely, if ever, do we see society torn apart by the exercise of individual human rights. Social disorder and decay are instead usually associated with the violation of individual human rights by the state or some other organized segment of society. Human rights are a rare and valuable intellectual and moral resource in the struggle to right the balance between society (and the state) and the individual. Unless we preserve their distinctive character, and stand firm on their character as individual rights, their positive role in the struggle for human dignity may be compromised.

13/ Nondiscrimination for All

The Case of Sexual Minorities

Article 1 of the Universal Declaration of Human Rights begins: "All human beings are born free and equal in dignity and rights." The right to protection against discrimination, recognized in Article 2, is an explicit guarantee of equal—and thus all—human rights for every person. It is thus central to the notion of "All human rights for all," the aptly chosen slogan of the High Commissioner for Human Rights for 1998, the fiftieth anniversary of the Universal Declaration.

Existing international human rights law, however, does not extend protection to all victims of systematic discrimination. This chapter critically examines the exclusion of gay men, lesbians, and members of other sexual minorities from the full protection of international human rights norms. In addition to being a topical issue of considerable substantive importance, it illustrates earlier arguments about changes in the substance of internationally recognized human rights and the appropriate limits on traditional rights-abusive practices.

1. The Right to Nondiscrimination

Article 2 of the Universal Declaration proclaims, "Everyone is entitled to all the rights and freedoms set forth in this Declaration, without distinction of any kind, such as race, colour, sex, language, religion, political or other opinion, national or social origin, property, birth or other status." This statement, however, is seriously exaggerated. Everyone cannot be entitled to all human rights without distinction of *any* kind. States are not prohibited from taking into account *any* status differences. Individuals are entitled only to protection against *invidious* discrimination, discrimination that tends to ill will or causes unjustifiable harm.

Social life is full of legitimate distinctions and discriminations. Individuals, groups, and even the state often not merely recognize but legitimately act on differences between groups of people. For example, all societies restrict the rights of children, a distinction based on age or mental capacity. Distinctions of nationality are deeply embedded in international human rights regimes: individuals ordinarily can claim human rights only against the government of which they are a national (or under whose jurisdiction they fall on the basis of residence). A variety of human rights are legitimately restricted for those who are incarcerated for criminal behavior.

The internationally recognized human right to nondiscrimination prohibits invidious public (or publicly supported or tolerated) discrimination that deprives target groups of the legitimate enjoyment of other rights. Although it may be hateful to choose one's friends on the basis of race, this is not an appropriate subject for regulation through antidiscrimination law. Only when friendships or social contacts systematically influence access to economic or political opportunities do they become a matter of legitimate state regulation. Likewise, discrimination in choice of marriage partners on the basis of family background does not fall within the confines of the right to nondiscrimination unless it is publicly supported or required (as, for example, in laws against miscegenation).

If human rights are paramount rights, not even all illegitimate discriminations fall under a human right to nondiscrimination. Human rights address egregious or widespread systematic practices—standard threats to human dignity, not every public indignity. The Universal Declaration thus highlights race, color, sex, language, religion, political or other opinion, national or social origin, property, and birth. The notion of suspect classifications in American constitutional jurisprudence nicely captures this idea. Because we know that race, for example, has been the basis for invidious discrimination in the past, practices that use racial categorizations are inherently suspect and thus subject to special judicial scrutiny.[1]

Article 2.2 of the International Covenant on Economic, Social, and Cultural Rights is slightly subtler:

> The States Parties to the present Covenant undertake to guarantee that the rights enunciated in the present Covenant will be exercised without discrimination of any kind as to race, colour, sex, language, religion, political or other opinion, national or social origin, property, birth or other status.

Distinction of any kind is replaced by *discrimination* of any kind. And rather than present the enumerated grounds as examples of prohibited discrimina-

1. Sexual orientation, however, has explicitly *not* been recognized as a suspect classification in the United States at the federal level. On current American legal and political practice see Gerstmann (1999) and D'Emilio, Turner, and Vaid (2000).

tion—"such as race . . ."—this formulation is exhaustive: "without discrimination . . . as to." (Flexibility is provided through the addition of "other status" at the end.)

In either formulation, however, the practical heart of the right is the list of prohibited grounds of invidious discrimination. Such explicit listing often is essential to strong and unambiguous protection, usually as the result of extended and difficult, often violent, political struggles. The list of protected groups provides a record of the successful struggles by excluded and despised groups to force full (or at least formally equal) inclusion in political society.

2. Nondiscrimination and Political Struggle[2]

Protections against discrimination based on birth and social origin take us back to the beginning of the modern Western struggle for human rights against aristocratic privilege. Although most societies have assigned rights in significant measure on the basis of birth, today we require that human rights be equally available to those born high and low on society's scale of social status or origins. But those who have forced their social "betters" to recognize their equal rights often denied the same rights to members of other social groups. For example, John Locke used the universal language of natural rights but developed a political theory that aimed largely to protect the rights of propertied European males. In the United States, whose Declaration of Independence declared that all men are created equal and endowed by their creator with certain unalienable rights, "until 1815, only those white males who owned property or paid taxes could vote; not allowed to vote were white males who did not own property; all women; all African Americans, including nonslaves; and all Native Americans." (Ropers and Pence 1995: 16)

Nonetheless, propertied white Christian European males were themselves forced to concede that differences of race, color, sex, language, religion, political or other opinion, national or social origin, and property are illegitimate grounds for differential basic rights. These previously accepted grounds of legal and political discrimination have been renounced. Today, through the right to nondiscrimination, we insist that such differences be treated as irrelevant in the assignment and enjoyment of rights. The state may no longer invidiously take these features into consideration when dealing with citizens and subjects.

Such changing conceptions of the criteria for full and equal membership in society have rested on and interacted with wider social, economic, and political

2. This section extends arguments initially developed in §4.1 and 4.3.

transformations. Consider Locke's link between property and citizenship. The rise of mass literacy seriously undercut arguments that those without property lacked the leisure required to develop their rational capacities sufficiently to participate fully in political society. So did mass electoral politics, which transformed political participation from direct decision making to authorizing and reviewing the actions of representative office holders. The claim that the unpropertied lacked a sufficient "stake" in society to be allowed full political participation fell to changing conceptions of political membership symbolized by the American and French revolutions, the rise of mass popular armies, and growing nationalist sentiments. Discrimination based on the lack of independence of the unpropertied gave way in the face of the increasingly impersonal relations between workers and employers and the general depersonalization of relations in urban settings. General processes of social leveling and mobility eroded the implicit assumption of the coincidence of wealth and virtue. Our expanded list of economic and social rights also reflects a growing appreciation of alternative means for realizing economic security and participation in a world of industrial capitalism.

Likewise, women and nonwhites were until well into this century widely seen as irreparably deficient in their rational or moral capacities and thus incapable of exercising the full range of human rights. These racial and gender distinctions, however, were in principle subject to moral and empirical counterarguments. Over the past several decades, dominant political ideas and practices in Western and non-Western societies alike have been transformed by national and international movements to end slavery and, later, colonialism; to grant women and racial minorities the vote; and to end discriminations based on race, ethnicity, and gender. A similar tale can be told in the case of Jews, nonconformist Christian sects, atheists, and other religious minorities.

In each case, a logic of full and equal humanity has overcome claims of group inferiority, bringing (at least formally) equal membership in society through explicitly guaranteed protections against discrimination. Signs of difference that previously were seen as marks of moral inferiority and grounds for justifiable subordination have been excluded from the realm of legally and politically legitimate discriminations. Adherents of different, even despised, religions have come to be recognized as (nonetheless) fully human, and thus entitled to the same rights as other (dominant groups of) human beings. Africans, Arabs, and Asians have come to be recognized as no less human than white Europeans, and so forth.

Such an account emphasizes the progressive development of the right to nondiscrimination—and human rights more generally—through processes of social and political struggle. It implicitly raises the question of other groups currently subject to discrimination, of victims of invidious public discrimination whose suffering remains legally and politically accepted. The remainder of this chapter focuses on those subject to discrimination because of their sexual behavior or orientation.

3. Discrimination against Sexual Minorities

Let us begin with the matter of linguistic conventions. "Homosexual" and "gay" have become relatively neutral and fairly inclusive terms in the American mainstream. Among activists in these communities, the formula of "gay, lesbian, bisexual, and transgendered (GLBT)" has considerable currency at the moment. In addition to being more inclusive, this formulation has the virtue of emphasizing *differences* among those who engage in same-sex erotic behavior or relationships, and by explicitly including transvestites and transsexuals it undermines conventional links between sex (defined by genitalia or chromosomes), behavior, gender, sexual orientation, and personal identity.[3]

Following the logic laid out in the preceding section, however, I will adopt the language of sexual minorities. This terminology is even more inclusive, being open to any group (previously, now, or in the future) stigmatized or despised as a result of sexual orientation, identity, or behavior. Furthermore, the language of minorities explicitly focuses our attention on the issue of discrimination, and at least the possibility of political action to eliminate it.[4]

Sexual minorities are not merely people who engage in "deviant" sexual behavior—for example, fetishists of various types—or even those who adopt "deviant" (sexual) identities (e.g., "swingers"). They are those despised and targeted by "mainstream" society because of their sexuality, victims of systematic denials of rights because of their sexuality (and, in most cases, for transgressing gender roles). Like victims of racism, sexism, and religious persecution, they are human beings who have been identified by dominant social groups as somehow less than fully human, and thus not entitled to the same rights as "normal" people, "the rest of us."

Discrimination against sexual minorities is widespread and deep in almost all societies today. In many countries, the intimate behavior and loving rela-

3. For a provocative and eclectic set of essays challenging the conventional male-female dichotomy, see Herdt (1994).

4. The drawback of this language, as Kees Waaldijk has pointed out to me in private conversation, is that by including those engaging in generally despised sexual practices that are not related to gender roles it moves away from the implicit emphasis on gender in the GLBT formulation. For example, were sadomasochists or rubber fetishists to be targets of systematic discrimination, they would fall under my definition of sexual minorities. I am not convinced, however, that discriminations based on sexual behavior unrelated to gender should not be included. To the extent that "sex" or sexual behavior is part of the issue, as I believe it is, the alternative of "gender minorities," besides its rhetorical shortcomings, has its own conceptual problems. Also, the special association of the language of gender with women's rights raises the likelihood of unintended analytical ambiguities and confusion.

tionships of sexual minorities are defined as crimes. They are singled out for official, quasi-official, and private violence. In almost all countries, sexual minorities suffer under substantial civil disabilities.

In numerous countries sexual relations among adult members of the same sex are legally prohibited. In revolutionary Iran and Taliban Afghanistan the proscribed penalty of death has been imposed.[5] In Zimbabwe, President Robert Mugabe has pursued an unusually active and vocal campaign, claiming that "animals in the jungle are better than these people" and calling homosexuals "worse than dogs and pigs."[6] A number of gay men have been convicted and received lengthy prison sentences.

Such examples are (sadly) easily multiplied.[7] In Romania, Mariana Cetiner was adopted by Amnesty International as a prisoner of conscience after her incarceration (solely) for homosexual activity. Gabriel Presnac and Radu Vasiliu were beaten by police, prosecuted, and imprisoned for holding hands and kissing in public.[8] In India, where homosexual acts are punishable by life in prison, two men recently were arrested after attempting to be married in public, amid public calls by religious leaders for their execution.[9] China's first gay salon was closed by the authorities because it "was spreading erroneous points of view, and instead of opposing, advocating homosexuality."[10] While I was making final revisions to this chapter, several gay men in Egypt were sentenced to prison.

In addition to the direct threat of prosecution, criminalization leads to restrictions on a wide range of other rights. For example, freedoms of speech and association are limited by laws that punish advocating or organizing to engage in "criminal" behavior.[11] This often creates an environment of pervasive fear in

5. On the Afghan practice of execution by collapsing a stone wall on the victims, see http://www.lgirtf.org/newsletters/Summer98/SU98-4.html. On Iran, where ILGA estimates more than 800 sodomy executions, see http://www.qrd.org/qrd/world/asia/Iran/ILGA.asks.end.execution.of.homosexuals-08.06.97. See also (Wilets 1994a: 28–29). In 2000, three Yemeni men were executed in Saudi Arabia. In 2001, a Nigerian man was sentenced to death by stoning. See Lexis-Nexis Middle East Newsfile (July 15, 2000) and Africa News Service (27 September 2001).

6. http://www.qrd.org/qrd/world/wockner/news.briefs/210-05.04.98 and http://www.qrd.org/qrd/world/africa/zimbabwe/mugabe.renews.attacks. Such high-level vilification seems to be spreading regionally, for example, to Namibia (http://www.iglhrc.org/news/features/1997_review.html and Lexis-Nexis Africa New Service, 20 March 2001), Zambia, (http://www.lgirtf.org/newsletters/Summer98/SU98-4.html), Kenya(http://www.qrd.org/qrd/world/wockner/news.briefs/226-08.24.98), and Uganda (Lexis-Nexis Africa News Service, 11 November 1999).

7. For additional case material, and reviews of national legal practices, see Amnesty International United Kingdom (1997) and Amnesty International (2001a).

8. See Amnesty International *Romania: A Summary of Human Rights Concerns* (AI INDEX: EUR 39/06/98) and http://www.iglhrc.org/world/easteurope/Romania1998Jan_2.html.

9. http://www.lgirtf.org/newsletters/Summer98/SU98-4.html.

10. http://www.qrd.org/qrd/world/asia/china/china.cracks.down-5.31.93.

11. Wilets (1994b: 22; 1994a: 45–48, 76–81). In September 1998, Zambia's Home Affairs Minister, Peter Machungwa, threatened to arrest leaders of a newly formed movement of gays and les-

which jobs, housing, and social benefits are constantly at risk. In some cases, sexual minorities are targets of active intimidation. For example, in Petaling Jaya Selangor state in Malaysia, political authorities and religious leaders have supported and encouraged local vigilante groups hunting out immoral activities, including homosexuality, in their neighborhoods.[12] An ad in a state-sponsored Zimbabwean newspaper in 1997 read "CRUSADE AGAINST RAPISTS AND HOMOSEXUALS. God commands the death of sexual perverts. Our culture and traditional justice system condemns them to death. Our religion condemns them to death."[13]

Such attitudes regularly lead to violence. In some cases, it is quasi-official (Wilets 1994a: 29–34, 40–42). Perhaps the most notorious example is "social cleansing" in Colombia (Ordonez 1994) and Ecuador (Amnesty International 2001b), where a general climate of official and quasi-official political violence against "disposable" people spilled over into death squad attacks on gays, lesbians, and transvestites. In other countries, violence is tolerated but official involvement is more indirect. For example, in Brazil, Luis Mott (1996) has documented more than 100 murders based on sexual orientation every year for more than a decade.

Even where violence against sexual minorities is prosecuted, "gay bashing" is often sadly common (Comstock 1991).[14] Occasionally a case achieves widespread public prominence. For example, in the United States in the fall of 1998, Matthew Shepherd, a Wyoming college student, was brutally beaten and left to die, tied to a fence like a scarecrow, simply because he was gay. More often, it is lost in the everyday flow of crime[15] or simply unreported.

Even where members of sexual minorities need not fear violence or criminal prosecution they usually are subject to civil disabilities and social discrimination. For example, soon after Fiji became only the second country in the world to prohibit discrimination on the basis of sexual orientation in its constitution, legislation was introduced to ban same-sex marriages.

---

bians for illegal activity, and the registrar of societies, Herbert Nyendwa, indicated that he would not even consider their application. "The proposed gays' association will not be registered . . . it is an illegal activity" http://www.lgirtf. org/newsletters/Summer98/SU98-4.html and http://www.qrd.org/qrd/world /wockner/news.briefs/229-09.14.98.

12. http://www.qrd.org/qrd/world/asia/malaysia/squads.target.gays-02.23.95. In Zimbabwe as well, the government has encouraged citizens to turn homosexuals over to the authorities. http://www.qrd.org/qrd/world /africa/zimbabwe/mugabe.renews.attacks.

13. See http://www.qrd.org/qrd/world/africa/zimbabwe/homophobic.ad-03.03.97.

14. Homosexual advances have even been accepted as excuses for manslaughter. For a discussion of U.S. practice, see Mison (1992).

15. For recent illustrative examples from Jamaica, Latvia, and Italy, see http://www.qrd.org/qrd/world/americas/jamaica/jamaica.homophobia-UPI, http://www.qrd.org/qrd/world/wockner/news.briefs /209-04.27.98, http://www.qrd.org/qrd/world/wockner/news.briefs/200-02.23.98, and http://www.qrd.org/qrd/world/wockner/news.briefs/198-02.09.98.

In most countries, sexual orientation is an accepted ground for discrimination in employment,[16] housing, or access to public facilities and social services. With a few recent exceptions, same-sex couples are denied civil status, resulting in discrimination in inheritance, adoption, and social insurance. In the United States, where health insurance is provided principally through employers, same-sex partners often are denied health care that would be routinely available were the couple male-female. Evan Wolfson nicely summarizes the contemporary American situation:

> Our society forbids gay people to marry, denies us equal pay for equal work, throws us off the job, forbids us from serving our country in the armed forces, refuses us health insurance, forces us into the closet, arrests us in our bedrooms, harasses our daily associations, takes away our children, beats and kills us in the streets and parks, smothers images of ourselves and others like us, and then tells us we are irresponsible, unstable, and aberrant (1991: 31–32).

Discrimination against sexual minorities also has international dimensions (beyond the exclusion of sexual minorities from the protections of international human rights law). Many countries deny entry to homosexuals as threats to public health or morals.[17] Qatar recently deported foreign homosexuals, reportedly even using forced rectal examinations as "proof."[18] Only recently have a few countries begun to recognize sexual orientation or behavior as a grounds for asylum, which in international law requires establishing that one has a well-founded fear of persecution back "home."[19]

Such officially mandated or tolerated discrimination reflects deep currents

16. For a recent discussion in the context of trade union activity, see Hunt (1999). Teachers in particular are regularly dismissed. See http://www.iglhrc.org/world/centralamerica/CostaRica 1998May.htmland http://www.qrd.org/qrd/world/wockner/news.briefs/208-04.20.98. In Thailand, homosexuals have been prohibited from entering the state teacher training colleges (http://www.iglhrc.org/world/asia/Thailand1997Mar.html). Cheng Chung-cheng, a director of student affairs at the Ministry of Education in Taiwan, recently said in a public meeting that "homosexuals should not pollute others with their relationships" and questioned whether they should have basic human rights (http://www.qrd.org/qrd/world/asia/taiwan/gays.in.taiwan).

17. For example, in 1967 the United States Supreme Court upheld deportation of aliens on grounds that homosexuality counted as "afflicted with psychopathic personality" and thus excludable. This ruling remained in force until the Immigration Act of 1990. See Foss (1994).

18. http://www.qrd.org/qrd/world/wockner/news.briefs/193-01.05.98.

19. In the United States, the first case was a Brazilian, Marcelo Tenorio, who was severely beaten and hospitalized in a gay bashing incident in Rio de Janeiro in 1989, refused a U.S. visa, and then entered illegally in 1990 (Grider 1994). A recently prominent case involved a gay Iranian refugee to Sweden, who received asylum in 1998 after initially being denied in 1996. See http://www.qrd.org/qrd/world/asia/iran/gay.iranian.granted.asylum.in.sweden-06.22.98. On Australia, see (De Waal 1998). For more information, with a primarily American orientation, see http://www.glirtf.org.

of social prejudice against sexual minorities. But, as I argued in Part II, the cultural depth of a practice cannot justify systematic denials of human rights. The remainder of this chapter argues that gays, lesbians, and others of "deviant" gender or sexuality are, as Evelyn Kallen puts it, "a stigmatized minority requiring [and deserving] protection" (1996: 209).

4. Nature, (Im)morality, and Public Morals

The common charge that homosexuality is "against nature" is hardly worth arguing against here. Sexuality and sexual orientation are constructed sets of social roles.[20] Many societies, including currently homophobic societies, have for extended periods tolerated, or even highly valued, (male) homoerotic relationships.

In the West, the best known examples come from ancient Greece.[21] But even the Christian tradition does not seem to have been consistently homophobic during its first millennium.[22] Melanesia, South Asia, and the Muslim Near East also have traditions of male homoerotic relations (Herdt 1984; Ratti 1993; Schmitt and Sofer 1992).

Homoerotic relations in Asia are of special interest because of the prominence of arguments against homosexuality in recent debates over "Asian values" (see Chapter 7). In Singapore and Malaysia in particular, homosexuality is regularity presented as a distinctively Western form of degeneracy. In fact, however, certain male-male sexual relationships have a traditional basis in both China (Lau and Ng 1989) and Japan (Schalow 1989; Hinsch 1990; Leupp 1995, Pflugfelder, 1999). There even seems to be evidence of same-sex marriage in Ming dynasty (1368–1644) Fujian (Hinsch 1990: 127–134).

Nonetheless, as the evidence of discrimination reviewed in the preceding section clearly indicates, homosexuality is widely considered—by significant segments of society in all countries, and by most people in most countries—to be profoundly immoral. The language of perversion and degeneracy is standard.

Drawing on such attitudes, advocates of discrimination are likely to point to provisions in the International Human Rights Covenants that permit restric-

20. The most influential version of this argument is Foucault (1990). See also Stein (1990), Abramson and Pinkerton (1995), Berger, Wallis, and Watson (1995), Parker and Gagnon (1995), Lochrie, McCracken, and Schultz (1997), Wijngaard (1997), Mort (2000), and Nardi (2000). With special reference to the law, see Walker (1994). Blackwood and Wieringa (1999) provide an interesting selection of contemporary cross-cultural case studies.

21. The standard scholarly study is Dover (1986). See also Cantarella (1992) and, with explicit reference to contemporary debates, Nussbaum (1994).

22. See, for example, Boswell (1980), Brooten (1996), Jordan (1997), and Kuefler (2001). More controversial is Boswell (1994).

tions on a number of recognized rights on the grounds of "public morals."[23] All the groups explicitly recognized as covered by the right to nondiscrimination today, however, were at one time perceived to be a threat to public morals. Consider some more or less randomly selected historical material from my own country concerning discrimination against those of African and Asian descent.

As is well known, slavery was explicitly permitted (and racial discrimination was not prohibited) in the U.S. Constitution and its Bill of Rights. In fact, for purposes of taxation and legislative representation, slaves—which James Madison described in *The Federalist Papers* (Number 54) as a mixture of persons and property and thus "divested of two fifths of the man"—counted as three fifths of a person. And just one year after the founding of the republic, a 1790 law confined naturalization to free white persons, a restriction that remained on the statute books until 1952.

In the infamous Dred Scott case of 1857 (60 US [19 How.]), Chief Justice Taney held that even emancipated Negroes do not "compose a portion of this people" and are not "constituent members of this sovereignty" but rather are a permanently "subordinate and inferior class of beings." From colonial times, Taney argued, "a perpetual and impassable barrier was intended to be erected between the white race and the ones which they had reduced to slavery." In fact, he argued, throughout American history Negroes had been considered by whites as "below them in the scale of created beings."

More than three quarters of a century later, Senator James O. Eastland, on the floor of the United States Senate, publicly proclaimed

> I believe in white supremacy, and as long as I am in the Senate I expect to fight for white supremacy. . . . The cultural debt of the colored peoples to the white race is such as to make the preservation of the white race a chief aim of the colored, if these latter but understood their indebtedness. That the colored race should seek to "kill the goose that lays the golden egg" is further proof that their inferiority, demonstrated so clearly in cultural attainments, extends to their reasoning processes in general. (quoted in Kennedy 1959: 32)

Making resistance to domination the decisive sign of inferiority is a rhetorical move as brilliant as it is frightening.

When U.S. law was changed in 1870 to permit naturalization of freed blacks,

23. For example, Article 19 of the International Covenant on Civil and Political Rights permits restrictions on the right to freedom of expression that are "provided for by law and are necessary . . . for the protection of . . . public health or morals." Similar limitations are allowed in Articles 12, 14, 18, 21, and 22.

foreign-born Asians continued to be denied the right to American nationality. A provision was proposed at the California Constitutional Convention of 1878–1879 to prevent Chinese immigration in order to protect Californians "from moral and physical infection from abroad" (Ringer 1983: 590).

> The Chinese bring with them habits and customs the most vicious and demoralizing. . . . They are, generally, destitute of moral principle. They are incapable of patriotism, and are utterly unfitted for American citizenship. Their existence here, in great numbers, is a perpetual menace to republican institutions, a source of constant irritation and danger to the public peace. (Ringer 1983: 606–607)

In the same year, a California State Senate Special Committee on Chinese Immigration found that

> the Chinese seem to be antediluvian men renewed. Their code of morals, their forms of worship, and their maxims of life, are those of the remotest antiquity. In this aspect they stand as a barrier against which the elevating tendency of a higher civilization exerts itself in vain. . . . there can be no hope that any contact with our people, however long continued, will ever conform them to our institutions, enable them to comprehend or appreciate our form of government, or to assume the duties or discharge the functions of citizens. (Ringer 1983: 604)

Almost half a century later, V.S. McClatchy, publisher of the *Sacramento Bee,* the leading paper in California's state capital, delivered a speech in Honolulu where he argued that Japanese migrants were "an alien, unassimilable element"; "their racial characteristics, heredity and religion prevent assimilation." McClatchy even went so far as to appeal to "the biological law which declares that races of widely different characteristics perpetuate through intermarriage, not their good, but their less desirable categories" (1979 [1921]: 5, 10). And U.S. citizens of Japanese origin were forcibly interned in the American west during World War II.

Such examples could be readily multiplied for other groups and other countries. Jews have long been a special target of attack in the Western world. Women were almost universally considered morally inferior to men until well into the twentieth century—and in many places of the world still are. In all such cases, certain marks of difference came to be constructed as "permissions-to-hate" (Woodward 1966: 81), grounds that authorize treating members of a group as less than fully human. Erik Erikson's notion of "psuedospeciation" nicely captures the dehumanizing logic, which we saw above in Mugabe's (unfavorable) comparison between gays and dogs.

Returning to the case of homosexuals, compare an interim report of a U.S. Senate subcommittee in 1950 investigating "Employment of Homosexuals and Other Sex Perverts in Government." The subcommittee's charge was "to determine the extent of the employment of homosexuals and other sex perverts in Government; to consider reasons why their employment by the Government is undesirable; and to examine into the efficacy of the methods used in dealing with the problem" (Katz 1975: 1). There was no question that these people were perverts who needed to be kept out of government (if they could not be fully purged from society). The only issue was whether enough reasons had been developed to achieve this unquestioned end and whether sufficiently strenuous efforts were being undertaken.[24]

The subcommittee found that employment was inappropriate because "first, they are generally unsuitable, and second, they constitute security risks." "Those who engage in overt acts of perversion lack the emotional stability of normal persons. . . . sex perversion weakens the moral fiber of an individual to a degree that he is not suitable for a position of responsibility." And because homosexuals "frequently attempt to entice normal individuals to engage in perverted practices" and show a strong "tendency to gather other perverts about [them]," they must be rigorously sought out. "One homosexual can pollute a Government office" (Katz 1975: 4). This is the same logic of incorrigible degradation and fear of pollution we saw above with Africans and Asians.

Even accepting, for the purposes of argument, that voluntary sexual relations among adults of the same sex are a profound moral outrage, discrimination against sexual minorities cannot be justified from a human rights perspective. "Perverts," "degenerates," and "deviants"[25] have the same human rights as the morally pure and should have those rights guaranteed by law. Members of sexual minorities are still human beings, no matter how deeply they are loathed by the rest of society. They are therefore entitled to equal protection of the law and the equal enjoyment of all internationally recognized human rights.

Human rights rest on the idea that *all* human beings have certain basic rights simply because they are human. How one chooses to lead one's life,[26]

24. The committee, with a logic strikingly reminiscent of the Red scare that was building at the same time, found that the government was insufficiently vigilant. The State Department, as during the McCarthy witch hunt, came in for special attack for allowing "known homosexuals" to resign for "personal reasons" without properly noting their homosexuality in their official personnel files (Katz 1975: 11).

25. I trust it is clear that I use this language not to be inflammatory or because it expresses my own views, but rather to engage some standard moral condemnations of homosexuality.

26. I am implicitly assuming here that sexual orientation is "chosen" and thus more like religion than race—although, of course, racial identity is largely socially constructed. If homosexuality is "genetic," the case for discrimination is even more tenuous.

subject only to minimum requirements of law and public order,[27] is a private matter—no matter how publicly one leads that life. Human rights do not need to be earned, and they cannot be lost because one's beliefs or way of life are repugnant to most others in a society. In fact, the real test of human rights comes when a state or society deals with unpopular or despised deviants rather than those comfortably in the mainstream. Likewise, it is those on the social margins—especially when they have been forced to the margins—who have the greatest need and the most important uses for human rights.

Rhoda Howard's interviews with Canadian civic leaders canvass some of the psychological and sociological barriers to acceptance of this moral position even within relatively "enlightened" or "liberal" groups in a country with a (generally deserved) reputation for tolerance, compassion, and a commitment to human rights (1999). And it is disheartening, if historically and sociologically understandable, to see leaders such as Mugabe, who came to power by opposing racist denials of his full humanity, resorting to vicious sexual hate mongering. But such resistance, however widespread, has no more moral force than past and present attitudes of racism, sexism, and religious intolerance. Just as other despised minorities have had to struggle against a dominant oppressive mainstream, ultimately forcing them to renounce their permissions to hate, homosexuals and other sexual minorities face just such a struggle today.

Popular attitudes of hatred and contempt are the problem to be overcome, not the solution to anything. Whatever the state of popular moral sentiments, we must remain committed to the overriding objective of all human rights for all. Sexual minorities, however, have to struggle not only against local attitudes and laws. They also face a body of international human rights law that accepts discrimination against them, in clear contradiction to the human rights logic of equality for *all.*

5. Strategies for Inclusion

The moral and conceptual case for extending nondiscrimination protection to gay men, lesbians, and other sexual minorities is overwhelming. They are adult human beings exercising their rights of personal autonomy to behave as they choose, and to associate, in public and private, with whom they choose, as they choose. Until the deep social prejudice against "perverts" is broken down, however, they will be subject to continued victimization and there is no chance for explicit inclusion of sexual orientation among internationally prohibited grounds of discrimination.

27. For example, sexual relations with children may be legitimately prohibited so long as both homosexual and heterosexual relations are prohibited.

As in most other areas of human rights, the central battlegrounds are local and national. The international dimension of the human rights movement is, in general, supplementary to and supportive of national struggles. Nonetheless, it will be my focus here. I want to consider briefly some of the tactical and strategic issues involved in bringing sexual minorities under international nondiscrimination protections.

A. INCORPORATION INTO INTERNATIONAL HUMAN RIGHTS LAW

The International Human Rights Covenants are largely fixed standards that reflect attitudes of the 1950s and early 1960s, when no country had a substantial gay rights movement. In principle it is possible to "amend" the Covenants, as has been done with the Second Optional Protocol (which outlaws the death penalty). But this process is extremely difficult. Even supplementary norm creation, through a separate declaration (as, for example, was done for disappearances and the right to development) is not promising. In the short and medium run, there is no chance of anything even close to an international consensus on even a working text for a draft declaration on the rights of homosexuals.

If I am correct that explicit listing as a prohibited ground of discrimination makes a significant difference, this relative inflexibility in the international "legislative" mechanisms poses serious problems for sexual minorities. But explicit inclusion under Article 2 should be seen as the end point of a long struggle, rather than an immediate aim. For the next decade at least, and probably much longer, central attention needs to be focused elsewhere.

If the text can't be changed directly and explicitly, we need to rely instead on interpretation. Sexual orientation is on its face an obvious case of an "other status" by which human beings are singled out for invidious discrimination. A campaign to emphasize these status disabilities can at least highlight the suffering publicly imposed on sexual minorities.[28] This strategy may be particularly promising if some linkage can be established with struggles of those subject to discrimination on the basis of disability or age. The idea would be to emphasize that the list of explicitly prohibited grounds in Article 2 is illustrative, not exhaustive, and that there remain a number of other statuses that are still widely used to justify invidious public discrimination.

A more radical strategy of interpretative incorporation would to be read "sex" in Article 2 to include sexual orientation. This was done by the Human

28. Of course, for those who consider such suffering appropriate, this is likely to have little impact. But it is hard to see what sort of political action is likely to be effective against those who consider sexual minorities sufficiently degenerate to merit systematic deprivations of their rights. The only hope would seem to be that pressure created by a widespread social attitude of tolerance would keep such views in the closet.

Rights Committee in the Toonen case.[29] Although a clever and provocative move, the Committee provided no grounds for such a finding. In its report, it simply stated, without further elaboration, "that in its view the reference to 'sex' in Articles 2, paragraph 1, and 26 is to be taken as including sexual orientation."[30] But this certainly was *not* what was intended at the time the provision was drafted; it is not even a widely held view in legally "advanced" European countries. It is also substantively problematic. Sexual minorities are in many ways no more analogous to women—the initially intended reference of "sex"—than they are to religious minorities. They suffer in systematically, even fundamentally, different ways from women, and those differences deserve to be highlighted rather than obscured.[31]

There are also procedural problems with existing international mechanisms for interpretation. The Human Rights Committee and the Committee on Economic, Social and Cultural Rights are *not* authorized to make authoritative interpretations (let alone act to enforce their understandings of the meaning of the Covenants). It is not even clear that these bodies are authorized to use what within the European regime is called "evolutive interpretation," a reading of the meaning of the text based on current understandings rather than on those at the time of drafting.

B. NATIONAL MECHANISMS OF INCORPORATION

The other principal source of interpretation in our decentralized international legal system is national legislatures and courts. These are authoritative—but only nationally. As part of a long-term struggle, precedents set in one national jurisdiction may be drawn on by others. As more and more national systems are changed, pressure for international changes may increase and resistance may be eroded. Although much better than nothing, this is only a start, not a solution. In the long run, we must work back up to the global dimension of the Universal Declaration and the Covenants.

One other prominent place for international action should be noted. Article 17 of the International Covenant on Civil and Political Rights includes a right to privacy. Toonen brought his case against a Tasmanian sodomy law criminalizing consensual sex among members of the same sex. The Human Rights Committee found that "it is undisputed that adult consensual sexual ac-

29. Human Rights Committee, Communication 488/1992, submitted by Nicholas Toonen against Australia. UN Document CCPR/C/50/D/488/1992, 4 April 1994. http://www.unhchr.ch/html/menu2/8/oppro/vws488.htm.

30. http://www.unhchr.ch/html/menu2/8/oppro/vws488.htm par. 8.7.

31. A strong *tactical* counterargument would advocate pursuing similarities first, taking advantage of the entrenched nature of women's rights in many legal systems, and then moving on later to dealing with differences.

tivity in private is covered by the concept of 'privacy'."[32] Although perhaps true in this particular case, where Australia did not deny the private nature of the acts, such an understanding, as we have seen above, is anything but undisputed in many countries of the world—although in such countries, privacy and the decriminalization of same sex relations would represent an important foot in the door.

The limited nature of the progress represented by mere decriminalization needs to be emphasized. It does nothing directly to eliminate civil disabilities, let alone social prejudice. Real *protection* for sexual minorities must involve inclusion within the right to nondiscrimination (and probably also incorporation under the rubric of equal protection of the laws). Nonetheless, while struggling for full protection and inclusion, an expanding sphere of privacy and protection against criminal prosecution are valuable resources.

We have thus worked backward from an ultimate aim of explicit recognition as a prohibited ground of discrimination to the very minimal toleration of decriminalization of private same-sex relations. If we think historically and politically, rather than conceptually and theoretically, we can reverse the direction of the flow and see an implicit strategy for achieving full inclusion.

C. PATHS OF INCREMENTAL CHANGE

Kees Waaldijk has identified an interesting pattern in the recognition of legal rights for homosexuals in European countries:

> The law in most countries seems to be moving on a line starting at (0) total ban on homo-sex, then going through the process of (1) the decriminalisation of sex between adults, followed by (2) the equalisation of ages of consent, (3) the introduction of anti-discrimination legislation, and (4) the introduction of legal partnership. A fifth point on the line might be the legal recognition of homosexual parenthood. (Waaldijk 1994: 51–52)

The basic logic is one of gradual inclusion, moving through increasingly active measures of nondiscrimination in a wide range of areas of public activity.

Waaldijk identifies ten principal areas of legal change: touching, safety, organizations, leisure, information, nondiscrimination, services, employment, partnerships, and parenthood. Within each domain there is a similar functional logic of progress from minimal toleration through active recognition and support. For example, within the category of homosexual safety he identifies three principal areas of activity, ranging from ending of official repression (e.g., police raids, safety in prisons, official registration), through the applica-

32. http://www.unhchr.ch/html/menu2/8/oppro/vws488.htm par. 8.2.

tion of general laws to crimes against homosexuals, to special provisions to protect lesbians and gays. In the area of lesbian/gay organizations, progress can be measured from permission to organize, through official recognition as legal persons, to support from the authorities (Waaldijk 1994: 69–72).

Waaldijk's concluding advice for national activists bears repeating here:

> 1. Think of the legal recognition of homosexuality as a number of parallel developments in more than ten different fields.
> 2. Think of the developments in each field as a series of many small steps.
> 3. Look at the experiences in other countries to find out what these steps normally are, and what their standard sequence is.
> 4. Look at the experiences in other foreign countries to find out where, at this moment of time, political pressure for legal reform can be most effectively applied.
> 5. Do not try too hard to make your legal system jump; be content with it only taking steps. But do keep the system walking. (Waaldijk 1994: 68)

At the international level, similar advice seems warranted. Keep in mind the ideal of full explicit inclusion under international nondiscrimination law, but don't expect miracles. Take advantage of whatever avenues are available to transform international human rights norms in ways that can contribute to lifting the burden imposed on sexual minorities. Remain ready for a long struggle. And as the continuing problems of women, racial and ethnic minorities, and some religious minorities remind us, even after formal protection is granted the struggle for effective enjoyment of rights to nondiscrimination is likely to remain difficult.

All human rights for all is a goal to which, even in the best of circumstances, we will always be aspiring. While striving to close the gap between ideal and reality, we can never expect practice to conform completely to theory. The case of sexual minorities also reminds us that progress in one area—in this case, discrimination against women and racial minorities—often allows, and by example perhaps even encourages, attention to shift to new problems.

14/ Humanitarian Intervention against Genocide

The "prodigious" stream of post–Cold War humanitarian interventions, (Kritsiotis 1998: 1007) running from Somalia, through Bosnia and Rwanda, to Kosovo and East Timor, provides a striking example of the complex interaction of theory and practice in the politics of international human rights. This chapter examines the legal, moral, and political dimensions of humanitarian intervention—which, as we will see, regularly conflict. I argue that the normative priority previously given to the legal prohibition of (humanitarian) intervention has eroded in contemporary international society. As a result, justifying either humanitarian intervention or nonintervention today seems problematic. When faced with massive suffering, both intervening and not intervening often seem both demanded and prohibited.

1. Intervention and International Law

Intervention is ordinarily defined in international relations as coercive foreign involvement in the internal affairs of a state; violation, short of war, of a state's sovereign rights; "dictatorial interference in the domestic or foreign affairs of another state which impairs that state's independence" (Friedmann 1971: 40). "Intervene" also has broader senses, as when we speak of intervening in a discussion. To count even diplomatic expressions of concern as intervention, though, as many governments have in response to human rights criticism, renders the concept of little interest.

Foreign policy usually aims to influence the behavior of other states, thus "interfering" with their decision making. Diplomatic "interference," however, seeks to persuade a state to alter its behavior. Intervention is coercive; it seeks to impose one's will. Although nonviolent coercion is possible—an economic boycott may remain entirely peaceful, yet be sufficiently punishing to be more coercive than persuasive—I will be concerned here only with armed (humanitarian) intervention.

Thus defined, intervention is, on its face, illegal. Nonintervention is the duty correlative to the rights of sovereignty. As Article 2(7) of the United Nations Charter puts it, "Nothing contained in the present Charter shall authorize the United Nations to intervene in matters which are essentially within the domestic jurisdiction of any state." Article 2(4) reinforces this: "All members shall refrain in their international relations from the threat or use of force against the territorial integrity or political independence of any state."

The legal presumption against intervention, however, can be overcome. For example, Article 2(7) concludes with the proviso that "this principle shall not prejudice the application of enforcement measures under Chapter VII." Furthermore, as we will see below (§5), what is considered to be "essentially within the domestic jurisdiction of any state" may change over time.

2. Humanitarian Intervention and International Law

An intervention is typically called humanitarian[1] if undertaken to halt, prevent, or punish systematic and severe human rights violations or in response to humanitarian crises, such as famines or massive refugee flows.[2] The nationality of those aided is also relevant. Rescue missions to save one's own nationals, although sometimes called humanitarian interventions,[3] are more accurately seen as self-defense or self-help: they rest on the special bond between states and their nationals, as is underscored by the fact that rescuing states typically fail to assist local citizens facing similar suffering. Humanitarian interventions, to borrow the title of Nick Wheeler's fine recent book (2000), are about saving strangers.

Is there a humanitarian exception to the general international legal prohibition of intervention? Before the end of the Cold War there clearly was not.[4]

Enterprising international lawyers have tried to find precedents in the behavior of the European Great Powers in the Ottoman and Chinese Empires in the mid-nineteenth and early twentieth centuries (e.g., Stowell 1921: 154–159). But even a casual student of history must be amused—or shocked—by this notion.

1. (Murphy 1996: 8–20) provides a good overview of definitional issues.

2. We have already discussed (§2.4.A) the legal and conceptual distinction between human rights violations, which are caused by the state (through either action or inaction), and comparable suffering for which the state is not so directly responsible. Although some interventions for other purposes might also plausibly be called humanitarian, here I consider only these two kinds of cases, which have been the focus of most recent discussions.

3. See, for example, McDougal, Lasswell, and Chen (1980: 245–246). For a good, brief critical review of such arguments, see Pease and Forsythe (1993: 298). On the current legal status of rescue missions, see Wingfield (2000).

4. Franck and Rodley (1973) provide a classic statement (and defense) of this standard interpretation. See also Brownlie (1973; 1974). Lillich (1974) offers the best Cold War era argument for the legality of humanitarian intervention.

These interventions usually were restricted to protecting conationals or coreligionists. Many sought not even to alleviate suffering or eliminate discrimination but rather to impose preferential treatment for Westerners or Christians.[5]

Turning to the half century following World War II, although we find literally hundreds of regimes guilty of gross, systematic, and persistent violations of internationally recognized human rights, we can count on our fingers, with digits to spare, the interventions with a central humanitarian intent.[6] The regular practice of states when faced with grossly repressive regimes was *not* to intervene, and this was almost universally seen as a matter of obligation. As General Assembly Resolution 2625 (XXV) put it, "no state or group of states has the right to intervene, directly or indirectly, for any reason whatever, in the internal or external affairs of any other state." And the United Nations Security Council, which might have had the legal authority, undertook no humanitarian interventions during the Cold War.

Contemporary international human rights law, as we saw earlier (§2.4 and Chapter 8), has left implementation of the extensive body of international human rights obligations largely to individual states, typically with only modest supervision by international committees of experts lacking coercive enforcement powers. "Governments by and large (and most jurists) would not assert a right to forcible intervention to protect the nationals of another country from atrocities carried out in that country" (Schachter 1984: 1629). "It is not possible to construct a persuasive argument to legitimate the use of force for humanitarian purposes while remaining within the idiom of classical international law" (Damrosch 1991: 96).

I will argue, however, that a very limited humanitarian exception has emerged over the past decade and that, all things considered, this is probably a desirable development. First, though, we must consider the moral and political dimensions of humanitarian intervention.[7]

3. The Moral Standing of the State

Does the state have a moral standing, or are its foundations purely political and legal? Michael Walzer (1977; 1980) presents a social contract justification of sov-

5. For a generally critical but slightly less jaundiced reading of pre-Charter practice see Murphy (1996: 49–64).

6. There are only three prominent candidates: India's intervention in East Pakistan, Tanzania's intervention in Uganda, and Vietnam's intervention in Cambodia. Wheeler (2000: chap. 2–4) provides useful descriptions and thoughtful evaluations. More briefly, see Murphy (1996: chap. 4).

7. There is considerable artificiality in the separation of law, morality, and politics. Nonetheless, it is a convenient shorthand device to emphasize that considerations of (moral) rectitude, (legal) authority, and (political) self-interest interact in decisions to intervene and in judgments of the legitimacy of intervention. I thus overdraw the distinctions to emphasize the interaction of these different types of considerations.

ereign states, based on self-determination, that I find largely persuasive,[8] perhaps because it fits so nicely with the general approach to human rights that I have adopted in this volume.

A. SELF-DETERMINATION AND NONINTERVENTION

Drawing heavily on John Stuart Mill's "A Few Words on Non-Intervention," Walzer argues that the sovereign rights of states "derive ultimately from the rights of individuals" (1977: 53). A sovereign state expresses the right of citizens collectively to choose their form of government.

But self-determination, Walzer argues (quoting Mill), is only

> the right of a people "to become free by their own efforts" if they can, and nonintervention is the principle guaranteeing that their success will not be impeded or their failure prevented by the intrusions of an alien power. It has to be stressed that there is no right to be protected against the consequences of domestic failure, even against a bloody repression (Walzer 1977: 88).

Our obligation is (only) to respect the autonomous choices of other political communities. "A state is self-determining even if its citizens struggle and fail to establish free institutions, but it has been deprived of self-determination if such [free] institutions are established by an intrusive neighbor" (Walzer 1977: 87).

States that systematically infringe the human rights of their citizens violate both their international legal obligations and their moral and legal obligations to their citizens. These offenses, however, do not authorize foreign states or international organizations to intervene. "As with individuals, so with sovereign states: there are things that we cannot do to them, even for their own ostensible good" (Walzer 1977: 89). Citizens have no right to good government, or (ordinarily) even to protection against bad government. And foreign states (and nationals) have neither a right nor an obligation to save citizens from their own government.

In grappling with the competing moral demands of human rights and self-determination, Walzer emphasizes respect for autonomy. His critics[9] give priority to the universality of the moral claims of the victims of suffering. This dispute reflects competing conceptions of "the international community." Walzer's critics give priority to the cosmopolitan moral community to which

8. Kant offers an alternative route to a similar conclusion in Parts II and III of "Theory and Practice" and the Definitive Articles of "Perpetual Peace" (1983: 71–89, 111–119).

9. See especially Beitz (1979; 1980), Doppelt (1978; 1980), Luban (1980a; 1980b), Slater and Nardin (1986), and Wasserstrom (1978).

all individual human beings belong, without the mediation of states. Walzer, however, focuses on the society of states, the (ethical as well as political) community of sovereign states, which has its own body of ethical norms.

We thus have a dispute over the relative weights to be given to competing ethical principles and obligations. Even Walzer accepts humanitarian intervention in response to genocidal massacres. In fact, some humanitarian interventions *must* be morally permissible if the moral standing of the state rests on self-determination, respect for autonomy, or respect for the rights of citizens. Even strong cosmopolitans grant some moral standing to at least some states.

B. PLURALISM, PATERNALISM, AND POLITICAL COMMUNITY

Robert Jackson offers the closest thing that we have in the recent literature to a principled blanket denial of the legitimacy of humanitarian intervention. Jackson presents a powerful ethical, legal, and political argument based on the values of normative pluralism and antipaternalism. He argues that a full appreciation of the ethical and political basis of international society requires us (regrettably but inescapably) to conclude that atrocities such as those in Bosnia and Kosovo are local tragedies rather than matters of international responsibility. "Sovereignty is no guarantee of domestic well-being; it is merely the framework of independence within which the good life can be pursued and hopefully realized" (2000: 308). A people has no right to be rescued from misrule, and international society has no right to come between a people and its government, even a brutal, tyrannical government.

Although I have considerable sympathy with the general thrust of this argument, Jackson clearly goes too far. Whatever the political or legal reasons to deny a humanitarian exception to a strong principle of nonintervention, such a position is ethically untenable—at least in a world of universal human rights.

We value pluralism not so much for itself but insofar as it reflects the autonomous choices of free moral agents. Not all choices deserve even our toleration, let alone our respect. The spread of international human rights values has substantially reduced the range of defensible appeals to normative pluralism. Unusually severe human rights violations thus may overcome a pluralist presumption against intervention.

In much the same way, we rebel against paternalism because it denies autonomous agency. Unusually severe and heinous human rights violations, such as genocide and slavery, however, are such profound denials of individual autonomy that even a strong presumption against paternalism must give way.

As Walzer puts it, "when a government turns savagely upon its own people, we must doubt the very existence of a political community to which the idea of self-determination might apply" (1977: 101). When human rights violations are "so terrible that it makes talk of community or self-determination . . . seem cynical and irrelevant" (Walzer 1977: 90), the moral presumption against intervention may be overcome. Human rights violations that "shock the moral conscience of mankind" (Walzer 1977: 107) conclusively demonstrate that there are no moral bonds between a state and its citizens that demand the respect of outsiders.

In the post–Cold War era, such violations, especially genocide, are increasingly seen as offenses not simply against cosmopolitan values but also against the ethical norms of the society of states. Before considering whether international law is moving closer to international ethics (and how we should resolve the competing claims of law and morality), though, we must consider the political dimensions of humanitarian intervention, which introduce a third set of relevant norms.

4. Politics, Partisanship, and International Order

States (and international organizations), in addition to being moral and legal agents, are political actors. Therefore, they should (also) be evaluated by political standards, which include not only the national interests of particular states but also the interests of states and international society in international order.

One need not be a raving realist to suggest that political leaders are supposed to take into account the interests of their own states, in addition to acting in light of the demands of law, morality, and humanity. If the society of states has interests as well as values of its own, its members (states) may also appropriately take them into consideration. States thus may have good, even sufficient, political reasons for not intervening when they are morally and legally authorized—especially if we are talking of a right, rather than a duty,[10] of humanitarian intervention. Right-holders ordinarily are at liberty to choose not to exercise their rights, for reasons that include their own costs or (in)convenience.

No less important, even successful, purely humanitarian interventions may threaten international order. The exclusive spheres of domestic jurisdiction provided by territorial sovereignty dramatically reduce the occasions for interstate conflict. Humanitarian intervention reintroduces human rights violations and humanitarian crises as legitimate subjects of violent international conflict. Although perhaps desirable, all things considered, this is not without cost.[11]

I want to focus here, however, on the political problem of partisan abuse. Throughout the Cold War era both the United States and the Soviet Union appealed to "humanitarian" concerns and principles such as "democracy" largely as masks for geopolitical, economic, and ideological interests. There is thus

10. Weisburd (2001) develops an extended argument against the idea of a duty of humanitarian intervention. More briefly, see Murphy (1996: 294–297).

11. Bull (1977: chap. 4) provides a classic discussion of the tension between order and justice in international society.

strong historical support for Ian Brownlie's claim that "a rule allowing humanitarian intervention . . . is a general license to vigilantes and opportunists to resort to hegemonial intervention" (1973: 147–148).[12]

Moral principles (alone) rarely determine political behavior. International legal precepts regularly are interpreted and applied with an eye to power. Adequately evaluating either individual interventions or proposals for a general authorizing rule thus requires political knowledge of how doctrines and precedents are likely to be used by those with the power to intervene.[13]

In the political circumstances of the Cold War (and the immediate post–Cold War era), I argued strongly against a humanitarian exception to the principle of nonintervention (1984; 1993). Despite the strong moral case, the political and legal environments were so unpromising that giving priority to the danger of partisan abuse seemed the best course. There was a clear international normative consensus, across the First, Second, and Third Worlds, that humanitarian intervention was legally prohibited. And genuinely humanitarian intervention was politically unlikely, not only because of the veto in the Security Council but because neither superpower had much of an inclination to intervene, for reasons that were centrally, let alone primarily, humanitarian. The problem during the Cold War was less one of too little intervention of the right kind than too much of the wrong kind. A pattern of superpower *anti*humanitarian intervention, in places such as Guatemala, Hungary, Czechoslovakia, and Nicaragua, was well established.

Normative and political changes in post–Cold War international society, however, suggest reconsidering such a blanket rejection. Partisanship remains a serious problem that is likely to increase when bipolar or multipolar political rivalry reasserts itself. Interventions not authorized by the Security Council may undermine respect for international law and order, even if they have genuinely humanitarian motivations and consequences. The United Nations has proved no humanitarian panacea, as Rwanda so tragically illustrates. Nonetheless, changing conceptions of security and sovereignty—which are closely connected to the growing penetration of international human rights norms into the political thinking of ruling elites, political opposition movements, and ordinary citizens around the globe—do seem to be moving international society

12. Dino Kritsiotis, however, rightly points out that the potential for abuse does not establish that humanitarian intervention is illegal. The proper legal response to concerns of abuse should be to develop clear criteria for identifying abuse and safeguards against its occurrence (1998: 1022–1023). In other words, we are dealing here with a political or policy issue.

13. For arguments that even in the post–Cold War era the language of humanitarianism remains a mask for great power domination, see Mutua (2001), Hadjor (1998), and, with special reference to Kosovo, Nambiar (2000). Mutua argues that universal human rights claims are a symptom of "a seemingly incurable virus" that leads the West to assert its "cultural and conceptual dominance" (2001: 210).

closer to accepting an antigenocide exception to the prohibition of intervention.

5. Changing Conceptions of Security and Sovereignty

The standard referent of "security" in international relations is national or state security, defined in primarily military and economic terms. Thus understood, there is no necessary or even obvious connection between security and human rights.[14] In fact, ruling regimes have frequently viewed (national) security and human rights as competing concerns. Consider, for example, the national security states of Latin America in the 1970s, the states of the Soviet bloc during the Cold War, and the United States during the McCarthy era.

The 1975 Helsinki Final Act of the Conference on Security and Cooperation in Europe (CSCE) was one of the earliest concrete expressions of an international political vision of security directly linked to human rights.[15] The states of Europe, plus the United States and Canada, met primarily to ratify the European borders established after World War II and to lay the foundations for a more stable policy of détente. The most important elements of the Helsinki process, however, proved to be its human rights provisions (Thomas 2001).

Human rights were not merely addressed in a major security agreement between the superpowers, they were treated as a security issue. The central concern for national security was not supplanted. It was, however, supplemented by a conception of personal security.[16] In a series of CSCE follow-up conferences, Western states emphasized the security of individuals and drew attention to the threats to that security, defined in terms of internationally recognized human rights, posed by (Soviet bloc) states.

The Helsinki process, however, did not challenge reigning conceptions of sovereignty. Other than public shaming, foreign states had no direct role in implementing human rights. Challenges to a rigid, legal positivist conception of sovereignty emerged from a more general diffusion of human rights values.

Sovereignty is typically defined as supreme authority: to be sovereign is to be

14. On alternative ways to conceptualize the relationship between human rights and security, see Forsythe (1993).

15. The United Nations Charter, especially in the Preamble and Article 1, explicitly links human rights to international peace and security. These statements of moral and political aspirations, however, did not solidify into legal and political norms—let alone practice—in the following decades.

16. Today it is becoming standard to talk of "human security." (For a useful annotated bibliography, see http://www.humansecurity-chs.org/first/BIBLIOGRAPHY.html.) The Helsinki era conception, however, was substantially narrower. And "human security" is so frequently used in expansive senses to include almost all good things that I prefer this narrower (although less familiar) language.

subject to no higher authority. States often present their sovereignty as a natural right or an inescapable logical feature of their existence. In fact, however, it is a matter of mutual recognition: sovereigns are those who are recognized as sovereign by other sovereigns, and that recognition never has been unconditional (compare Linklater 2000: 485–487). At minimum, states are required to control their territory and be willing to participate in the system of international law. Historically, other tests have been applied as well.

In the nineteenth century, full sovereign rights were extended only to states that met minimum standards of "civilization" (Gong 1984; Schwarzenberger 1955). In contrast to imperial domination or colonial rule, Western states recognized (rather than denied or extinguished) the sovereignty of China, Japan, the Ottoman Empire, and Siam, but the sovereignty of these "uncivilized" states was treated as impaired. The Chinese description of this period as the era of unequal treaties nicely captures the situation: treaties were between sovereigns but not equals.[17] I would suggest that human rights—or, more precisely, avoidance of genocide—is emerging as something like a new standard of civilization.[18]

Aggression provides another model for understanding changing conceptions of sovereignty. States guilty of aggression forfeit their right to nonintervention, as Iraq so dramatically illustrates. Although they remain sovereign, their aggression authorizes international action that infringes their territorial integrity and political independence. States guilty of, or about to embark on, genocide may likewise forfeit the protections of the principle of nonintervention.

We might also think of individuals—or at least large groups of victims of violence—acquiring some sort of international legal standing. Even under classical positivist conceptions of sovereignty, massacring *foreign* nationals in one's own territory was prohibited (as an offense against the state of which they were nationals). A comparable right for one's own nationals may be emerging. International society is in effect asserting a legitimate interest in the rights of all human beings threatened by genocide. Genocide is coming to be seen as an offense against international society as well as those directly attacked.

Perhaps the best evidence for such changing international understandings of sovereignty comes from a most unlikely source, the executive head of the

17. Although this practice reflected crude Western self-interest, it was not simply hypocritical. Japan provides the classic example of a country "graduating" to full status after having made the changes necessary to meet Western standards of "civilization" (Gong 1984: chap. 6; Suganami 1984).

18. I develop such an argument in Donnelly (1998). The uncomfortable overtones of abusive paternalism in this language underscore the potential for partisan abuse. Past abuse, however, is no reason to avoid doing the right thing in the future—although it does demand careful, skeptical scrutiny of allegedly principled behavior.

United Nations, an institution that traditionally has treated sovereignty with the respect due to the holiest of religious relics. Kofi Annan argues that individual sovereignty, rooted in human rights, is taking its place in international relations alongside state sovereignty. "When we read the charter today, we are more than ever conscious that its aim is to protect individual human beings, not to protect those who abuse them" (1999). And the December 2001 report of the International Commission on Intervention and State Sovereignty to the General Assembly promises to be a watershed event in international discussions of humanitarian intervention.[19]

The Kosovo intervention, along with those in Bosnia and East Timor, and the strong international reaction against inaction in Rwanda suggest that substantial parts of the international community, including some leading powers, are increasingly uncomfortable with, and perhaps even unwilling to accept, continued national authority for implementing the internationally recognized human right to protection against genocide. As Thomas Franck put it, "egregious repression of minorities is not a risk-free venture, particularly for smallish states. That cannot be a statement of law, but, like law, it *is* a fairly accurate predictor of state behavior" (1999: 859).[20] To that I would add that such behavior may signal, and help to generate, significant changes in the law.

6. Justifying the Antigenocide Norm

The 1948 Convention on the Prevention and Punishment of the Crime of Genocide defines genocide as "acts committed with intent to destroy, in whole or in part, a national, ethnical, racial or religious group, as such" (Art. 1). Many mass killings do not meet this authoritative international legal definition. For example, most of the victims of the Khmer Rouge were targeted for political reasons (although certain minority ethnic groups, such as the Cham, were singled out for special attacks that probably did meet the treaty definition). And in at least some humanitarian crises—perhaps Somalia in 1992 or Eastern Zaire in 1996—suffering has been largely unintended.

I will use "genocide" in a looser sense to refer to any killing of large numbers of people in a particular place in a short time. Although international law and many national legal systems provide greater protection against racial and ethnic discrimination than against political discrimination, the trend in recent discussions seems to be toward treating mass killing as mass killing ("genocide"), whatever the reason or modality. (The technically more correct term "politicide" has not caught on outside of its use among a narrow group of scholars.)

19. See http://www.iciss.gc.ca/menu-e.asp.

20. For an at least partially dissenting view, suggesting that the costs of humanitarian intervention will preclude a serious rethinking of sovereignty by states, see James (2000: 341–342).

The moral case for intervention against "genocide" is relatively unproblematic. The nature of the crime even allows us to circumvent the notorious incommensurability of competing moral theories.

As we saw in §3.2, John Rawls usefully distinguishes "comprehensive religious, philosophical, or moral doctrines" from "political conceptions of justice" (1996: xliii–xlv, 11–15, 174–176; 1999: 31–32, 172–173). Adherents of different comprehensive doctrines may reach an "overlapping consensus" (1996: 133–172, 385–396) on a political conception of justice. I want to suggest that such an overlapping consensus exists today on the prohibition of genocide.

Whatever one's moral theory—or at least across most of today's leading theories and principles—*this* kind of suffering cannot be morally tolerated. Some such notion seems to underlie Jarat Chopra and Tom Weiss's (1995) idea of "humanitarian space." It seems implicit in Walzer's appeal to abuses that shock the moral conscience of mankind. I would suggest that the restriction of post–Cold War humanitarian intervention to action against genocide rests on the limits of strong overlapping international consensus.

The interdependence of all human rights, and the underlying idea that human rights are about a life of dignity and not mere life, makes acting *only* against genocide highly problematic. We place ourselves in the morally paradoxical position of failing to respond to comparable or even greater suffering so long as it remains geographically or temporarily diffuse. As uncomfortable as this may be, though, it seems to me the least indefensible option when we take into account the full range of moral, legal, and political claims in contemporary international society.

In the absence of a clear overlapping consensus—which I think exists today only for genocide[21]—the moral hurdle of respect for the autonomy of political communities is very hard to scale. Politically and legally, the restriction to genocide reflects the continuing centrality of state sovereignty. Whatever the impact of "globalization," state sovereignty remains central to international law and politics, and sovereign states remain insistent on asserting and enjoying their internationally recognized rights. In addition, an active sense of cosmopolitan moral community remains very thin. There is no logically necessary, let alone automatic, spillover from coercive international action against genocide to a broader right of humanitarian intervention on other grounds.

7. Changing Legal Practices

The Genocide Convention (Art. 6) specifies enforcement through trial before "a competent tribunal of the State in the territory of which the act was com-

21. In particular, there is nothing like a consensus on a right to democratic governance, which has been strongly championed by Thomas Franck (1992) and has considerable resonance in U.S. foreign policy. For a good discussion of the legal status of such a right, see Fox and Roth (2000).

mitted, or by such international penal tribunal as may have jurisdiction"—of which there were none until the 1990s. Nuremberg set a precedent for international judicial action, not armed intervention. And, as we have seen, before the 1990s there was no evidence of a customary right to intervene against genocide.

Today, however, we have both ad hoc and permanent international criminal tribunals. In addition, an emerging body of state practice can be read to support an argument for the emergence of an international legal right of humanitarian intervention. Debate in the legal literature thus increasingly addresses not whether humanitarian intervention is ever legally permissible but who has a right to intervene against genocide and when.

"Collective humanitarian intervention, when undertaken or authorized by the UN, now meets with little controversy" (Nanda, Muther, and Eckert 1998: 862).[22] Although still something of an exaggeration, it is only in the past decade that such a claim has become even plausible. During the Cold War, genocide simply was not treated as a threat to or breach of international peace and security (the only ground explicitly provided by the Charter for enforcement action). The Security Council, however, does seem to be moving toward an understanding of security closer to that outlined above—although, as Frederick Kirgis discreetly notes, the Council has been "disinclined to explain what it saw as the threat to international peace" in its more humanitarian actions (1995: 513).

Actions not authorized by the Security Council, however, still are almost universally considered illegal. Louis Henkin spoke for most commentators when he wrote, following the Kosovo intervention, that "the law is, and ought to be, that unilateral intervention by military force by a state or group of states is unlawful unless authorized by the Security Council" (Henkin 1999: 826).

But the moral arguments for humanitarian intervention should not be ignored. A world of lawyer kings would not be all that much more attractive than one of philosopher kings. If we are to confront seriously the problems posed by humanitarian intervention, we must weigh the full range of competing norms and claims against one another.

Over the past decade, international society has begun to allow for an increasingly complex interaction of law, morality, and politics in assessing claims for the legitimacy of humanitarian intervention. Consider Kosovo in light of the "precedent" of Rwanda. The Council's refusal to authorize intervention until most of the damage was done provoked a powerful mixture of outrage and shame both within the UN and in many member states. In Kosovo, having "learned the lesson of Rwanda," NATO neither waited until the bodies were piled high nor was deterred by the lack of Security Council authorization. The response was outrage in many circles and substantial unease even among many who accepted the intervention as justified.

22. For partially dissenting views, see Alvarez (1996) and Gardam (1996).

Both sets of reactions seem to me appropriate. We see much the same tension in the conclusion of the Independent International Commission on Kosovo that the NATO intervention was "illegal but legitimate" (2000: 4).[23] To capture these crucial ambiguities and ambivalences, discussions of the "justification" of humanitarian intervention need to be much more subtle and complex than they often have been, especially in the legal and moral literatures (which, understandably but ultimately unhelpfully, tend to focus on a single set of norms).

8. "Justifying" Humanitarian Intervention

A humanitarian intervention might be held to be justified only if (fully) *authorized* in the sense that it meets the demands of all relevant standards. The force of the moral principle of self-determination and the legal principle of sovereignty gives such a stringent conception considerable appeal, but there are other important and relevant senses of justification.

Contested justifications arise when different standards point in different directions.[24] Positive authorization, as I have defined it, requires that all relevant standards be satisfied: where *a* prohibits action but *b* permits it, *a* trumps *b*. But it is no less plausible to see *a* and *b* as offsetting, making the intervention both "justified" and "unjustified."[25] This seems to me the right way to assess genuinely humanitarian interventions not authorized by the Security Council: they are legally prohibited but may be morally authorized. Contested interventions are particularly interesting because they are likely to be the focal points of change, the locus of the most important struggles over dominant norms and practices.

Two kinds of contested justifications merit special note. Some interventions are clearly prohibited but nonetheless *excusable*. Stealing food to feed one's family, for example, is clearly illegal. But we are disinclined to say that it is simply, or perhaps even all things considered, unjustified. Even in a court of law (let alone the court of public opinion) the moral obligation to one's family may carry considerable weight, especially at the time of sentencing. Thus the Tanzanian intervention that overthrew Idi Amin in Uganda, although a clear viola-

23. Simma (1999) and Cassese (1999) develop similar arguments. For arguments in favor of the legality of the Kosovo intervention, see Mertus (2000) and Alexander (2000). On the issue of anticipatory intervention, see Charney (1999) and Joyner and Arend (1999).

24. Almost all interventions are likely to be contested in the sense that someone (other than the target) objects. I distinguish here between interventions that are *relatively* uncontested and those where leading powers or a large number of states plausibly reject or counter a plausibly advanced claim of authorization.

25. The abstract theoretical possibility of something being neither authorized nor prohibited has no apparent relevance to humanitarian interventions, given existing norms of sovereignty and nonintervention.

tion of international and regional law, met with only relatively modest verbal condemnation—and received considerable informal and popular support—because it removed a barbarous regime at relatively modest cost (assuming that we need not attribute the atrocities of the second Obote regime to the Tanzanians).

Contrast this with Vietnam's intervention that removed the Khmer Rouge in Cambodia. Read (as I think it can plausibly be seen) as an effort to impose a quasi-imperial regional hegemony, it was, at best, (merely) *tolerable*. If excusable interventions intentionally produce desirable outcomes, tolerable interventions produce good results largely unintentionally. Although good consequences carry some weight, intentions are also important to our evaluation.

An excusable act reflects an underlying norm with which we have considerable sympathy. We may even want to commend that norm: you *ought* to steal if that is truly the only way to feed your family. The principle underlying a merely tolerable act, however, cannot be widely endorsed. The positive humanitarian consequences are largely a fortunate accident. However thankful we may be for the results, we should not give much credit to those who produce them.[26]

These varied senses of "justified" reflect the pull of competing norms. The resulting confusion and complexities have led to regular efforts to formulate tests or criteria for permissible humanitarian interventions.[27] Such lists are in many ways helpful. They do not, however, specify necessary and sufficient conditions that define a unambiguous threshold of justifiability. Rather, they identify factors that ought to be considered in any evaluation of an intervention's justifiability.

There is no simple, mechanical means for resolving the competing moral, legal, and political considerations raised by most humanitarian interventions. "The calculations are tortuous, and the mathematics far from exact" (Weiss 1999: 22). Usually we can only appeal to our best-considered judgment and strive for arguments that, although not decisive, have a certain force. In §11 I offer an illustration of such as assessment in the case of Kosovo.

9. Mixed Motives and the Problem of Consistency

A different kind of conflict of standards arises when interveners have mixed motives. A growing number of states see preventing, stopping, or punishing

26. These references to consequences remind us that a full evaluation of an intervention must take into account how it was carried out. For reasons of simplicity and economy I have focused solely on the decision to intervene, with the proviso that good humanitarian consequences may provide some sort of mitigation in the case of otherwise unjustifiable interventions.

27. See, for example, Lillich (1967: 347-350), Fonteyne (1974: 235, 258–268), Fairley (1980: 60–61), Hassan (1981: 865, 890–900), Nanda (1992), and Charney (1999: 838–840).

genocide as part of their national interest. Such interests, however, rarely determine foreign policy when soldiers must be put at risk or when interveners face high financial or political costs. Humanitarian interventions thus are likely only when humanitarian motives are supported by more selfish national interests.

Any suggestion that such economic and political interests invalidate humanitarian motives and render an intervention unjustified, however, reflects an absurd moral perfectionism that is dubious even in individual action and is certainly misguided when applied to states. Even when political motives conflict with moral or legal norms—which is not always the case—we need to *balance* the competing motives for and consequences of both action and inaction. The degree of humanitarian motivation certainly should be taken into account when judging an intervention, but the presence, even centrality, of nonhumanitarian motives does not necessarily reduce its justifiability.

A variant on the theme of mixed motives is the charge of selectivity or inconsistency: because one did not intervene in A, which is in all essential ways similar to B, intervening in B is somehow unjustified. Consistency is desirable, for many political, psychological, and even moral reasons.[28] But as Peter Baehr nicely puts it, "one act of commission is not invalidated by many acts of omission" (2000: 32 n.75). The fact that I have acted badly in the past ought not to compel me to act badly in the future.

Faced with multiple conflicting standards, the very notion of consistency becomes problematic. A state that supports genocide when committed by friends but intervenes against it when committed by an enemy may merit disdain, but not for inconsistency. Such behavior shows great political consistency, a consistent lack of central humanitarian motivation. Inconsistency arguments usually prove to be instead arguments that give categorical priority to one set of standards—in the case of humanitarian intervention, usually law or morality—over another (compare §9.6).

I have argued, by contrast, for an appreciation of the complex and contingent interaction of often competing moral, legal, and political considerations.[29] We may, all things considered, have good reasons to give priority to concerns of (il)legality or moral purity. But simple answers to the question "Is this humanitarian intervention justified?" rarely are good answers, at least where either genuine humanitarian motives or significant humanitarian consequences are involved.

28. For a thoughtful discussion of when selective interventions are problematic and why, see Brilmayer (1995).

29. Damrosch (2000) offers a thoughtful discussion and limited defense of "selectivity" in the context of the Kosovo intervention.

10. Politics and the Authority to Intervene

The problem of the authority to intervene can also be reformulated in terms of competing standards of evaluation. The Security Council has the legal authority to intervene but has been, and is likely to remain, extremely reluctant to exercise it. Other actors, such as NATO in Kosovo, may have the will and the capabilities to intervene but they lack the legal authority. When faced with a conflict between legal and moral norms, I would argue that political considerations, rather than a corrupting influence, ought to weigh heavily in decisions to act and in judgments of such actions.

Enforcement action by the Security Council, beyond its legal attractions, has the political virtue of being unlikely in the absence of a central humanitarian aim. Although Council-authorized action may in principle reflect merely the shared selfish interests of the great powers, in practice this is improbable. A similar logic may apply to regional organizations that are not hegemonically dominated. The likelihood of partisan abuse is reduced by the need to build coalitions across states.

Great powers acting alone have historically engaged in many more *anti*humanitarian than humanitarian interventions. Therefore, multilateral rather than unilateral intervention is on its face to be preferred. But unilateral state power may save lives that would be lost while waiting for a more "pure" multilateral intervention that never comes.

Order, security, and even justice in the anarchical society of states cannot be separated from state power—which may be used for good as well as evil. Where intervention rests almost entirely on selfish national interests, with little broader support among other states or in the target country, the "authority" of the intervening state is much like that of the highwayman. But the action may be more that of a policeman when a state or group of states intervenes as a de facto representative of victims or of broader communities. Even a single state may act on behalf of broader moral or political communities—which may offer active or passive support, or the indirect "support" of not opposing the intervention.

How should we handle claims of moral or political authority in the absence of the legal authority of Security Council authorization? The dangers of partisan abuse still seem to me sufficiently great that, even when genuinely humanitarian motives are central, such interventions usually should be considered only excusable. We should deal with them case by case, as they arise, being especially wary of treating them as precedents. Developing a *doctrine* of humanitarian intervention without Security Council authorization, whatever its moral attractions, seems to me profoundly unwise.

This admittedly leaves regional and unilateral interveners in an awkward position. That seems to me not merely preferable to the alternatives but fundamentally correct; they *should* bear an additional justificatory burden. We should take seriously, but not too seriously, the illegality of (humanitarian) intervention not authorized by the Security Council.

11. Judging the Kosovo Intervention

With all of these considerations in mind, let us return to the case of Kosovo. To sharpen the argument, let us give the NATO decision to intervene the most favorable possible interpretation. In particular, let us agree that genocide was either imminent or already under way.[30] Without that, even the moral case is seriously undermined (except for some radical cosmopolitans).

Security Council action was blocked by the relatively "principled" objections of Russia and China, as well as Russia's selfish political interests in its relationship with Serbia. The OSCE, the most obvious regional actor, had neither the desire nor the legal authority to use force. A similar combination of legal and political constraints blocked action through the European Union or the Council of Europe. Unilateral action by the United States, however, was unacceptable to almost all states.

Nonetheless, the United States, Britain, and many states of continental Western European were unwilling to stand by and allow genocide in Kosovo. Faced with a genuine dilemma, the members of NATO decided, not implausibly it seems to me, that intervention was the lesser of two evils. The decision to intervene can thus be seen as at least tolerable, perhaps even excusable.

Interveners in such cases, however, ought to bear the burden of demonstrating that their illegal behavior is not ultimately culpable.[31] The leading powers were less than clear in their self-justifications (see Shinoda 2000), although in large part it seems to me because of their reticence to appeal centrally to humanitarian concerns.[32] Nonetheless, the United States in this case acted like a

30. In support of this interpretation, see Mertus (1999), Physicians for Human Rights (1999), Independent International Commission on Kosovo (2000: Annexe 1), and Human Rights Watch (2001). If the reader cannot accept this account, what follows can be read as an illustrative discussion of a hypothetical case loosely modeled on "the real" Kosovo.

31. A more complete assessment would require considering the rights of innocents, which were infringed by the excessive reliance on high-altitude bombing, and the obligations of proportionality. The picture, however, is complicated by political realities. Could the intervention have been carried to its conclusion if several NATO pilots had been shot down? If not, did the positive humanitarian consequences that were achieved outweigh the costs to innocent civilians? These seem to me profoundly difficult questions.

32. Vital national interests, in the classical realist sense of that term, played a surprisingly peripheral, tenuous, and shifting role in the arguments of both the United States and Britain. Even David Rieff, who has been generally critical of U.S. policy in the region and who specifically attacked the handling of the Kosovo intervention after it was launched, allows that it was "undertaken more in the name of human rights and moral obligation than out of any traditional concep-

hegemon—a leader acting with normative authority and a collective purpose (in addition, of course, to power and self-interest)—rather than unilaterally or imperially.[33] A Russian resolution rejecting the NATO intervention was not vetoed but defeated (on March 26, 1999) by a vote of 12 to 3.

As a liberal American whose political views were shaped during the Vietnam war, I must admit to being more than a bit uncomfortable with this (limited) defense of the Kosovo intervention. Although I think that it is substantively sound in this particular case, it has considerable potential for partisan abuse and a very troubling "selectivity." In most of the world there is neither a regional organization nor a dominant actor with the power, legitimacy, and commitment needed to intervene successfully. The effective exemption of the permanent members of the Security Council from United Nations action, and a comparable effective exemption of leading regional powers such as Nigeria and India (and their clients or allies), only increases the problem of selectivity. Kosovo also raises the specter of what might be called coercive regionalism, in which the target of action is not a member of the intervening "regional" community.

Regionalism, and even ad hoc coalitions, however, may fill a gap when global institutions are unwilling or unable to aid victims.[34] And regional intervention is likely to increase the role of genuine humanitarian motivations, if only by increasing the number of (potentially competing) national interests that must be accommodated. Selective humanitarian intervention, for all its problems, may be preferable to no humanitarian intervention at all.

Caution is in order. The presumption always ought to be against intervention not authorized by the Security Council. But that presumption may in rare cases be overcome.

Problems of authority, selectivity, and inequality are likely to recur so long as we retain an international system structured around sovereign states—that

---

tion of national interest" (1999: 1). Of course, it is not obvious that this is a good thing. As Coral Bell notes, "the most chilling, alarming, or exasperating aspect of Western policy . . . may have been that it was visibly 'norm driven' rather than 'interest driven'" because norms tend to be "universal and not subject to compromise" (2000: 460).

33. The ancient Greeks usefully distinguished *hegemonia* from *arche*, "rule," the standard term for what we translate as "empire." (Contemporary Gramscians draw a similar, although somewhat different, distinction between *hegemony* and *force*.) The common use of "hegemonic" to mean dominant obscures the crucial distinction between various senses of and means to domination. It also systematically slights the role of norms and authority in, and the reality of, international society in favor of a crude materialism that obscures the variety of international political practices and processes.

34. Some system of after-the-fact review, by the Security Council or even the General Assembly, might reduce the risks of partisan abuse. Unfortunately, there is no evidence that even an informal practice of review is emerging and good reason to expect strong and, in the short run at least, fatal, resistance to any such proposals, especially (but by no means only) from the United States.

is, for the foreseeable future. Perhaps, though, we are finally beginning to grapple with them, rather than leaving complete authority to sovereign states, even when they choose to exercise that authority genocidally. Giving full weight to both the moral limitations of intervening only against genocide and the very real dangers of partisan politics, this still seems to me a small but significant step forward for international human rights.

References

Abdelkader, Dina. 2000. *Social Justice in Islam.* Herndon, Va.: International Institute of Islamic Thought.

Abramson, Paul R., and Steven D. Pinkerton, eds. 1995. *Sexual Nature, Sexual Culture.* Chicago: University of Chicago Press.

Adams, Kirstine, and Andrew Byrnes, eds. 1999. *Gender Equality and the Judiciary: Using International Standards to Promote the Human Rights of Women and the Girl Child at the National Level.* London: Commonwealth Secretariat.

Alexander, Klinton W. 2000. "NATO's Intervention in Kosovo: The Legal Case for Violating Yugoslavia's National Sovereignty in the Absence of Security Council Approval." *Houston Journal of International Law* 22 (Spring): 403–449.

Alfredsson, Gudmundur, and Erika Ferrer. 1999. *Minority Rights: A Guide to United Nations Procedures and Institutions.* London: Minority Rights Group International.

Ali, Shaheen Sardar. 2000. *Gender and Human Rights in Islam and International Law: Equal Before Allah, Unequal Before Man?* Boston: Kluwer Law International.

Al-Marzouqi, Ibrahim Abdulla. 2000. *Human Rights in Islamic Law.* Abu Dhabi.

Alston, Philip. 1984. "Conjuring up New Human Rights: A Proposal for Quality Control." *American Journal of International Law* 78 (July): 607–621.

Alston, Philip, ed. 1999. *The EU and Human Rights.* Oxford: Oxford University Press.

Alston, Philip, and Bridget Gilmour-Walsh. 1996. *The Best Interests of the Child: Towards a Synthesis of Children's Rights and Cultural Values.* Florence: International Child Development Centre, UNICEF.

Alston, Philip, Stephen Parker, and John Seymour, eds. 1992. *Children, Rights, and the Law.* Oxford: Clarendon Press.

Alvarez, Jose E. 1996. "Judging the Security Council." *American Journal of International Law* 90 (January): 1–39.

Ames, Roger. 1997. "Continuing the Conversation on Chinese Human Rights." *Ethics and International Affairs* 11: 177–205.

Amnesty International. 2001a. *Crimes of Hate, Conspiracy of Silence: Torture and Ill-Treatment Based on Sexual Identity.* AI Index ACT 40/016/2001.

———. 2001b. *Ecuador: No to "Social Cleansing of People because of their Sexual Orientation.* AI Index AMR 28/011/2001.

———. 2001c. *Egypt: Torture and Imprisonment for Actual or Perceived Sexual Orientation.* AI Index MDE 12/034/2001.

Amnesty International United Kingdom. 1997. *Breaking the Silence: Human Rights Violations Based on Sexual Orientation.* London: Amnesty International United Kingdom.

Anand, Sudhir, and Amartya K. Sen. 1996. *Sustainable Human Development: Concepts and Priorities.* New York: United Nations Development Programme, Office of Development Studies.

Angle, Stephen C. 2002. *Human Rights and Chinese Thought: A Cross-Cultural Inquiry.* Cambridge: Cambridge University Press.

Ankumah, Evelyn A. 1996. *The African Commission on Human and Peoples' Rights: Practice and Procedures.* Dordrecht: Martinus Nijhoff.

An-Na'im, Abdullahi. 1987. "Religious Minorities under Islamic Law and the Limits of Cultural Relativism." *Human Rights Quarterly* 9 (February): 1–18.

———. 1990. *Toward an Islamic Reformation: Civil Liberties, Human Rights, and International Law.* Syracuse: Syracuse University Press.

———. 1992. "Toward a Cross-Cultural Approach to Defining International Standards of Human Rights: The Meaning of Cruel, Inhuman, or Degrading Treatment or Punishment." In *Human Rights in Cross-Cultural Perspectives: A Quest for Consensus.* Edited by Abdullahi An-Na'im. Philadelphia: University of Pennsylvania Press.

———. 2001. "The Legal Protection of Human Rights in Africa: How to Do More with Less." In *Human Rights: Concepts, Contests, Contingencies.* Edited by Austin Sarat and Thomas R. Kearns. Ann Arbor: University of Michigan Press.

Annan, Kofi. 1999. "Two Concepts of Sovereignty." *The Economist* (September 18): http://www.economist.com/displayStory.cfm?Story=_ID=324795.

Anwar, Ibrahim. 1994. Luncheon Address. Paper read at JUST International Conference, "Rethinking Human Rights," at Kuala Lampur.

Apffel-Marglin, Frederique, and Stephen A. Marglin, eds. 1990. *Dominating Knowledge: Development, Culture, and Resistance.* Oxford: Clarendon Press.

Apodaca, Clair, and Michael Stohl. 1999. "United States Human Rights Policy and Foreign Assistance." *International Studies Quarterly* 43 (March): 185–198.

Appiah, K. Anthony. 2001. "Grounding Human Rights." In Amy Gutmann, ed. *Human Rights as Politics and Idolatry, by Michael Ignatieff.* Princeton: Princeton University Press.

Apter, David. 1965. *The Politics of Modernization.* Chicago: University of Chicago Press.

Arkes, Hadley. 1998. "The Axioms of Public Policy." In *Natural Law and Contemporary Public Policy.* Edited by David F. Forte. Washington, D.C.: Georgetown University Press.

Asante, S. K. B. 1969. "Nation Building and Human Rights in Emergent Africa." *Cornell International Law Journal* 2 (Spring): 72–107.

Askin, Kelly D., and Dorean N. Koenig, eds. 1999. *Women and International Human Rights Law.* Ardsley, N.Y.: Transnational.

Asquith, Stewart, and Malcolm Hill, eds. 1994. *Justice for Children.* Dordrecht: Martinus Nijhoff.

Austin, John. 1954 [1832]. *The Province of Jurisprudence Determined.* New York: Noonday Press.

Baehr, Peter R. 1997. "Problems of Aid Conditionality: The Netherlands and Indonesia." *Third World Quarterly* 18 (June): 363–376.

———. 2000a. "Controversies in the Current International Human Rights Debate." *Human Rights Review* 2 (October–December): 7–32.

———. 2000b. "Trials and Errors: The Netherlands and Human Rights." In *Human Rights and Comparative Foreign Policy.* Edited by David P. Forsythe. Tokyo: United Nations University Press.

Banerjee, Sanjoy. 2000. "India's Human Rights Diplomacy: Crisis and Transformation." In *Human Rights and Comparative Foreign Policy*. Edited by David P. Forsythe. Tokyo: United Nations University Press.

Bank, Roland. 2000. "Country-Oriented Procedures under the Convention against Torture: Toward a New Dynamism." In *The Future of UN Human Rights Treaty Monitoring*. Edited by Philip Alston and James Crawford. Cambridge: Cambridge University Press.

Banton, Michael. 1996. *International Action Against Racial Discrimination*. Oxford: Clarendon Press.

———. 2000. *Combating Racial Discrimination: The UN and Its Member States*. London: Minority Rights Group.

Barnhart, Michael G. 2001. "Getting Beyond Cross-Talk: Why Persisting Disagreements are Philosophically Nonfatal." In *Negotiating Human Rights and Culture*. Edited by Lynda Bell, Andrew J. Nathan, and Ilan Peleg. New York: Columbia University Press.

Bauer, Joanne R., and Daniel A. Bell, eds. 1999. *The East Asian Challenge for Human Rights*. Cambridge: Cambridge University Press.

Baxi, Upendra. 1999. "Voices of Suffering, Fragmented Universality, and the Future of Human Rights." In *The Future of International Human Rights*. Edited by Burns H. Weston and Stephen P. Marks. Ardsley, N.Y.: Transnational Publishers.

Bay, Christian. 1977. "Human Needs and Political Education." In *Human Needs and Politics*. Edited by Ross Fitzgerald. Rushcutters Bay: Pergamon Press (Australia).

———. 1982. "Self-respect as a Human Right: Thoughts on the Dialectics of Wants and Needs in the Struggle for Human Community." *Human Rights Quarterly* 4 (February): 53–75.

Bayefsky, Anne F., ed. 2000. *The UN Human Rights Treaty System in the 21st Century*. The Hague: Kluwer Law International.

Bayley, David. 1964. *Public Liberties in New States*. Chicago: Rand McNally.

Bayly, Susan. 1999. *Caste, Society and Politics in India from the Eighteenth Century to the Modern Age*. Cambridge: Cambridge University Press.

Bedau, Hugo Adam. 1979. "Human Rights and Foreign Assistance Programs." In *Human Rights and U.S. Foreign Policy*. Edited by Peter G. Brown and Douglas Maclean. Lexington, Va.: Lexington Books.

Beer, Lawrence W. 1976. "Freedom of Expression in Japan, with Comparative Reference to the United States." In *Comparative Human Rights*. Edited by Richard P. Claude. Baltimore: Johns Hopkins University Press.

Beitz, Charles R. 1979. "Bounded Morality: Justice and the State in World Politics." *International Organization* 33 (Summer): 405–420.

———. 1980. "Nonintervention and Communal Integrity." *Philosophy and Public Affairs* 9 (Summer): 385–391.

Bell, Coral. 2000. "Force, Diplomacy, and Norms." In *Kosovo and the Challenge of Humanitarian Intervention: Selective Indignation, Collective Action, and International Citizenship*. Edited by Albrecht Schnabel and Ramesh Thakur. Tokyo: United Nations University Press.

Bell, Daniel A. 1996. "The East Asian Challenge to Human Rights: Reflections on an East-West Dialogue." *Human Rights Quarterly* 18 (August): 641–667.

———. 2000. *East Meet West: Human Rights and Democracy in East Asia*. Princeton: Princeton University Press.

Bell, Lynda, Andrew J. Nathan, and Ilan Peleg. 2001. "Introduction: Culture and Human

Rights." In *Negotiating Culture and Human Rights*. Edited by Lynda Bell, Andrew J. Nathan, and Ilan Peleg. New York: Columbia University Press.

Bell, Lynda S. 2001. "Who Produces Asian Identity? Discourses, Discrimination, and Chinese Peasant Women in the Quest for Human Rights." In *Negotiating Culture and Human Rights*. Edited by Lynda Bell, Andrew J. Nathan, and Ilan Peleg. New York: Columbia University Press.

Benn, Stanley I. 1967. "Rights." In *The Encyclopedia of Philosophy*. New York: Macmillan.

Berger, Maurice, Brian Wallis, and Simon Watson, eds. 1995. *Constructing Masculinity*. New York: Routledge.

Berger, Peter L., and Thomas Luckmann. 1967. *The Social Construction of Reality: A Treatise in the Sociology of Knowledge*. New York: Doublcday.

Beteille, Andre. 1965. *Caste, Class, and Power: Changing Patterns of Stratification in a Tanjore Village*. Berkeley: University of California Press.

Bhagwati, Jagdish N. 1966. *The Economics of Underdeveloped Countries*. New York: McGraw-Hill.

Bhatti, Akhtar Khalid, and Jannat Gul e. 1996. *The Holy Quran on Human Rights*. Karachi: Royal Book Company.

Blackburn, Robert, ed. 1996. *The European Convention on Human Rights: The Impact of the European Convention on Human Rights on Human Rights in the Legal and Political Systems of Member States*. London: Mansell.

Blackburn, Robert, and Jörg Polakiewicz. 2001. *Fundamental Rights in Europe: The European Convention on Human Rights and its Member States, 1950–2000*. Oxford: Oxford University Press.

Blackwood, Evelyn, and Saskia E. Wieringa, eds. 1999. *Female Desires: Same-Sex Relations and Transgender Practices across Cultures*. New York: Columbia University Press.

Boaz, David. 1997. *Libertarianism: A Primer*. New York: Free Press.

Booth, Ken. 1999. "Three Tyrannies." In *Human Rights in Global Politics*. Edited by Tim Dunne and Nicholas J. Wheeler. Cambridge: Cambridge University Press.

Boswell, John. 1980. *Christianity, Social Tolerance and Homosexuality: Gay People in Western Europe from the Beginning of the Christian Era to the Fourteenth Century*. Chicago: University of Chicago Press.

———. 1994. *Same-Sex Unions in Premodern Europe*. New York: Villard Books.

Bougle, Celestin. 1971 [1908]. *Essays on the Caste System*. Cambridge: Cambridge University Press.

Boulding, Kenneth E. 1958. *Principles of Economic Policy*. Englewood Cliffs, N.J.: Prentice-Hall.

Brilmayer, Lea. 1995. "What's the Matter with Selective Intervention?" *Arizona Law Review* 37 (Winter): 955–970.

Brooten, Bernadette J. 1996. *Love Between Women: Early Christian Responses to Female Homoeroticism*. Chicago: University of Chicago Press.

Brown, Chris. 1999. "Universal Human Rights: A Critique." In *Human Rights in Global Politics*. Edited by Tim Dunne and Nicholas J. Wheeler. Cambridge: Cambridge University Press.

Brownlie, Ian. 1973. "Thoughts on Kind-Hearted Gunmen." In *Humanitarian Intervention and the United Nations*. Edited by Richard B. Lillich. Charlottesville: University Press of Virginia.

———. 1974. "Humanitarian Intervention." In *Law and Civil War in the Modern World*. Edited by John Norton Moore. Baltimore: Johns Hopkins University Press.

Brysk, Alison. 2000. *From Tribal Village to Global Village: Indian Rights and International Relations in Latin America.* Stanford: Stanford University Press.

Buchheit, Lee C. 1978. *Secession: The Legitimacy of Self-Determination.* New Haven: Yale University Press.

Buckley, William F. Jr. 1980. "Human Rights and Foreign Policy: A Proposal." *Foreign Affairs* 58 (Spring): 775–796.

Buergenthal, Thomas, and Dinah Shelton. 1995. *Protecting Human Rights in the Americas: Cases and Materials,* 4th ed. Arlington, Va.: N. P. Engel.

Bull, Hedley. 1977. *The Anarchical Society: A Study of Order in World Politics.* New York: Columbia University Press.

Burns, Peter. 2000. "The Committee against Torture." In *The UN Human Rights Treaty System in the 21st Century.* Edited by Anne F. Bayefsky. The Hague: Kluwer Law International.

Busia, Nana Kusi Appea Jr. 1994. "The Status of Human Rights in Pre-Colonial Africa: Implications for Contemporary Practices." In *Africa, Human Rights, and the Global System: The Political Economy of Human Rights in a Changing World.* Edited by George W. Shepherd, Eileen McCarthy-Arnolds, David R. Penna, and Debra Joy Cruz Sobrepena. Westport, Conn.: Greenwood Press.

Bustelo, Mara R. 2000. "The Committee on the Elimination of Discrimnationa against Women at the Crossroads." In *The Future of UN Human Rights Treaty Monitoring.* Edited by Philip Alston and James Crawford. Cambridge: Cambridge University Press.

Buultjens, Ralph. 1980. "Human Rights in Indian Political Culture." In *The Moral Imperatives of Human Rights: A World Survey.* Edited by Kenneth W. Thompson. Washington, D.C.: University Press of America.

Byrnes, Andrew. 2000. "An Effective Complaints Process in the Context of International Human Rights Law." In *The UN Human Rights Treaty System in the 21st Century.* Edited by Anne F. Bayefsky. The Hague: Kluwer Law International.

Byrnes, Andrew, Jane Connors, and Lum Bik, eds. 1997. *Advancing the Human Rights of Women: Using International Human Rights Standards in Domestic Litigation.* London: The Commonwealth Secretariat.

Callaghy, Thomas M. 1980. "State-Subject Communication in Zaire: Domination and the Concept of Domain Consensus." *Journal of Modern African Studies* 18 (September): 469–492.

Campos, Jose Edgardo, and Hilton L. Root. 1996. *The Key to the Asian Miracle: Making Shared Growth Credible.* Washington, D.C.: The Brookings Institution.

Cantarella, Eva. 1992. *Bisexuality in the Ancient World.* New Haven: Yale University Press.

Cardoso, Fernando Henrique, and Enzo Faletto. 1979. *Dependency and Development in Latin America.* Berkeley: University of California Press.

Carleton, David, and Michael Stohl. 1985. "The Foreign Policy of Human Rights: Rhetoric and Reality from Jimmy Carter to Ronald Reagan." *Human Rights Quarterly* 7 (May): 205–229.

Cassese, Antonio. 1999. "*Ex iniuria ius oritur*: Are We Moving Towards International Legitimation of Forcible Humanitarian Countermeasures in the World Community?" *European Journal of International Law* 10: http://www.ejil.org/journal/Vol10/No1/com.html.

Cauquelin, Josiane, Paul Lim, and Birgit Mayer-Konig, eds. 1998. *Asian Values: An Encounter with Diversity.* Richmond, Sydney: Curzon.

Charney, Jonathan I. 1999. "Anticipatory Humanitarian Intervention." *American Journal of International Law* 93 (October): 834–841.

Chatterjee, Satischandra. 1950. *The Fundamentals of Hinduism: A Philosophical Study.* Calcutta: Das Gupta and Company.

Chenery, Hollis B., and Moises Syrquin. 1975. *Patterns of Development, 1950–1970.* London: Oxford University Press.

China. 1991. *Human Rights in China.* Beijing: Information Office of the State Council.

———. 1993. Statement by H. E. Mr. Liu Hiaqui. Paper read at Second World Conference on Human Rights, at Vienna.

Chkhidvadze, V. 1980. "Constitution of True Human Rights and Freedoms." *International Affairs (Moscow)* (October): 13–20.

Chopra, Jarat, and Thomas G. Weiss. 1995. "Sovereignty under Siege: From Intervention to Humanitarian Space." In *Beyond Westphalia? State Sovereignty and International Intervention.* Edited by Gene M. Lyons and Michael Mastanduno. Baltimore: Johns Hopkins University Press.

Chua, Beng-Huat. 1992. "Australian and Asian Perceptions of Human Rights." In *Australia's Human Rights Diplomacy.* Edited by Ian Russell, Peter Van Ness, and Beng-Huat Chua. Canberra: Australian National University Press.

Cingranelli, David L., and Thomas E. Pasquarello. 1985. "Human Rights Practices and the Distribution of U.S. Foreign Aid to Latin American Countries." *American Journal of Political Science* 29 (August): 539–563.

Clapham, Andrew. 2000. "UN Human Rights Reporting Procedures: An NGO Perspective." In *The Future of UN Human Rights Treaty Monitoring.* Edited by Philip Alston and James Crawford. Cambridge: Cambridge University Press.

Claude, Inis L. Jr. 1955. *National Minorities: An International Problem.* Cambridge, Mass.: Harvard University Press.

Collier, David, and Steven Levitsky. 1997. "Democracy with Adjectives: Conceptual Innovation in Comparative Research." *World Politics* 49 (April): 430–451.

Comstock, Gary David. 1991. *Violence Against Lesbians and Gay Men.* New York: Columbia University Press.

Connors, Jane. 2000. "An Analysis and Evaluation of the System of State Reporting." In *The UN Human Rights Treaty System in the 21st Century.* Edited by Anne F. Bayefsky. The Hague: Kluwer Law International.

Cook, Rebecca J., ed. 1994. *Human Rights of Women: National and International Perspectives.* Philadelphia: University of Pennsylvania Press.

Coomaraswamy, Radhika. 1980. "Human Rights Research and Education: An Asian Perspective." In *International Congress on the Teaching of Human Rights: Working Documents and Recommendations.* Paris: UNESCO.

Cooper, John F. 1994. "Peking's Post-Tiananmen Foreign Policy: The Human Rights Factor." *Issues and Studies* 30 (October): 49–73.

Cotran, Eugene, and Adel Omar Sherif, eds. 1999. *Democracy, the Rule of Law and Islam.* London: Kluwer Law International.

Cox, Robert W. 1996. *Approaches to World Order.* Cambridge: Cambridge University Press.

Cranston, Maurice. 1964. *What Are Human Rights?* New York: Basic Books.

———. 1973. *What are Human Rights?* New York: Taplinger Publishing.

Crawford, James. 2000. "The UN Human Rights Treaty System: A System in Crisis?" In *The Future of UN Human Rights Treaty Monitoring.* Edited by Philip Alston and James Crawford. Cambridge: Cambridge University Press.

Cumper, Peter, and Steven Wheatley, eds. 1999. *Minority Rights in the "New" Europe*. The Hague: M. Nijhoff.

Dahl, Robert. 1971. *Polyarchy: Participation and Opposition*. New Haven: Yale University Press.

———. 1989. *Democracy and Its Critics*. New Haven: Yale University Press.

Damrosch, Lori Fisler. 1991. "Changing Conceptions of Intervention in International Law." In *Emerging Norms of Justified Intervention*. Edited by Laura W. Reed and Carl Kaysen. Cambridge: American Academy of Arts and Sciences.

———. 2000. "The Inevitability of Selective Response: Principles to Guide Urgent Action." In *Kosovo and the Challenge of Humanitarian Intervention: Selective Indignation, Collective Action, and International Citizenship*. Edited by Albrecht Schnabel and Ramesh Thakur. Tokyo: United Nations University Press.

Dandan, Virginia. 2000. "The Committee on Economic, Social and Cultural Rights and Non-Governmental Organizations." In *The UN Human Rights Treaty System in the 21st Century*. Edited by Anne F. Bayefsky. The Hague: Kluwer Law International.

Davidson, Scott. 1992. *The Inter-American Court of Human Rights*. Aldershot, Hants: Dartmouth.

Davidson, J. Scott. 1997. *The Inter-American Human Rights System*. Aldershot, Hants.: Dartmouth.

De Waal, Peter. 1998. *When Only the Best Will Do: A Study of Lesbian and Gay Immigration*. Darlinghurst: GLITF NSW.

Degener, Theresia, and Yolan Koster-Dreese, eds. 1995. *Human Rights and Disabled Persons: Essays and Relevant Human Rights Instruments*. Dordrecht: Martinus Nijhoff.

DeMartino, George. 1996. "Industrial Policies versus Competitiveness Strategies: In Pursuit of Prosperity in the Global Economy." *International Papers in Political Economy* 3 (2): 1–42.

D'Emilio, John, William B. Turner, and Urvashi Vaid, eds. 2000. *Creating Change: Sexuality, Public Policy, and Civil Rights*. New York: St. Martin's Press.

D'Entreves, A. P., ed. 1959. *Aquinas: Selected Political Writings*. New York: Macmillan.

Detrick, Sharon. 1999. *A Commentary on the United Nations Convention on the Rights of the Child*. The Hague: Boston: M. Nijhoff Publishers.

———. 2000. *A Children's Rights Bibliography based on the Convention on the Rights of the Child*. Florence: UNICEF Innocenti Research Centre.

Detrick, Sharon, Jaap Doek, and Nigel Cantwell, eds. 1992. *The United Nations Convention on the Rights of the Child: A Guide to the "Travaux Preparatoires"*. Dordrecht: Martinus Nijhoff.

Dickson, Anna K. 1997. *Development and International Relations: A Critical Introduction*. Cambridge: Polity Press.

Dijk, P. van, G. J. H. van Hoof, and A. W. Heringa. 1998. *Theory and Practice of the European Convention on Human Rights*, 3rd ed. The Hague: Kluwer Law International.

Donnelly, Jack. 1980. "Natural Law and Right in Aquinas' Political Thought." *Western Political Quarterly* 33 (December): 520–535.

———. 1984. "Human Rights, Humanitarian Intervention, and American Foreign Policy: Law, Morality and Politics." *Journal of International Affairs* 37 (Winter): 311–328.

———. 1985a. *The Concept of Human Rights*. London/New York: Croom Helm/St. Martin's Press.

———. 1985b. "In Search of the Unicorn: The Jurisprudence of the Right to Development." *California Western International Law Review* 15 (Summer): 473–509.

———. 1989. *Universal Human Rights in Theory and Practice*. Ithaca: Cornell University Press.

———. 1993a. "Human Rights, Humanitarian Crisis, and Humanitarian Intervention." *International Journal* 48 (Autumn): 607–640.

———. 1993b. "Third Generation Rights." In *Peoples and Minorities in International Law*. Edited by Catherine Brolmann, Rene Lefeber, and Marjoleine Zieck. The Hague: Kluwer.

———. 1998. "Human Rights: A New Standard of Civilization?" *International Affairs* 74 (January): 1–24.

Donnelly, Jack, and Rhoda E. Howard. 1988. "Assessing National Human Rights Performance: A Theoretical Framework." *Human Rights Quarterly* 10 (May): 214–248.

Doppelt, Gerald. 1978. "Walzer's Theory of Morality in International Relations." *Philosophy and Public Affairs* 8 (Autumn): 3–26.

———. 1980. "Statism Without Foundations." *Philosophy and Public Affairs* 9 (Summer): 398–403.

Douglas, Gillian, and Leslie Sebba, eds. 1998. *Children's Rights and Traditional Values*. Aldershot: Ashgate Dartmouth.

Douzinas, Costas. 2000. *The End of Human Rights*. Oxford: Hart Publishing.

Douzinas, Costas, and Ronnie Warrington. 1991. *Postmodern Jurisprudence: The Law of Texts in the Texts of Law*. London: Routledge.

Dover, K. 1986. *Greek Homsexuality*, 2d ed. Cambridge: Harvard University Press.

Dreze, Jean, and Amartya Sen. 1990. *Hunger and Public Action*. Oxford: Clarendon Press.

Dumont, Louis. 1980. *Homo Hierarchicus: The Caste System and Its Implications*. Chicago: University of Chicago Press.

Dworkin, Ronald. 1977. *Taking Rights Seriously*. Cambridge: Harvard University Press.

———. 1985. *A Matter of Principle*. Cambridge: Harvard University Press.

Dwyer, Kevin. 1991. *Arab Voices: The Human Rights Debate in the Middle East*. London: Routledge.

Dyck, Arthur J. 1994. *Rethinking Rights and Responsibilities: The Moral Bonds of Community*. Cleveland: The Pilgrim Press.

Economist, The. 2001. "Righting Wrongs." *The Economist* (August 18–24): 18–20.

Egorov, A. G. 1979. "Socialism and the Individual—Rights and Freedoms." *Soviet Studies in Philosophy* 18: 3–51.

Eide, Asbjorn, and Theresa Swinehart, eds. 1992. *The Universal Declaration of Human Rights: A Commentary*. New York: Oxford University Press.

Elder, Jospeph. 1996. "Hindu Perspectives on the Individual and the Collectivity." In *Religious Diversity and Human Rights*. Edited by Irene Bloom, J. Paul Martin, and Wayne L. Proudfoot. New York: Columbia University Press.

Enke, Stephen. 1963. *Economics for Development*. Englewood Cliffs, N.J.: Prentice-Hall.

Escobar, Arturo. 1995. *Encountering Development: The Making and Unmaking of the Third World*. Princeton: Princeton University Press.

Espiell, Hector Gros. 1979. "The Evolving Concept of Human Rights: Western, Socialist and Third World Approaches." In *Human Rights: Thirty Years After the Universal Declaration*. Edited by B. G. Ramcharan. The Hague: Martinus Nijhoff.

Evans, Malcolm D., and Rod Morgan. 1998. *Preventing Torture: A Study of the European Convention for the Prevention of Torture and Inhuman or Degrading Treatment or Punishment*. New York: Oxford University Press.

Evans, Malcolm, and Rachel Murray, eds. (2002). *The African Charter on Human and Peoples' Rights: The System in Practice, 1986-200*. Cambridge: Cambridge University Press.

Evatt, Elizabeth. 2000. "Ensuring Effective Supervisory Procedures: The Need for Resources." In *The Future of UN Human Rights Treaty Monitoring*. Edited by Philip Alston and James Crawford. Cambridge: Cambridge University Press.

Fairbank, John King. 1972. *The United States and China*, 3d ed. Cambridge: Harvard University Press.

Fairley, H. Scott. 1980. "State Actors, Humanitarian Intervention, and International Law: Reopening Pandora's Box." *Georgia Journal of International and Comparative Law* 10 (Winter): 29–63.

Falk, Richard A. 2000. *Human Rights Horizons: The Pursuit of Justice in a Globalizing World*. New York: Routledge.

Faucheux, Sylvie, Martin O'Connor, and Jan van der Staaten, eds. 1998. *Sustainable Development: Concepts, Rationalities, and Strategies*. Dordrecht: Kluwer.

Fein, Helen. 1984 [1979]. *Accounting for Genocide: National Responses and Jewish Victimization during the Holocaust*. Chicago: University of Chicago Press.

Feinberg, Joel. 1980. *Rights, Justice and the Bounds of Liberty: Essays in Social Philosophy*. Princeton: Princeton University Press.

Femia, Joseph V. 1981. *Gramsci's Political Thought: Hegemony, Consciousness, and the Revolutionary Process*. Oxford: Clarendon Press.

———. 1993. *Marxism and Democracy*. Oxford: Clarendon Press.

Fenton, John Y., Norvin Hein, Frank E. Reynolds, et al. 1983. *Religions of Asia*. New York: St. Martin's Press.

Fernyhough, Timothy. 1993. "Human Rights and Precolonial Africa." In *Human Rights and Governance in Africa*. Edited by Ronald Cohen, Goran Hyden, and Winston P. Nagan. Gainesville: University Press of Florida.

Finnis, John. 1980. *Natural Law and Natural Rights*. Oxford: Clarendon Press.

Flinterman, Cees. 1990. "Three Generations of Human Rights." In *Human Rights in a Pluralist World: Individuals and Collectivities*. Edited by Jan Berting, Peter R. Baehr, J. Herman Burgers et al. Westport, Conn.: Meckler.

Fonteyne, Jean-Pierre L. 1974. "The Customary International Law Doctrine of Humanitarian Intervention: Its Current Validity under the UN Charter." *California Western International Law Review* 4 (Spring): 203–270.

Foot, Rosemary. 2000. *Rights Beyond Borders: The Global Community and the Struggle over Human Rights in China*. Oxford: Oxford University Press.

Forsythe, David P. 1993. *Human Rights and Peace: International and National Dimensions*. Lincoln: University of Nebraska Press.

Fortin, Ernest. 1982. "The New Rights Theory and the Natural Law." *Review of Politics* 44 (October): 590–612.

Fortin, Ernest L., and J. Brian Benestad, eds. 1996. *Human Rights, Virtue, and the Common Good: Untimely Meditations on Religion and Politics*. Lanham, Md: Rowman & Littlefield.

Foss, Robert J. 1994. "The Demise of Homosexual Exclusion: New Possibilities for Gay and Lesbian Immigration." *Harvard Civil Rights—Civil Liberties Law Review* 29 (Summer): 439–475.

Fottrell, Deirdre, ed. 2000. *Revisiting Children's Rights: 10 Years of the UN Convention on the Rights of the Child*. The Hague: Kluwer Law International.

Foucault, Michel. 1990. *The History of Sexuality: Volume I: An Introduction*. New York: Vintage Books.

Franck, Thomas M. 1992. "The Emerging Right to Democratic Governance." *American Journal of International Law* 86 (January): 46–91.

———. 1999. "Lessons of Kosovo." *American Journal of International Law* 93 (October): 857–860.

Franck, Thomas M., and Nigel S. Rodley. 1973. "After Bangladesh: The Law of Humanitarian Intervention by Military Force." *American Journal of International Law* 67 (April): 275–305.

Fredman, Sandra, Philip Alston, and Grainne Burca, eds. 2001. *Discrimination and Human Rights: The Case of Racism*. Oxford: Oxford University Press.

Freeman, Michael. 1994. "The Philosophical Foundations of Human Rights." *Human Rights Quarterly* 16 (August): 491–514.

———. 1997. *The Moral Status of Children: Essays on the Rights of the Child*. The Hague: Martinus Nijhoff.

Friedmann, Wolfgang. 1971. "Intervention and International Law." In *Intervention in International Politics*. Edited by Louis G. M. Jaquet. The Hague: Martinus Nijhoff.

Frost, Mervyn. 1996. *Ethics in International Relations: A Constitutive Theory*. Cambridge: Cambridge University Press.

Galenkamp, Marlies. 1996. "The Rationale of Minority Rights: Wishes rather than Needs?" In *Do we Need Minority Rights? Conceptual Issues*. Edited by Juha Raikka. The Hague: Martinus Nijhoff.

Gallie, W. B. 1968. "Essentially Contested Concepts." In *Philosophy and the Historical Understanding*. New York: Schocken Books.

Gardam, Judith G. 1996. "Legal Restraints on Security Council Military Enforcement Action." *Michigan Journal of International Law* 17 (Winter): 285–322.

Gerstmann, Evan. 1999. *The Constitutional Underclass: Gays, Lesbians, and the Failure of Class-Based Equal Protection*. Chicago: University of Chicago Press.

Gewirth, Alan. 1982. *Human Rights: Essays on Justification and Applications*. Chicago: University of Chicago Press.

———. 1996. *The Community of Rights*. Chicago: University of Chicago Press.

Gilbert, Felix. 1961. *To the Farewell Address: Ideas of Early American Foreign Policy*. Princeton: Princeton University Press.

Gill, Stephen, ed. 1993. *Gramsci, Historical Materialism and International Relations*. Cambridge: Cambridge University Press.

Ginther, Konrad, Erik Denters, and Paul J. I. M. de Waart, eds. 1995. *Sustainable Development and Good Governance*. Dordrecht: Martinus Nijhoff.

Glendon, Mary Ann. 1991. *Rights Talk: The Impoverishment of Political Discourse*. New York: The Free Press.

Gong, Gerrit W. 1984. *The Standard of 'Civilisation' in International Society*. Oxford: Clarendon Press.

Goodin, Robert E., Bruce Headley, Ruud Muffels, and Henk-Jan Dirven. 1999. *The Real Worlds of Welfare Capitalism*. Cambridge: Cambridge University Press.

Goodman, Roger, Gordon White, and Huck-ju Kwon, eds. 1998. *The East Asian Welfare Model: Welfare Orientalism and the State*. New York: Routledge.

Gordon, Joy. 1998. "The Concept of Human Rights: The History and Meaning of its Politicization." *Brooklyn Journal of International Law* 23 (January): 689–791.

Gore, Charles. 2000. "The Rise and Fall of the Washington Consensus as a Paradigm for Developing Countries." *World Development* 28 (May): 789–804.

Gramsci, Antonio. 1971. *Selections from the Prison Notebooks*. Translated by Quintin Hoare and Geoffrey Nowell Smith. New York: International Publishers.

Grant, Stefanie. 2000. "The NGO Role: Implementing, Expanding Protection and Monitoring the Monitors." In *The UN Human Rights Treaty System in the 21st Century*. Edited by Anne F. Bayefsky. The Hague: Kluwer Law International.

Green, Reginald Herbold. 1981. "Basic Human Rights/Needs: Some Problems of Categorical Translation and Unification." *Review of the International Commission of Jurists* 27 (December): 53–58.

Grider, Stuart. 1994. "Sexual Orientation as Grounds for Asylum in the United States." *Harvard International Law Journal* 35 (Winter): 213–224.

Grillo, R. D., and R. L. Stirrat, eds. 1997. *Discourses of Development: Anthropological Perspectives*. Oxford: Berg.

Grimshaw, Patricia, Katie Holmes, and Marilyn Lake, eds. 2001. *Women's Rights and Human Rights: International Historical Perspectives*. Basingstoke, Hampshire: Palgrave.

Grossman, Claudio. 1999. "The Inter-American System of Human Rights and the New Hemispheric Reality." In *Innovation and Inspiration: Fifty Years of the Universal Declaration of Human Rights*. Edited by Peter R. Baehr, Cees Flinterman, and Mignon Senders. Amsterdam: Royal Academy of Arts and Sciences.

Gupta, Akhil, and James Ferguson. 1997. "Culture, Power, Place: Ethnography at the End of an Era." In *Culture, Power, Place: Explorations in Critical Anthropology*. Edited by Akhil Gupta and James Ferguson. Durham: Duke University Press.

Gupta, Dipankar. 1992. "Hierarchy and Difference: An Introduction." In *Social Stratification*. Edited by Dipankar Gupta. New York: Oxford University Press.

Gutmann, Amy, ed. 1994. *Multiculturalism: Examining the Politics of Recognition*. Princeton: Princeton University Press.

———. 2001. Introduction. In Amy Gutmann, ed. *Human Rights as Politics and Idolatry, by Michael Ignatieff*. Princeton: Princeton University Press.

Haas, Ernst B. 1970. *Human Rights and International Action: The Case of Freedom of Association*. Stanford: Stanford University Press.

Habermas, Jurgen. 1993. *Justification and Application: Remarks on Discourse Ethics*. Cambridge: MIT Press.

———. 1996. *Between Facts and Norms: Contributions to a Discourse Theory of Law and Democracy*. Translated by William Rehg. Cambridge: MIT Press.

———. 1998. "Remarks on Legitimation through Human Rights." *Philosophy and Social Criticism* 24 (2/3): 157–171.

Hadjor, Kofi Buenor. 1998. "Whose Human Rights?" *Journal of Asian and African Studies* 33 (November): 359–368.

Haggard, Stephan, and Beth A. Simmons. 1987. "Theories of International Regimes." *International Organization* 41 (Summer): 491–517.

Hakim, Khalifa Abdul. 1955. *Fundamental Human Rights*. Lahore: Institute of Islamic Culture.

Han, Yanlong. 1996. "Legal Protection of Human Rights in China." In *Human Rights: Chinese and Dutch Perspectives*. Edited by Peter R. Baehr, Fried van Hoof, Liu Nanlai et al. The Hague: Martinus Nijhoff.

Harris, David. 2000. "Lessons from the Reporting System of the European Social Char-

ter." In *The Future of UN Human Rights Treaty Monitoring.* Edited by Philip Alston and James Crawford. Cambridge: Cambridge University Press.
Harris, David J., and Stephen Livingstone, eds. 1998. *The Inter-American Human Rights System.* New York: Oxford University Press.
Harris, D. J., M. O'Boyle, and Colin Warbrick. 2001. *Law of the European Convention on Human Rights* 2d ed. London: Butterworths.
Hartney, Michael. 1995. "Some Confusions Concerning Collective Rights." In *The Rights of Minority Cultures.* Edited by Will Kymlicka. Oxford: Oxford University Press.
Hasenclever, Andreas, Peter Mayer, and Volker Rittberger, eds. 1997. *Theories of International Regimes.* Cambridge: Cambridge University Press.
Hasenclever, Andreas, Peter Mayer, and Volker Rittberger. 2000. "Integrating Theories of International Regimes." *Review of International Studies* 26: 3–33.
Hassan, Farooq. 1981. "Realpolitik in International Law: After the Tanzanian-Ugandan Conflict 'Humanitarian Intervention' Revisited." *Willamette Law Review* 17 (Fall): 859–912.
Held, David. 1987. *Models of Democracy.* Stanford: Stanford University Press.
Henkin, Louis. 1999. "Kosovo and the Law of 'Humanitarian Intervention'." *American Journal of International Law* 93 (October): 824–828.
Henrard, Kristin. 2000. *Devising an Adequate System of Minority Protection: Individual Human Rights, Minority Rights and the Right to Self-Determination.* The Hague: Martinus Nijhoff.
Herdt, Gilbert H., ed. 1984. *Ritualized Homosexuality in Melanesia.* Berkeley: University of California Press.
———, ed. 1994. *Third Sex, Third Gender: Beyond Sexual Dimorphism in Culture and History.* New York: Zone Books.
———. 1997. *Same Sex, Different Cultures : Gays and Lesbians across Cultures.* Boulder, Colo.: Westview Press.
Hernandez-Truyol, Berta Esperanza. 1996–1997. "International Law, Human Rights, and Latcrit Theory: Civil and Political Rights—An Introduction." *University of Miami Inter-American Law Review* 28 (Winter): 223–243.
Hewlett, Sylvia Ann. 1980. *The Cruel Dilemmas of Development: Twentieth-Century Brazil.* New York: Basic Books.
Hinsch, Bret. 1990. *Passions of the Cut Sleeve: The Male Homosexual Tradition in China.* Berkeley: University of California Press.
Hobart, Mark, ed. 1993. *An Anthropological Critique of Development: The Growth of Ignorance.* London: Routledge.
Holt, Robin. 1997. *Wittgenstein, Politics, and Human Rights.* London: Routledge.
Howard, Rhoda E. 1984. "Women's Rights in English-Speaking Sub-Saharan Africa." In *Human Rights and Development in Africa.* Edited by Claude E. Welch Jr. and Ronald I. Meltzer. Albany: State University of New York Press.
———. 1986. *Human Rights in Commonwealth Africa.* Totowa N.J.: Rowman & Littlefield.
———. 1995a. *Human Rights and the Search for Community.* Boulder, Colo.: Westview Press.
———. 1995b. "Occidentalism, Human Rights, and the Obligations of Western Scholars." *Canadian Journal of African Studies* 29 (1): 111–125.
———. 1999. "Gay Rights and the Right to a Family: Conflicts between Liberal and Illiberal Belief Systems." In *Innovation and Inspiration: Fifty Years of the Universal Dec-*

laration of Human Rights. Edited by Peter R. Baehr, Cees Flinterman, and Mignon Senders. Amsterdam: Royal Academy of Arts and Sciences.

Hsiung, James C. 1985. "Human Rights in an East Asian Perspective." In *Human Rights in East Asia: A Cultural Perspective*. Edited by James C. Hsiung. New York: Paragon House Publishers.

Hughes, Marissa Leigh. 2000. "Indigenous Rights in the Philippines: Exploring the Intersection of Cultural Identity, Environment, and Development." *Georgetown International Environment Law Review* 13 (Fall): 3–21.

Hunt, Gerald. 1999. *Laboring for Rights: Unions and Sexual Diversity Across Nations*. Philadelphia: Temple University Press.

Huntington, Samuel P. 1968. *Political Order in Changing Societies*. New Haven: Yale University Press.

Huntington, Samuel P., and Joan M. Nelson. 1976. *No Easy Choice: Political Participation in Developing Countries*. Cambridge: Harvard University Press.

Hussein, A. M. 1994. "The Impact of Western Hegemonic Policies Upon the Rights of People in West Asia and North Africa." Paper read at JUST International Conference, "Rethinking Human Rights", at Kuala Lampur.

Hutton, J. H. 1963. *Caste in India: Its Nature, Function and Origins*, 4th ed. Bombay: Oxford University Press.

Ignatieff, Michael. 2001. *Human Rights as Politics and Idolatry*. Princeton: Princeton University Press.

Independent International Commission on Kosovo. 2000. *The Kosovo Report: Conflict, International Response, Lessons Learned*. New York: Oxford University Press. http://www.kosovocommission.org/index.html.

Inoue, Tatsuo. 1999. "Liberal Democracy and Asian Orientalism." In *The East Asian Challenge for Human Rights*. Edited by Joanne R. Bauer and Daniel A. Bell. Cambridge: Cambridge University Press.

International Commission of Jurists. 1996. *The Participation of NGOs in the Work of the African Commission on Human and Peoples' Rights: A Compilation of Basic Documents*. Geneva: International Commission of Jurists.

Ishaque, Khalid M. 1974. "Human Rights in Islamic Law." *The Review of the International Commission of Jurists* 12 (June): 30–39.

Jackson Preece, Jennifer. 1998. *National Minorities and the European Nation-States System*. New York: Oxford University Press.

Jackson, Robert. 2000. *The Global Covenant: Human Conduct in a World of States*. Oxford: Oxford University Press.

Jacobsen, Michael, and Ole Bruun, eds. 2000. *Human Rights and Asian Values: Contesting National Identities and Cultural Representations in Asia*. Richmond, Australia: Curzon.

James, Alan. 2000. "The Concept of Sovereignty Revisited." In *Kosovo and the Challenge of Humanitarian Intervention: Selective Indignation, Collective Action, and International Citizenship*. Edited by Albrecht Schnabel and Ramesh Thakur. Tokyo: United Nations University Press.

James, Paul. 1997. "Postdependency? The Third World in an Era of Globalization and Late-Capitalism." *Alternatives* 22 (April–June): 205–226.

Johnson, Harry G. 1962. *Money, Trade, and Economic Growth*. Cambridge: Harvard University Press.

Jordan, Mark D. 1997. *The Invention of Sodomy in Christian Theology*. Chicago: University of Chicago Press.

Joseph, Sarah, Jenny Schultz, and Melissa Castan. 2000. *The International Covenant on Civil and Political Rights: Cases, Materials, and Commentary*. New York: Oxford University Press.

Kallen, Evelyn. 1996. "Gay and Lesbian Rights Issues: A Comparative Analysis of Sydney, Australia and Toronto, Canada." *Human Rights Quarterly* 18 (February): 206–223.

Kant, Immanuel. 1983. *Perpetual Peace and Other Essays*. Translated by Ted Humphrey. Indianapolis: Hackett.

Katz, Jonathan, ed. 1975. *Government versus Homosexuals*. New York: Arno Press.

Kausikan, Bilahari. 1993. "Asia's Different Standard." *Foreign Policy* 92 (Fall): 24–41.

———. 1997. "Governance That Works." *Journal of Democracy* 8 (April): 24–24.

Keck, Margaret E., and Kathryn Sikkink. 1998. *Activists Beyond Borders: Advocacy Networks in International Politics*. Ithaca: Cornell University Press.

Kennan, George F. 1985/86. "Morality and Foreign Policy." *Foreign Affairs* 63 (Winter): 205–218.

Kennedy, Stetson. 1959. *Jim Crow Guide to the U.S.A.: The Laws, Customs and Etiquette Governing the Conduct of Nonwhites and Other Minorities as Second-Class Citizens*. London: Lawrence & Wishart.

Kent, Ann. 1993. *Between Freedom and Subsistence: China and Human Rights*. Hong Kong: Oxford University Press.

Keohane, Robert O. 1982. "The Demand for International Regimes." *International Organization* 36 (Spring): 325–355.

———. 1984. *After Hegemony: Cooperation and Discord in the World Political Economy*. Princeton: Princeton University Press.

Khadduri, Majid. 1946. "Human Rights in Islam." *The Annals* 243 (January): 77–81.

Khushalani, Yougindra. 1983. "Human Rights in Asia and Africa." *Human Rights Law Journal* 4 (4): 403–442.

Kirgis, Frederic L. Jr. 1995. "The Security Council's First Fifty Years." *American Journal of International Law* 89 (July): 506–539.

Kirkpatrick, Colin, and Norman Lee, eds. 1997. *Sustainable Development in a Developing World: Integrating Socio-Economic Appraisal and Environmental Assessment*. Cheltenham, Eng.: Edward Elgar.

Kolenda, Pauline. 1978. *Caste in Contemporary India: Beyond Organic Solidarity*. Menlo Park, Calif.: Benjamin/Cummings Publishing.

Krasner, Stephen D. 1982. "Structural Causes and Regime Consequences: Regimes as Intervening Variables." *International Organization* 36 (Spring): 185–206.

Kritsiotis, Dino. 1998. "Reappraising Policy Objections to Humanitarian Intervention." *Michigan Journal of International Law* 19 (Summer): 1005–1049.

Kuefler, Mathew. 2001. *The Manly Eunuch: Masculinity, Gender Ambiguity, and Christian Ideology in Late Antiquity*. Chicago: University of Chicago Press.

Kuznets, Simon. 1955. "Economic Growth and Income Inequality." *American Economic Review* 45 (March): 1–28.

Kymlicka, Will, ed. 1995. *The Rights of Minority Cultures*. Oxford: Oxford University Press.

Kymlicka, Will, and Wayne Norman, eds. 2000. *Citizenship in Diverse Societies*. New York: Oxford University Press.

Lakatos, Imre. 1970. "Falsification and the Methodology of Scientific Research Programmes." In *Criticism and the Growth of Knowledge*. Edited by Imre Lakatos and Alan Musgrave. Cambridge: Cambridge University Press.

———. 1978. *The Methodology of Scientific Research Programmes*. Cambridge: Cambridge University Press.

Langlois, Anthony J. 2001. *The Politics of Justice and Human Rights*. Cambridge: Cambridge University Press.

Lau, M. P., and M. L. Ng. 1989. "Homosexuality in Chinese Culture." *Culture, Medicine and Psychiatry* 13 (December): 465–488.

Lawyers Committee for Human Rights. 1997. *Islam and Justice: Debating the Future of Human Rights in the Middle East and North Africa*. New York: Lawyers Committee for Human Rights.

LeBlanc, Lawrence J. 1991. *The United States and the Genocide Convention*. Durham: Duke University Press.

———. 1995. *The Convention on the Rights of the Child: United Nations Lawmaking on Human Rights*. Lincoln: University of Nebraska Press.

Leckie, Scott. 2000. "The Committee on Economic, Social and Cultural Rights: Catalyst for Change in a System Needing Reform." In *The Future of UN Human Rights Treaty Monitoring*. Edited by Philip Alston and James Crawford. Cambridge: Cambridge University Press.

Lee, Manwoo. 1985. "North Korea and the Western Notion of Human Rights." In *Human Rights in East Asia: A Cultural Perspective*. Edited by James C. Hsiung. New York: Paragon House Publishers.

Legesse, Asmarom. 1980. "Human Rights in African Political Culture." In *The Moral Imperatives of Human Rights: A World Survey*. Edited by Kenneth W. Thompson. Washington, D.C.: University Press of America.

Lehmbruch, Gerhard, and Philippe C. Schmitter, eds. 1982. *Patterns of Corporatist Policy-Making*. Beverly Hills: Sage Publishers.

Leipziger, Danny M., and Vinod Thomas. 1997. "An Overview of East Asian Experience." In *Lessons from East Asia*. Edited by Danny M. Leipziger. Ann Arbor: University of Michigan Press.

Lemons, John, and Donald A. Brown, eds. 1995. *Sustainable Development: Science, Ethics, and Public Policy*. Dordrecht: Kluwer.

Leupp, Gary P. 1995. *Male Colors: The Construction of Homosexuality in Tokugawa Japan*. Berkeley: University of California Press.

Levy, Jacob T. 1997. "Classifying Cultural Rights." In *Ethnicity and Group Rights*. Edited by Ian Shapiro and Will Kymlicka. New York: New York University Press.

Lijphart, Arend. 1977. *Democracy in Plural Societies: A Comparative Exploration*. New Haven: Yale University Press.

Lillich, Richard B. 1967. "Forcible Self-Help by States to Protect Human Rights." *Iowa Law Review* 53: 325–351.

———. 1974. "Humanitarian Intervention: A Reply to Ian Brownlie and a Plea for Constructive Alternatives." In *Law and Civil War in the Modern World*. Edited by John Norton Moore. Baltimore: Johns Hopkins University Press.

Lindholt, Lone. 1997. *Questioning the Universality of Human Rights: The African Charter of Human and Peoples' Rights in Botswana, Malawi and Mozambique*. Aldershot, Eng.: Ashgate.

Linklater, Andrew. 2000. "The Good International Citizen and the Crisis in Kosovo." In *Kosovo and the Challenge of Humanitarian Intervention: Selective Indignation, Collective Action, and International Citizenship*. Edited by Albrecht Schnabel and Ramesh Thakur. Tokyo: United Nations University Press.

Lipschutz, Ronnie D. 1996. *Global Civil Society and Global Environmental Governance: The Politics of Nature from Place to Planet*. Albany: State University of New York Press.

Lipset, Seymour Martin. 1959. "Some Social Requisites for Democracy: Economic Development and Political Legitimacy." *American Political Science Review* 53 (March): 69–105.

Lo, Chung-Sho. 1949. "Human Rights in the Chinese Tradition." In *Human Rights: Comments and Interpretations*. Edited by UNESCO. New York: Columbia University Press.

Lochrie, Karma, Peggy McCracken, and James A. Schultz, eds. 1997. *Constructing Medieval Sexuality*. Minneapolis: University of Minnesota Press.

Londregan, John Benedict, and Keith T. Poole. 1996. "Does High Income Promote Democracy?" *World Politics* 49 (October): 1–30.

Luard, Evan. 1981. *Human Rights and Foreign Policy*. Oxford: Pergamon Press.

Luban, David. 1980a. "Just War and Human Rights." *Philosophy and Public Affairs* 9 (Winter): 160–181.

———. 1980b. "The Romance of the Nation-State." *Philosophy and Public Affairs* 9 (Summer): 392–397.

Machan, Tibor R. 1989. *Individuals and their Rights*. La Salle, Ill.: Open Court.

———. 1999. *Private Rights and Public Illusions*. New Brunswick, N.J.: Transaction Publishers.

MacIntyre, Alasdair C. 1988. *Whose Justice? Which Rationality?* Notre Dame: University of Notre Dame Press.

———. 1990. *Three Rival Versions of Moral Enquiry: Encyclopaedia, Genealogy, and Tradition*. Notre Dame: University of Notre Dame Press.

Macpherson, C. B. 1962. *The Political Theory of Possessive Individualism: Hobbes to Locke*. Oxford: Clarendon Press.

Magnarella, Paul J., ed. 1999. *Middle East and North Africa: Governance, Democratization, Human Rights*. Aldershot, Eng.: Ashgate.

Mahathir bin Mohamad. 1994. Keynote Address. Paper read at JUST International Conference, "Rethinking Human Rights," at Kuala Lampur.

Mahbubani, Kishore. 1998. "Can Asians Think?" *The National Interest* 52 (Summer): 27–35.

Mangalpus, Raul. 1978. "Human Rights are Not a Western Discovery." *Worldview* 4 (October): 4–6.

Maritain, Jacques. 1943. *The Rights of Man and Natural Law*. New York: C. Scribner's Sons.

Marks, Stephen P. 1981. "Emerging Human Rights: A New Generation for the 1980s?" *Rutgers Law Review* 33 (Winter): 435–452.

Maslow, Abraham. 1970. *Motivation and Personality*. New York: Harper & Row.

———. 1971. *The Farther Reaches of Human Nature*. New York: The Viking Press.

Mawdudi, Abul A'la. 1976. *Human Rights in Islam*. Leicester: The Islamic Foundation.

Mayer, Ann Elizabeth. 1999. *Islam and Human Rights: Tradition and Politics*. Boulder, Colo.: Westview Press.

McClatchy, V.S. 1979 [1921]. "Assimilation of Japanese: Can They Be Moulded Into American Citizens." In *Four Anti-Japanese Pamphlets*. Edited by Valentine Stuart McClatchy. New York: Arno Press.

McDougal, Myres S., Harold D. Lasswell, and Lung-chu Chen. 1980. *Human Rights and World Public Order: The Basic Policies of an International Law of Human Dignity*. New Haven: Yale University Press.

McGoldrick, Dominic. 1994. The *Human Rights Committee: Its Role in the Development of the International Covenant on Civil and Political Rights*. Oxford: Clarendon Press.

McHale, John, and Magda Cordell McHale. 1979. "Meeting Basic Human Needs." *The Annals* 442 (March): 13–27.

Medina Quiroga, Cecilia. 1988. *The Battle of Human Rights: Gross, Systematic Violations and the Inter-American Regime*. Dordrecht: Martinus Nijhoff.

Mertus, Julie. 2000. "Reconsidering the Legality of Humanitarian Intervention: Lessons from Kosovo." *William and Mary Law Review* 41 (May): 1743–1787.

———. 1999. *Kosovo: How Myths and Truths Started a War*. Berkeley: University of California Press.

Messer, Ellen. 1997. "Pluralist Approaches to Human Rights." *Journal of Anthropological Research* 53 (Fall): 293–317.

Miller, Richard W. 1986. "Democracy and Class Dictatorship." *Social Philosophy and Policy* 3 (Spring): 59–78.

Mison, Robert B. 1992. "Homophobia in Manslaughter: The Homosexual Advance as Insufficient Provocation." *California Law Review* 80 (January): 133–178.

Mitra, Kana. 1982. "Human Rights in Hinduism." *Journal of Ecumenical Studies* 19 (Summer): 77–84.

Monshipouri, Mahmood. 1998. *Islamism, Secularism, and Human Rights in the Middle East*. Boulder, Colo.: Lynne Rienner.

Morgan, Rod, and Malcolm Evans. 1999. *Protecting Prisoners: The Standards of the European Committee for the Prevention of Torture in Context*. New York: Oxford University Press.

Morgenthau, Hans J. 1954. *Politics Among Nations: The Struggle for Power and Peace*, 2d ed. New York: Alfred A. Knopf.

———. 1962. *Politics in the Twentieth Century. Volume I: The Decline of Democratic Politics*. Chicago: University of Chicago Press.

———. 1979. *Human Rights and Foreign Policy*. New York: Council on Religion and International Affairs.

Morris, Kenneth E. 2001. "Western Defensiveness and the Defense of Rights: A Communitarian Alternative." In *Negotiating Culture and Human Rights*. Edited by Lynda Bell, Andrew J. Nathan, and Ilan Peleg. New York: Columbia University Press.

Morriss, Bruce R. 1967. *Economic Growth and Development*. New York: Pitman Publishing.

Morsink, Johannes. 1999. *The Universal Declaration of Human Rights: Origins, Drafting, and Intent*. Philadelphia: University of Pennsylvania Press.

Mort, Frank. 2000. *Dangerous Sexualities: Medico-Moral Politics in England since 1830*. London: Routledge.

Mott, Luiz R. B. 1996. *Epidemic of Hate: Violations of the Human Rights of Gay Men, Lesbians, and Transvestites in Brazil*. San Francisco: International Gay and Lesbian Human Rights Commission.

Moussalli, Ahmad. 2001. *The Islamic Quest for Democracy, Pluralism, and Human Rights*. Gainesville: University Press of Florida.

Mowbray, Alastair, and David Harris. 2001. *Cases and Materials on the European Convention on Human Rights*. London: Butterworths.

Murphy, Sean D. 1996. *Humanitarian Intervention: The United Nations in an Evolving World Order*. Philadelphia: University of Pennsylvania Press.

Murray, Rachel. 2000. *The African Commission on Human and Peoples' Rights in International Law*. Oxford: Hart Publishing.

Mutua, Makau wa. 1995. "The Banjul Charter and the African Cultural Fingerprint: An Evaluation of the Language of Duties." *Virginia Journal of International Law* 35 (Winter): 339–380.

———. 1996. "The Ideology of Human Rights." *Virgina Journal of International Law* 36 (Spring): 589–657.

———. 1998. "Looking Past the Human Rights Committee: An Argument for De-Marginalizing Enforcement." *Buffalo Human Rights Law Review* 4: 211–260.

Mutua, Makau 1999. "The African Human Rights Court: A Two-Legged Stool?" *Human Rights Quarterly* 21 (May): 342–363.

———. 2001. "Savages, Victims, and Saviors: The Metaphor of Human Rights." *Harvard International Law Journal* 42 (Winter): 201–245.

Muzaffar, Chandra. 1994. From Human Rights to Human Dignity. Paper read at JUST International Conference, "Rethinking Human Rights," at Kuala Lampur.

———. 1999. "From Human Rights to Human Dignity." In *Debating Human Rights: Critical Essays from the United States and Asia.* Edited by Peter Van Ness and Nikhil Aziz. London: Routledge.

———. 2002. *Rights, Religion, and Reform: Enhancing Human Dignity through Spiritual and Moral Transformation.* London: Routledge.

Naim, Moises. 2000. "Fads and Fashion in Economic Reforms: Washington Consensus or Washington Confusion?" *Third World Quarterly* 21 (June): 505–528.

Nambiar, Satish. 2000. "India: An Uneasy Precedent." In *Kosovo and the Challenge of Humanitarian Intervention: Selective Indignation, Collective Action, and International Citizenship.* Edited by Albrecht Schnabel and Ramesh Thakur. Tokyo: United Nations University Press.

Nanda, Ved P. 1992. "Tragedies in Iraq, Liberia, Yugoslavia and Haiti: Revisiting the Validity of Humanitarian Intervention under International Law—Part I." *Denver Journal of International Law and Policy* 20 (Winter): 305–334.

Nanda, Ved P., Thomas F. Jr. Muther, and Amy E. Eckert. 1998. "Tragedies in Somalia, Yugoslavia, Haiti, Rwanda and Liberia: Revisiting the Validity of Humanitarian Intervention under International Law, Part II." *Denver Journal of International Law and Policy* 26 (Winter): 827–868.

Nardi, Peter M., ed. 2000. *Gay Masculinities.* Thousand Oaks, Calif.: Sage Publications.

Nardin, Terry. 1983. *Law, Morality, and the Relations of States.* Princeton: Princeton University Press.

Nathan, Andrew J. 1986. "Sources of Chinese Rights Thinking." In *Human Rights in Contemporary China.* Edited by R. Randle Edwards, Louis Henkin, and Andrew J. Nathan. New York: Columbia University Press.

———. 2001. "Universalism: A Particularistic Account." In *Negotiating Culture and Human Rights.* Edited by Lynda Bell, Andrew J. Nathan, and Ilan Peleg. New York: Columbia University Press.

Nickel, James W. 1987. *Making Sense of Human Rights: Philosophical Reflections on the Universal Declaration of Human Rights.* Berkeley: University of California Press. http://spot.colorado.edu/~nickelj/msohr-welcome.htm.

———. 1997. "Group Agency and Group Rights." In *Ethnicity and Group Rights.* Edited by Ian Shapiro and Will Kymlicka. New York: New York University Press.

Nolan, Cathal. 1988. "Canada at the Commission on Human Rights." In *Canadian Foreign Policy and Human Rights.* Edited by Robert Matthews and Cranford Pratt. Montreal: McGill-Queens University Press.

Nussbaum, Martha. 1994. "Platonic Love and Colorado Law: The Relevance of Ancient Greek Norms to Modern Sexual Controversies." *Virginia Law Review* 80 (October): 1515–1651.

O'Boyle, Michael. 2000. "Reflections on the Effectiveness of the European System for Protecting Human Rights." In *The UN Human Rights Treaty System in the 21st Century*. Edited by Anne F. Bayefsky. The Hague: Kluwer Law International.

Ordonez, Juan Pablo. 1994. *No Human Being Is Disposable: Social Cleansing, Human Rights, and Sexual Orientation in Colombia*. San Francisco: International Gay and Lesbian Human Rights Commission.

Orend, Brian. 2002. *Human Rights: Concept and Context*. Peterborough, Ont.: Broadview Press.

Organ, Troy Wilson. 1974. *Hinduism: Its Historical Development*. Woodbury, N.Y.: Barron's Educational Series.

Othman, Norani. 1999. "Grounding Human Rights Arguments in Non-Western Culture: Shari'a and the Citizenship Rights of Women in a Modern Islamic State." In *The East Asian Challenge for Human Rights*. Edited by Joanne R. Bauer and Daniel A. Bell. Cambridge: Cambridge University Press.

Palma, Gabriel. 1977. "Dependency: A Formal Theory of Underdevelopment or a Methodology for the Analysis of Concrete Situations of Underdevelopment?" *World Development* 6 (July–August): 881–924.

Pandeya, R.C. 1986. "Human Rights: An Indian Perspective." In *Philosophical Foundations of Human Rights*. Edited by UNESCO. Paris: UNESCO.

Parekh, Bhikhu. 1999. "Non-ethnocentric Universalism." In *Human Rights in Global Politics*. Edited by Tim Dunne and Nicholas J. Wheeler. Cambridge: Cambridge University Press.

Parker, Richard G., and John H. Gagnon, eds. 1995. *Conceiving Sexuality: Approaches to Sex Research in a Postmodern World*. New York: Routledge.

Pease, Kelly Kate, and David P. Forsythe. 1993. "Human Rights, Humanitarian Intervention, and World Politics." *Human Rights Quarterly* 15 (May): 290–314.

Penna, David R., and Patricia J. Campbell. 1998. "Human Rights and Culture: Beyond Universality and Relativism." *Third World Quarterly* 19 (March): 7–27.

Perry, Michael J. 1998. *The Idea of Human Rights: Four Inquiries*. New York: Oxford University Press.

Pflugfelder, Gregory M. 1999. *Cartographies of Desire: Male-Male Sexuality in Japanese Discourse, 1600–1950*. Berkeley: University of California Press.

Phillips, Alan, and Allan Rosas, eds. 1995. *Universal Minority Rights*. Turku/Abo: Institute for Human Rights, Abo Akademi University.

Physicians for Human Rights. 1999. *War Crimes in Kosovo: A Population Based Assessment of Human Rights Violations Against Kosovar Albanians*. Boston: Physicians for Human Rights.

Pitkin, Hanna Fenichel. 1972. *Wittgenstein and Justice: On the Significance of Ludwig Wittgenstein for Social and Political Thought*. Berkeley: University of California Press.

Poe, Steven C. 1990. "Human Rights and U.S. Foreign Aid: A Review of Quantitative Studies and Suggestions for Future Research." *Human Rights Quarterly* 12 (November): 499–512.

Poe, Steven C., Suzanne Pilatovsky, and Brian Miller. 1994. "Human Rights and US Foreign Aid Revisited: The Latin American Region." *Human Rights Quarterly* 16 (August): 539–558.

Poe, Steven C., and Rangsima Sirirangsi. 1994. "Human Rights and U.S. Economic Aid During the Reagan Years." *Social Science Quarterly* 75 (September): 494–509.

Pogge, Thomas W. 2001 [1995]. "How Should Human Rights Be Conceived?" In *The Philosophy of Human Rights.* Edited by Patrick Hayden. St. Paul: Paragon House.

Pollis, Adamantia. 1996. "Cultural Relativism Revisited: Through a State Prism." *Human Rights Quarterly* 18 (May): 316–344.

Pollis, Adamantia, and Peter Schwab. 1980a. "Human Rights: A Western Construct with Limited Applicability." In *Human Rights: Cultural and Ideological Perspectives.* Edited by Adamantia Pollis and Peter Schwab. New York: Praeger.

———. 1980b. "Introduction." In *Human Rights: Cultural and Ideological Perspectives.* Edited by Adamantia Pollis and Peter Schwab. New York: Praeger.

Pomerance, Michla. 1982. *Self-Determination in Law and Practice: The New Doctrine in the United Nations.* The Hague: Martinus Nijhoff.

Preis, Ann-Belinda S. 1996. "Human Rights as Cultural Practice: An Anthropological Critique." *Human Rights Quarterly* 18 (May): 286–315.

Price, Daniel E. 1999. *Islamic Political Culture, Democracy, and Human Rights : A Comparative Study.* Westport, Conn.: Praeger.

Przeworski, Adam, and Fernando Limongi. 1997. "Modernization: Theories and Facts." *World Politics* 49 (January): 155–183.

Quigley, Declan. 1993. *The Interpretation of Caste.* New York: Oxford University Press.

Raj, M. Sundara. 2000. "Awakening of Human Rights." In *Human Rights in India: Historical, Social and Political Perspectives.* Edited by C. J. Nirmal. New Delhi: Oxford University Press.

Ratti, Rakesh, ed. 1993. *A Lotus of Another Color: An Unfolding of the South Asian Gay and Lesbian Experience.* Boston: Alyson Publications.

Rawls, John. 1955. "Two Concepts of Rules." *Philosophical Review* 64 (January): 3–32.

———. 1971. *A Theory of Justice.* Cambridge: Harvard University Press.

———. 1980. "Kantian Constructivism in Moral Theory." *Journal of Philosophy* 77 (September 9): 515–572.

———. 1996. *Political Liberalism.* New York: Columbia University Press.

———. 1999a. *Collected Papers.* Cambridge: Harvard University Press.

———. 1999b. *The Law of Peoples.* Cambridge: Harvard University Press.

Rehman, Javaid. 2000. *The Weakness in the International Protection of Minority Rights.* The Hague: Kluwer Law International.

Rieff, David. 1999. "Moral Imperatives and Political Realities." *Ethics and International Affairs* 13: 35–42.

Ringer, Benjamin B. 1983. *"We the People" and Others: Duality and America's Treatment of its Racial Minorities.* New York: Tavistock Publications.

Risse, Thomas, Steven C. Ropp, and Kathryn Sikkink, eds. 1999. *The Power of Human Rights: International Norms and Domestic Change.* Cambridge: Cambridge University Press.

Ritter, Matthew A. 1999. "Human Rights: The Universalist Controversy. A Response to Are the Principles of Human Rights 'Western' Ideas? An Analysis of the Claim of the 'Asian' Concept of Human Rights from the Perspectives of Hinduism, by Dr. Surya P. Subedi." *California Western International Law Journal* 30 (Fall): 71–90.

Rittberger, Volker, and Peter Mayer, eds. 1993. *Regime Theory and International Relations.* Oxford: Clarendon Press.

Ropers, Richard H., and Dan J. Pence. 1995. *American Prejudice: With Liberty and Justice for Some.* New York: Plenum Press.

Rosanvallon, Pierre. 1995. "The History of the Word 'Democracy' in France." *Journal of Democracy* 6 (October): 140–154.

Ross, W. D. 1930. *The Right and the Good.* London: Oxford University Press.

Rostow, Walt. 1960. *The Stages of Economic Growth: A Non-Communist Manifesto.* Cambridge: Cambridge University Press.

Rowen, Henry S., ed. 1998. *Behind East Asian Growth: The Political and Social Foundations of Prosperity.* New York: Routledge.

Roxborough, Ian. 1979. *Theories of Underdevelopment.* London: Macmillan.

Ruffin, Patricia. 1982. "Socialist Development and Human Rights in Cuba." In *Towards a Human Rights Framework.* Edited by Peter Schwab and Adamantia Pollis. New York: Praeger Publishers.

Sachs, Wolfgang, ed. 1992. *The Development Dictionary: A Guide to Knowledge as Power.* London: Zed Books.

Said, Abdul Aziz. 1979. "Precept and Practice of Human Rights in Islam." *Universal Human Rights* 1 (1): 63–80.

———. 1980. "Human Rights in Islamic Perspectives." In *Human Rights: Cultural and Ideological Perspectives.* Edited by Adamantia Pollis and Peter Schwab. New York: Praeger.

Saksena, S. K. 1967. "The Individual in Social Thought and Practice." In *The Indian Mind: Essentials of Indian Philosophy and Culture.* Edited by Charles A. Moore. Honolulu: University of Hawaii Press.

Samnoy, Ashlid. 1990. *Human Rights and International Consensus: The Making of the Universal Declaration of Human Rights, 1945–1948.* Bergen: Department of History, University of Bergen.

Sawczuk, Konstantyn. 1979. "Soviet Juridical Interpretation of International Documents on Human Rights." *Survey* 24: 86–91.

Schabas, William A. 2000. *Genocide in International Law: The Crime of Crimes.* Cambridge: Cambridge University Press.

Schachter, Oscar. 1984. "The Right of States to Use Armed Force." *Michigan Law Review* 82 (April–May): 1620–1646.

Schalow, Paul Gordon. 1989. "Male Love in Early Modern Japan: A Literary Depiction of the 'Youth'." In *Hidden From History: Reclaiming the Gay and Lesbian Past.* Edited by Martin Baumal Duberman, Martha Vicinus, and George Chauncey. New York: New American Library.

Schlesinger, Arthur, Jr. 1979. "Human Rights and the American Tradition." *Foreign Affairs* 57 (Summer): 503–526.

Schmidt, Markus. 2000. "Servicing and Financing Human Rights Supervision." In *The Future of UN Human Rights Treaty Monitoring.* Edited by Philip Alston and James Crawford. Cambridge: Cambridge University Press.

Schmitt, Arno, and Jehoeda Sofer, eds. 1992. *Sexuality and Eroticism Among Males in Moslem Societies.* Binghamton, N.Y.: Harrington Park Press.

Schmitter, Philippe C., and Terry Lynn Karl. 1991. "What Democracy Is . . . and Is Not." *Journal of Democracy* 2 (Summer): 75–88.

Schulte Nordholt, Nico G. 1995. "Aid Conditionality: The Case of Dutch-Indonesian Relationships." In *Aid and Political Conditionality.* Edited by Olav Stokke. London: Frank Cass.

Schwarzenberger, Georg. 1955. "The Standard of Civilisation in International Law." *Current Legal Problems* 17: 212–234.

Sen, Amartya. 1981. *Poverty and Famines: An Essay on Entitlement and Deprivation.* New York: Oxford University Press.

Shalev, Carmel. 2000. "State Reporting and the Convention on the Elimination of All Forms of Discrimination against Women." In *The UN Human Rights Treaty System in the 21st Century.* Edited by Anne F. Bayefsky. The Hague: Kluwer Law International.

Sharma, Miriam. 1985. "Caste, Class, and Gender: Production and Reproduction in North India." *Journal of Peasant Studies* 12 (July): 57–88.

Shelton, Dinah L. 1984. "Individual Complaint Machinery under the United Nations 1503 Procedure and the Optional Protocol to the International Covenant on Civil and Political Rights." In *Guide to International Human Rights Practice.* Edited by Hurst Hannum. Philadelphia: University of Pennsylvania Press.

Shinoda, Hideaki. 2000. "The Politics of Legitimacy in International Relations: A Critical Examination of NATO's Intervention in Kosovo." *Alternatives: Social Transformation and Humane Governance* 25 (October–December): 515–536.

Shue, Henry. 1979. "Rights in the Light of Duties." In *Human Rights and U.S. Foreign Policy.* Edited by Peter G. Brown and Douglas Maclean. Lexington, Mass.: Lexington Books.

———. 1980. *Basic Rights: Subsistence, Affluence, and U.S. Foreign Policy.* Princeton: Princeton University Press.

Shyllon, Folarin. 1998. "The Right to a Cultural Past: African Viewpoints." In *Cultural Rights and Wrongs.* Edited by Halina Niec. Paris: UNESCO.

Simma, Bruno. 1999. "NATO, the UN and the Use of Force: Legal Aspects." *European Journal of International Law* 10: http://www.ejil.org/journal/Vol10/No1/ab1.html.

Skurbaty, Zelim. 2000. *As If Peoples Mattered: Critical Appraisal of "Peoples" and "Minorities" from the International Human Rights Perspective and Beyond.* The Hague: Martinus Nijhoff.

Slater, Jerome, and Terry Nardin. 1986. "Nonintervention and Human Rights." *Journal of Politics* 48 (February): 86–96.

Stackhouse, Max L. 1984. *Creeds, Society, and Human Rights: A Study in Three Cultures.* Grand Rapids, Mich.: William B. Eerdmans.

Steger, Manfred. 2002. *Globalism: The New Market Ideology.* Lanham, Md: Rowman & Littlefield.

Stein, Edward, ed. 1990. *Forms of Desire: Sexual Orientation and the Social Constructionist Controversy.* New York: Garland Publishing.

Steiner, Henry J. 2000. "Individual Claims in a World of Massive Violations: What Role for the Human Rights Committee." In *The Future of UN Human Rights Treaty Monitoring.* Edited by Philip Alston and James Crawford. Cambridge: Cambridge University Press.

Stewart, Frances. 1985. *Basic Needs in Developing Countries.* Baltimore: Johns Hopkins University Press.

Stiefel, Matthias, and Marshall Wolfe. 1994. *A Voice For the Excluded: Popular Participation in Development.* London: Zed (in association with the United Nations Research Institute for Social Development).

Stokke, Olav, ed. 1989. *Western Middle Powers and Global Poverty: The Determinants of the Aid Policies of Canada, Denmark, the Netherlands, Norway and Sweden.* Uppsala: Almquist and Wiksell International.

Stowell, Ellery C. 1921. *Intervention in International Law*. Washington, D.C.: John Byrne & Co.

Strauss, Leo. 1953. *Natural Right and History*. Chicago: University of Chicago Press.

Strawson, John. 1997. "A Western Question to the Middle East: 'Is there a Human Rights Discourse in Islam?'." *Arab Studies Quarterly* 19 (Winter): 31–58.

Subedi, Surya P. 1999. "Are the Principles of Human Rights 'Western' Ideas? An Analysis of the 'Asian' Concept of Human Rights from the Perspectives of Hinduism." *California Western International Law Journal* 30 (Fall): 45–69.

Suganami, Hidemi. 1984. "Japan's Entry into International Society." In *The Expansion of International Society*. Edited by Hedley Bull and Adam Watson. Oxford: Clarendon Press.

Symonides, Janusz. 2000. "Cultural Rights." In *Human Rights: Concept and Standards*. Edited by Janusz Symonides. Paris: UNESCO.

Tabandeh, Sultanhussein. 1970. *A Muslim Commentary on the Universal Declaration of Human Rights*. Guildford: F. J. Goulding.

Tai, Hung-Chao. 1985. "Human Rights in Taiwan: Convergence of Two Political Cultures?" In *Human Rights in East Asia: A Cultural Perspective*. Edited by James C. Hsiung. New York: Paragon House Publishers.

Taylor, Charles. 1994. "The Politics of Recognition." In *Multiculturalism: Examining the Politics of Recognition*. Edited by Amy Gutmann. Princeton: Princeton University Press.

Taylor, Lance, and Ute Pieper. 1996. *Reconciling Economic Reform and Sustainable Human Development: Social Consequences of Neo-Liberalism*. New York: Office of Development Studies, United Nations Development Programme.

Thapar, Romila. 1966. "The Hindu and Buddhist Traditions." *International Social Science Journal* 18 (1): 31–40.

Thomas, Daniel C. 2001. *The Helsinki Effect: International Norms, Human Rights, and the Demise of Communism*. Princeton: Princeton University Press.

Todaro, Michael P. 1994. *Economic Development*, 5th ed. New York: Longman.

Tolley, Howard Jr. 1987. *The U.N. Commission on Human Rights*. Boulder, Colo.: Westview Press.

Travieso, Juan Antonio. 1996. *La Corte Interamericana de Derechos Humanos: opiniones conslutivas y fallos: la jurisprudencia de la Corte Interamericana de Derechos Humanos*. Buenos Aires: Abeledo Perrot.

United Nations, Centre for Human Rights. 1992. *The Committee against Torture*. Geneva: United Nations Centre for Human Rights.

United Nations, Centre for Human Rights. 1996. *Fourth Workshop on Regional Human Rights Arrangements in the Asian and Pacific Region: Report, Kathmandu, 26–28 Feburary 1996*. Geneva: United Nations Centre for Human Rights.

United Nations Conference on Environment and Development. 1993. *Agenda 21: Programme of Action for Sustainable Development*. New York: United Nations Department of Public Information.

United Nations Development Program. 1998. *Integrating Human Rights with Sustainable Human Development: A UNDP Policy Document*. New York: http://magnet.undp.org/Docs/policy5.html#Human.

United Nations, Division for the Advancement of Women. 2000. *Bringing International Human Rights Law Home: Judicial Colloquium on the Domestic Application of the Convention on the Elimination of All Forms of Discrimination against Women and the Convention on the Rights of the Child*. New York: United Nations.

Van Beuren, Geraldine. 1998. *International Law on the Rights of the Child.* Dordrecht: M. Nijhoff.

van Hoof, Fried. 1996. "Asian Challenges to the Concept of Universality: Afterthoughts on the Vienna Conference on Human Rights." In *Human Rights: Chinese and Dutch Perspectives.* Edited by Peter R. Baehr, Fried van Hoof, Liu Nanlai et al. The Hague: Martinus Nijhoff.

Van Ness, Peter, and Nikhil Aziz, eds. 1999. *Debating Human Rights: Critical Essays from the United States and Asia.* New York: Routledge.

Vasak, Karel. 1984. "Pour une troisième génération des droits de l'homme." In *Studies and Essays on International Humanitarian Law and Red Cross Principles in Honour of Jean Pictet.* Edited by C. Swinarski. The Hague: Martinus Nijhoff.

———. 1991. "Les différentes catégories des droits de l'homme." In *Les Dimensions universelles des droits de l'homme.* Edited by A. Lapeyre, F. de Tinguy, and K. Vasak. Bruxelles: Émile Bruylant.

Veatch, Henry B. 1985. *Human Rights: Fact or Fancy?* Baton Rouge: Louisiana State University Press.

Vidal-Naquet, Pierre. 1986. *The Black Hunter: Forms of Thought and Forms of Society in the Greek World.* Baltimore: The Johns Hopkins University Press.

Vincent, R. J., ed. 1986. *Foreign Policy and Human Rights.* Cambridge: Cambridge University Press.

Waaldijk, Kees. 1994. "Standard Sequences in the Legal Recognition of Homosexuality: Europe's Past, Present, and Future." *Australasian Gay and Lesbian Law Journal* 4: 50–72.

Wafi, Ali Abdu al-Wahid. 1998. *Human Rights in Islam.* Riyadh: Naif Arab Academy for Security Sciences.

Wai, Dunstan M. 1980. "Human Rights in Sub-Saharan Africa." In *Human Rights: Cultural and Ideological Perspectives.* Edited by Adamantia Pollis and Peter Schwab. New York: Praeger.

Waldron, Jeremy. 1995. "Minority Cultures and the Cosmopolitan Alternative." In *The Rights of Minority Cultures.* Edited by Will Kymlicka. Oxford: Oxford University Press.

Walker, Kristen. 1994. "The Participation of the Law in the Construction of (Homo)Sexuality." *Law in Context* 12 (1): 52–75.

Wallace, Rebecca, ed. 1997. *International Human Rights: Text and Materials.* London: Sweet & Maxwell.

Waltz, Susan (1995). *Human Rights and Reform: Changing the Face of North African Politics.* Berkeley: University of California Press.

———. 2001. "Universalizing Human Rights: The Role of Small States in the Construction of the Universal Declaration of Human Rights." *Human Rights Quarterly* 23 (February): 44–72.

Walzer, Michael. 1977. *Just and Unjust Wars: A Moral Argument with Historical Illustrations.* New York: Basic Books.

———. 1980. "The Moral Standing of States: A Response to Four Critics." *Philosophy and Public Affairs* 9 (Spring): 209–229.

———. 1994. "Comment." In *Multiculturalism: Examining the Politics of Recognition.* Edited by Amy Gutmann. Princeton: Princeton University Press.

Wasserstrom, Richard A. 1978. "Review of Walzer, *Just and Unjust Wars.*" *Harvard Law Review* 92: 536–545.

Weiner, Myron. 1987. "The Goals of Development." In *Understanding Political Development: An Analytic Study*. Edited by Myron Weiner, Samuel P. Huntington, and Gabriel A. Almond. Boston: Little Brown.

Weisburd, A. Mark. 2001. "International Law and the Problem of Evil." *Vanderbilt Journal of Transnational Law* 34 (March): 225–281.

Weiss, Thomas G. 1999. "Principles, Politics, and Humanitarian Action." *Ethics and International Affairs* 13: 1–22.

Welch, Claude E. Jr. 1995. *Protecting Human Rights in Africa: Roles and Strategies of Non-Governmental Organizations*. Philadelphia: University of Pennsylvania Press.

Wellman, Carl. 1997. *The Proliferation of Rights: Moral Progress or Empty Rhetoric?* Boulder, Colo.: Westview Press.

Wheeler, Nick. 2000. *Saving Strangers: Humanitarian Intervention in International Society*. Oxford: Oxford University Press.

White, Gordon, and Roger Goodman. 1998. "Welfare Orientalism and the Search for an East Asian Welfare Model." In *The East Asian Welfare Model: Welfare Orientalism and the State*. Edited by Roger Goodman, Gordon White, and Huck-ju Kwon. New York: Routledge.

Wight, Martin. 1966. "Western Values in International Relations." In *Diplomatic Investigations: Essays in the Theory of International Politics*. Edited by Herbert Butterfield and Martin Wight. Cambridge: Harvard University Press.

———. 1992. *International Theory: The Three Traditions*. New York: Holmes & Meier (for the Royal Institute of International Affairs).

Wijngaard, Marianne van den. 1997. *Reinventing the Sexes: The Biomedical Construction of Femininity and Masculinity*. Bloomington: Indiana University Press.

Wilets, James D. 1994a. "International Human Rights Law and Sexual Orientation." *Hastings International and Comparative Law Review* 18 (Fall): 1–120.

———. 1994b. "Pressure From Abroad: U.N. Human Rights Ruling Strengthens Hopes for U.S. Gays and Lesbians." *Human Rights* 21 (Fall): 22–23ff.

Williamson, John. 1993. "Democracy and the 'Washington Consensus'." *World Development* 21 (August): 1329–1336.

Wilson, Richard. 1997. "Introduction." In *Human Rights, Culture and Context: Anthropological Perspectives*. Edited by Richard Wilson. London: Pluto Press.

Wingfield, Thomas C. 2000. "Forcible Protection of Nationals Abroad." *Dickinson Law Review* 104 (Spring): 439–469.

Wolf, Francis. 1984. "Human Rights and the International Labor Organization." In *Human Rights in International Law: Legal Policy Issues*. Edited by Theodor Meron. Oxford: Clarendon Press.

Wolfson, Evan. 1991. "Civil Rights, Human Rights, Gay Rights: Minorities and the Humanity of the Different." *Harvard Journal of Law and Public Policy* 14 (Winter): 21–39.

Woodward, C. Vann. 1966. *The Strange Career of Jim Crow*, 2d ed. New York: Oxford University Press.

World Bank. 1992. *Governance and Development*. Washington, D.C.: World Bank.

Xie, Bohua, and Lihua Niu. 1994. Review and Comments on the Issue of Human Rights. Paper read at JUST International Conference, "Rethinking Human Rights", at Kuala Lampur.

Xin, Chunying. 1996. "Can the Pluralistic World Have a Unified Concept of Human Rights?" In *Human Rights: Chinese and Dutch Perspectives*. Edited by Peter R. Baehr, Fried van Hoof, Liu Nanlai et al. The Hague: Martinus Nijhoff.

Yates, Steven. 1995. "'Righting' Civil Wrongs: Toward a Libertarian Agenda." In *Liberty for the 21st Century: Contemporary Libertarian Thought*. Edited by Tibor R. Machan and Douglas B. Rasmussen. Lanham, Md: Rowman & Littlefield.

Zakaria, Fareed. 1994. "Culture Is Destiny: A Conversation with Lee Kuan Yew." *Foreign Affairs* 73 (March/April): 109–126.

Zechenter, Elizabeth M. 1997. "In the Name of Cultural Relativism and the Abuse of the Individual." *Journal of Anthropological Research* 53 (Fall): 319–347.

Zuijdwijk, Ton J. 1982. *Petitioning the United Nations: A Study in Human Rights*. Aldershot, Eng.: Gower.

Index

Active respect, 9
African conceptions of human rights, 78–79
African regional regime, 143–144
Aggression, 250
American regional regime, 141–143
Analytic theory, 16–17, 21
Annan, Kofi, 251
antihumanitarian intervention, 248
Aquinas, Thomas, 76–77
Arab regional regime, 144–145
Arkes, Hadley, 19
Asian regional regime, 144
Asian values and human rights, 233
Asserting rights, 8, 9
Assertive exercise, 9
Autonomy, 32, 37, 44–45, 47, 50–51, 52, 98, 121 n. 11, 206–208, 245

Barnhart, Michael, 84 n. 18
Bay, Christian, 13
Being right, 7–8, 76–77
Bell, Daniel, 70, 99–100
Benefits (and rights), 8, 37, 81, 190
Booth, Ken, 51 n. 19, 117 n. 9
Brown, Chris, 20, 204, 205

Cambodia, humanitarian intervention in, 255
Caste and human rights, 81–84, 87
Children's rights regime, 149–150
Chopra, Jarat, 252
Collective rights. *See* group rights
Committee on Economic, Social, and Cultural Rights, 133 n. 10
Communications. *See* complaint procedures
Complaint procedures, 134–135, 138–139, 147, 149, 176–177
Comprehensive doctrines, 40–41
Concept (substance) of a right, 94–95
Conceptual theory. *See* analytic theory
Confucian China and human rights, 79–81, 115–116
Consistency. *See* inconsistency
Constitutive rules, 16
Constructivist theory of human rights, 16
Cranston, Maurice, 28–30, 31
Cultural identity, right to, 220–221
Cultural rights, 218–221
Culture and human rights, 71–72, 76, 78, 86–88, 97, 100–103, 119–123

Declaratory regimes, 128, 136, 151–152
Democracy, 186, 188–194, 202–203
  definitions, 188–191
  electoral, 190–191, 192–194
  liberal, 49, 192–194, 201, 202–203
  peoples', 192
  substantive and procedural, 190–191
Development, 109–110, 111, 186, 194–203
  definitions, 194–196
  tradeoffs with human rights, 196–199
Dignity, human, 14, 18, 19, 27, 41, 57, 61, 74, 79, 81, 83, 85, 86, 91, 92, 94, 111–112, 116, 203, 215, 219, 225, 226
Distributive justice, and human rights, 79, 81, 87
Duties (and rights), 8, 25 n. 4, 46, 71, 72–74, 82, 114–115
Dworkin, Ronald, 8, 43–44, 47
Dyck, Arthur, 19

Economic and social rights, 27–33, 60–61, 64–65, 68, 110–112, 196–199, 200–203
Empowerment and (human) rights, 8, 12, 121, 122, 191–192
Enforcement regimes, 128, 152–153
Enforcing rights, 8–10, 35–36
English School of international studies, 66
Enjoying rights, 8–10
Entitlement, 7–10, 12–13, 23, 45, 76, 77 n. 9
Equal concern and respect, 43–46, 51, 123, 201, 206–207
Equal protection, 206
Equal rights, human rights as, 10
Equality, 10, 36, 41, 44–45, 47, 48, 50–51, 52–53, 58–59, 120–121, 208, 237

Equality tradeoff, 197, 200–202
Essentially contested concepts, 96
European regional regime, 138–141,
Exercising rights, 8–9
External judgments, 92–93

Fein, Helen, 74
Feinberg, Joel, 12
Finnis, John, 19
Foreign aid, 165
Foreign policy, 177–179
  choice of means, 164–166
  tradeoffs, 162–164
Forms of rights, 97–98
Foundations, 18–21, 43
Franck, Thomas, 243n. 4, 251, 252n. 21
Free speech, 115
Freedom of association, 208
Frost, Mervyn, 38

Galenkamp, Marlies, 209
Gender equality, 120–121, 211
Genetic fallacy, 69–70
Genocide, 150–151, 251–252, 252–253
Global human rights regime, 129–138
Goodin, Robert, 65
Goods and rights, 10–11
Group agency, 210
Group human rights, arguments against, 209–211, 217–218
Group rights, 25. *See also* indigenous peoples, self-determination
  and group identity, 214–215
  of minorities, 212–214, 220
  of women, 211–212

Having a right, 7–10, 81
Hegemony, 38–40, 142–143, 153–154, 259n. 33
Held, David, 188, 189
Helsinki process, 39, 249
Hindu India and human rights, 81–84, 87
Hobbes, Thomas, 9, 204
Howard, Rhoda, 25n. 5, 79, 105
Human being, concept of, 19, 51–52, 83, 91
Human nature, 13–17, 83, 90–91
Human goods and human rights, 10–11
Human Rights Committee, 133–135, 238–239, 239–240
Humanitarian intervention
  and international law, 243–244
  collective versus unilateral, 253, 257–258
  justifications, 254–255
  right not duty, 247
Humanitarian space, 252

Implementations of rights, 97–98
Inalienable rights, 10
Inconsistency, 166–167, 168–173, 255–256
Independent International Commission on Kosovo, 254
Indian conceptions of human rights, 81–84, 87
Indigenous peoples, 215–217
Individual rights, 23–27, 112–114, 204–208
Interdependence and indivisibility, 23, 27–33, 169
Internal judgments, 92–93
International Labor Organization, 145–146
International normative universality, 1
Interpretations of rights, 96–97
Intervention, 242–244
Ishaque, Khalid, 72
Islam and human rights, 72–76

Jackson, Robert, 246–247
Justification, senses of, 254–255

Kant, Immanuel, 42, 66–67
Kennan, George, 156–157, 158
Keohane, Robert O., 135, 142
Khadduri, Majid, 73
Kosovo, 253, 258–259

Lee Kawn Yew, 116
Legal positivism, 13n. 7
Legal rights, relation to human rights, 11–13
Legitimacy, and human rights, 12, 27, 36, 38–39, 43, 63, 77, 167–168, 186–188, 206
Liberal democracy, 49, 192–194, 201, 202–203
Liberal democratic welfare state, 188, 202–203,
Liberalism, and human rights, 46–51, 61, 202–203, 204–208,
Libertarianism, 48–49
Liberty. *See* autonomy
Liberty trade-off, 198, 199–200
Limited government and human rights, 80
Lists of human rights, 45–46, 57–58, 60–61, 227–229
Locke, John, 47, 60, 228

Manifesto rights, 12
Markets, and human rights, 58–59, 62, 67–69, 200–203
Maslow, Abraham, 13
Minimalist liberalism, 48–49
Minorities, sexual, 229–241
Minority rights regime, 151
Mixed motives, -inconsistency
Modernity, and human rights, 58, 59
Moral interdependence, 137
Moral theory and human rights, 41–43
Moral universality of human rights, 1
Morgenthau, Hans, 155–156, 158
Mugabe, Robert, 230
Multiculturalism, 206
Muzaffar, Chandra, 116–117

Nardin, Terry, 66
Nathan, Andrew, 119
National action, priority of, 137, 141, 152
National identity and international human rights, 159–162
National implementation of international human rights, 34–35
National security, 163
Needs, 13–14, 18
Needs tradeoff, 197, 200–202
Negative rights, 30–31
Neoliberalism, 48, 68
Neutrality, 49–51, 206–208
Niebuhr, Reinhold, 156
Nondiscrimination, 121, 206
 and sexual minorities, 237–241
 international legal right to, 225–227
Nongovernmental organizations, 148

Objective enjoyment, 9
Overlapping consensus, 40–41, 43, 51–53, 63, 75, 98, 207, 252

Paramount rights, 11–12, 28, 226
Parekh, Bhikhu, 51
Peoples' rights, 221–224
Philosophical anthropology, 17
Pitkin, Hanna, 16 n. 12
Pluralism (relativism), 66–67, 158–159, 246–247
Political theory and human rights, 41–43
Pollis, Adamantia, 71, 84
Pornography, 98
Positive rights, 30–31
Possession paradox, 9, 12
Preis, Ann-Belinda, 86–88
Progress, moral, 21
Promotional regimes, 128, 135, 138, 151–152
Property, right to, 31–32, 60–61, 77 n. 9, 228

Racial discrimination regime, 146–147
Racial discrimination in the United States, 234–235
Rawls, John, 16 n. 12, 21 n. 21, 40, 47, 252
Realism, 155–157, 158, 169,
Rechtstaat, 64
Rectitude, 7–8, 76, 77 n. 9
Reflective equilibrium, 21 n. 21
Regimes, international human rights, evolution of, 151–154
Regional human rights regimes, 138–145
Regulative rules, 16
Relative universality of human rights, 98, 106, 107
Relativism (pluralism) and foreign policy, 158–159
Relevance of human rights, 84–86, 88
Reporting procedures, 134, 146, 173–175
Respecting rights, 8–10
Rights, human rights as, 10–11. *See also* entitlement
Rousseau, Jean Jacques, 52, 190
Rule of law, 64
Rwanda, 133, 253

Said, Abdul Aziz, 73
Schwab, Peter, 71, 84
Security, and human rights, 249
Self-determination, 221–224, 244
Self-fulfilling prophecy, human rights as, 15
Settled norms of international society, 38
Sexual minorities, 229–241
 discrimination against, 231–233, 236–237
 nondiscrimination against, 237–241
 violence against, 231
Shue, Henry, 30–31, 57
Single-issue human rights regimes, 145–151
Slavery, 104–105
Social construction, 14–17, 61, 102
Social contract theory, 35
Social democratic liberalism, 48–49
Society of states, 38–40, 65–67
Solidarism, 66–67
Source of human rights, 13–14
Sovereignty, 66, 67, 108–109, 157–158, 191, 249–251
Standard threats, 57, 69, 215, 221, 226
States, and human rights, 33–37, 58–59, 62, 64, 65–66, 67
Statism (legalism), 157–158
Strauss, Leo, 204
Sub-Commission on the Promotion and Protection of Human Rights, 132
Substance of rights, 94–95

Tempered universalism, 119
1503 procedure, 129–132
Thematic procedures, 132
Third generation rights, 65 n. 9, 221
Toleration, 50, 52, 105, 206
Toonen case, 238–240
Torture regime, 147–148
Trade-offs. *See* development. foreign policy
Trumps, 8

Uganda, humanitarian intervention in, 254–255
UN Commission on Human Rights, 129–133
UN High Commissioner for Human Rights, 135
Universal Declaration, and equal concern and respect, 45–46
Universal Declaration, non-Western influences on, 22 n. 2
Universe of obligation, 74

Vietnam, intervention in Cambodia, 255

Waaldijk, Kees, 229 n. 4, 240–241
Walzer, Michael, 207, 244–245, 246–247, 252
Weiss, Thomas, 252
Welfare state, 48–49, 65, 201–203
West, and human rights, 61–65, 67–70, 71, 76–78
Wheeler, Nick, 243
Wight, Martin, 66
Witness, 168
Wittgenstein, Ludwig, 16 n. 12
Women's rights regime, 148–149
Workers' rights regime, 145–146